State Interest and the Sources of International Law

This book addresses the disparity between positive non-treaty law and its scholarly assessment in the area of moral concepts, understood as altruistic as opposed to reciprocal legal obligations. It shows how scholars are generously willing to assert the existence of a rule of international law, thereby moving further away from actual state practice, not taking into account the factors of legal rhetoric and the core survival interests of the state in the formation of custom and general principles of law. The main argument is that such moral concepts can simply not manifest themselves as non-treaty sources of international law from a dogmatic perspective. The reason is the inherent connection between the formation of the non-treaty sources of international law and state interest that makes it difficult, if not impossible, to assess state practice or *opinio juris* in the case of altruistic obligations. The book further demonstrates this finding by looking at two cases in point: Human rights and humanitarian exceptions to the prohibition of force.

As opposed to the majority of existing works on the subject, *State Interest and the Sources of International Law* takes a bigger-picture approach to a number of distinct problems in international law scholarship by looking at the building blocks of international relations on the one hand, and merging this with sources doctrine on the other. It will be of interest to researchers, academics, and students in the fields of international law, human rights, international relations, political science, legal philosophy, and legal theory.

Markus P. Beham is an Assistant Professor at the Chair of Constitutional and Administrative Law, Public International Law, European, and International Economic Law at the University of Passau, Germany.

Routledge Research in International Law

For a full list of titles in this series, visit www.routledge.com/Routledge-Research-in-International-Law/book-series/INTNLLAW

Available:

Regionalism in International Law
Ján Klučka

The International Criminal Court and Nigeria
Implementing the Complementarity Principle of the Rome Statute
Muyiwa Adigun

Armed Conflict and Forcible Displacement
Individual Rights under International Law
Edited by Elena Katselli Proukaki

The Rule of Unwritten International Law
Customary Law, General Principles, and World Order
Peter G. Staubach

State Interest and the Sources of International Law
Doctrine, Morality, and Non-Treaty Law
Markus P. Beham

Demilitarization and International Law in Context
The Åland Islands
Sia Spiliopoulou Åkermark and Saila Heinikoski

International Criminal Law and Sexual Violence against Women
The Interpretation of Gender in the Contemporary International Criminal Trial
Daniela Nadj

Regional Developmentalism Through Law
The Use of Law to Support the Effective Establishment of an African Economic Community
Jonathan Bashi Rudahindwa

State Interest and the Sources of International Law

Doctrine, Morality, and Non-Treaty Law

Markus P. Beham

Routledge
Taylor & Francis Group
LONDON AND NEW YORK

First published 2018
by Routledge

2 Park Square, Milton Park, Abingdon, Oxfordshire OX14 4RN
52 Vanderbilt Avenue, New York, NY 10017

Routledge is an imprint of the Taylor & Francis Group, an informa business

First issued in paperback 2020

Library of Congress Cataloging-in-Publication Data
Names: Beham, Markus Peter, author.
Title: State interest and the sources of international law : doctrine, morality, and non-treaty law / Markus P. Beham.
Description: Abingdon, Oxon [UK] ; New York, NY : Routledge, 2018. | Series: Routledge research in international law | Includes bibliographical references and index.
Identifiers: LCCN 2017055529 | ISBN 9781138298781 (hardback) | ISBN 9781351579964 (web pdf) | ISBN 9781351579957 (epub) | ISBN 9781351579940 (mobipocket)
Subjects: LCSH: International law. | State, The. | International law–Moral and ethical aspects.
Classification: LCC KZ3410 .B44 2018 | DDC 341/.1–dc23
LC record available at https://lccn.loc.gov/2017055529

ISBN: 978-1-138-29878-1 (hbk)
ISBN: 978-0-367-59079-6 (pbk)

Typeset in Galliard
by Taylor & Francis Books

In memory of Christian Fiammengo (1989–2014) who would have been a great international lawyer, and who saw more of the world in 25 years than most diplomats I know

Contents

List of Treaties

List of Cases

Permanent Court of International Justice

International Court of Justice

Arbitral Awards

European Court of Human Rights

International Criminal Tribunal for Yugoslavia

United Kingdom Cases

United States Cases

List of Documents

League of Nations

United Nations

International Labour Organization

European Union

United States

Miscellaneous

Foreword

Sir Karl Popper once observed that the progress of science depends on scholars putting the right questions. But that does not mean that such questions are always appreciated, especially when they call ingrained ideas of the scholarly community into question, or cast doubt on well-loved methods of using them.

Markus Beham sets out to do just that: putting questions – better to say question marks – to hallowed mainstream theories that dominate two areas which are notorious for unsubstantiated claims to the existence of legal rules: certain parts of human rights and humanitarian exceptions to the prohibition of the use of force. With a realistic positivist method, he proposes to separate existing rules of international law from those merely imagined or desired by academics or activists. To establish a firm basis for his examination, he deals first with some pertinent preliminary questions, particularly thorough with source doctrine. Then he uses his findings as tools in the analysis of the subjects. His intrinsic aim is to discover whether "non-treaty" sources support the contention that moral conceptions can make law. In both instances he rejects assertions that binding international law has emerged, either through custom or through the application of general principles of law, arguing that none of the asserters have proven their submissions with any source material, but left it at the assertion. In sum, the book repudiates the thesis that certain moral concepts have, by themselves, generated law.

Persuasive as his conclusions are, they leave the reader nevertheless with an uneasy feeling because that branch of the law needs an undisputed content and, whilst the methods hitherto used to establish it are shown as inappropriate, there seems to be no prospect of legal certainty because of the prevailing illusion that the asserted content is the law. But when the primary aim of the author was "to raise the appeal of analytical honesty and show the benefit of emphasizing positive law and legal methodology for the sake of the credibility of the discipline", he has achieved it.

Even so, his conclusions are disturbing and some might even seem provocative through their pointed formulation. Yet mere indignation is not an appropriate reaction. For those disagreeing with Markus Beham the proper answer is to disprove his conclusions. The book deserves this sort of serious and profound discussion.

Karl Zemanek

Preface

One of the persons I thank in this foreword once told me of the experience of reading publications on the League of Nations from the interwar years, in particular the 1930s. As opposed to the expected eschatological fatalism, his impression was that of listening to the musicians on the Titanic. The reason for writing this book is that this is my impression when reading publications on human rights, the responsibility to protect, or much else on the progressive development of customary international law.

The present work is not only the result of my doctoral thesis at the Université Paris Ouest – Nanterre La Défense and the University of Vienna but, in a sense, a personal coming of age in the study of international law. It reflects the journey of maturing from a young student of international law, passionate about the fads and fashions of the field from international criminal law to the use of force and the responsibility to protect, to a – still somewhat young – researcher accustomed to the discourses and mechanics of a legal system that still fascinates in spite of – or because of – its many deficiencies. Through my socialization at the Section for International Law and International Relations of the University of Vienna, it also stands in the tradition of a long line of thought in legal scholarship developed there, though not often fully recognized as such, that may be placed somewhere between positivism and realism – what one of the anonymous peer-reviewers referred to as "pragmatic positivism".

The opportunities that I have been given both at home and abroad have been as wonderful as they have been generous. I cannot overstate the effect this has had on my outlook on international law. From working with Irmgard Marboe and August Reinisch at the Section for International Law and International Relations to later receiving a fellowship with my thesis supervisor Christian Stadler at the Department of Legal Philosophy, the University of Vienna has proven an optimal hub. Hans-Georg Dederer of the University of Passau, Lori F. Damrosch and Anthea Roberts of Columbia Law School granted me the opportunity of experiencing international law within a transnational context. Joachim Gruber, now at the Westsächsische Hochschule Zwickau, and Jean-Marc Thouvenin of the Université Paris Ouest – Nanterre La Défense allowed me to develop my thesis under the supervision of

the Centre de Droit International de Nanterre. I am grateful to all of my mentors for their encouragement.

The thesis which provided the basis for this book was generously supported by Pro Scientia, the Theodor Körner Foundation, the Université Paris Ouest – Nanterre La Défense, and the University of Vienna. I greatly appreciated the luxury of not having to worry about how to make ends meet.

In the writing process, I was deeply humbled by the honor of having Gerhard Hafner and Karl Zemanek offer comments on my introductory chapter as well as the fruitful discussion with my Austrian colleagues during the presentation of that chapter and the thesis at the Section for International Law and International Relations at the University of Vienna in January 2016. In particular, Stephan Wittich carefully read the entire manuscript and took the time to share his views. Helmut Tichy of the Austrian Foreign Ministry not only took the time to read the manuscript but also, changing hats, played an active role as professor at the University of Graz during the submission of my thesis, for which I am overly grateful. At the Department of Philosophy, I thank Alexander Somek as well as René Kuppe for generously sharing their perspectives on the ideas developed in this book.

My two co-authors on a previous occasion, Melanie Fink and Ralph Janik,[1] were kind enough to provide comments on a number of aspects. I deeply appreciate that they were willing to go over even more of my writing than they already have to by way of a publishing contract. I thank them for their friendship and critical eye to both issues of theory and of style, which greatly improved this contribution.

Finally, I am indebted to the three anonymous peer-reviewers for their comments and suggestions. While many of their comments have been incorporated, the original character of the work has been left to represent the results of my doctoral thesis. Apart from minor additions regarding the literature, most changes concern structure and style of the book.

Needless to say, while the views taken within this publication have greatly benefitted from interacting with all of the inspiring personalities just mentioned, all flaws to the present argument remain the sole responsibility of the author.

Brianna Ascher, Mary Del Plato, Ronnie Morgan, and Nicole Sharpe of Routledge were essential in realizing this book project. Lusana Taylor was a wonderful copy editor to work with. On the way towards the finished product, I must also thank the many employees of the Columbia Law School Library, the Peace Palace Library – in particular the ever-helpful Niels van Tol – and the various libraries of the University of Vienna that I frequented in the writing process. At the University of Passau, Susann Burger, Lisa Paul, and Christiane Schleich made sure to find all necessary publications in the library on the final stretch of the manuscript. The same goes for Patricia Trapp who also provided

1 Markus Beham, Melanie Fink, and Ralph Janik, *Völkerrecht verstehen* (Vienna: Facultas, 2015).

invaluable help in the redaction of the footnotes for publication. Susann Burger and Christiane Schleich were equally active in reading and correcting the final proofs.

Beyond the scope of this book, there is an infinite list of colleagues, friends, and more often both, that I wish to thank for their constant advice, inspiration, and support. I must omit an attempt at an enumerative list for fear of forgetting any one of you. I must, however, explicitly thank Gabriele Buchta and Scarlett Ortner at the University of Vienna as well as Aloisia Falk and Ramona Maier in my new position at the University of Passau for relieving me of the burdens of administrative obligations.

Finally, I thank Lidi – who also took the time to read the entire manuscript – for all her patience, guidance, and attentiveness.

Markus P. Beham

Abbreviations

For the sake of readability, abbreviations have been avoided both within the text and the notes. Where abbreviations are in common use, both in the text, within citations, and for specific forms of reference, they are included in the following list for easy reference.

2d Cir.	United States Court of Appeals for the Second Circuit
add.	addendum
CIL	customary international law
doc.	document
e.g.	*exempli gratia* ("for the sake of example")
ed. / eds	editor / editors
et seq.	*et sequitur* ("and the following")
F.2d	Federal Reporter, Second Series
FIFA	Fédération Internationale de Football Association
fn. / fns	footnote / footnotes (referring to footnotes within a reference)
i.e.	*id est* ("that is")
ibid.	*ibidem* ("in the same place")
ICJ	International Court of Justice
ICTY	International Criminal Tribunal for the former Yugoslavia
id.	*idem* ("the same")
ILC	International Law Commission
L.Ed.	United States Supreme Court Reports, Lawyers' Edition
L.R.	Law Reports (UK)
n. / ns	note / notes (referring to footnotes *supra* or *infra*)
NATO	North Atlantic Treaty Organization
NGO	non-governmental organization
no. / nos	number / numbers
p. / pp.	page / pages
para. / paras	paragraph / paragraphs
PCIJ	Permanent Court of International Justice

R	*Regina* ("queen", UK)
Res.	Resolution
S.Ct.	Supreme Court Reporter (US)
SVN	Satzung der Vereinten Nationen ("Charter of the United Nations")
UK	United Kingdom
UN / U.N.	United Nations
UNGAOR	United Nations General Assembly Official Records
US / U.S.	United States / United States Reports
v.	*versus* ("against")
VCLT	Vienna Convention on the Law of Treaties
VGR	Völkergewohnheitsrecht ("customary international law")
Vol. / Vols	volume / volumes
VR	Völkerrecht ("public international law")
WVK	Wiener Vertragsrechtskonvention ("Vienna Convention on the Law of Treaties")

1 Introduction

A Do You Believe in International Law?

International law has a credibility issue.[1] And it is grounded in its very foundations, the use of its "non-treaty" sources, customary international law, and general principles of law,[2] as rhetorical gap fillers to push the progressive development of international law. A simple comparison between scholarly articles, commentaries, and textbooks with the realities of international relations reveals a disparity that cannot simply be brushed aside.

This fact, in essence, drives the main question of this book: Are these manifestations of international law the optimal vehicle for the pursuit of normative projects; or is their content an unredacted reflection of international relations and domestic legislation? Is international law as it is taught and written illustrative of Plato's allegory of the cave? Is there custom and "custom"? Are there principles and "principles"?

Two case studies, human rights and exceptions to the prohibition of the use of force, have been chosen to illustrate the phenomenon and to argue that there is an inherent connection between state interest and the formation of customary international law respective the identification of general principles of

1 See also on this idea of "international law in crisis" Jean D'Aspremont, 'Send Back the Lifeboats: Confronting the Project of Saving International Law', 108 *American Journal of International Law* (2014) 680.

2 Throughout this book, customary international law is used, on and off, as a *pars pro toto* for "non-treaty" obligations, as it often is. See, *e.g.*, Daniel Bodansky, 'Customary (and Not So Customary) International Environmental Law', 3 *Indian Global Legal Studies Journal* (1995–1996) 115–116; Martti Koskenniemi, 'Introduction', in Martti Koskenniemi (ed.), *Sources of International Law* (Aldershot: Ashgate, 2000) xxi; *id.*, *From Apology to Utopia. The Structure of International Legal Argument,* 2nd edn (Cambridge: Cambridge University Press, 2005) 389 and 392. On the usefulness of the term "non-treaty" law see Daniel Bodansky, 'Prologue to a Theory of Non-Treaty Norms', in Manush H. Arsanjani, Jacob Katz Cogan, Robert D. Sloane, and Siegfried Wiessner (eds), *Looking to the Future. Essays on International Law in Honor of W. Michael Reisman* (Leiden: Martinus Nijhoff, 2011) 120, fn. 7. In addition, Bodansky also includes "soft law". See *ibid.*, at 121.

law. This, in turn, might disfavor moral concepts from becoming non-treaty law altogether.

The idea is to reassess "mainstream" views on the topic and to reconstruct a credible foundation for normative change, rested in positive law. A sound assessment of substantive law equally requires a sound assessment of its manifestations. Thereby, this book makes an argument that spans across a broad stretch of international legal and international relations theory, passing a number of doctrinal roadworks along the way.

1 The Quest for the Status Quo

What the international legal landscape requires is pragmatic "law reform", not just in the sense of tunnel-visioned, forward-moving development, but by taking a step back to reassess and discard norms and ideas that have not managed to acquire any footing in the real world of international relations; what has, in effect, become "out-moded law".[3]

Instead, by putting the cart before the horse, sources doctrine has been gradually redrawn to match the blueprint of whichever agenda requires a legal determination. The discourse takes place both at the level of legal argument and international relations theory; two questions that are inextricably linked, if one must answer to the effectivity of what has been drawn up as a supposed system of rules.

Of course, international law will always have – and should have – a normative component. Without it, there would be stagnation. Yet, any such "utopian"[4] notions must be grounded on a dogmatically[5] sound assessment of the legal *status*

3 See Robert Jennings, 'International Law Reform and Progressive Development', in Gerhard Hafner, Gerhard Loibl, Alfred Rest, Lilly Sucharipa-Behrmann, and Karl Zemanek (eds), *Liber Amicorum Professor Ignaz Seidl-Hohenveldern. In Honour of his 80th Birthday* (The Hague: Kluwer Law International, 1998) 325–326. Here, one might want to add "creation", as much of this credibility issue revolves around the determination of what constitutes customary international law or general principles of law. See also Theodore Funck-Brentano and Albert Sorel, *Précis du Droit des Gens,* 3rd edn (Paris: Librairie Plon, 1900) 2:

> Le droit des gens théorique ne crée point d'obligations positives et ne trace point de règles pratiques, puisqu'il est interprété diversement et qu'il n'est ni observé ni même reconnu par tous les peuples dont il est appelé à diriger la conduite et à régler les relations. Il varie selon les temps, les pays, les écoles de philosophie. Tout traité de droit des gens théorique est un système de politique internationale; il n'engage que l'auteur qui l'a écrit, et toute sa force est dans les idées qu'il renferme.

4 See on this as part of a dichotomy in the international legal argument, most prominently, Koskenniemi, *From Apology to Utopia, supra* n. 2.

5 One of the main agendas of "Rechtsdogmatik" is quality assurance as to the use of certain principles and standards within the legal argument. Unfortunately, the English legal language lacks a corresponding term to the German "Dogmatik" or

quo. Even a policy- or process-oriented approach to international law must first acknowledge the true mechanisms within which a given scenario will take place.[6]

As Lassa Oppenheim already observed in 1912, the task of legal scholars should be, "in the first place, to ascertain and to give precision to the rules which have grown up in custom, and in the second place to formulate the enacted rules in their full content and in their full bearing" in order to bring "to light that there are many gaps not yet regulated by law".[7] Thereby, it may be legitimate "to make proposals *de lege ferenda* of a politico-juridical character", not, however, to "fill up the gaps".[8]

Once the point of departure has been agreed upon, normative efforts may be pursued, so long as they are grounded in the body of positive law. The post-medieval world cannot rely on the Aquinian unity of morality and law.[9] What is right and proper, what is good, must be transposed into law.[10] This basic exercise is a fundamental necessity, for the sake of *Vertrauensschutz* and an overarching rule of law.[11]

"Rechtsdogmatik". Indeed, the term "Dogmatik" is an offspring of the continental law tradition, although it is most probably a uniquely German phenomenon that can be traced back to the attempt to structure the law towards the end of the eighteenth century. See Nils Jansen, 'Rechtsdogmatik im Zivilrecht', *Enzyklopädie zur Rechtsphilosophie* <www.enzyklopaedie-rechtsphilosophie.net/inhaltsverzeichnis/19-beitraege/98-rechtsdogmatik-im-zivilrecht>, paras 1 and 4. See further, generally, Aleksander Peczenik, 'Scientia Iuris – An Unsolved Philosophical Problem', 3/3 *Ethical Theory and Moral Practice* (2000) 273–302. However, to avoid confusion with ideas such as "doctrine", "interpretation", and "legal theory" in the Anglophone legal tradition, the term "dogmatic" will be used throughout this book, although the definitions of the *Concise Oxford English Dictionary* for "dogmatics" as either "inclined to assert principles or opinions as inconvertibly true" or "a system of dogma, especially one laid down by the Roman Catholic Church" have nothing to do with what is meant by the corresponding German *terminus technicus*. On the differentiation between legal theory and dogmatics see also Michael Potacs, *Rechtstheorie* (Vienna: Facultas, 2015) 24–26. See also the elaborations on the German academic tradition in Anthea Roberts, *Is International Law International?* (Oxford: Oxford University Press, 2017).

6 See Oscar Schachter, *International Law in Theory and Practice* (Developments in International Law, Vol. 13; Dordrecht: Martinus Nijhoff, 1991) 34.

7 Lassa Oppenheim, *The Future of International Law* (Pamphlet Series of the Carnegie Endowment for International Peace, Division of International Law, No. 39; Oxford: Oxford University Press, 1921) 57. The original German version was first published in 1912, the English first edition in 1914.

8 *Ibid*., at 57.

9 See on the differentiation between morality and legality *infra* pp. 46 *et seq*. and extensively elaborated pp. 114 *et seq*.

10 Then the rule might even be that "what is right and proper is the law", conditional upon the evidence that this rule exists in some manifestation of international law (*quod non*, unfortunately).

11 In the broad sense that the (black letter) law takes precedent. Used in this broad sense, legitimate expectations are equally a part of the rule of law. For a basic definition see also Philip R. Wood, *The Fall of the Priests and the Rise of the Lawyers* (Oxford: Hart Publishing, 2016) 54.

It might be helpful as a starting point of this discussion to recall a truism formulated by Emerson Tiller and Frank Cross in their article on legal doctrine, that "[p]olitical researchers have too often focused on outcomes and ignored doctrine", whereas "[l]egal researchers have studied doctrine as pure legal reasoning, without recognizing its political component".[12] While this latter element plays a role in the formation of international law, it should not guide those seeking to identify the body of positive law.

At the same time, norms and ideas that have not managed to acquire any footing in the real world of international relations – not in the theory of international relations – must be recognized as "out-moded law",[13] activists distinguished from academics.

2 Methodology as Added Value

This is not to say that obsessing over methodology[14] should become a self-purpose, as Anthony D'Amato suggests that "excessive preoccupation with the tools (the law-words) of the legal system distorts, in some students' minds perhaps irrevocably, what law is all about and what it is for".[15] He goes on to state that this "elevates tools over goals, form over substance, manipulations over justice".[16]

However, the exact opposite should be the case: Normative goals must be achieved through a dogmatically sound assessment of the legal *status quo* – it is simply a form of quality assurance as to the use of certain principles and standards within the legal argument.[17] Without this, "substance" and "justice" can only be a form of agenda or policy, not law. However, the purpose of the present argument is not analytic clarity alone.

3 Pending Added Value

The added value of this exercise should be the reconstruction of a credible foundation for normative change, both for the sake of satisfying

12 Frank B. Cross and Emerson H. Tiller, 'What is Legal Doctrine?', 100/1 *Northwestern University Law Review* (2006) 528.

13 See *supra* n. 3.

14 On the complexities of methodology, generally, see Jean D'Aspremont, *Epistemic Forces in International Law. Foundational Doctrines and Techniques of International Legal Argumentation* (Cheltenham: Edward Elgar, 2015) 177–198.

15 Anthony A. D'Amato, *Introduction to Law and Legal Thinking* (Irvington-on-Hudson: Transnational, 1996) 186.

16 *Ibid.*

17 See *supra* n. 5. Just as law journals serve the purpose of ensuring quality of publications contained therein. See on this Jean D'Aspremont and Larissa van den Herik, 'The Public Good of Academic Publishing in International Law', 26/1 *Leiden Journal of International Law* (2013) *passim.*

legitimate expectations of its subjects[18] and the rule of law. At the same time, it is a call to channel the rhetorical and scholarly energies towards goals that are achievable under an existent system, the legal *status quo*, as opposed to creating what W. Michael Reisman has referred to as "*lex simulata*".[19]

One suggestion concerning the rule of law might be that states are to be encouraged to ratify[20] and withdraw reservations to treaties, if they should be bound, as opposed to reliance on the proposition that there are customary obligations or general principles of law in place that make non-committal attitudes to treaty efforts acceptable. Equally, treaty rules alone should be sufficient without the need to find that they are "strengthened" by additional non-treaty law.[21]

Of course, the immediate rebuke would be that uncertainties would only transition from the use of non-treaty sources to the question of subsequent practice or treaty interpretation.[22] Yet unless one engages in dynamic teleological interpretation, which is, in any case, usually aimed at normative expansion of the application of a treaty provision, a textual or systematic reading will not leave the door wide open, where a rule is sufficiently clear.[23]

18 Not in the narrow sense of international investment law as an emanation of the fair and equitable treatment standard but more generally as the expectation of the individual subjects that administrative and judicial decisions will be based on what has been the representation of the (black letter) law.

19 W. Michael Reisman, 'International Law-making: A Process of Communication', 75 *American Society of International Law Proceedings* (1981) 102.

20 See with regard to humanitarian intervention Philip C. Jessup, 'The Defense of Oppressed Peoples', 31/1 *American Journal of International Law* (1938) 117.

21 See, *e.g.*, Javaid Rehman, *International Human Rights Law*, 2nd edn (Harlow: Pearson, 2010) 810, who writes that the treaty prohibitions of torture are "strengthened by international customary law". He goes on to add: "Furthermore it can also be asserted forcefully that the prohibition on torture is a norm of *jus cogens*, a norm from which no derogation is permissible". In this logic, normativity follows a three-prong test: Is there a treaty rule? Is there a corresponding customary international law rule? Does this rule also enjoy *ius cogens* status?

22 See on this also the agora on 'Court Generated State Practice?' 20 *Austrian Review of International and European Law* (2015) to which the present author has also contributed.

23 See *Competence of the General Assembly for the Admission of a State to the United Nations*, Advisory Opinion of 3 March 1950, ICJ Reports 1950, p. 4, at 8: "If the relevant words in their natural and ordinary meaning make sense in their context, that is an end of the matter". Cf., however, Koskenniemi, *From Apology to Utopia*, *supra* n. 2, at 340–341. A second, follow-up suggestion to this might be to focus on the elimination or, at least, avoidance of such drafting tools as "constructive ambiguity", where it will likely result in non-compliance with the object and purpose of the rule.

If the International Court of Justice rules that torture[24] and the prohibition of genocide[25] constitute *ius cogens*[26] in an *obiter dictum*,[27] this could lead to the belief that international law has a capacity to protect individuals from such acts. As opposed to treaty bodies and regimes, there is no institution at the international level where individuals can bring up violations of customary international law or *ius cogens*. An international legal system that seeks to place the rule of law at its centre and honors the legitimate expectations of both its subjects and its observers[28] – and manages not to disappoint – is an effective international legal system.

One need not be a cynic to realize that a farmer in North Korea, a sub-Saharan refugee on the Sinai Peninsula, or a Yazidi girl in Iraq will doubt the capacity of international law to alleviate their suffering. The findings of international courts, tribunals, and scholars may constitute the "legal *status quo*" for an academic elite, but not for those that hope to rely on it. Irrespective of the moral gravity of a certain rule, the assessment of a rule as *ius cogens* or as non-treaty law in light of contrary practice might blind scholars and practitioners from deficiencies in the level of protection that need to be addressed.

4 Immediate Goals

Normative efforts in international law must be grounded on a dogmatically sound assessment of the legal *status quo*. This book is not the manifest of a heretic on a "crusade against the growing impact of international law on our lives",[29] but the attempt of an apologetic of international law to convince one's peers of the need

24 See *Questions Relating to the Obligation to Prosecute or Extradite* (Belgium *v.* Senegal), Judgment of 20 July 2012, ICJ Reports 2012, p. 422, at 457, para. 99.

25 See *Case Concerning Armed Activities on the Territory of the Congo (New Application: 2002)* (Democratic Republic of the Congo *v.* Rwanda), Judgment of 3 February 2006 (Jurisdiction and Admissibility), ICJ Reports 2006, p. 6, at 32, para. 64. See, more recently, also *Application of the Convention on the Prevention and Punishment of the Crime of Genocide* (Croatia *v.* Serbia), Judgment of 3 February 2015, ICJ Reports 2015, p. 3, at 48, para. 87.

26 At this point the author feels obliged to comment that it is regrettable that the majority of the literature, as well as the VIENNA CONVENTION ON THE LAW OF TREATIES itself, adds the letter "j" to the Latin alphabet. The correct term is "*ius cogens*", not "*jus cogens*"; as everyone who has watched *Indiana Jones and the Last Crusade* should know: "But in the Latin alphabet, Jehovah begins with an 'I.'" Of course, the test here is academic debate and not "three instruments of lethal cunning", which is probably why people do not take such great issue with the use of the letter "j".

27 On instances of other, in particular regional human rights courts see Tawhida Ahmed and Israel de Jesús Butler, 'The European Union and Human Rights: An International Law Perspective', 17/4 *European Journal of International Law* (2006) 779–780, fns 49–59 and accompanying text.

28 In the case of international law, the population in so far as these individuals are not themselves subjects.

29 See Jens David Ohlin, *The Assault on International Law* (Oxford: Oxford University Press, 2015) 9 with regard to the movement of the "new realists".

for scholarly restraint in determining the positive law[30] – as difficult as this may seem in light of the phenomenon that Bruno Simma once called "Normenhunger".[31] Norms need some form of social validation.[32]

The analysis is motivated by the powerful force that positive law could have as a stabilizer of international relations as well as the harm it has been done by the mushrooming of agenda and opinion over sound academic analysis.[33] Agenda and

30 See the conclusion of Jörg Kammerhofer in his pointed analysis of the issue 'Law-Making by Scholarship? The Dark Side of 21st Century Legal "Methodology"', in James Crawford and Sarah Nouwen (eds), *Select Proceedings of the European Society of International Law: Third Volume: International Law 1989–2010: A Performance Appraisal* (Oxford: Hart Publishing, 2012) 125.

31 See Bruno Simma, *Das Reziprozitätselement in der Entstehung des Völkergewohnheitsrechts* (München: Wilhelm Fink, 1970) 28.

32 See Charles de Visscher, *Theory and Reality in Public International Law. Revised Edition* (Princeton: Princeton University Press, 1968) 137 and 143:

> Every rule of positive international law thus presents two essential aspects for critical examination on different planes: the degree in which its content corresponds to social needs, and the accuracy of its formal expression compared with the practice of States. The rule of international law retains its full force in application, and consequently all its positiveness, only insofar as it satisfies this double requirement. This is a fact of experience particularly well illustrated in treaty regulation. A normative (law-making) treaty the content of which is too far in advance of development in international relations is stillborn, just as a treaty that ceases to be exactly observed in the practice of governments is no longer valid in its formal expression. [...] If abstraction carried to an extreme degenerates into unreality, individualization pushed to excess leads to the destruction of the rule. International justice expecially [*sic*] must maintain a proper relationship between social data and the rules designed to govern them.

See also Philip Alston, 'Conjuring Up New Human Rights: A Proposal for Quality Control', 78/3 *American Journal of International Law* (1984) 614. This must, however, not be mistaken with the assumption that something is "law just because it is (alleged to be) socially necessary: here be the lions (as maps used to say) of natural law and policy-oriented jurisprudence". See Maurice Mendelson, 'The Subjective Element in Customary International Law', 66/1 *British Yearbook of International Law* (1995) 197.

33 It has been pointed out that this is not necessarily intentional but that agenda may simply block the path to a correct assessment of the law. See Kammerhofer, *supra* n. 30, at 116. See the potential effects of this pointed out by Alexander Somek:

> [T]he normative premises of doctrine require, lest they claim to represent natural law, social validation. Without such validation, doctrine is likely to behave in the manner reminiscent of the demeanour that Machiavelli observed in oligarchs vis-à-vis the lesser sort. It becomes insolent and boisterous. When unleashed from political authority, doctrine runs a high risk of becoming indistinguishable from exuberant prophecies and divinations of supreme principles. Doctrine without practice is fanciful; it begins to design projects of legal reform, for it is always inclined to purify the system of those principles that threaten to render it murky. Doctrine must protect itself against its own insolence vis-à-vis politics.

opinion must be detracted from the scholarship of international law. Purely normative and progressive assessments of an assumed "legal *status quo*" come at the cost of formal determinacy of positive law. Loss of determinacy comes at the cost of credibility. Loss of credibility comes at the cost of relevance. *E contrario*, analytical clarity of a subject may, in effect, pave the way towards higher compliance.

While some of the following propositions may seem "conservative" and "out-dated" at a first glance – as "positivist" or "realist" ideas often do[34] – they are not grounded in a revisionist mind-set. Much rather, they seek to assist the debate to focus on what is really – and realistically – necessary to give international law a credible normative component. The analysis is no less than a proposal to rethink the building blocks of international law[35] through an unfiltered lens, unburdened by "mainstream" doctrine[36] and, thereby, reconstruct a credible foundation for normative change. Karl Zemanek has called for "mehr Realismus und Wahrheit", "more realism and truth", in the scholarship of international law.[37] This is the immediate goal and, in itself, an added value. Depending on whether these considerations will be accepted, lofty goals await.

5 *The Factual*

a *Irrelevance of Words*

While "rethinking the building blocks of international law" might seem a rather pompous proposition, it requires little more than looking past the words

See *id.*, 'Beyond Kelsen and Hart', in Jean D'Aspremont and Jörg Kammerhofer (eds), *International Legal Positivism in a Post-Modern World* (Cambridge: Cambridge University Press, 2014) 177. See also James C. Hathaway, *The Rights of Refugees Under International Law* (Cambridge: Cambridge University Press, 2005) 31–32.

34 See, *e.g.*, the introduction by Andreas L. Paulus and Bruno Simma, 'The Responsibility of Individuals for Human Rights Abuses in Internal Conflicts: A Positivist View', 93/2 *American Journal of International Law* (1999) 302.

35 See also Prosper Weil, 'Toward Relative Normativity in International Law?', 77 *American Journal of International Law* (1983) 440: "A system builder by vocation, the jurist cannot dispense with a minimum of conceptual scaffolding".

36 On this idea of "mainstream doctrine" see, in particular, Martti Koskenniemi, 'The Pull of the Mainstream', Review of Theodor Meron, *Human Rights and Humanitarian Norms as Customary Law* (Oxford: Clarendon Press, 1989), 88 *Michigan Law Review* (1990) 1946–1962.

37 See Karl Zemanek, 'Für mehr Offenheit und Realismus in der Völkerrechtslehre', in Klaus Dicke, Stephan Hobe, Karl-Ulrich Meyn, Anne Peters, Eibe Riedel, Hans-Joachim Schütz, and Christian Tietje (eds), *Weltinnenrecht. Liber amicorum Jost Delbrück* (Veröffentlichungen des Walther-Schücking-Instituts für Internationales Recht an der Universität Kiel, Vol. 155; Berlin: Duncker & Humblot, 2005) 907 *et passim*. See also Funck-Brentano and Sorel, *supra* n. 3, at 49:

> Ce n'est pas en spéculant sur les rapports abstraits de nations idéales que les hommes apporteront plus d'ordre et de justice dans les relations des États; c'est en considérant les faits dans leur réalité et en recherchant, sans illusion, sans passion et sans défaillance, les lois qui les régissent.

of international law textbooks, judgments, and decisions of human rights bodies as well as the voices of state representatives in the media and the bodies of international organizations to simply take acts of states for what they are, when determining non-treaty law.[38]

Uncoated by rhetoric and stereotypical assessments, Occam's razor will easily help the "extra-terrestrial observer" or, one could say in this context, "agendaless observer"[39] to either identify the true intentions of states or determine that these are indeterminable (by matter of fact) or indistinguishable (by matter of ulterior motives).[40] Hortatory rhetoric has become the habit in international discourse.[41] More often than not, a common-sense appreciation of the obvious – "pragmatic positivism" – will lead to a more honest assessment of what states consider to be the law.[42]

b Relevance of Words

This does not mean that one must fully ignore the rhetoric of scholars and states. Words may assist our "extra-terrestrial observer" in making an inclusive determination of a certain act. Just like the Pied Piper led rats through the street, teachers of international law, often also active as officials in the foreign service or international organizations,[43] have made a deep impression upon

38 As Charles de Visscher pointedly remarked: "Every political enterprise is clothed in some kind of moral justification, every program of expansion combines with the use of force the formulas of a civilizing ideal". See *id., supra* n. 32, at 95. See also Ingo Venzke and Jochen von Bernstorff, 'Ethos, Ethics, and Morality in International Relations', in *Max Planck Encyclopedia of Public International Law*, para. 10 <http://opil.ouplaw.com/view/10.1093/law:epil/9780199231690/law-9780199231690-e936?rskey=v1zt5J&result=2&prd=EPIL>, who hold that

> [a]ppeals to morality serve to conceal self-interested action, and an international morality is likely to be the product of dominant groups that succeed in aligning a sense of what is right and good with their interests and views.

39 On this approach see also Bodansky, 'Customary (and Not So Customary) International Environmental Law', *supra* n. 2, at 110–111.

40 On the disparity between what states say and what they do see also Jack L. Goldsmith and Eric A. Posner, *The Limits of International Law* (Oxford: Oxford University Press, 2005) 167–184; J. Shand Watson, 'Legal Theory, Efficacy and Validity in the Development of Human Rights Norms in International Law', *University of Illinois Law Forum* (1979) 632–633.

41 See also Jack Donnelly, 'Human Rights, Democracy, and Development', 21/3 *Human Rights Quarterly* (1999) 611: "Whatever the gap between theory and practice, most states today prominently feature appeals to human rights, democracy, and development in their efforts to establish national and international legitimacy".

42 See Kammerhofer, *supra* n. 30, at 125.

43 See Ohlin, *supra* n. 29, at 11.

how questions of international relations and international law are discussed. They have provided a discoursive framework.[44]

Notwithstanding, it is obvious that not each and every statement by the "most highly qualified publicist"[45] will reflect the reality of what states believe the law to be[46] and, of course, this may, in turn, equally suit states that do not willingly grant insight into what they really believe.[47] Discoursive frameworks such as that provided by the technical terms of international law alleviate "doublespeak".

Yet sometimes words do speak out for themselves, explicitly or through contradiction, in a single instance or through a behavioral pattern, to allow for brief snapshots of what states actually consider to be the law.[48] As an international legal professional, in practice or in academia, it is essential to be the photographer that hits the button at just the right moment to capture these instances of "honest" states in action. The "Pulitzer Prize for Positive Law" awaits for those who determine the legal *status quo*.

c Baseline

Why do international law textbooks, judgments, and decisions of human rights bodies or state representatives and the representatives of international organizations say what they do? In answering this question, apart from the lawyer's hat, one may need some understanding of linguistic, psychological, and sociological processes to differentiate between the words states use, as "[a]ny study of the action of power on international law [...] demands knowledge of all the social realities that determine this action as well as knowledge of the processes of formal elaboration by which it takes effect".[49]

Not each and every public proposition that bolsters or defies "mainstream" doctrine and jurisprudence – and may thus seem more "honest" than others – goes beyond political opportunism. There may be an infinite number of reasons why states say what they do, ranging from carefully voiced statements to completely random outbursts.

44 See Jean D'Aspremont, 'If International Judges Say So, It Must Be True: Empiricism or Fetishism?', 4/9 *ESIL Reflections* (2015) fn. 9 and accompanying text <www.esil-sedi.eu/node/1134>. See also, generally, *id.*, 'Wording in International Law', 25/3 *Leiden Journal of International Law* (2012) *passim*; Nicholas Greenwood Onuf, *World of Our Making: Rules and Rule in Social Theory and International Relations* (Studies in International Relations; Columbia: University of South Carolina, 1989) 252.

45 See Article 38(1)(d) of the Statute of the International Court of Justice.

46 As Sir Christopher Greenwood put it in one of his contributions to the UN Lecture Series: "And it's very important to keep in mind that international law is made by what states do, not by what professors like me say". See *id.*, 'The Sources of International Law', Original Lecture, Sources of Law, United Nations Audiovisual Library of International Law <http://legal.un.org/avl/ls/Greenwood_IL.html#>.

47 See also Goldsmith and Posner, *supra* n. 40, at 167–184; Koskenniemi, *From Apology to Utopia*, *supra* n. 2, at 386–387.

48 See also Onuf, *supra* n. 44, at 228–229.

49 De Visscher, *supra* n. 32, at 138.

For this reason, it is not possible to stop at the mere factual level. The analysis would have to conclude with either finding a formal mechanism to determine what states actually believe – an endeavor highly unlikely to be blessed with success – or to take an exclusive black-letter approach to the external expressions of states.[50]

6 The Abstract

The issue must also be confronted at an abstract level by taking a step back and reassessing the teachings of "mainstream" doctrine in light of the cast of actors of international law. It is absolutely quintessential to understand who the relevant stakeholders are and what makes them "tick", if one wants to attempt a reliable determination of positive law.

If the question involves customary international law and general principles of law, this necessitates not just a knowledge of these two manifestations of international law but also an understanding of the main entities that take the stage to participate in the formation process. It is, therefore, essential to include considerations such as to the nature and function of states[51] – for they are the primary actors of international law.[52]

50 See on the latter view, for example, Michael Akehurst, 'Custom as a Source of International Law', 47 *British Yearbook of International Law* (1974–1975) 36: "[W]hat matters is statements, not beliefs". Cf., however, Bodansky, 'Prologue to a Theory of Non-Treaty Norms', *supra* n. 2, at 125: "[T]he issue is not what states believe, but whether they in fact engage in rule-governed behavior". See also the view shared by Bruno Simma and Alfred Verdross, *Universelles Völkerrecht. Theorie und Praxis,* 3rd edn (Berlin: Duncker & Humblot, 1984) 355, § 562:

> Die Organe, die, [*sic*] für den Staat handeln und VR anwenden, sind Menschen. Nur um *ihr* Rechtsbewußtsein und um jenes der Experten, die ihnen in Völkerrechtsfragen zur Seite stehen, geht es. Ähnliches gilt für den Einwand, daß das Rechtsbewußtsein als innerseelischer Vorgang kaum nachzuweisen sei. Denn dabei wird übersehen, daß es sich bei der Ermittlung einer Norm des VGR nicht um einen psychologischen Befund, sondern immer nur um die Deutung von Erklärungen, Duldungen oder Unterlassungen der maßgeblichen Organe drehen kann, die uns über deren Rechtsauffassung Auskunft geben.

As a trade-off against indeterminacy in the formation of customary international law, this view does not consider the factor of rhetoric in international law, however.

51 See also Koskenniemi, *From Apology to Utopia, supra* n. 2, at 305: "Sources doctrine must, in some way, link itself to concrete State behavior, will and interest".

52 See on this the references given *infra* n. 75 and ns 683–684. As subjects of international law derivative of states, international organizations will – in accordance with the general principle of law *nemo plus iuris transferre potest quam ipse habet* – at a minimum not carry out functions beyond those of states, even if their nature may be somewhat different. This may become more nuanced in constellations, in which NGOs, multi- or transnational corporations, or individuals are integrated into the decision-making process.

B What if I Told You...

Of course, opposed to what the "dinner-party staple"[53] question inherent in the supposed *Matrix* movie reference suggests, international law exists. It is evidenced by the legion of employees of international organizations and the legal staff of foreign ministries around the world.

The question is only whether international law should constitute a constructive and stabilizing force in international relations or if it should merely offer the discoursive framework or the vocabulary for states to conduct their relations amongst each other.

While it may, in fact, do both, hortatory phrases alone will do little good in strengthening the rule of law; too much may rather lead to the decrease of international law language as an expression of authority in international relations.[54] On the contrary, it will increase its perception as "doublespeak".

1 External Perspectives

Outsiders to the field more often than not view international law as a charade, put in place to add formality or a fickle sense of orderliness to the politics of international relations.[55] As the "father of classical realism", Hans Morgenthau, remarked, "[i]t is a strange paradox that the lay public has observed a much more sceptical and realistic, therefore scientific, attitude toward international law than the science of international law itself".[56]

53 Gerry Simpson, 'On the Magic Mountain: Teaching Public International Law', 10 *European Journal of International Law* (1999) 74.
54 See Hathaway, *supra* n. 33, at 31–32.
55 See James Leslie Brierly, *The Outlook for International Law* (Oxford: Clarendon Press, 1944) 1–2; Zemanek, *supra* n. 37, at 895. See also de Visscher, *supra* n. 32, at 144:

> Having their source in governmental practices inaccessible to the immense majority of men, the rules of international law bear for the most part no clearly perceptible relation to the necessarily very summary ideas that opinion forms of international relations.

56 See Hans J. Morgenthau, 'Positivism, Functionalism and International Law', 34/2 *American Journal of International Law* (1940) 260. See also J. Shand Watson, *Theory & Reality in the International Protection of Human Rights* (Ardsley: Transnational Publishers, 1999) 1, who uses this quote as an introduction to the first chapter of his critique of human rights scholarship, and Brian D. Lepard, 'Towards a Normative Theory of Customary International Law as Law', 103 *American Society of International Law Proceedings* (2009) 379. To the quote from Morgenthau one has to add "by the 'lay public'" that understands what public international lawyers mean when they say "public international law". Just moments before putting these lines to paper, a friendly conversation at the airport baggage claim after recognizing apparel from a common *alma mater*, resulted in a complaint about those practising "international law" (*i.e.* the author of these lines) for so unfairly deciding custody cases between parents of different nationalities. See also the anecdote by David Kennedy, *A World of Struggle. How Power, Law,*

Any teacher of international law will know the difficulty of explaining to students that the subject one is so passionate about fits firmly within their law school curriculum, while forcing them to accept that a political whim can strike down centuries-old practice and leave those unfortunate enough to have relied on the protection of the "international legal system" without redress.[57] The exercise can be as challenging as it is frustrating.

A further illuminating perspective would be the exposure of scholars and employees of governmental and international organizations to classic "private practice". While some corporate lawyers will frown at anything including the words "human rights" or "corporate social responsibility",[58] oftentimes perceiving it as burdensome sugar-coating, litigators will bask in the vast multitude of legitimate arguments that survive the laugh test in international adjudication.[59] Too easily, one might feel driven back to that "dinner-party staple" question.[60]

2 *The International College of Legal Illusionists*

Yet these very same aspects – in addition to an often insurmountable dose of idealism[61] – are what draw an ever-growing crowd of scholars and – another

and Expertise Shape Global Political Economy (Princeton: Princeton University Press, 2016) 174. Cf., however, *ibid.*, at 198. For an attempt to raise awareness of the importance of international law among the public for such situations see American Society for International Law (ed.), *International Law: 100 Ways it Shapes our Lives* <www.asil.org/sites/default/files/100%20Ways%20Booklet_2011.pdf>.

57 See on this dilemma, generally, Simpson, *supra* n. 53, *passim*.

58 This is, of course, more a caricature than an academic appraisal but it has been witnessed by the present author on numerous occasions, may that be a representative sample or not. See on this also Simpson, *ibid.*, at 74, fn. 25.

59 Also referred to as the "giggle test" or "straight face test" to see whether a legal argument can be made without the proponent breaking out in laughter due to its lack of seriousness. See James W. McElhaney, 'The Giggle Test', *ABA Journal. The Lawyer's Magazine* (1 October 1988) 90–92. During a career event at Columbia Law School in the spring term of 2015, the partner of a very prominent, internationally active law firm, was heard by the present author to say: "The best thing about international law is that most of the time you are making things up".

60 See *supra* n. 53.

61 On the problematic consequences of idealism in international law see Jennings, *supra* n. 3, at 326:

> The principal reason for this neglect of the subject [law reform] by international lawyers themselves is surely that the whole public international law culture that we have inherited from previous generations of international lawyers is calculated to discourage any thought of reform of the core subjects of the system. Those previous generations were inspired by an almost missionary spirit of zeal and enthusiasm; and this was an understandable and indeed sometimes effective reaction to a general scepticism about the subject often amounting to a disbelief in the very existence of any international law that was truly law. [...] It was natural and proper therefore that international lawyers should have put

peculiarity of international law – a smaller crowd of practitioners to the field.[62] The legion of unpaid interns at international organizations such as the United Nations are living proof of this transcendent appeal.[63] Why else digress from other more immediately financially rewarding careers in securities transactions or M&A? Of course, there are realists awaiting the larger spoils of working in top-tier investment arbitration practices. But the impression prevails that the gravitational pull is emitted by the fascination of doing work that smells like policy, less like law.

The result is, of course, paradoxical – and some might think even frightening: ending up either with lawyers trying to make policy in their juridical capacity or policy makers shaping the law as they go along,[64] "[t]he cosmopolitan scholar as law-giver".[65] In academic scholarship and international adjudication this has led to a normative turn,[66] in which the agenda surpasses any sense of legal

much energy into believing and propagating the message that international law is truly law, and that it is good and necessary law; and the great need was for more of it and for the development and elaboration of that which we had. International law became not just a subject of study but a cause to be energetically protected and propagated. [...] This was an admirable attitude at a time when the great need was for the elaboration and development of law. But this legal culture, still immensely powerful, hardly produces an intellectual climate in which the shortcomings and inadequacy of some of the core areas of international law could easily command attention and sympathy. To attempt to do so has often been rather regarded as a sort of treachery to the subject. It is perhaps not then surprising that law reform is so little heard of amongst public international lawyers.

62 See on this, generally, Martti Koskenniemi, 'Between Commitment and Cynicism: Outline for a Theory of International Law as Practice', in Martti Koskenniemi (ed.), *The Politics of International Law* (Oxford: Hart Publishing, 2011) 271–293, originally published in Office of Legal Affairs (ed.), *Collection of Essays by Legal Advisers of States, Legal Advisers of International Organizations and Practitioners in the Field of International Law / Recueil d'Articles de Conseillers Juridiques d'États, d'Organisations Internationales et de Praticiens du Droit International* (New York: United Nations, 1999) 495–523. See also Kammerhofer, *supra* n. 30, at 116–118.

63 Which can easily be witnessed every Friday at the Delegates Lounge at the UN Headquarters in New York, where interns flock to enjoy the privilege of drinking with diplomats and UN staff within the inviolable walls of an international organization building. On the dilemma of unpaid internships see 'Why the UN Doesn't pay its Interns', *The Economist* (20 August 2015) <www.economist.com/blogs/economist-explains/2015/08/economist-explains-15>.

64 As Jörg Kammerhofer writes, "we will be reduced to second-rate politicians". See *id., supra* n. 30, at 125.

65 Jan Paulsson, 'Scholarship as Law', in Manush H. Arsanjani, Jacob Katz Cogan, Robert D. Sloane, and Siegfried Wiessner (eds), *Looking to the Future. Essays on International Law in Honor of W. Michael Reisman* (Leiden: Martinus Nijhoff, 2011) 183.

66 See also Martti Koskenniemi, '"The Lady Doth Protest Too Much". Kosovo, and the Turn to Ethics in International Law', 65/2 *Modern Law Review* (2002) 159, 170–171 *et passim*. This phenomenon has also been referred to as "confidence in

positivism.[67] As a consequence, a select number of academic legal elite – flatteringly fashioned as an "invisible college of international lawyers"[68] or a "guild of international lawyers"[69] – has gradually created a body of law that runs parallel to, rather than intersecting with the realities of a state-centred international political system.

It would be pretentious, however, to try and sell this as a novel observation. Already in 1909, John Chipman Gray observed: "On no subject of human interest, except theology, has there been so much loose writing and nebulous speculation as on International Law".[70]

Against the background of such an epistemic community, the need is great for the lawyer to refrain from "facilitat[ing] the decision maker's dilemma between law and politics (and, occasionally, between law and morals), but to clarify the legal side of things".[71]

3 *The "Is" and the "Ought"*

While a purely descriptive legal regime is little more than a subservient justification device,[72] a body of "law" completely detached cannot succeed in

progress". See Alexander Somek, 'From the Rule of Law to the Constitutionalist Makeover: Changing European Conceptions of Public International Law', 18/4 *Constellations* (2011) 581. Of course, such a "normative turn" is not necessarily negative, if it is grounded in *lex lata*. Already Hersch Lauterpacht, in his seminal work on the role of the International Court of Justice in determining international law held: "Judicial legislation, so long as it does not assume the form of deliberate disregard of the existing law, is a phenomenon both healthy and unavoidable". See *id.*, *The Development of International Law by the International Court* (London: Stevens & Sons, 1958) 156.

67 See Mary Ellen O'Connell, 'Taking *Opinio Juris* Seriously, a Classical Approach to International Law on the Use of Force', in Enzo Cannizzaro and Paolo Palchetti (eds), *Customary International Law on the Use of Force. A Methodological Approach* (Leiden: Martinus Nijhoff, 2005) 9–10, in particular fn. 1 with further references.

68 On this idea of the profession as an "invisible college of international lawyers" see Oscar Schachter, 'The Invisible College of International Lawyers', 72 *Northwestern University Law Review* (1977–1978) 217–226. See also Richard B. Lillich, 'The Growing Importance of Customary International Human Rights Law', 25/1 *Georgia Journal of International and Comparative Law* (1995–1996) 30. For a more recent appraisal of this idea see Santiago Villalpando, 'The "Invisible College of International Lawyers" Forty Years Later', *European Society of International Law. Conference Paper Series*, No. 5/2013, Amsterdam Research Forum (23–25 May 2013) <http://papers.ssrn.com/sol3/papers.cfm?abstract_id=2363640>.

69 Jean D'Aspremont and Jörg Kammerhofer, 'Introduction: The Future of International Legal Positivism', in *id.* (eds), *International Legal Positivism in a Post-Modern World* (Cambridge: Cambridge University Press, 2014) 1–3.

70 John C. Gray, *The Nature and Sources of the Law. The Carpenter Lectures. 1908–1909* (New York: Columbia University Press, 1927) 122.

71 Paulus and Simma, *supra* n. 34, at 307.

72 See Martti Koskenniemi, 'The Normative Force of Habit: International Custom and Social Theory', 1 *Finnish Yearbook of International Law* (1990) 83.

creating a functioning rule of law,[73] let alone further legitimacy. The goal is to find the prescriptive between the normative and the descriptive:

> [Customary international law] prohibits torture, but torture is epidemic in the international system. [Customary international law] prohibits the use or threat of force, but States clearly still consider, and use force as, [*sic*] an instrument of national policy. [Customary international law] prescribes humanitarian behavior in international and civil conflict, but atrocities occur in virtually every conflict on appalling scales. Transboundary harm from pollution is prohibited, but States continue to pollute with adverse transboundary effects.[74]

73 This is particularly the case with regard to non-treaty sources such as customary international law. See Gérard Cahin, 'Le Rôle des Organes Politiques des Nations Unies', in Cannizzaro and Palchetti (eds), *supra* n. 67, at 147:

> S'il est vrai que pour faire état de règles du droit international en vigueur, "il faut qu'il existe une certaine concordance entre les mots qui expriment ces règles et les conduites étatiques visées par celles-ci", cette exigence ne revêt pas exactement la même portée pour le droit conventionnel et pour le droit coutumier: à la différence du premier, qui existe sans avoir à démontrer une pratique conforme au moment de la conclusion du traité, le second ne se conçoit pas en dehors de cette pratique, inhérente à la notion même de coutume, et dont la conformité à la règle invoquée est précisément censée attester l'existence et la vigueur continue.

See also Anthea Elizabeth Roberts, 'Traditional and Modern Approaches to Customary International Law: A Reconciliation', 95 *American Journal of International Law* (2001) 762. On the general dilemma between "concreteness" and "normativity" in this sense see Martti Koskenniemi, 'The Politics of International Law', in Martti Koskenniemi (ed.), *The Politics of International Law* (Oxford: Hart Publishing, 2011) 39, originally published in 1 *European Journal of International Law* (1990) 8:

> This argumentative structure, however, which forces jurists to prove that their law is valid because it is concrete and normative [...], both creates and destroys itself. For it is impossible to prove that a rule, principle or doctrine (in short, an argument) is both concrete and normative simultaneously. The two requirements *cancel each other out*. An argument about concreteness is an argument about the closeness of a particular rule, principle or doctrine to state practice. However, the closer to state practice an argument is, the less normative and the more political it seems. The more it seems just another uncritical apology for existing power. An argument about normativity, on the other hand, is an argument which intends to demonstrate the rule's distance from state will and practice. The more normative (ie critical) a rule, the more political it seems because the less it is possible to argue it by reference to social context. It seems utopian and – like theories of natural justice – manipulable at will.

74 David P. Fidler, 'Challenging the Classical Concept of Custom: Perspectives on the Future of Customary International Law', 39 *German Yearbook of International Law* (1998) 227.

Who determines what is the law? Non-state actors and individuals may play an ever-increasing role in the development of international law, but it is ultimately up to states to implement what has been thought up by international organizations, treaty bodies, NGOs, think-tanks, and scholars.[75] This is arguably also inherent in the formation of customary international law with its focus on state practice[76] and the take on the question of attribution by the International Law Commission in its Articles on State Responsibility.[77] As to the role of the individual in the formation of non-treaty sources of law, Charles de Visscher went so far as to state that "[t]here is no customary law that individuals take so little a part in forming as international custom".[78]

75 After all, it is also states that bear the brunt of obligations. See René Cassin, 'La Declaration Universelle et la Mise en Œuvre des Droits de l'Homme', 79 *Recueil des Cours de l'Académie de Droit International de La Haye* (1951-II) 327. See also the assessment by Santiago Villalpando, 'The Legal Dimension of the International Community: How Community Interests Are Protected in International Law', 21/2 *European Journal of International Law* (2010) 414–415:

> The world community is not yet ready to change the legal order which rules its activities, namely an international law centred on the figure of the state as the principal subject, and the preservation of sovereignty continues to be one of the fundamental objectives of the system.

See further, *e.g.*, Martin Dixon, *Textbook on International Law,* 6th edn (Oxford: Oxford University Press, 2007) 13; Gerhard Hafner, 'Some Thoughts on the State-Oriented and Individual-Oriented Approaches in International Law', 14 *Austrian Review of International and European Law* (2009) 39. Torsten Gihl, 'The Legal Character and Sources of International Law', 1 *Scandinavian Studies in Law* (1957) 85, quotes Thomas E. Holland, *Letters to 'The Times' Upon War And Neutrality (1881–1920) With Some Commentary,* 3rd edn (London: Longmans, Green and Co., 1921) 119:

> The ignorance, by the by, which certain of my critics have displayed of the nature and claims of international law is not a little surprising. Some seem to identify it with treaties; others with "Vattel". Several, having become aware that it is not law of the kind which is enforced by a policeman or a County Court bailiff, have hastened, much exhilarated, to give the world the benefit of their discovery. Most of them are under the impression that it has been concocted by "bookworms", "jurists", "professors", or other "theorists", instead of, as is the fact, mainly by statesmen, diplomatists, prize courts, generals and admirals.

This should, however, not be mistaken with the "positivist doctrine", as Hersch Lauterpacht called it, that states are the only subjects of international law. On this proposition and its rejection see Hersch Lauterpacht, *International Law and Human Rights* (London: Stevens & Sons, 1950) 6–9, in particular fn. 2.

76 See *infra* pp. 61 *et seq.*

77 See Draft Articles on Responsibility of States for Internationally Wrongful Acts, U.N. Doc. A/CN.4/SER.A/2001/Add.1 (2001), *Yearbook of the International Law Commission* (2001-II), Articles 4–11.

78 De Visscher, *supra* n. 32, at 154. Contrary, *e.g.*, Jordan J. Paust, 'The Complex Nature, Sources and Evidences of Customary Human Rights', 25 *Georgia Journal of International Law* (1995/1996) 158.

Still, scholars push the continuous development of international law by emphasizing the role that non-state actors play,[79] attempting to create the impression – or actually convinced – that norms exist, irrespective of the legal process. This deficiency in the identification of positive law is what Alexander Somek has called "an ideology of law, that is, an image of law concealing its own disintegration".[80]

Yet international law academia is well aware that in any positive law discussion *de lege lata, de lege in statu nascendi*, or *de lege ferenda*,[81] the source of obligations should be grounded in one of the potential manifestations of international law. As it seems difficult, even to such "highly qualified illusionists" to conjure an inexistent treaty, non-treaty sources have become the weapon of choice.

Even within the sphere of obligations springing from existing treaties, the additional flavor of universal application through customary international law or general principles of law has led to rhetoric bootstrapping and bolstering of rules, in order to close the doors on any remaining doubt.[82] The external perspective, unaccustomed to the rules on formation of international law, fails to pierce this veil of "doublespeak". This might not, as Bin Cheng writes, be doing the development of international law a favor:

> International law may be our subject of study, but we are not personally, or even collectively, responsible for what it is today. We would hardly be performing a service to our profession by pretending that international law is something different from what we find it to be. We can no more improve international law this way than the pathologist who hopes that, simply by reporting that a growth is benign when in fact it is malignant, the patient will therefore recover.[83]

79 See, most recently, Anne Peters, *Beyond Human Rights. The Legal Status of the Individual in International Law* (Cambridge Studies in International and Comparative Law; Cambridge: Cambridge University Press, 2016).

80 Somek, *supra* n. 33, at 157.

81 Already Karl Zemanek lamented the loss of the term "*de lege ferenda*" from the vocabulary of scholars. See *id., supra* n. 37, at 901. See also Bin Cheng, 'Custom: The Future of General State Practice in a Divided World', in Douglas M. Johnston and Ronald St. J. Macdonald, *The Structure and Process of International Law Essays in Legal Philosophy, Doctrine and Theory* (The Hague: Martinus Nijhoff, 1983) 514; Weil, *supra* n. 35, at 415.

82 See Theodor Meron, *Human Rights and Humanitarian Norms as Customary Law* (Oxford: Clarendon Press, 1989) 9. He refers in particular to the wording of the International Court of Justice in the *Tehran Hostages* case: "In the view of the Court, the obligations of the Iranian Government here in question are not merely contractual obligations established by the Vienna Conventions of 1961 and 1963, but also obligations under general international law". See *Case Concerning United States Diplomatic and Consular Staff in Tehran* (United States of America *v.* Iran), Judgment of 24 May 1980, ICJ Reports 1980, p. 3, at 32, para. 62.

83 Cheng, *supra* n. 81, at 515.

C Customary International Law and "Customary International Law"

The ultimate litmus test of any argument regarding the development of international law seems to have become whether a particular right or exception has indeed finally become customary international law or – even better – *ius cogens*,[84] as has already been pointed out by Nicholas Onuf:

> While this may often be a manipulation of metaphors to increase the chances of particular directives being accepted, the very fact that they are legalized in this fashion contributes to the likelihood of future performative sufficiency, in which case they have indeed become law of uncertain, even clandestine authorship. The preoccupation with custom as a source of international law is recognition that by some mysterious process practice yields laws. The alchemy of custom in international law can now be seen as the displacement of directive rule-candidates into a setting which is classically legal, so that legal discourse about those speech acts expedites their acceptance as precedent to be noted in acknowledging matters of principle, claiming rights, and justifying conduct.[85]

Alternatively, other non-treaty sources such as general principles of law have been suggested; a position that has never reached mainstream acceptance, however.[86]

1 Formation

Every student of international law has, at one stage or other, memorized the simple formula: customary international law consists of state practice and *opinio iuris*.[87] That it is indeed not that simple is evidenced by the metres of book shelves filled with literature and studies on either of these two elements[88] and by the fact that the

84 See, *e.g.*, Meron, *supra* n. 82, at 8–9.

85 Nicholas Onuf, 'Do Rules Say What They Do? From Ordinary Language to International Law', 26/2 *Harvard International Law Journal* (1985) 410. See also Philip Alston and Bruno Simma, 'The Sources of Human Rights Law: Custom, Jus Cogens, and General Principles', 12 *Australian Yearbook of International Law* (1992) 88, who at 103, however, themselves claim that "fundamental human rights prescriptions [...] belong to the body of international *jus cogens*".

86 See Christine Chinkin, 'Sources', in Daniel Moeckli, Sangeeta Shah, and Sandesh Sivakumaran (eds), *International Human Rights Law* (Oxford: Oxford University Press, 2010) 115.

87 See Christian J. Tams, 'Meta-Custom and the Court: A Study in Judicial Law-Making', 14/1 *The Law and Practice of International Courts and Tribunals* (2015) 58.

88 Apart from the works cited throughout this book, in particular Chapter 2, pp. 57 *et seq.*, see the references given in Malcolm N. Shaw, *International Law*, 7th edn (Cambridge: Cambridge University Press, 2014) 51, fn. 7. See also the select bibliography in the Report of the International Law Commission on the Work of the Sixty-third Session, U.N. Doc. A/66/10, Add. 1 (2011), at 310–314.

International Law Commission only recently, in 2012, added the topic of "Formation and evidence of customary international law" to its program of work.[89]

Generalising, the camps are divided into the voluntarists, who assume some form of consent or indeed a tacit agreement in the process of customary international law formation, and the empiricists, who deny such an element by assuming a bird's eye view of the elements of customary international law[90] or, instead, resort to alternative explanations such as rational choice theory, for example.[91]

2 *Two "Is"*

Independent of the respective theory of customary international law to which one adheres, the creation of a custom *ex machina* that has become so popular in recent times[92] cannot convince. As Robert Jennings observes, "most of what we perversely persist in calling customary international law is not only *not* customary law: it does not even faintly resemble a customary law".[93]

For the classic voluntarist as well as the empiricist, customary international law is essentially grounded in the behavior of states.[94] Yet the "invisible college of

89 See Report of the International Law Commission on the Work of the Sixty-third Session, U.N. Doc. A/66/10 (2011), at 7, para. 32, and Report of the International Law Commission on the Work of the Sixty-fourth Session, U.N. Doc. A/67/10 (2012), at 6, para. 19.

90 Classically, the empirical analysis of state practice and *opinio iuris*. On this terminology see also Bodansky, 'Customary (and Not So Customary) International Environmental Law', *supra* n. 2, at 109; Simma, *supra* n. 31, at 71. The scale between these two elements can, of course, be sliding. Although this view of the empiricists necessarily includes a quasi-consensual element – for states can "decide" to some extent how they will act and what their opinion is – it does not go so far as to make outright consent a constitutive element. See on this issue in detail *infra* pp. 57 *et seq.*

91 See, most prominently, Goldsmith and Posner, *supra* n. 40. See also Andrew T. Guzman, 'Saving Customary International Law', 27 *Michigan Journal of International Law* (2005) *passim*. For an overall rebuttal of Goldsmith and Posner see Ohlin, *supra* n. 29, *passim*. For an early criticism of rationality as a factor in international relations see Joseph Frankel, *National Interest* (London: Macmillan, 1970) 144:

> The rationality of political decisions is highly suspect as even the most cursory analysis reveals a high incidence of non-rational, emotive elements, of sheer stupidity and of chance. Nevertheless, it is a recurrent notion in political argument, both in terms of praise and of opprobrium; some political evaluations are directly centred upon it, most of them at least refer to it. A statement that an interest is "rational" or "irrational" need not be fully meaningless but on the whole it is the accepted way of arguing about our political likes and dislikes.

92 See *infra* pp. 101 *et seq.*

93 Robert Y. Jennings, 'The Identification of International Law', in Bin Cheng (ed.), *International Law: Teaching and Practice* (London: Stevens & Sons, 1982) 5.

94 See Jan Klabbers, 'International Organizations in the Formation of Customary International Law', in Cannizzaro and Palchetti (eds), *supra* n. 67, at 188–189 on the analysis of customary international law by the International Court of Justice in

international lawyers" has become convinced that it knows better. Just as medieval alchemists thought they could transmute common metals into gold, this academic elite has conjured up rules through cherry picking among non-binding legal instruments, shifting away from "traditional international law".[95]

The friction, it seems, is, therefore, no longer between an "is" and an "ought", but rather between two alternate "is":[96] An *avant-garde* body of "customary international law" created by an academic legal elite, on the one side, and the legal principles adhered to by states in their international relations, on the other[97] – "real rules and paper rules".[98]

Risk-averse by nature, what should the lawyer do? Trust in the wisdom of generations past or go where the wild things are? If the internal perspective is unclear, what effects will it have upon those on the outside looking in? There appear to be two layers of normativity.

This is exactly where international law risks its external reputation as a stabilizer of international relations.[99] Expectation is alienated. Such a loss of credibility

the *Nicaragua* case and at 190–191 on the Court's advisory opinion on the *Legality of the Threat or Use of Nuclear Weapons*. See also *supra* n. 75.

95 See, *e.g.*, for an early instance of the approach taken in the *South West Africa Cases* (Ethiopia *v.* South Africa; Liberia *v.* South Africa), Dissenting Opinion of Judge Tanaka, ICJ Reports 1966, p. 250, at 291–294 (irrespective of whether the outcome may be favorable at the moral level, which, of course, it would).

96 Or two "oughts" for that matter.

97 See Watson, *supra* n. 56, at 13; *id.*, 'Normativity and Reality in International Human Rights Law', 13 *Stetson Law Review* (1983–1984), 224.

98 Watson, *supra* n. 40, at 626. The words that Prosper Weil used in his Hague lectures to describe the changing role of custom in light of General Assembly resolutions come to mind:

> Tant et si bien – et c'est là le plus important – que la fonction stratégique de la coutume se trouve radicalement modifiée. L'observation en a été si souvent faite dans la littérature récente qu'elle en devient banale: à la coutume conservatrice et traditionaliste, fondée sur la stabilité et la consolidation, a succédé la coutume innovatrice et révolutionnaire, levier de changement de l'ordre international. De la lente maturations d'une sagesse pragmatique on a glissé à la formation quasi immédiate d'une règle nouvelle qui paraît socialement désirable; d'une "coutume sage", facteur de permanence, on est passé à une 'coutume sauvage', instrument de contestation et de révisionnisme.

See *id.*, 'Le Droit International en Quête de Son Identité', 237 *Recueil des Cours de l'Académie de Droit International de La Haye* (1992-VI) 178, citing René-Jean Dupuy's pointed distinction between "coutume sage" and "coutume sauvage". See René-Jean Dupuy, 'Coutume Sage et Coutume Sauvage', in *La Communauté Internationale. Mélanges Offerts à Charles Rousseau* (Paris: Éditions A. Pedone, 1974) 75–87.

99 Karl Zemanek criticized the use of such different layers of normativity with regard to the CHARTER OF THE UNITED NATIONS for exactly this reason:

> The undifferentiated conglomeration of "principles" in the Charter is unfortunate. Collecting principles of different normativeness without clearly indicating

and legitimate expectation eventually translates into a lack of leverage, when it comes to building an international rule of law.

3 Ensuring Effectivity

Of course, international legal scholarship alone is not to blame. Some of the great hypocrisies of international relations – and, thus, non-compliance with the law – lie well outside any educated capacity to foresee the possible. The difference between the violator punished and the violator unscathed is more often than not the result of political opportunism – yet fair to say, not dissimilar to the rogue actions of individuals within a domestic legal system, whenever it may seem opportune. However, this is exactly where progressive development should start, not where it should end.

4 The Downward Spiral

What do we expect of customary international law? Blind parroting of the *Nicaragua* paradigm that "instances of State conduct inconsistent with a given rule should generally have been treated as breaches of that rule, not as indications of the recognition of a new rule", if they are at least accompanied by *opinio iuris* to the contrary,[100] will not raise the credibility of the international

> their difference carries the risk of deluding lay opinion. When people cannot distinguish between imperative and hortative principles, they may develop uniform expectations warranted only by the former, which reality will almost necessarily disappoint. That may, in turn, lead to a cynical attitude towards the United Nations in general.

See id., 'The Basic Principles of UN Charter Law', in Ronald St. John Mcdonald and Douglas M. Johnston (eds), Towards World Constitutionalism. Issues in the Legal Ordering of the World Community (Leiden: Martinus Nijhoff, 2005) 406.

100 *Case Concerning Military and Paramilitary Activities in and Against Nicaragua* (Nicaragua *v.* United States of America), Judgment of 27 June 1986 (Merits), ICJ Reports 1986, p. 14, at 98, para. 186. Of course, the Court made this statement in a very specific context and with an eye to general compliance (the full citation is:

> The Court does not consider that, for a rule to be established as customary, the corresponding practice must be in absolutely rigorous conformity with the rule. In order to deduce the existence of customary rules, the Court deems it sufficient that the conduct of States should, in general, be consistent with such rules, and that instances of State conduct inconsistent with a given rule should generally have been treated as breaches of that rule, not as indications of the recognition of a new rule. If a State acts in a way prima facie incompatible with a recognized rule, but defends its conduct by appealing to exceptions or justifications contained within the rule itself, then whether or not the State's conduct is in fact justifiable on that basis, the significance of that attitude is to confirm rather than to weaken the rule.).

legal system.[101] In effect, it encourages cherry picking in the identification of a manifestation of international law, where the respective normative project makes it opportune to do so.[102]

From a dogmatic perspective, an approach that favors "a largely shared understanding on the normative validity of a given behavioral model"[103] is

But the ruling has not necessarily been received that way. See, for instance, Enzo Cannizzaro and Paolo Palchetti, 'Customary International Law on the Use of Force … At a Time of Perplexity', in *id.* (eds), *supra* n. 67, at 3:

> By stating that a breach of the rule prohibiting the use of force – if it is not presented as such but as a permitted exception thereto – confirms rather than weakens the existence of such rule, the Court sanctioned a methodological approach where *opinio iuris ac necessitatis* plays a decisive role.

That the approach of the International Court of Justice is, in any case, a deviation from the orthodox definition of customary international law is self-evident. See also the observation by Christine Gray:

> The gap between the prohibition of the use of force and the practice seems striking to some commentators, but this divergence should not necessarily be taken as proving the ineffectiveness or pointlessness of the law in this area. Conversely, international law should not be assumed to be effective in the sense of controlling or influencing state behaviour just because state behaviour is in fact in compliance with it.

See *id.*, *International Law and the Use of Force*, 3rd edn (Foundations of Public International Law; Oxford: Oxford University Press, 2008) 25.

101 See also Roberts, *supra* n. 73, at 770: "[N]orms that are honored in the breach do not yield reliable predictions of future conduct and are likely to bring themselves, and possibly custom as a whole, into disrepute".

102 Interestingly enough, in the *Nuclear Weapons* advisory opinion, the International Court of Justice held that refraining from a particular action does not in and of itself convey *opinio iuris* that this action is prohibited under international law. See *Legality of the Threat or Use of Nuclear Weapons*, Advisory Opinion of 8 July 1996, ICJ Reports 1996, p. 226, at pp. 253–254, paras 65–67. For an early discussion of this problem see Walter Heinrich, 'Zur Problematik des Gewohnheitsrechts', in Charles Appleton (ed.), *Recueil d'Études sur les Sources du Droit en l'Honneur de François Gény. Tome II. Les Sources Générales des Systèmes Juridiques Actuels* (Paris: Sirey, 1934) 300, fn. 17:

> Was soll der Rechtsanwender mit der […] vorausgesetzten allgemeinen Ueberzeugung von der Notwendigkeit einer bestimmten Handlungsweise anfangen, wenn sich "zufälligerweise" noch niemals eine Gelegenheit zur praktischen Betätigung dieser Handlungsweise geboten hat? Woran soll er das Vorhandensein eines bezüglichen Sozialwillens, solange keine Uebungsakte vorliegen, auch nur mit einiger Sicherheit erkennen und, was für die richterliche Praxis von nicht zu unterschätzender Bedeutung ist, wie soll er davon seine Volksgenossen überzeugen?

103 Giuseppe Palmisano, 'Determining the Law on the Use of Force: The ICJ and Customary Rules on the Use of Force', in Cannizzaro and Palchetti (eds), *supra* n. 67, at 207–208.

inconsistent, let alone with regard to the permissive message it conveys. If a state generally complies with a certain rule, the prohibition of torture, for example, it may deviate from time to time, as long as it makes sure to express its *opinio iuris* that there was some kind of "exception or justification" even if it is "in fact [not] justifiable on that basis". The existence of the rule that should derive its legitimacy from the empirical assessment of state practice and *opinio iuris* is not put into question. *E contrario*, this would allow for the assumption that states may torture from time to time, as long as they do not place their stamp of approval on the act. The idea that practice on the basis of an alleged yet non-existent exception or justification could strengthen the overall rule seems elaborately artificial, if not cynical.

The *Nicaragua* case also leaves open just how much short of "rigorous conformity"[104] compliance needs to be.[105] From the point of view of states seeking justifications for non-compliance, this can only result in a downward spiral. Alexander Somek points out the effects of such a paradoxical approach in assessing international law:

> This view raises the question, to be sure, how much deviation is acceptable until the broken norms cease to have any normative force. It could be argued that even if all states disrespected their international obligations these obligations would be *effective enough* for the international legal system to exist as long as universal non-compliance is universally *perceived* as legally wrongful. The whole system would be, at best, a system of universal hypocrisy. It would not be worthy of praise from a Kantian perspective.[106]

5 State Interest

As Louis Henkin convincingly laid out in his seminal work *How Nations Behave*, states act according to carefully calculated interests[107] and dependent upon the consequences of their conformity to or violation of international law.[108] This approach is, generally, quite similar to the economic theory of

104 See *Case Concerning Military and Paramilitary Activities in and Against Nicaragua* (Nicaragua *v.* United States of America), Judgment of 27 June 1986 (Merits), ICJ Reports 1986, p. 14, at 98, para. 186.

105 See also Bodansky, 'Customary (and Not So Customary) International Environmental Law', *supra* n. 2, at 109: "If a purported rule says one thing and states generally do something else, one can no longer say that the rule 'governs' behavior. Nevertheless, mistakes and violations of rules are possible".

106 Alexander Somek, 'Kelsen Lives', 18/3 *European Journal of International Law* (2007) 430–431. See also *ibid.*, at 439.

107 On the definition of state interest see *infra* pp. 121 *et seq.*

108 Louis Henkin, *How Nations Behave. Law and Foreign Policy*, 2nd edn (New York: Columbia University Press, 1979). For a rational choice model of this view see, prominently, Goldsmith and Posner, *supra* n. 40. For an overview of the various

negligence that "[w]hen the cost of accidents is less than the cost of prevention, a rational profit-maximizing enterprise will pay tort judgments to the accident victims rather than incur the larger cost of avoiding liability".[109] In assessing state practice, it is impossible to avoid dipping into such "law and ..." approaches, if one wants to make any determination to the likelihood of certain acts.[110] After all, it is not just international law that guides the behavior of states, but politics of interest. In turn, interest determines the formation of international law.[111]

This is not to say that interest alone is determinative of state behavior, as Jack Goldsmith and Eric Posner argue.[112] However, if customary international

compliance theories see Markus Burgstaller, *Theories of Compliance With International Law* (Leiden: Martinus Nijhoff, 2005).

109 Richard Posner, 'A Theory of Negligence', 1 *Journal of Legal Studies* (1972) 32.

110 See Cheng, *supra* n. 81, at 550.

111 See Somek, *supra* n. 106, at 446:

> The usual view is that international law is a check on state interests, causing a state to behave in a way that is contrary to its interests. In our view, the causal relationship between international law and state interests runs in the opposite direction. International law emerges from states' pursuit of self-interested policies on the international stage. International law is, in this sense, endogenous to state interests. It is not a check on state self-interest; it is a product of state self-interest.

112 See Goldsmith and Posner, *supra* n. 40, at 39:

> Although most international law scholars acknowledge that states are more likely to violate customary international law as the costs of compliance increase, they insist that the sense of legal obligations puts some drag on such deviations. Our theory, by contrast, insists that payoffs from cooperation or deviation are the sole determinants of whether states engage in the cooperative behaviors that are labeled customary international law is an exogenous influence on states' behavior. And because we are skeptical about the possibility of cooperation by custom in multiplayer prisoner's dilemmas, we are skeptical that customary international law fosters true multilateral cooperation.

The view of Goldsmith and Posner has been rightly criticized by George Norman and Joel P. Trachtman for ignoring that compliance with legal obligation may in itself be considered an "exogenous influence". See *id.*, 'The Customary International Law Game', 99/3 *American Journal of International Law* (2005) 571:

> The mistake here is that compliance with international law resulting from a sense of legal obligation is, in fact, consistent with extrinsic reasons: there may well be utility in upholding a particular rule or in upholding the rule of law in general. That is, indeed, precisely what our model demonstrates.

Cf., contrary as to the inclusion of state interest as a determinative factor, Alexander Orakhelashvili, *The Interpretation of Acts and Rules in Public International*

law is in any way dependent upon state practice and states act primarily according to their interests, then the result may well be that customary international law can only exist for norms that states require being followed.[113]

Of course, the elaboration of these interests sometimes necessitates complex forms of cooperation that go beyond the strictly personal sphere.[114] Thereby, trade-offs become unavoidable. The pragmatic predicament, in which states may often find themselves, while trying to assert their own interests can also be summed up by the alleged Franklin D. Roosevelt quote regarding Nicaraguan dictator Somoza: "He may be a son of a bitch, but he's our son of a bitch".[115]

6 Reciprocity

A well-known trade-off in international law is compliance on the grounds of reciprocal obligation. Reciprocity serves as a "motivation" for state action,[116] as a "starting mechanism" that "helps to initiate social

Law (Oxford: Oxford University Press, 2008) 179. This other side of the spectrum again falls short of the realities of international relations. Only because state interest is "elusive and indeterminate", which is surely not unique to that particular concept, does not mean that it does not have a role to play. See on the vast multitude of reasons for state behavior also Bodansky, 'Prologue to a Theory of Non-Treaty Norms', *supra* n. 2, at 124.

113 Cf., however, Isabelle R. Gunning, 'Modernizing Customary International Law: The Challenge of Human Rights', 31 *Vanderbilt Journal of International Law* (1990–1991) *passim*, who provides a feminist and "Afrocentric" critique of this "needs-based" state-oriented view.

114 See Villalpando, *supra* n. 75, at 393. See also Frankel, *supra* n. 91, at 143:

> Political debates are now much more frequent and the arguments advanced in them more elaborate but confusion is caused by the convergence of several factors. The domestic reasons are both procedural and substantive: the greatly increased complexity of the decision-making machinery as well as the abandonment of the simple equation of national interest with national security. The obvious international reasons are the growing interdependence as well as the complexity of the world.

115 As a recent 'Letter From the Editors' in *Foreign Policy* (Jan/Feb 2014) commented:

> The quote may well be apocryphal, but it succinctly (and colorfully) sums up the knottiest and most persistent tension in U.S. foreign policy: how to balance the cold demands of the national interest with the moral obligations of a superpower established as a beacon of liberty.

See *ibid.*, at 1.

116 See Simma, *supra* n. 31, at 51: "Der psychologische Faktor der Gegenseitigkeitserwartung bildet damit eine Motivation staatlichen Verhaltens; er kann eine konstruktive Funktion, eine Schrittmacherrolle ausüben". See also *ibid.*, at 59:

interaction".[117] That is surely the case for the rules of diplomatic immunity,[118] diplomatic protection,[119] or the outlawing of piracy.[120] A number

> Auch hier [im Modell der allmählichen unbewußten Rechtserzeugung] kann also das gegenseitige parallele (identische) Interesse der Beteiligten als Triebkraft zu immer umfangreicheren Beschränkungen der ursprünglich positivrechtlich noch ungehemmten Handlungsfreiheit der Staaten dienen: die Schmälerung dieser Freiheit wird durch die Einsicht vertretbar, ja vorangetrieben, daß die daraus resultierenden Nachteile durch die Vorteile, die sich aus der gleichen Zurückhaltung seitens anderer Völkerrechtssubjekte ergeben, zumindestens aufgewogen werden.

117 Alan W. Gouldner, 'The Norm of Reciprocity: A Preliminary Statement', 25/2 *American Sociological Review* (1960) 176. See also *Delimitation of the Maritime Boundary in the Gulf of Maine Area* (Canada *v.* United States of America), Judgment of 12 October 1984 Given by the Chamber Constituted by the Order Made by the Court on 20 January 1982, ICJ Reports 1984, p. 246, at 299, para. 111.

118 In this respect, bilateral immunity must be differentiated from immunity in multilateral situations. Here, the reasons for compliance may be different from mere reciprocity. For an analysis of diplomatic relations as a traditionally custom-governed field see Eugene Kontorovich, 'Inefficient Customs in International Law', 48 *William and Mary Law Review* (2006) 916–917.

119 See Hathaway, *supra* n. 33, at 34, who also brings international humanitarian law into play on the same grounds as diplomatic protection.

120 Cf. also, critically, Joel P. Trachtman, 'The Obsolescence of Customary International Law' (2014) <http://papers.ssrn.com/sol3/papers.cfm?abstract_id=2512757> 16–17. Santiago Villalpando writes:

> With respect to piracy, international criminal responsibility expressed less a universal concern of a moral nature than a solution to a practical difficulty in protecting a community interest, namely the lack of effective means of punishment of a crime which took place outside national territorial jurisdictions and endangered the freedom and security of the high seas.

See Villalpando, *supra* n. 75, at 406. However, he also contrasts "a different category of crimes under international law [...] justified by the emergence of ethical values common to all humankind", listing the abolition of slavery and the earliest attempt at prosecuting a head of state, German Emperor Wilhelm II, following the end of World War I. See *ibid.*, at 407. This assessment ignores that both the abolition of slavery and the criminal prosecution of the German Emperor did not originate from moral considerations alone. Therefore, they could just as easily be listed among the same "category" as piracy. For a concise discussion of the reasons for abolition and the current state of research on the topic, see Barbara L. Solow, reply by David Brion Davis, 'The British & the Slave Trade', *The New York Review of Books* (12 January 2012) <www.nybooks.com/articles/archives/2012/jan/12/british-slave-trade/>.

of more "conservative"[121] or expansive lists[122] have been presented in the literature.[123]

In a primarily horizontal legal system such as public international law, the elements of state interest and reciprocity are key factors in

121 For such a "conservative" list of rules of customary international law see Georg Schwarzenberger, *The Inductive Approach to International Law* (London: Stevens & Sons, 1965) 53:

> Moreover, sufficient evidence is available to permit the formulation of a fair number of rules and the abstraction from them of seven fundamental principles of international customary law: the principles of Sovereignty, Recognition, Consent, Good Faith, International Responsibility, Self-Defence, and the Freedom of the Seas.

See also Simma and Verdross, *supra* n. 50, at 49, § 65, who list the law of armed conflict, diplomatic respective consular privileges and immunities, international economic law as well as diplomatic protection, in particular. See also, along these lines, Simma, *supra* n. 31, at 30–31, who speaks of the additional element of "*vetustas*" as the gradual development of *opinio iuris* over time and mentions the legal status of diplomats and consuls as well as other state officials abroad, the conclusion and entry into force of international treaties, the treatment of foreign states before domestic courts, and the treatment of aliens in this regard. See also *ibid.*, at 60. For an early assessment see Oppenheim, *supra* n. 7, at 24–25, who already in 1921 mentions "the law of ambassadors and consuls, the law concerning the open sea and territorial waters, the law about merchantmen and men-of-war in foreign territorial waters" as areas of international law regulated by custom.

122 For a more expansive list, surprisingly also including human rights, considering his approach to international law, see Guzman, *supra* n. 91, at 116, fn. 1:

> Though treaties have come to govern large areas of international law, there remain important areas of international law governed wholly or partially by CIL either because no treaties are in place or because treaties are not universal or do not cover all relevant issues. These areas include, for example, the law of state responsibility, foreign direct investment, the jurisdiction to apply law, diplomatic immunity, human rights, and state immunity.

See also Ted L. Stein, 'The Approach of the Different Drummer: The Principle of the Persistent Objector in International Law', 26/2 *Harvard International Law Journal* (1985) 464:

> The classical process for generating international rules of general applicability produced a body of rules that were generally unwritten. Up through the end of the nineteenth century and into the beginning of the twentieth, the law in many areas of central concern to international lawyers remained *lex non scripta*. Questions relating to the law of the sea, the law of arbitral procedure, the law of state succession, and the law of state responsibility all had to be resolved without reference to any text that could claim special authority.

123 See also *Delimitation of the Maritime Boundary in the Gulf of Maine Area* (Canada *v.* United States of America), Judgment of 12 October 1984 Given by the Chamber Constituted by the Order Made by the Court on 20 January 1982, ICJ Reports 1984, p. 246, at 299, para. 111.

determining whether a state will comply with or allow for the enforcement of a norm against itself.[124] It is the "essence of customary law-making".[125] Anthea Roberts makes the distinction here between "facilitative and moral customs" to describe norms regulating the international relations of states and those of normative substance.[126]

However, there might also exist areas of law, in which compliance is not necessarily rewarded by reciprocal behavior, but it seems that customary international law will, at least, likely reflect an equilibrium of interests:

> Essentially, one may call the concept embodied in Article 38(1)(b) of the Statute of the ICJ a pragmatic one. Its genius is to strike a bridge between the world of the being and the world of the ought. Whatever is consistently practised and has in addition found general acceptance as reasonable and rightful conduct should at the same time be the yardstick for the future. Proven practice is the best test for the suitability as a standard of behaviour. What is done repeatedly by a large number of States without eliciting objections cannot be fundamentally detrimental to anyone's interests. Even if an individual State has not participated in the practice concerned, it does not suffer any major injustice if what others have established is held against it.[127]

124 See Anthony D'Amato, 'Trashing Customary International Law', 81 *American Journal of International Law* (1987) 102; David J. Bederman, 'Acquiescence, Objection and the Death of Customary International Law', 21 *Duke Journal of Comparative and International Law* (2010) 42; Kontorovich, *supra* n. 118, at 867–868, 893–894, and *passim*; Hugh Thirlway, 'Human Rights in Customary Law: An Attempt to Define Some of the Issues', 28/3 *Leiden Journal of International Law* (2015) 498; Watson, 'Normativity and Reality in International Human Rights Law', *supra* n. 97, at 228; *id.*, *supra* n. 40, at 619. See, generally, Simma and Verdross, *supra* n. 50, at 48–49, §§ 64–65. See also the views reproduced, though critically, by Simma, *supra* n. 31, at 16–18. See, however, *ibid.*, 63–64: "Dabei darf jedoch eines nicht aus dem Auge verloren werden: daß es niemals die Gegenseitigkeitserwägungen selber sind, die schließlich diese Verwandlung in verbindliche Rechtsnormen hervorrufen, sondern das Aufkommen der *opinio iuris*".

125 Hathaway, *supra* n. 33, at 34. See also Alston and Simma, *supra* n. 85, at 99, and *The Case of the S.S. 'Lotus'* (France *v.* Turkey), Judgment of 7 September 1927, PCIJ Series A. – No. 10, p. 4, at 18, in which the Permanent Court of International Justice defines customary international law ("usages generally accepted") "as expressing principles of law and established in order to regulate the relations between these co-existing independent communities or with a view to the achievement of common aims". See, however, Gihl, *supra* n. 75, at 85.

126 See Roberts, *supra* n. 73, at 764.

127 Christian Tomuschat, 'Obligations Arising for States Without or Against Their Will', 241 *Recueil des Cours de l'Académie de Droit International de La Haye* (1993-IV) 290–291. See also D'Amato, *supra* n. 124, at 102.

7 Moral Concepts

This begs a whole number of questions: What about human rights? What about prohibitions on the capacity of a state to exercise force, when it would be in its own interest? Or even exceptions to such a prohibition that call upon the international community to take action, independent of any individual state interest? What is the prospect of these areas of law becoming embedded in the body of non-treaty sources of international law?

Eugene Kontorovich goes as far as claiming that customary law is inherently unpredestined to father altruistic norms or moral obligations, holding that "customs are not designed to improve welfare or for any other normative goal" and "are not designed at all, but rather emerge from a system of interactions within a group".[128]

So what if such "interactions within a group", a group that inevitably bases its decisions upon state interest, make it unlikely that moral concepts[129] will become enshrined in non-treaty law? Then it may just be the case that the existence of a body of customary international human rights law or general human rights principles of law – or of any other "moral custom", altruistically motivated – are simply an illusion: "real rules and paper rules".[130] This is the illusion of a non-treaty law of moral concepts.

D Case Studies

Two areas of international law, in which the great divide between the "is" and the "ought" has been most visible in this respect, are human rights and basically anything to do with the regulation of the use of force. Nowhere in the Colosseum of international law has the crowd[131] been more generous in raising their thumbs up than in the field of human rights and humanitarian exceptions to the prohibition of the use of force.[132]

Whereas human rights treaties often face the choice between a low number of ratifications and a high number of reservations, neither "humanitarian intervention" nor the "responsibility to protect" have even gone to such high

128 Kontorovich, *supra* n. 118, at 863.
129 On the definition of the idea see *infra* pp. 118 *et seq.*
130 See *supra* n. 98.
131 Or, to borrow a term adapted from literary theory, the "interpretive community". See, *inter alia*, Andrea Bianchi, 'Looking Ahead: International Law's Main Challenges', in David Armstrong (ed.), *Routledge Handbook of International Law* (London: Routledge, 2009) 404; Oscar Schachter, 'Metaphors and Realism in International Law', 96 *Proceedings of the American Society of International Law at its Annual Meeting* (2002) 269; Michael Waibel, 'Interpretive Communities in International Law', *University of Cambridge. Faculty of Law. Legal Studies Research Paper Series*, No. 62/2014 (October 2014) <http://papers.ssrn.com/sol3/papers.cfm?abstract_id=2513411##>.
132 On this observation of agenda driven through means of discourse see also Waibel, *ibid.*, at 7, citing to Dirk Pulkowski, *The Law and Politics of International Regime Conflict* (Oxford: Oxford University Press, 2014) 16.

levels of formalization, if one leaves aside a small number of "soft law" instruments such as non-binding General Assembly resolutions. Either way, scholars will take recourse to the non-treaty sources of international law. They have, thereby, created a new "customary international law" or, as Hugh Thirlway calls it, "custom with a special 'flavour'".[133]

After all, human rights and humanitarian motivation behind the use of force have a common denominator: they are driven by moral considerations which seem difficult to refuse as an educated humanist. It seems that even "underdog topics" such as environmental protection or the protection of cultural heritage[134] that battle with mainstream acceptance as well as technical "soft law" provisions that indeed acquire a broad following and acceptance,[135] have been assessed more humbly as to their legal *status quo*.[136]

1 Human Rights

a Best Test Object

Among the two case studies, human rights, understood here in the broad sense of obligations of the state owed to the individual on the basis of international law,[137] may serve as the prime example for the proposition that "moral concepts" are unlikely to manifest themselves as non-treaty sources of law.

133 Thirlway, *supra* n. 124, at 503.

134 See, for example, Patricia Birnie, Alan Boyle, and Catherine Redgwell, *International Law and the Environment*, 3rd edn (Oxford: Oxford University Press, 2009) 108–109; Philippe Sands and Jacqueline Peel, *Principles of International Environmental Law* (Cambridge: Cambridge University Press, 2012) 111–112. See Bodansky, 'Customary (and Not So Customary) International Environmental Law', *supra* n. 2, at 105. For an alternative model of legal development in international environmental law see, *e.g.*, Ivano Alogna, 'The Circulation of Legal Models: Toward the Evolution of Environmental Law', in Maša Kovič Dine and Vasilka Sancin (eds), *International Environmental Law: Contemporary Concerns and Challenges in 2014* (Ljubljana: GV Založba, 2014) 59–69.

135 See, *e.g.*, with regard to such provisions in the field of space law the volume edited by Irmgard Marboe, *Soft Law in Outer Space: The Function of Non-Binding Norms in International Space Law* (Studien zu Politik und Verwaltung, Vol. 102; Vienna: Böhlau, 2012).

136 One reason might be that courts such as the European Court of Human Rights or the Inter-American Court of Human Rights can address human rights violations, baiting the inference that these rules also exist as a matter of non-treaty law. While these bodies may have raised the level of human rights protection, the fact remains that their jurisdiction is conferred by a treaty, not the fact that human rights supposedly exist as customary international law or general principles of law.

137 Including "civil and political" as well as "cultural, economic, and social" rights but also the many "soft law" standards such as the labor standards that are being codified and developed by the International Labour Organization, for example. See International Labour Organization, Labour Standards <www.ilo.org/global/standards/lang–en/index.htm>. Not included are those rights conferred upon the individual by way of domestic (constitutional) law.

What makes them such an ideal candidate for the purpose of the main research question? One aspect that has already been pointed out[138] is the tendency of human rights scholarship to engage in the creation of a body of law that runs parallel to, rather than intersecting the realities of a state-centred international system. Already in 1921, Lassa Oppenheim identified "fundamental rights" as the "arena" for a "tyranny of phrases".[139] However, that is surely not a mutually exclusive phenomenon of human rights scholarship. Neither is the phenomenon of international law "doublespeak" a unique feature of the field.

As opposed to many other areas of international law related to the treatment of the individual such as the "proto-human rights" of diplomatic protection or humanitarian law,[140] human rights are neither based on reciprocity,[141] nor are they widely contaminated with other state interests at the level of international relations,[142] as humanitarian grounds for the use of force most necessarily are.

138 See *supra* pp. 19 *et seq.*

139 Oppenheim, *supra* n. 7, at 58–59.

140 Including, in particular, a minimum treatment standard. Investor-state protection could also be mentioned here, although the issue is more complex due to the fact that it is grounded in bilateral treaties and a small number of multilateral frameworks alone. See *supra* n. 119 and accompanying text.

141 See Meron, *supra* n. 82, at 99–100, and *verbatim* first sentence of 246:

> Unlike most other fields of international law, the observance of human rights is not based on reciprocal interests of states, but on the broader goal of states to establish orderly and enlightened international and national legal orders. In human rights instruments, the contractual (interstate) elements are far less important than those which are objective and normative. The customary law of human rights is not established by a record of claims and counterclaims between the foreign ministries of countries concerned with the protection of their right as states and the rights of their respective nationals.

See also Niels Petersen, 'Customary Law Without Custom? Rules, Principles, and the Role of State Practice in International Norm Creation', 23/2 *American University International Law Review* (2007) 305, arguing that "reciprocity plays no role whatsoever" in human rights protection.

142 Although, of course, human rights are often fashioned in a way as to take into account the balancing with competing state interests (*e.g.*, derogation in cases of emergency or other exceptions). See also the pronouncement of the International Court of Justice with regard to the Convention on the Prevention and Punishment of the Crime of Genocide of 1948 in its *Reservations to the Convention on the Prevention and Punishment of the Crime of Genocide*, Advisory Opinion of 28 May 1951, ICJ Reports 1951, p. 15, at 23:

> The objects of such a convention must also be considered. The Convention was manifestly adopted for a purely humanitarian and civilizing purpose. It is indeed difficult to imagine a convention that might have this dual character to a greater degree, since its object on the one hand is to safeguard the very existence of certain human groups and on the other to confirm and endorse the most elementary principles of morality. In such a convention the contracting States do not have any interests of their own; they merely have, one and all,

At their core, human rights are, in a sense, purely altruistic norms. Although they spring from international obligations, they are primarily owed to individuals, often irrespective of their nationality even. By their very nature, a violation can only be addressed against another state, if they concern the nationals of the claimant or if they are considered *erga omnes* obligations.[143] From a strictly claim-based intra-state view of international law,[144] human rights norms are presumed "innocent".[145] Ideally, the state implements human rights

> a common interest, namely, the accomplishment of those high purposes which are the *raison d'être* of the convention. Consequently, in a convention of this type one cannot speak of individual advantages or disadvantages to States, or of the maintenance of a perfect contractual balance between rights and duties. The high ideals which inspired the Convention provide, by virtue of the common will of the parties, the foundation and measure of all its provisions.

143 See John Cerone, 'Out of Bounds? Considering the Reach of International Human Rights Law', *NYU School of Law Center for Human Rights and Global Justice Working Paper*, No. 6 (2006), at 2 *et seq.* <http://chrgj.org/wp-content/uploads/2012/07/WPS_NYU_CHRGJ_Cerone_Final.pdf>.
144 See, *e.g.*, Mendelson, *supra* n. 32, at 201.
145 See Kontorovich, *supra* n. 118, at 919–920:

> To the extent the CIL process can be expected to generate efficient norms, it is through repeated interactions between players. The higher the density of interaction, the stronger the claim for efficiency. With human rights law, no reason exists to expect the "customary" development of such law to move towards efficiency, because it is not at all based on substantive interactions between nations. The accounts of customary efficiency do not explain why regularities in the separate human rights practices of states should be elevated to the status of international obligation. By any account, custom is a social phenomenon. To be sure, in the Hayekian account customs are good because they incorporate the diffuse information available to a multitude of individual actors. But they do this through a process of *inter*actions among the disparate elements, with each actor bringing his private information to bear on each interaction. Custom can arise from repeated transactions between pairs of atomistic actors and grow to coordinate the interactions of a complex web of actors. In the spontaneous order model, customs develop towards efficiency, because in each separate transaction one of the parties to the transaction would defect from a practice not advantageous to him. The practices that persist are those that both sides of a transaction have deemed advantageous. Thus judges can be confident that, in legalizing a customary norm, they are merely enforcing a rule developed by the parties themselves in their mutual dealings. Human rights lack this crucial mutuality. Human rights norms do not arise from dealings between states. Rather, they are the sum of the entirely individual actions of each state, not with respect to other states but with respect to itself. Thus their utility as a means of social ordering on the international level is entirely untested. The crucial tension between competing private interests whose resolution suggests an efficient outcome is missing. State A and state B do not have competing interests as to their separate treatment of their own nationals.

See also Alston and Simma, *supra* n. 85, at 99; Schachter, *supra* n. 6, at 336.

for the sole reason of fostering welfare among the individuals under its control. They are upheld for their own sake in the full Kantian sense.[146]

The proposition formulated within the "Vienna Declaration and Programme of Action" of 1993 that human rights are "universal, indivisible and inter-dependent and interrelated"[147] is not just a truism, philosophically grounded in moral universalism, but the very foundation upon which a diverse global community can live together peacefully. Who in their sane mind would contest the existence of this body of law?

b Les "Droits-de-l'Hommistes"...

It is not the "if" that has tarnished the credibility of international law as a force of change, but the "how".[148] While scholarship is still pervaded by cultural relativists[149] and reality by violators of human rights, a large number of human rights treaty bodies, international organizations, and scholars are adamant in claiming customary international law status for an expanding catalogue of human rights.[150] Are these postulations grounded in a sound assessment of the legal *status quo*? It is doubtful, to say the least:

146 See Immanuel Kant, *Grundlegung zur Metaphysik der Sitten. Kritik der praktischen Vernunft nebst den Abhandlungen zur Philosophie der Geschichte* (Leipzig: Baumann und Modes, 1838) 53. See also Paul Vinogradoff, 'Historical Types of International Law', in *The Collected Papers of Paul Vinogradoff. With a Memoir by H.A.L. Fisher. Vol. II. Jurisprudence* (London: Wildy & Sons Ltd., 1964) 313.

147 Vienna Declaration and Programme of Action. Adopted by the World Conference on Human Rights in Vienna on 25 June 1993, at para. 5.

148 See Alain Pellet, '"Human Rightism" and International Law', 20 *Italian Yearbook of International Law* (2000) 4:

> It [human rights law respective the international law of human rights] is, and can only be, the art of the possible, and by wanting to ask the impossible of it, the "human rightists" harm the cause that they intend to defend more than they serve it. Often, they would do better to leave changes in the law to the "human rights activists", who have this objective as their respectable function, rather than try and do it themselves, and in so doing hamper progress in both human rights and international law.

See also Alston, *supra* n. 32, at 607 and 614; J. Shand Watson, 'Autointerpretation, Competences, and the Continuing Validity of Article 2(7) of the UN Charter', 71/1 *American Journal of International Law* (1977) 61.

149 See, for an extreme example, Abdulmumini A. Oba, 'Female Circumcision as Female Genital Mutilation: Human Rights or Cultural Imperialism?' 8/3 *Global Jurist* (2008) 1–38.

150 See the list of examples given by Alston, *supra* n. 32, at 610–611, even identifying the "frivolous claim" of tourism as a human right. See also Alston and Simma, *supra* n. 85, at 82, 84–85, and 90–96 with further references. Alternatively, the claim is made for an equally undeterminable "core" of human rights. For a typical textbook example, see Simma and Verdross, *supra* n. 50, at 76–77, § 97:

> Den zweiten Grundsatz des VR der Vereinten Nationen [in the sense of new *ius cogens* through elevation from the CHARTER OF THE UNITED NATIONS by virtue

> Yet, every passing day more and more purported rules are labelled customary law if this helps to support an argument that cannot otherwise be sustained under the law. [...] Bad as this situation tends to be with respect to general issues of international law, it turns only worse in certain fields where idealism, and occasionally political interest, needs to find a rule of law even where there is none, or reach an interpretation of a rule that does not even remotely allow for such a development. A desired outcome is then substituted for the strict rule of law.[151]

As the lawyer behind the original draft of the Universal Declaration of Human Rights, John Peters Humphrey, himself proclaimed: "Human rights lawyers are notoriously wishful thinkers".[152] Statements such as that "customary international law constitutes an alternative basis for human rights obligations" and that "[it] provides a robust external legal obligation upon the Security Council"[153] may sound great if read aloud and often enough, but definitely stretch the term "robust", when considered in light of actual practice.

More than any other field of international law, human rights scholarship has slowly but surely established itself as an independent discipline that stretches far beyond the confines of the study of law and prides itself on being interdisciplinary, breaching the confines of general international law.[154] This not only gives it such a strong appeal but also an even stronger lobby across the disciplines. As Myres McDougal once pointedly

> of Article 103 of the CHARTER] bildet die Achtung der sich aus der Würde des Menschen ergebenden *grundlegenden* Menschenrechte "für alle ohne Unterschied der Rasse, des Geschlechts, der Sprache oder der Religion", wozu nicht nur die Freiheitsrechte, sondern auch die sozialen und kulturellen Rechte gehören.

See on this phenomenon also Kammerhofer, *supra* n. 30, at 117; Zemanek, *supra* n. 100, at 420 with references to Oscar Schachter, Theodor Meron, and Mohamed El Kouhene.

151 Francisco Orrego-Vicuña, 'Customary International Law in a Global Community: Tailor Made?' 38/148 *Revista de Estudios Internacionales* (2005) 21–22.

152 John P. Humphrey, 'Foreword', in Richard B. Lillich (ed.), *Humanitarian Intervention and the United Nations* (Charlottesville: University Press of Virginia, 1973) vii.

153 Catherine Bevilacqua and Scott Sheeran, 'The UN Security Council and International Human Rights Obligations: Towards a Theory of Constraints and Derogation', in Nigel Rodley and Scott Sheeran (eds), *Routledge Handbook of International Human Rights Law* (London: Routledge, 2013) 386.

154 This has been equated with a tendency to ignore general rules of international law:

> Was sich in den Gesprächen mit den Menschen- und Umweltrechtlern aber ebenfalls zeigen würde, ist eine Tendenz zur Spezialisierung, die die den Sonderbereichen des Völkerrechts zugrunde liegenden allgemeinen Normen vernachlässigt, ja diese unter Umständen ignoriert. Hier fragmentiert sich also nicht nur das Völkerrecht selbst, sondern auch der völkerrechtliche Sachverstand.

See Bruno Simma, 'Gestaltwandel im Völkerrecht und in der Organisation der Vereinten Nationen', in Waldemar Hummer (ed.), *Paradigmenwechsel im Völkerrecht*

commented, "[o]ne way of making a policy into law is for influential people to assert in a very loud voice that it is law".[155] It is this behavior that led the often combative[156] Alain Pellet to speak of "human rightism"[157] and the "*droits-de-l'hommiste*".[158]

c ... et la Réalité

If customary international law should be more than a rhetoric trick or a figure of speech and *ius cogens* is to carry any real meaning, these manifestations must carry the acceptance of the states that are called upon to follow and implement them.[159] Where signatures on international human rights treaties are accompanied by reservations to key provisions,[160] one cannot speak of customary international law by virtue of a rule "of a fundamentally normcreating character such as could be regarded as forming the basis of a general rule of law" as

zur Jahrtausendwende. Ansichten österreichischer Völkerrechtler zu aktuellen Problemlagen (Vienna: Manzsche Verlags- und Universitätsbuchhandlung, 2002) 62.

155 Myres S. McDougal, 'Law and Minimum World Public Order: Armed Conflict in Larger Context', 3 *Pacific Basin Law Journal* (1984) 24. See also Venzke and von Bernstorff, *supra* n. 38, at para. 10.

156 A concession he himself makes. See Pellet, *supra* n. 148, at 4.

157 See *ibid., passim.* For a differing, "positive" use of the word see Arnold N. Pronto, '"Human-Rightism" and the Development of General International Law', 20 *Leiden Journal of International Law* (2007) 753 *et passim.*

158 Alain Pellet, 'La Mise en Œuvre des Normes Relatives aux Droits de l'Homme. "Souveraineté du Droit" Contre Souveraineté de l'État?', in Hubert Thierry and Emmanuel Decaux (eds), *Droit international et Droits de l'Homme. Actes du Colloque des 12 et 13 Octobre. La Pratique Juridique Française Dans le Domaine de la Protection Internationale des Droits de l'Homme* (Cahiers du CEDIN 5; Paris: Édition Montchrestien, 1990) 126.

159 See Meron, *supra* n. 82, at 247–248: "It is only when rights are not only rhetorically asserted but are pressed seriously as legal entitlements, that human rights and humanitarian norms will become truly effective protections of human dignity".

160 See, *e.g.*, the reservation behavior of Qatar with regard to the CONVENTION AGAINST TORTURE AND OTHER CRUEL, INHUMAN OR DEGRADING TREATMENT OR PUNISHMENT. See United Nations Treaty Collection, Database <https://treaties.un.org/Pages/ViewDetails.aspx?src=treaty&mtdsg_no=iv-9&chapter=4&lang=en#EndDec>. This is not a random rogue state, but the host of the 2022 FIFA World Cup, organized by an association that holds "building a better future for all through football" as one of its core missions. See FIFA.com., *About FIFA. Who We Are* <www.fifa.com/about-fifa/who-we-are/explore-fifa.html>. See, generally, Liesbeth Lijnzaad, *Reservations to UN Human Rights Treaties. Ratify and Ruin?* (International Studies in Human Rights; Dordrecht: Martinus Nijhoff, 1995). On the issue of "*sharia* reservations" and the example of Qatar see also Markus P. Beham, 'Islamic Law and International Criminal Law', in Marie-Luisa Frick and Andreas Th. Müller (eds), *Islam and International Law* (Brill's Arab and Islamic Law Series, Vol. 7; The Hague: Martinus Nijhoff, 2013) 360, fn. 95 with further references.

contemplated in the *North Sea Continental Shelf Cases.*[161] Even in the case that states do not raise reservations, it is doubtful that they comply in the way which human rights scholars have in mind.[162]

Is the undoubted normative appeal of universal human rights sufficient to trump the framework of international law?[163] Again: Who in their sane mind would contest the existence of human rights? Yet it is exactly this apparent truism that should make the "extra-terrestrial observer" wary of the conclusions that are drawn from it.

The normative appeal of human rights easily blinds the observer to dogmatic discrepancies,[164] a fact that human rights activists may use as a handy tool in pushing their agenda. As the infamous[165] Carl Schmitt pointedly held, "[w]er Menschheit sagt, will betrügen"[166] – "whoever speaks of humanity, seeks to

161 *North Sea Continental Shelf Cases* (Federal Republic of Germany *v.* Denmark/ Federal Republic of Germany *v.* Netherlands), Judgment of 20 February 1969, ICJ Reports 1969, p. 3, at 42, para. 72.

162 See Karl Zemanek, 'How to Identify Peremptory Norms of International Law', in Pierre-Marie Dupuy, Bardo Fassbender, Malcolm N. Shaw, and Karl-Peter Sommermann (eds), *Völkerrecht als Wertordnung. Common Values in International Law. Festschrift für / Essays in Honour of Christian Tomuschat* (Kehl: N.P. Engel Verlag, 2006) 1115:

> In spite of this impressive state of ratifications or accessions it would be preposterous to suggest that the human rights protected by these conventions are uniformly observed. States may "condemn discrimination against women in all forms" but they will understand the resulting obligations differently, in accordance with their own cultural/religious background, as the numerous and sometimes crippling reservations to these conventions testify, and still feel that they are correctly implementing them.

163 See Somek, *supra* n. 66, at 579:

> Most importantly, from the perspective of this value system, the state is viewed as its agent – more precisely, an agent whose task is to realise the "blueprint" of the international value system. In the words of Tomuschat, this means that "[...] States are no more than instruments whose inherent function is to serve the interests of their citizens as legally expressed in human rights". Wow. Consequently, it is assumed that attributing a constitutional structure to public international law presupposes transcending the horizon of the mere co-ordination of state interests in favour of recognising the greater autonomy of public international law vis-à-vis the professed will of states. In any event, there has to be "something fundamental" about norms for them to become eligible to fall within the remit of international constitutional law. The legacy of the natural law tradition is quite evident here.

164 Although difficulties in this respect are conceded in the literature. See, *inter alia*, Carl Wellman, *The Moral Dimension of Human Rights* (Oxford: Oxford University Press, 2011).

165 It has again become quite *en vogue* to cite him, possibly for that dubious reason.

166 Carl Schmitt, *Der Begriff des Politischen* (Wissenschaftliche Abhandlungen und Reden zur Philosophie, Politik und Geistesgeschichte, X; Duncker & Humblot: München, 1932) 42.

deceive".[167] If international human rights law wants to be taken seriously, it must address deficiencies, draw its conclusions, and find new consequences to violations;[168] not let condemnation follow violation follow condemnation … and so on. At the doctrinal level, this means to correctly assess the legal *status quo* and from that starting point devise proper legal instruments to create a credible international system of human rights protection (not necessarily based on legal instruments alone[169]); not "*ius cogens*" derived from "customary international law" derived from a non-binding resolution.

d "Meta-Effects"

Seen against the background of human rights violations, this seemingly strictly academic feat might appear as either cynical or an ivory tower exercise with the sole goal of analytical clarity, a "human rightist Glasperlenspiel"[170] so to speak; but that would ignore the interrelatedness between scholars and practitioners in international law who often exist in a transitional state between the two, if not in a constant dual role.[171] The results are unintentional "meta-effects"[172] that influence what happens in the "real world". In that sense, it is also not feasible that doctrine is and should be "accountable […] only to ideal entities such as the scientific community".[173] In the words of Philip Alston: "If international law is unable to respond to challenges to principles at the very apex of the system, its credibility in all other fields will be seriously, perhaps irrevocably, damaged".[174] Why should human rights be singled out in this respect? Is it not equally the case in other areas of international law that methodological inconsistencies arise? There is one very good reason to deconstruct the issue in

167 Translation by the present author.

168 This is not to be mistaken with the proposition that the lack of enforcement of human rights is proof of the absence of a body of customary international human rights law, which is arguably one of the main weaknesses of J. Shand Watson's critique of the international human rights regime. See Watson, *supra* n. 56, *passim*.

169 See Philip Alston, 'Against a World Court for Human Rights', 28/2 *Ethics and International Affairs* (2014) 197–212.

170 On the idea of the *Glasperlenspiel* ("glass bead game") see Hermann Hesse, *Das Glasperlenspiel. Versuch einer Lebensbeschreibung des Magister Ludi Josef Knecht samt Knechts hinterlassenen Schriften* (Zurich: Fretz & Wasmuth, 1943).

171 See *supra* n. 43 and accompanying text.

172 On the concept see Markus P. Beham, '"Borrowed" Concepts: The Pitfalls of "Atrocity Labelling" in Contemporary Historiography', in *id.* and Marija Wakounig (eds), *Transgressing Boundaries: Humanities in Flux* (Vienna: LIT Verlag, 2013) 76 and 88.

173 Anne Peters, 'Realizing Utopia as a Scholarly Endeavour', 24/2 *European Journal of International Law* (2013) 540. Cf. Onuf, *supra* n. 44, at 105–106.

174 Philip Alston and Euan MacDonald, 'Sovereignty, Human Rights, Security: Armed Intervention and the Foundational Problems of International Law', in Philip Alston and Euan MacDonald (eds), *Human Rights, Intervention, and the Use of Force* (The Collected Courses of the Academy of European Law, Vol. X/2; Oxford: Oxford University Press, 2008) 29. See also Kammerhofer, *supra* n. 30, at 125.

this particular area: Apart from the prohibition of the use of force, human rights are the benchmark by which the lay public measures the effectivity of international law.[175] People will care when the international human rights regime does not provide the right answers to the concerns of the world.

The surge of ethnic and religious violence across the African continent, be it in Nigeria or Southern Sudan, the rise of the so-called Islamic State throughout Northern Africa and the Middle East, and violations against freedom of speech or persecution for reasons of sexual orientation across the globe, make it seem like this normative development of international law and the realities on the ground are in fact inversely proportional. Should a more credible approach to the development of human rights not aim at the achievable, rather than following a "human rightist"[176] equivalent to "Moore's law"?[177] In no other field will the disappointment of legitimate expectations and a functioning rule of law so permanently damage the credibility of international law.

This correlation has been pointed out before.[178] "Meta-effects" will rise from the growing fault line between reality and a completely detached body of "law". To take but one example: While the last decade has seen a growing number of scholars assert a human right to internet access and freedom of speech within the cloud,[179] China has managed to keep up its "Great

175 See *supra* pp. 12 *et seq.*
176 See *supra* ns 157–158.
177 "Moore's law" is the prediction made by Gordon E. Moore on the constant doubling of transistors in integrated electronics. See Gordon E. Moore, 'Cramming More Components onto Integrated Circuits', 38/8 *Electronics* (1965) 114–117.
178 See, *e.g.*, Hathaway, *supra* n. 33, at 31–32:

> As the gap between declared universal law and the practice of states widens, advocates of an expansive interpretation of universal human rights norms may inadvertently be contributing to the destruction of a meaningful system of general interstate obligation toward humankind. The net result of the persistent overstatement of the reach of custom, general principles, and *jus cogens* is not, as presumably hoped, the effective incorporation of new standards into a clear and practical system of enforceable duties. Instead, wishful legal thinking sends the signal that the very notion of universal human rights law is essentially rhetorical, thereby diluting the force of whatever standards truly command (or may one day command) the respect of states. In the end, this melding of international law and politics yields little beyond politics.

179 See, prominently, a number of Austrian scholars: Wolfgang Benedek and Matthias C. Kettemann, *Freedom of Expression and the Internet* (Straßburg: Council of Europe Publishing, 2014); Matthias C. Kettemann, *The Future of Individuals in International Law. Lessons from International Internet Law* (The Hague: Eleven International Publishing, 2013); Matthias C. Kettemann, 'Endlich bestätigt: Menschenrechte gelten online wie offline', *jusPortal.at. Das Fachportal für Juristen* (24 July 2012) <www.jusportal.at/endlich-bestatigt-menschenrechte-gelten-online-wie-offline_matthias-c-kettemann/>.

Firewall"[180] and bloggers around the globe are subject to anything from harassment and arbitrary detention to torture, disappearance, or death.[181]

e Wrong Instruments?

The world and its most vulnerable inhabitants are in dire need of a functional international human rights regime and each individual human being should be able to rely upon states and, ultimately, as the guardian watchmen, the international community to provide for human rights protection[182] – and this is not even going as far as to call for any form of redress in case of their violation.[183] But constantly cutting and overtaking reality by cooking the books to assert customary international law or even *ius cogens* for even the most far-fetched human right benefits neither the individual nor the academic and international political discourse.[184] Perhaps customary international law or general principles of law are simply not the right instruments to implement such change?[185]

If human rights lawyers want to make policy – and, indeed, they should criticize what is wrong in the world and what should be done about it – then this should be done only following a sound assessment of the legal *status quo*; not as "wishful thinkers".[186] Only on such a foundation can legal scholarship contribute to the formation of international law, as "the cause of human

180 Again, this is not a random rogue state, but one of the permanent five members of the UN Security Council. The term "Great Firewall" was first coined in a *Wired* article by Geremie R. Barme and Sang Ye, 'The Great Firewall of China', 5/6 *Wired* (June 1997) <www.wired.com/wired/archive/5.06/china.html>.

181 See, *e.g.*, Joseph Allchin, 'Cut Down in Their Prime', *Foreign Policy* (29 May 2015) <http://foreignpolicy.com/2015/05/29/cut-down-in-their-prime-bangladesh-atheist-bloggers/>, or Angus McDowall, 'Saudi Arabia Rejects Rights Criticism After Flogging of Blogger', *Reuters* (7 March 2015) <www.reuters.com/article/2015/03/07/us-saudi-rights-badawi-idUSKBN0M30SP20150307>.

182 See General Assembly Resolution 60/1, '2005 World Summit Outcome', U.N. Doc. A/RES/60/1 (24 October 2005), at paras 138–139.

183 Although it has been held before that any right without the possibility of judicial checks is nothing more than "hortatory fluff". See the dissenting opinion of Justice O'Connor in *Kelo v. City of New London*.

184 See also the critique by Karl Zemanek on the use of *ius cogens* in such a fashion:

> The concept should not be overstretched. It suits nobody's purpose if any rule of international law is artificially raised to the level of *jus cogens*, apparently to make its violation look more loathsome. It should be remembered that sanctioning a factual violation is not the primary aim of the concept. It aims at *normative* acts, for the proper and only sanction of the violation of a peremptory norm is the nullity of the infringing normative act.

Id., supra n. 162, at 1116.

185 See Alston and Simma, *supra* n. 85, at 96 and 104; Emily Kadens and Ernest A. Young, 'How Customary is Customary International Law?', 54 *William and Mary Law Review* (2012–2013) 914–920.

186 See *supra* n. 152.

dignity is best served by the maintenance of a credible distinction between the law and the politics of international human rights".[187] Alternatively, scholars may ignore the lack of change and, in the words of Noam Chomsky, "live in a world of comforting illusion".[188] Comforting for scholars at least.

2 *Use of Force*

a A Circular Dead End?

If it is doubtful that customary international human rights law exists, where should the discourse on the regulation of the use of force be placed within the landscape of the sources of international law? On what basis are potential exceptions such as humanitarian intervention or even obligations such as a "responsibility to protect" discussed? Or might the character of the sources of international law be to blame for a debate that has been going on for more than half a century without hope for any firm conclusion? This second case study allows for the expansion of the argument of this book to a number of additional dogmatic questions related to the identification of state interest.

b Discourse

It is a truism that Francis Fukuyama's "end of history" has not come about and liberal democracy has not succeeded in making the world a more peaceful one.[189] The beginning of the twenty-first century is haunted by the ghosts of a bipolar world order and the current news headlines read like a history of the "Eastern Question" of the long nineteenth century: the Black Sea, the Crimea, and Turkey (with Ankara often, but not always, replacing Istanbul). At the same time, China is literally reshaping the landscape of Asia by building islands in the South China Sea to expand its territorial reach. Global policy is still dominated by the need for oil and gas, the threat of a nuclear Iran, and an already nuclear North Korea. Where do humanitarian and human rights considerations fit into

187 Hathaway, *supra* n. 33, at 33. See also Douglass Cassel, 'Does International Human Rights Law Make a Difference?', 2/1 *Chicago Journal of International Law* (2001) 121:

> The importance of these questions for rights protection is obvious: the institutions of international human rights law deserve our energetic support only to the extent they contribute meaningfully to protection of rights, or at least promise eventually to do so.

188 Noam Chomsky, *9–11* (New York: Seven Stories Press, 2001) 68.

189 The theory that has since entered common parlance was formulated by Francis Fukuyama, 'The End of History?', 16 *The National Interest* (Summer 1989) 3–18 and then *id., The End of History and the Last Man* (London: Penguin Books, 1992).

this global power play? How may they shape customary international law or general principles of law?

Even the most avid supporter of the idea of an international rule of law will notice the failure to transpose hortatory "UN-speak"[190] regarding the use of force and normative scholarship to the real world. While the discourse has shifted from "humanitarian intervention" in the 1990s to the "responsibility to protect" of the millennial years, legally speaking, nothing has changed, apart from the terminological vehicles that allow lawyers to discuss global policy in law school journals.[191]

c Indeterminacy of State Practice

Judging from what has been said with regard to non-treaty human rights law, it is very much possible that the discourse on the regulation of the use of force may suffer from the same deficiencies. However, as opposed to human rights, forceful acts of states are also almost always surrounded by a penumbra of competing interests and ulterior motives. It may simply not be possible to prove that states act solely upon altruistic or moral considerations in such cases.[192] Even if it were possible, the analyst would falter at the multitude of possible motivations for action.[193] In the terminology of Joseph Raz, even in light of the existence of an exclusionary reason, an actor may base his conduct on any parallel "first-order reason".[194] After all,

> [t]he fact that an authority requires performance of an action is a reason for its performance which is not to be added to all other relevant reasons

190 A derogatory term used off the record by some United Nations employees encountered by the present author to refer to the carefully worded phrases that recur in resolutions, reports, and other documents of the United Nations.

191 See Martti Koskenniemi, 'Miserable Comforters: International Relations as New Natural Law', 15/13 *European Journal of International Relations* (2009) 395: "Words are politics. When vocabularies change, things that previously could not be said, are now spoken by everyone; what yesterday seemed obvious, no longer finds a plausible articulation. With a change of vocabularies, new speakers become authoritative".

192 See Thomas M. Franck and Nigel S. Rodley, 'After Bangladesh: The Law of Humanitarian Intervention by Military Force', 67/2 *American Journal of International Law* (1973) 290; Peter Hilpold, 'Humanitarian Intervention: Is There a Need for a Legal Reappraisal?', 12/3 *European Journal of International Law* (2001) 464; Sean D. Murphy, *Humanitarian Intervention. The United Nations in an Evolving World Order* (Procedural Aspects of International Law Series, Vol. 21; Philadelphia: University of Pennsylvania Press, 1996) 85 and 143. See also Hathaway, *supra* n. 33, at 34.

193 This is not the result of a "half-baked" definition of positive law, but a result of how customary international law formation works. See *infra* pp. 57 *et seq.*

194 See Joseph Raz, *The Authority of Law: Essays on Law and Morality*, 2nd edn (Oxford: Oxford University Press, 2009) 26–27. On the terminology see further *ibid.*, at 22–23, and *id.*, *Practical Reason and Norms* (London: Hutchinson, 1975) 34 *et passim.*

> when assessing what to do, but should exclude and take the place of some of them.[195]

Did the NATO coalition have a humanitarian motivation in carrying out the bombing campaign against Serbia in 1999? Was the "international community" – not the collectivity of the abstract entities that are states, but the decision-makers that function as the organs of states – urged by a "responsibility to protect" the civilian population in Libya? Probably yes. And probably they have in each and every case, in which civilian populations are subject to war crimes, crimes against humanity, or even genocide. But this altruistic impulse seems, in most cases, too weak to spur any form of meaningful intervention in and as of itself.[196]

This raises the question: Were there any additional factors that served as a catalyst for intervention in Kosovo in 1999 or Libya in 2011? There surely were. May these have been the primary reason for intervention as opposed to humanitarian grounds? Maybe yes, maybe no. There is simply no way for the international lawyer to prove either proposition.[197] The idea of marrying moral authority with political opportunity has been around for a long time.[198]

This supports the proposition that it may just not be feasible to prove the existence of customary international law or general principles of law[199] with regard to forceful acts of states. The intervention devoid of any additional

195 *Id.*, 'Authority and Justification', 14/1 *Authority and Justification* (1985) 13, reprinted in *id.* (ed.), *Authority* (New York: New York University Press, 1990) 124.

196 Most recent examples include the inaction in Rwanda following the infamous "Dallaire cable" and throughout the ensuing genocide of 1994, Darfur as of 2003 and South Sudan in general, as well as the current situation in the states that have been destabilized throughout Northern Africa and the Middle East following the "Arab Spring". In other instances, the interest in warding off greater escalation deters action, as in the cases of North Korea or the Russian "annexation" of the Crimea as well as in the conflict in the eastern provinces of Ukraine. See Franck and Rodley, *supra* n. 192, at 279 and 291–298; Karl Zemanek, 'Hat die "humanitäre Intervention" Zukunft?', *Jahrbuch für internationale Sicherheitspolitik* (2000) 8 <www.bundesheer.at/wissen-forschung/publikationen/beitrag.php?id=857>.

197 See Cannizzaro and Palchetti, *supra* n. 100, at 3: "The difficulties related to the determination of customary law increase dramatically in fields where legal arguments have deep ethical and political implications, such as the international regulation of the use of force". See also Karl Zemanek, 'Ist das Gewaltverbot noch aktuell?', in Waldemar Hummer (ed.), *Paradigmenwechsel im Völkerrecht zur Jahrtausendwende. Ansichten österreichischer Völkerrechtler zu aktuellen Problemlagen* (Vienna: Manzsche Verlags- und Universitätsbuchhandlung, 2002) 68–69.

198 See Alfred P. Rubin, *Ethics and Authority in International Law* (Cambridge: Cambridge University Press, 1997) 82–83. See also *ibid.*, at 55–59.

199 After all, as Article 103 of the Charter of the United Nations bars any competing treaty regulation on the use of force within the Charter, customary international law or, alternatively, general principles of law would remain the only way of progressive change. See Olivier Corten, 'Breach and Evolution of Customary International Law on the Use of Force', in Cannizzaro and Palchetti (eds), *supra* n. 67, at 120 and 123; Zemanek, *supra* n. 99, at 416.

motives may be out there, but it escapes the knowledge of the present author.[200]

d Synthesis

Transposing the analysis regarding human rights as analogous moral concepts, the result would be that any humanitarian exceptions to the prohibition of the use of force cannot come into being as customary international law.

While it seems impossible to prove that a certain state practice was undertaken for humanitarian reasons alone, the conclusion arrived at with the "best test object",[201] human rights, suggests an inherent lack of imminent state interest with regard to such moral concepts. From "humanitarian intervention" to the "responsibility to protect", the underlying question necessarily procures a dead end. Eventually the discourse will be reframed and rebranded for the next academic expedition.

E Catch, Before the Fall

Taking into account the nature of the main question, a number of caveats and clarifications are in order before setting out.

1 Controversy and Apology

Of course, the present postulations may seem controversial – or even offensive to some – at first glance. This is only natural.[202] As Michael Waibel writes:

> Over time, the epistemic community associated with a particular regime develops its own views of what constitutes "reasonable" conduct in respect of that regime. Acculturation and learning among the actors within a regime lead to shared background understandings, shared preferences, and a common worldview.[203]

200 See also Michael Walzer, *Just and Unjust Wars: A Moral Argument with Historical Illustrations*, 4th edn (New York: Basic Books, 2006) 102.

201 See *supra* pp. 31 *et seq.*

202 See the reaction of Lillich to the critique of customary international human rights law by Alston and Simma, *supra* n. 68, at 11–20. See also the early reception of Koskenniemi's deconstruction of the international legal discourse as reflected by Jennings, Henkin, and Schachter. See Antonio Cassese, *Five Masters of International Law. Conversations with R-J Dupuy, E Jiménez de Aréchaga, R Jennings, L Henkin and O Schachter* (Oxford: Hart Publishing, 2011) 145–146, 220, and 240. See also Jean D'Aspremont, 'Martti Koskenniemi, the Mainstream, and Self-Reflectivity', *Amsterdam Law School Legal Studies Research Paper*, No. 2016–03 (2016) 17–19 <http://ssrn.com/abstract=2718846>.

203 See Waibel, *supra* n. 131, at 6–7, citing to the conclusions of German political scientist Alexander Wendt, *Social Theory of International Politics* (Cambridge Studies in International Relations; Cambridge: Cambridge University Press, 1999)

Even the otherwise soft-spoken and well-balanced treatise by Malcolm Shaw engages in footnote discreditation of scholars who question the "mainstream" view of human rights.[204] Fernando Tesón, a prominent supporter of humanitarian intervention, referred to any scholarly criticism of the NATO intervention in Kosovo as "a pathology that I call, for want of a better name, positivist stubbornness".[205]

At the outset stands the usually unquestioned, if not unquestionable consensus among international legal scholarship, in particular human rights scholars, that some, if not just the most "fundamental" human rights exist as customary international law. This assumption is almost solely carried today by an *argumentum ad populum* along the lines of "50,000,000 customary international human rights law fans can't be wrong".[206]

215–220. This is particularly the case for "activist" lawyers, as Martti Koskenniemi points out:

> [H]e or she is prepared to accept a legal argument only if it accords with his or her political objectives – in which case the activist's legal rhetoric looks like a manipulative-cynical facade to those whose commitment is to the law.

See *id.*, *supra* n. 62, at 291:

> Each regime, with its own language, background norms and shared understandings promotes varied policy goals. Each is primarily concerned with the pursuit of its own goals, be it the protection of the environment, human rights, or cross-border investment. The epistemic community associated with each regime has strong incentives to work towards the achievements of their regime's goals, as the effectiveness of the regime is likely to contribute to its own prestige and the influence of its members.

These observations essentially rest on theory advanced by French historian Michel Foucault on control and delimitation of the respective discourse. See Bianchi, *supra* n. 131, at 404. See also D'Aspremont, 'Wording in International Law', *supra* n. 44, *passim*; Koskenniemi, *supra* n. 36, at 1946–1962.

204 See Shaw, *supra* n. 88, at 194–195, in particular referencing the work of J.S. Watson:

> There are writers who regard the high incidence of non-compliance with human rights norms as evidence of state practice that argues against the existence of a structure of human rights principles in international law. Although sight must not be lost of violations of human rights law, such an approach is not only academically incorrect but also profoundly negative.

For some background on the debate underlying this comment see also Rosalyn Higgins, 'Reality and Hope in International Human Rights: A Critique', 9/5 *Hofstra Law Review* (1981) 1494–1499.

205 Fernando R. Tesón, 'Kosovo: A Powerful Precedent for the Doctrine of Humanitarian Intervention', 1 *Amsterdam Law Forum* (2008–2009) 44.

206 As in the title of the Elvis Presley LP, '50,000,000 Elvis Fans Can't Be Wrong: Elvis' Gold Records – Volume 2' (RCA Victor, 1959).

But the proposition of this book need not and should not be controversial or offensive. The conclusion is not a negation of human rights or humanitarian action, but a call to place them on a more solid foundation. It is meant as an apology for moral concepts in law, not in the sense of an excuse, but as an apologist that is concerned by the mushrooming of agenda and opinion over sound academic analysis; ultimately harming international law as the constructive and stabilizing force in international relations that it should be.

There are many examples of successful regional[207] – and non-judicial[208] – mechanisms currently in place. A focus could be on their expansion and the propagation of universally binding instruments, as opposed to simple "human rightism".[209]

Of course, one might argue that the European Court of Human Rights and the Inter-American Court of Human Rights have indeed been at the forefront of dynamically interpreting human rights treaties by ways of an *effet utile* to ensure a comprehensive protection that often goes beyond the letters of the word itself.[210] But it is also evident that these developments are only possible in a system consisting of both a treaty and a meaningful mechanism for adjudicating these rights that are simply non-existent at the universal level.

In both the European and the Inter-American cases, protection of human rights is not warranted by customary international law or general principles of law but by the existence of treaties paired with a culture of overall compliance over withdrawal.[211] The Council of Europe's mechanisms for human rights protection are role-models, on which normative change could be based.[212]

2 *"Legality" and "Morality"*

Generally, one has the impression that it has become unpopular to stand the ground for legal positivism. Hans Kelsen already was criticized for his legalist assessment of the Charter of the United Nations in his early commentary.[213] Although he had managed to convincingly repudiate the assumption that a

207 Such as the jurisdiction of the European Court of Human Rights or the Inter-American Court of Human Rights.
208 See Alston, *supra* n. 169, at 197–212.
209 See *supra* ns 157–158.
210 For the European Court of Human Rights see, most prominently, the finding that the European Convention of Human Rights is a "living instrument" in *Tyrer v. United Kingdom*, Judgment of 25 April 1978, § 31, Series A – No. 26. For the Inter-American Court of Human Rights see Antônio Augusto Cançado Trindade, 'Selected Aspects of the Case-Law Under the Inter-American System of Human Rights Protection', in Paulo Borba Casella (ed.), *Dimensão Internacional do Direito* (São Paulo: Editora LTR, 2000) 506–511.
211 See, however, *infra* ns 47–48, Chapter 3 and accompanying text.
212 See Rubin, *supra* n. 198, at 170.
213 See Bardo Fassbender, 'Hans Kelsen und die Vereinten Nationen', in Dupuy, Fassbender, Shaw, and Sommermann (eds), *supra* n. 162, at 775–776.

"political" instrument cannot be interpreted through legal means in his study of the COVENANT OF THE LEAGUE OF NATIONS,[214] this did not change much of the ensuing criticism. A methodological rebuttal was not on point; positivism is simply not attractive to those who aim to construe international law in political terms.

Equally, as "political" and ethereal human rights and other moral concepts may seem at first, they cannot escape a positivist legal assessment if their validity should be sought in the sources of law rather than in those of morality.[215] What seems so easy to accept within domestic law, is often viewed as a preposterous proposition in international law.

3 "Dogmatik", not "Pedantic"

Similarly, the emphasis on methodology within the legal assessment or, as German-speaking academia would call it, "Dogmatik" or "Rechtsdogmatik",[216] might seem pedantic, when weighed against the moral gravity of the legal substance that is human rights law and humanitarian action.

Such an approach has never been very fashionable within the field, nor is it popular in a scholarly setting that has devoted itself to critical theory, process, and other instruments of the social sciences. As Jean D'Aspremont remarked in the introduction to his book *Formalism and the Sources of International Law*:

> [T]he quest for a consensus on the criteria necessary for the identification of international legal rules no longer occupies a prominent position on the contemporary agenda of international legal scholars. Indeed, international legal scholars are becoming much less sensitive to the necessity of rigorously distinguishing law from non-law. [...] This growing acceptance of the idea of a penumbrance between law and non-law has provoked a move away from questions of law-ascertainment, increasingly perceived as irrelevant.[217]

214 See Hans Kelsen, *Legal Technique in International Law: A Textual Critique of the League Covenant* (Geneva Studies, Vol. X, No. 6; Geneva: Geneva Research Centre, 1939) 7–23.

215 See on this *South West Africa Cases* (Ethiopia *v.* South Africa; Liberia *v.* South Africa), Judgment of 18 July 1966 (Second Phase), ICJ Reports 1966, p. 6, at 34, paras 49–50. This differentiation was not even disputed by the large number of separate and dissenting opinions to the judgment. See, in particular, the explicit acknowledgement of the existence of such a distinction in the Dissenting Opinion of Vice-President Wellington Koo, ICJ Reports 1966, p. 216, at 228, and the Dissenting Opinion of Judge Jessup, ICJ Reports 1966, p. 325, at 441.

216 See *supra* n. 5 and accompanying text.

217 Jean D'Aspremont, *Formalism and the Sources of International Law. A Theory of the Ascertainment of Legal Rules* (Oxford Monographs in International Law; Oxford: Oxford University Press 2011) 1.

The approach of the present book combines a controversial topic with a seemingly unpopular quest, an emphasis on positive law and legal methodology for the sake of quality assurance as to the use of certain principles and standards within the legal argument. Yet it is not pedantic, but apologetic, when it favors sound academic analysis over agenda and opinion. It is a proposal to reconstruct a credible foundation for normative change that gets by without illusions.

2 Non-Treaty Sources

The title of this book speaks of non-treaty law. Rather than the immediate notion of an "unwritten" source that might spring to mind,[1] the term "non-treaty" seeks to emphasize the delineation between "consensual" and "non-consensual",[2] "unconsciously"[3] created manifestations of international law; what Robert Ago would call a formation "spontanée": Without a formal process.[4] The idea is that such non-consensual law is generated through social interaction or largely domestic processes, as opposed to the voluntary formation of will at the international level. The following chapter seeks to convey this particular understanding of non-treaty law.

A On the "Sources" of International Law

The term "source" itself, "figurative and highly ambiguous",[5] is problematic for a variety of reasons:[6] the failure of Article 38 of the STATUTE OF THE

1 Although it is true that they have no "authentic wording". See Ulrich Fastenrath, 'Relative Normativity in International Law', 4 *European Journal of International Law* (1993) 316. See also Jörg Kammerhofer, 'Uncertainty in the Formal Sources of International Law: Customary International Law and Some of Its Problems', 15/3 *European Journal of International Law* (2004) 524–525 and 552.

2 For the characterization of the sources of customary international law and general principles of law as non-consensual see James Leslie Brierly, 'The Basis of Obligation in International Law', in Hersch Lauterpacht and Humphrey Waldock, *The Basis of Obligation in International Law and Other Papers by the Late James Leslie Brierly* (Oxford: Clarendon Press, 1958) 18. See on this dichotomy also Koskenniemi, *From Apology to Utopia, supra* n. 2, Chapter 1, *passim.*

3 Dixon, *supra* n. 75, Chapter 1, at 26.

4 Robert Ago, 'Science Juridique et Droit International', 90 *Recueil des Cours de l'Académie de Droit International de La Haye* (1953) 929–945. See also Gihl, *supra* n. 75, Chapter 1, at 83:

> We are therefore driven to the conclusion that no source of law in a formal, that is to say proper, sense for international customary law can be pointed to. International customary law simply exists, and that indeed is quite sufficient.

5 Hans Kelsen, *Principles of International Law*, 2nd edn (New York: Holt, Rinehart and Winston, 1966) 437.

6 On the problem of the terminology "source" see *id., Das Problem der Souveränität und die Theorie des Völkerrechts. Beitrag zu einer reinen Rechtslehre*

INTERNATIONAL COURT OF JUSTICE to distinguish between rights and obligations[7] or the confusion regarding the character of the sources of international law as "formal" and "material" or what is even meant by one or the other.[8] As these

(Tübingen: J.C.B. Mohr [Paul Siebeck], 1920) 105–107; *id., supra* n. 5, at 437–438; Max Sørensen, *Les Sources du Droit International. Etude sur la Jurisprudence de la Cour Permanente de Justice Internationale* (Copenhagen: Einar Munksgaard, 1946) 13–14; more recently, Gennady M. Danilenko, *Law-making in the International Community* (Developments in International Law, Vol. 15; Dordrecht: Martinus Nijhoff, 1993) 23; Godefridus H.V. van Hoof, *Rethinking the Sources of International Law* (Deventer: Kluwer, 1983) 57–60, confirmed by Karol Wolfke, *Custom in Present International Law*, 2nd edn (Developments in International Law, Vol. 14; Dordrecht: Martinus Nijhoff, 1993) xv, fn. 8.

7 However, the distinction is rather superficial and of little added value to the present question. See on this Alain Pellet, 'Article 38', in Karin Oellers-Frahm, Christian J. Tams, Christian Tomuschat, and Andreas Zimmermann (eds), *The Statute of the International Court of Justice. A Commentary*, 2nd edn (Oxford: Oxford University Press, 2012) 761, para. 85.

8 See on this distinction George Abi-Saab, 'Les Sources du Droit International: Essai de Déconstruction', in Manuel Rama-Montaldo (ed.), *El Derecho Internacional en un Mundo en Transformacion. Liber Amicorum en Homenaje al Professor Eduardo Jiménez de Aréchaga / Le Droit International Dans un Monde en Mutation. Liber Amicorum en Hommage au Professeur Eduardo Jiménez de Aréchaga / International Law in an Evolving World. Liber Amicorum in Tribute to Eduardo Jiménez de Aréchaga* (Montevideo: Fundación de cultura universitaria, 1994) 30–32; Danilenko, *supra* n. 6, at 16–29; Pierre-Marie Dupuy, 'A Propos de l'Opposabilité de la Coutume Générale: Enquête Brève sur l' "Objecteur Persistant"', in *Le Droit International au Service de la Paix de la Justice et du Développement. Mélanges Michel Virally* (Paris: Éditions A. Pedone, 1991) 54–58; Shaw, *supra* n. 88, Chapter 1, at 51; Hugh Thirlway, 'The Sources of International Law', in Malcolm D. Evans (ed.), *International Law* (Oxford: Oxford University Press, 2010) 96–97; Raphael M. Walden, 'Customary International Law: A Jurisprudential Analysis', 13 *Israel Law Review* (1978) *passim*. For a general discussion on the distinction between formal and material sources in Article 38 of the STATUTE OF THE INTERNATIONAL COURT OF JUSTICE see, for example, Gerald G. Fitzmaurice, 'Some Problems Regarding the Formal Sources of International Law', in Frederik M. Van Asbeck (ed.), *Symbolae Verzijl. Présentées au Professeur J. H.W. Verzijl à l'Occasion de son LXX-ième Anniversaire* (La Haye: Martinus Nijhoff, 1958) 153–176, reprinted in Koskenniemi (ed.), *supra* n. 2, Chapter 1, at 57–80. See also the critique thereof by Anthony A. D'Amato, *The Concept of Custom in International Law* (Ithaca: Cornell University Press, 1971) 264–268. The problem goes further, of course, once one tries to justify the existence of the secondary rule: "The Statute [of the International Court of Justice] is in fact a material source of the secondary rule that treaties make law, but not a formal source of that rule". See Thirlway, *supra* n. 8, at 97. See also the comment by Martti Koskenniemi:

> It is impossible to pretend that the realist critiques concerning the indeterminacy of treaty interpretation, or the circularity and fluidity of custom and general principles would not have devastated formalism's credibility as a theoretical articulation of the business of law-application.

See *id., supra* n. 2, Chapter 1, at xxiv.

issues have been widely discussed elsewhere and would reach far beyond what is necessary or practical for the present argument, the term "source" is understood here simply as any conceivable appearance of the law,[9] the "outward manifestation" of a rule.[10]

To follow H.L.A. Hart's terminology, these manifestations might be referred to as, in a sense, the "secondary rules" of international law,[11] to which one must look in order to identify substantive law. However, as opposed to providing a blueprint for the creation of "primary rules", they only reveal in which guise they will appear.[12]

9 See also Bruno Simma, *Das Reziprozitätselement im Zustandekommen völkerrechtlicher Verträge* (Schriften zum Völkerrecht, Vol. 23; Berlin Duncker & Humblot, 1972) 24, who speaks of "Erscheinungsformen des Rechts". For a comprehensive discussion see Maarten Bos, 'The Hierarchy Among the Recognized Manifestations ("Sources") of International Law', 25/3 *Netherlands Law Review* (1978) 337 *et passim*. See further the definition of sources by the American Law Institute that points to such an understanding:

> § 102. Sources of International Law (1) A rule of international law is one that has been accepted as such by the international community of states (a) in the form of customary law; (b) by international agreement; (c) by derivation from general principles common to the major legal systems of the world. (2) Customary international law results from a general and consistent practice of states followed by them from a sense of legal obligation. (3) International agreements create law for the states parties thereto and may lead to the creation of customary international law when such agreements are intended for adherence by states generally and are in fact widely accepted. (4) General principles common to the major legal systems, even if not incorporated or reflected in customary law or international agreement, may be invoked as supplementary rules of international law where appropriate.

See American Law Institute, *Restatement of the Law. The Foreign Relations of the United States. Volume 1* (St. Paul: American Law Institute Publishers, 1987), further referred to simply as *Restatement of the Law (Third)*.

10 What Georges Scelle calls the "manifestation extérieure, le fait perçu et probant, l'élément captable et utilisable". See *id.*, 'Essai sur les Sources Formelles du Droit International', in Charles Appleton (ed.), *Recueil d'Études sur les Sources du Droit en l'Honneur de François Gény. Tome III. Les Sources des Diverses Branches du Droit* (Paris: Sirey, 1934) 400.

11 See Thirlway, *supra* n. 8, at 96. See also D'Amato, *supra* n. 8, at 41–44; Danilenko, *supra* n. 6, at 28. See, however, Hart's own determination of a society based on custom as one of "primary rules of obligation" alone. *Id., The Concept of Law* (Oxford: Oxford University Press, 2012) 91.

12 As Alain Pellet writes in his commentary to Article 38 of the STATUTE OF THE INTERNATIONAL COURT OF JUSTICE, the provision lists the "'formal' sources of international law, *i.e.* the manifestations of the rights and obligations of States". See *id., supra* n. 7, at 757, para. 78. See also *ibid.*, at 774, para. 111.

1 Article 38 of the Statute of the International Court of Justice

The sources of international law are given, though "not *eo nomine*"[13] and non-exhaustively[14] in the first paragraph of the "famous – or infamous –"[15] Article 38 of the STATUTE OF THE INTERNATIONAL COURT OF JUSTICE.[16]

This provision is not itself intended to be an enumerative list of the sources of international law, but a guideline for the International Court of Justice regarding which sources to look to in deciding the cases brought before it.[17] In any case, the catalogue with its origins in the STATUTE OF THE PERMANENT COURT OF INTERNATIONAL JUSTICE[18] has "stood the test of time".[19] Of course, "States can agree on international law being made in any way they wish",[20] but the categories contained in this catalogue seem

13 Hugh Thirlway, *International Customary Law and Codification: An Examination of the Continuing Role of Custom in the Present Period of Codification of International Law* (Leiden: A.W. Sijthoff, 1972) 36.

14 Most prominently, acts and documents of international organizations and unilateral acts of states, both now considered sources in their own right, are omitted. See Dixon, *supra* n. 75, Chapter 1, at 23–25.

15 Pellet, *supra* n. 7, at 733, para. 1.

16 The first paragraph reads:

> The Court, whose function is to decide in accordance with international law such disputes as are submitted to it, shall apply: (a) international conventions, whether general or particular, establishing rules expressly recognized by the contesting states; (b) international custom, as evidence of a general practice accepted as law; (c) the general principles of law recognized by civilized nations; (d) subject to the provisions of Article 59, judicial decisions and the teachings of the most highly qualified publicists of the various nations, as subsidiary means for the determination of rules of law.

17 See Ian Brownlie, *Principles of Public International Law*, 7th edn (Oxford: Oxford University Press, 2008), at 5, who also states that the provisions "represent the previous practice of arbitral tribunals, and Article 38 is generally regarded as a complete statement of the sources of international law". See also Dixon, *supra* n. 75, Chapter 1, at 23; Pellet, *supra* n. 7, at 748, para. 55, 759, para. 80, and accompanying footnotes; Thirlway, *supra* n. 8, at 98–99.

18 See Article 38 of the STATUTE OF THE PERMANENT COURT OF INTERNATIONAL JUSTICE:

> The Court shall apply: 1. International conventions, whether general or particular, establishing rules expressly recognized by the contesting States; 2. International custom, as evidence of a general practice accepted as law; 3. The general principles of law recognized by civilized nations; 4. Subject to the provisions of Article 59, judicial decisions and the teachings of the most highly qualified publicists of the various nations, as subsidiary means for the determination of rules of law.

See also Pellet, *ibid.*, at 738–745, paras 17–50; Thirlway, *ibid.*, at 98.

19 Jennings, *supra* n. 3, Chapter 1, at 331.

20 Louis B. Sohn, 'Sources of International Law', 25/1 *Georgia Journal of International Law* (1995–1996) 406.

to comprise what states and, in turn, courts find to be the conceivable forms in which this happens.[21]

2 Acceptance and Reception in the Literature

On review of the literature, Article 38 of the Statute of the International Court of Justice "is widely recognised as the most authoritative and complete statement as to the sources of international law",[22] "the cornerstone of positivist approaches to international law",[23] and "there is no serious contention that the provision expresses the universal perception as to the enumeration of sources of international law".[24] It may be viewed as "the criteria which international law uses in order to distinguish rules belonging to it".[25]

Other observers such as Jean D'Aspremont have described it as "misguidedly elevated into the overarching paradigm of all source doctrines in

21 As Edwin Borchard writes,

> [t]he classification of sources under Article 38 is mainly, it is believed, directory or possibly even academic in character; and the classification would be applied by any court even if not so specified, unless the treaty or compromise expressly barred the court from considering anything but treaties.

See *id.*, 'The Theory and Sources of International Law', in Appleton (ed.), *supra* n. 10, at 356.

22 Shaw, *supra* n. 88, Chapter 1, at 50. See Kammerhofer, *supra* n. 1, at 541, in particular fn. 93; Maurice Mendelson, 'The Formation of Customary International Law', 272 *Recueil des Cours de l'Académie de Droit International de La Haye* (1998) 364. Cf., however, Daniel Bethlehem, 'The Secret Life of International Law', 1/1 *Cambridge Journal of International and Comparative Law* (2012) 23–24, who gives a realist practitioner's perspective on the sources of international law:

> It seems to me that in fact there is a rather smaller subset of what constitutes the law and legal obligation than Article 38 of the Statute suggests. In practice, this comprises, first, treaties, namely, the text of the treaties. Second, there are principles of customary international law that have been declared by courts or by other authoritative bodies. By courts I mean both international courts and national courts. By other authoritative bodies, I mean, although with a question mark, bodies such as the treaty monitoring bodies in Geneva. Third, there are binding decisions of the UN Security Council. And fourth, perhaps, although a smaller category, there are binding decisions of other international organisations. In reality, everything else does not constitute law.

23 Anthea Roberts and Sandesh Sivakumaran, 'Lawmaking by Nonstate Actors: Engaging Armed Groups in the Creation of International Humanitarian Law', 37 *Yale Journal of International Law* (2012) 111.

24 Shaw, *supra* n. 88, Chapter 1, at 50. See also Danilenko, *supra* n. 6, at 34–36, listing a wide range of state practice and judicial decisions to support the proposition; Kammerhofer, *supra* n. 1, at 541, in particular fn. 96.

25 Gihl, *supra* n. 75, Chapter 1, at 73.

international law", while recognizing its value as a "handy toolbox for international lawyers in need of a list of sources of international law" and "the lens through which law-identification in international law has been – almost exclusively – construed".[26] Martti Koskenniemi has referred to sources doctrine "as a kind of user's manual; a practical checklist that professional lawyers have recourse to as part of their professional task and self-image".[27]

3 Two or Three "Main" Sources?

The three "main" sources are given in *litterae* (a) through (c) of Article 38(1) of the STATUTE OF THE INTERNATIONAL COURT OF JUSTICE as treaties, customary international law, and general principles of law. While there is little doubt that the first two stand on an equal footing, the legal status of general principles has been the subject of heated debate ever since the drafting of Article 38 of the STATUTE OF THE PERMANENT COURT OF INTERNATIONAL JUSTICE.[28]

a Hierarchy

While there is no inherent hierarchy within the sources listed in Articles 38(1) (a) through (c),[29] general principles of law have been seen as "[u]ne source

26 D'Aspremont, *supra* n. 217, Chapter 1, at 149. See also Pellet, *supra* n. 7, at 760, para. 82 and 845, para. 281.

27 Koskenniemi, 'Introduction', *supra* n. 2, Chapter 1, at xiii.

28 See on the origin of Article 38 of the STATUTE OF THE INTERNATIONAL COURT OF JUSTICE *supra* n. 18.

29 At least with regard to the relationship between treaties and customary international law. See Pellet, *supra* n. 7, at 841, para. 270, and 844, para. 278; Thirlway, *supra* n. 8, at 114. See also the Analytical Study of the Study Group of the International Law Commission on 'Fragmentation of International Law: Difficulties Arising from the Diversification and Expansion of International Law', finalized by Martti Koskenniemi, U.N. Doc. A/CN.4/L.682 (13 April 2006), at 166, para. 324, and Report of the Study Group of the International Law Commission on 'Fragmentation of International Law: Difficulties Arising from The Diversification and Expansion of International Law', U.N. Doc. A/CN.4/L.702 (18 July 2006), at 20, para. 31. Cf., however, Antonio Cassese:

> One should not be misled by this provision into believing that treaties override customary rules. In fact, the sources of international law are listed in Article 38 in the order in which they should be used by the Court. Treaties being special *ratione personae* and possibly even *ratione materiae vis-à-vis* customary rules, the Court should look into them before resorting to customary rules, if any.

Antonio Cassese, *International Law*, 2nd edn (Oxford: Oxford University Press, 2005), at 156, fn. 7. See on this also Sørensen, *supra* n. 6, at 237–250; Mark E. Villiger, *Customary International Law and Treaties: A Study of Their Interactions and Interrelations with Special Consideration of the 1969 Vienna Convention on the Law of Treaties* (Dordrecht: Martinus Nijhoff Publishers, 1985) 35, para. 85.

subsidiaire ou supplétive",[30] "complimenting custom and treaty law",[31] which are "obviously"[32] the "two most important",[33] "two main orthodox",[34] "the two",[35] "principal",[36] "primary",[37] or "main"[38] sources, with general principles of law standing "firmly in third place",[39] as they "largely disappear behind the two other [...] being transitory in nature",[40] functioning as a "fall-back source of law in the event that no treaty and no customary rule could be found to apply",[41] "only [...] resorted to in the rather exceptional cases where the dispute can be settled neither on the basis of treaties nor custom".[42] However, it has also been pointed out that such a view of Article 38(1)(c) of the Statute would violate the general principle of law *ut res magis valeat quam pereat*,[43] as this would not give the wording of Article 38 sufficient effect.

b Practice of the International Court of Justice

The ICJ itself has been found to apply the sources listed in Article 38(1) of the Statute of the International Court of Justice "in successive order and has organized a kind of complementarity between them".[44] This approach had already been envisaged in one of the original drafts.[45] As Cassese wrote with

30 Abi-Saab, *supra* n. 8, at 33.
31 Shaw, *supra* n. 88, Chapter 1, at 87–88.
32 Brownlie, *supra* n. 17, at 5.
33 Cassese, *supra* n. 29, at 183; *verbatim* Thirlway, *supra* n. 8, at 97.
34 Jennings, *supra* n. 93, Chapter 1, at 4.
35 Kontorovich, *supra* n. 118, Chapter 1, at 863.
36 Thirlway, *supra* n. 13, at 31.
37 D'Amato, *supra* n. 8, at 4; Guzman, *supra* n. 91, Chapter 1, at 116.
38 Guzman, *ibid.*, at 116; Klabbers, *supra* n. 94, Chapter 1, at 180; Pellet, *supra* n. 7, at 844, para. 278. See also Louis Le Fur, 'La Coutume et les Principes Généraux du Droit Comme Sources du Droit International Public', in Appleton (ed.), *supra* n. 10, at 372:

> La convention et la coutume priment les principes généraux: mais s'il n'y a pas de règle coutumière ou conventionelle applicable au litige, le juge peut et doit se référer aux principes généraux pour y chercher la solution des conflits que les Etats lui soumis. Les principes généraux viennent donc compléter les autres sources du droit.

39 Shaw, *supra* n. 88, Chapter 1, at 88.
40 Pellet, *supra* n. 7, at 848, para. 288. See also *ibid.*, at 850, para. 295, and 852, para. 300.
41 Thirlway, *supra* n. 8, at 114.
42 Pellet, *supra* n. 7, at 844, para. 278.
43 Tomuschat, *supra* n. 127, Chapter 1, at 314, fn. 283.
44 Pellet, *supra* n. 7, at 841, para. 270. On the question of application see further *ibid.*, at 841–844, paras 270–279, and 850, para. 296.
45 See the Permanent Court of International Justice, *Advisory Committee of Jurists, Procés-verbaux of the Proceedings of the Committee, 16 June-24 July 1920, with Annexes* (Van Langenhuysen Brothers: The Hague, 1920) 306. See on the origins of the Statute of the International Court of Justice also *supra* n. 18.

regard to the application of the sources contained in Article 38 of the STATUTE OF THE INTERNATIONAL COURT OF JUSTICE:

> Resort to these sources must be made based on specialty; that is, one should first look for the most specific provision applicable to a particular case and, if it is lacking, fall back on the more general rule. Thus, one must first look for a treaty or a source deriving from a treaty; failing an applicable rule, one should search for a customary rule or a general principle of international law. Only at that stage, if no relevant rule or principle can be found, may one apply general principles of law recognized by the domestic legal orders of States. This particular category of general principles makes up what one may term a "*subsidiary source*".[46]

He goes as far as arguing for a subsidiary application of general principles of law in relation to "general principles of international law" even.[47] Of course, this argument misses the conceivable possibility that customary international law could constitute *lex specialis* in relation to a treaty.

Although there are instances in which judges of the International Court of Justice have protested such an interpretation,[48] up until today, there has been no decision before the Court in which it has explicitly based its reasoning on general principles of law.[49] The same held true for its predecessor, the Permanent Court of International Justice.[50] Both courts, however, referred to the existence of such principles and applied principles generally considered to be general principles of law.[51] Additionally, "the [International] Court [of

46 Cassese, *supra* n. 29, at 183. He at least concedes that general principles "may be termed '*primary*', in that they are contemplated by general 'constitutional' rules". See *ibid.* as well as *infra* n. 65 and accompanying text. See on the subsidiarity of general principles of law also Max Sørensen, 'Principes de Droit International Public. Cours Général', 101 *Recueil des Cours de l'Académie de Droit International de La Haye* (1960-III) 34. With regard to the STATUTE OF THE PERMANENT COURT OF INTERNATIONAL JUSTICE see Alfred Verdross, *Die Verfassung der Völkerrechtsgemeinschaft* (Vienna: Julius Springer, 1926) 67.

47 See Cassese, *supra* n. 29, at 194.

48 See, *e.g.*, *Case Concerning Right of Passage over Indian Territory* (Portugal *v.* India), Dissenting Opinion of Judge Moreno Quintana, ICJ Reports 1960, p. 88, at 90.

49 See Brownlie, *supra* n. 17, at 17; Jonathan I. Charney, 'Universal International Law', 87/4 *American Journal of International Law* (1993) 537; Koskenniemi, 'Introduction', *supra* n. 2, Chapter 1, at xxi; *id.*, 'General Principles: Reflexions on Constructivist Thinking in International Law', in *id.* (ed.), *supra* n. 2, Chapter 1, at 362; Pellet, *supra* n. 7, at 833, para. 253, 839, para. 265, and 850, para. 295; Thirlway, *supra* n. 8, at 108–109; Tomuschat, *supra* n. 127, Chapter 1, at 311.

50 See Sørensen, *supra* n. 6, at 138–152. See Charney, *ibid.*, at 537; Koskenniemi, 'General Principles', *ibid.*, at 362. For a history of the application of general principles of law prior to their "formal" inclusion into the catalogue of sources of law see Simma and Verdross, *supra* n. 50, Chapter 1, at 380–382, §§ 597–98.

51 See, for example, *The Corfu Channel Case* (United Kingdom of Great Britain and Northern Ireland *v.* Albania), Judgment of 9 April 1949 (Merits), ICJ Reports 1949, p. 4, at 22. See also the instances of case law, including of the Permanent Court of

Justice] has frequently made reference to 'principles' without feeling a need to classify them under any other category of formal sources".[52]

B Customary International Law

1 Law of a Primitive Society

While having been replaced by treaties as the primary source of international law,[53] customary international law – also referred to as "usages[54] generally accepted as expressing principles of law"[55] or "general international law"[56] – is still considered to be "the foundation stone of the modern law of nations",[57] "the most basic source of rules to govern the activities of States",[58] the "oldest"[59] and "original source"[60] of international law, or even an "unquestioned authority",[61] "at the heart of what we mean by international law",[62] necessarily taking a primordial place among the different categories of legal norms.[63]

International Justice, mentioned by Cassese, *supra* n. 29, at 192–193; Robert Jennings and Arthur Watts (eds), *Oppenheim's International Law. Volume 1. Peace. Introduction and Part 1,* 9th edn (London: Longman, 1996) 37–38, fn. 5; Koskenniemi, 'General Principles', *ibid.*, at 362. See further Pellet, *supra* n. 7, at 833–834, para. 253, and 838–839, paras 265–266.

52 Koskenniemi, 'Introduction', *supra* n. 2, Chapter 1, at xxi. See Pellet, *ibid.*, at 835–836, para. 259, and 838–839, paras 265–266.

53 See Dixon, *supra* n. 75, Chapter 1, at 30. However, Kelsen held that "conventional law is inferior to the customary law" due to the fact that treaties based their validity on the customary principle of *pacta sunt servanda*. See Kelsen, *supra* n. 5, at 114.

54 See, however, Brownlie, *supra* n. 17, at 6, who insists on a strict division between the terms "custom" and "usage", the latter representing specifically "a general practice which does not reflect a legal obligation". On the confusion of terminology more generally see Wolfke, *supra* n. 6, at xv–xxi.

55 See, *e.g.*, *The Case of the S.S. 'Lotus'* (France *v.* Turkey), Judgment of 7 September 1927, PCIJ Series A. – No. 10, p. 4, at 18.

56 See, for example, reference throughout the *Fisheries Case* (United Kingdom *v.* Norway), Judgment of 18 December 1951, ICJ Reports 1951, p. 116.

57 Dixon, *supra* n. 75, Chapter 1, at 30.

58 Thirlway, *supra* n. 13, at 2.

59 Jennings and Watts, *supra* n. 51, at 25, §10. See also van Hoof, *supra* n. 6, at 85.

60 Paul Guggenheim, 'Contribution à l'Histoire des Sources du Droit des Gens', 94 *Recueil des Cours de l'Académie de Droit International de La Haye* (1958-II) 36; *verbatim* Jennings and Watts, *ibid.*, at 25, §10.

61 Koskenniemi, 'Introduction', *supra* n. 2, Chapter 1, at xx.

62 D'Amato, *supra* n. 8, at xii. For an earlier appraisal of customary international law in this respect see, *e.g.*, Elfried Härle, *Die allgemeinen Entscheidungsgrundlagen des Ständigen Internationalen Gerichtshofs. Eine kritisch-würdigende Untersuchung über Artikel 38 des Gerichtshof-Statuts* (Völkerrechtliche Monographien 10; Berlin Verlag von Franz Vahlen, 1933) 4: "Die internationale Gewohnheit ist die bedeutendste und umfassendste Rechtsquelle, auf die sich ein internationaler Richter berufen kann, um für den konkreten Fall eine rein rechtliche Entscheidung zu finden". See also Fidler, *supra* n. 74, Chapter 1, at 198.

63 See Sørensen, *supra* n. 46, at 35, writing that it "prend forcément une place primordiale parmi les differentes catégories de normes juridiques".

Malcolm Shaw summarizes the generation and legitimacy of custom within a community:

> In any primitive society certain rules of behaviour emerge and prescribe what is permitted and what is not. Such rules develop almost subconsciously within the group and are maintained by the members of the group, by social pressures and with the aid of various other more tangible implements. They are not, at least in the early stages, written down or codified, and survive ultimately because of what can be called an aura of historical legitimacy. [...] It is regarded as an authentic expression of the needs and values of the community at any given time.[64]

For Antonio Cassese, the authority of customary international law rested on a "constitutional" rule, lying "at the very apex of the legal order", namely that of "*consuetudo est servanda*".[65] This idea of customary international law as the *Grundnorm* of international law can be traced back to Kelsen himself together with a row of other prominent authors.[66] To paraphrase Georg Friedrich Puchta, customary international law is, in a way, the expression of the collective spirit of the international community.[67]

But customary international law has also been described as "the most cumbersome"[68] of the sources of international law, "wrapped in mystery and

64 Shaw, *supra* n. 88, at 51–52. On such categorizations of international law see also Hans Morgenthau and Kenneth W. Thompson, *Politics Among Nations: The Struggle for Power and Peace*, 6th edn (New York: Alfred A. Knopf, 1985) 295:

> International Law is a primitive type of law resembling the kind of law that prevails in certain preliterate societies, such as the Australian aborigines and the Yurok of northern California. It is a primitive type of law primarily because it is almost completely decentralized law.

See also Simpson, *supra* n. 53, Chapter 1, at 77, comparing international law with the "indigenous customary law in Australia and Canada". See also the beautifully written analogy used by Maurice Mendelson:

> Imagine a large island, inhabited by about two hundred families or clans. Fortune has not smiled equally on all of them. [...] I need hardly explain that our imaginary island is the Earth, and that the two hundred clans are States.

See *id., supra* n. 22, at 165–168.

65 Cassese, *supra* n. 29, at 183.

66 For more on this in detail see Gihl, *supra* n. 75, Chapter 1, at 62, in particular fn. 5.

67 See Georg Friedrich Puchta, *Das Gewohnheitsrecht. Erster Theil* (Erlangen: Palm'sche Verlagsbuchhandlung, 1828) 144–145.

68 Van Hoof, *supra* n. 6, at 85. For earlier examples of such statements see, *e.g.*, Heinrich, *supra* n. 102, Chapter 1, at 277:

> Das Gewohnheitsrecht gehört zu den schwierigsten Kapiteln der Rechtsquellenlehre. Das erklärt sich aus zwei Gründen: zunächst daraus, dass kein im

illogic".[69] More caricature than scholarly appraisal, it has had to put up with the characterization as an "amorphous but formidable jelly-fish".[70] Some have gone so far as to conclude that customary international law "is, quite literally, what states make of it".[71]

2 Theories on Custom

There is insufficient space here to give a full review of the bookshelves of theories of customary international law and their countless repetition in textbooks and articles trying to come up with ever-new solutions.[72] As Stefan Talmon holds, "[t]here are probably few topics in international law that are more over-theorized than the creation and determination of custom".[73] The obligatory accounts of prominent positions are to be found in the dozens of books and articles on the subject cited throughout this book.[74] And it is doubtful that a repetition of these would bring much clarity:

> Rahmen der Theorie der Rechtsquellen erörtertes Problem so eng mit grundlegenden erkenntnistheoretischen Fragen unserer Wissenschaft zusammenhängt wie gerade die Lehre vom Gewohnheitsrecht, und sodann daraus, dass kaum eine zweite rechtswissenschaftliche Spezialfrage so stark mit einer geradezu ins Uferlose gehenden Literatur belastet erscheint.

See also Fidler, supra n. 74, Chapter 1, at 198:

> CIL stands at the heart of modern international law while generating frustration and frictions in its identification and application. CIL appears indispensable and incomprehensible. In the contemporary international system, is CIL, to steal a phrase from Winston Churchill, a riddle inside a mystery wrapped in an enigma?

69 D'Amato, *supra* n. 8, at 4.
70 Eduardo Jimenéz de Aréchaga, 'International Law in the Past Third of a Century', 159 *Recueil des Cours de l'Académie de Droit International de La Haye* (1978) 9. See also Pierre-Marie Dupuy, 'Théorie des Sources et Coutume en Droit International Contemporain', in Rama-Montaldo (ed.), *supra* n. 8, at 51.
71 See Dixon, *supra* n. 75, Chapter 1, at 31.
72 For a very concise presentation of theories on customary international law see Petersen, *supra* n. 141, Chapter 1, at 294–297. For a historical appraisal see Kadens and Young, *supra* n. 185, Chapter 1, at 888–906.
73 Stefan Talmon, 'Determining Customary International Law: The ICJ's Methodology Between Induction, Deduction and Assertion', 26/2 *European Journal of International Law* (2015) 429.
74 See also *supra* ns 88–89 in Chapter 1 as well as the International Law Association, 'Final Report on Formation of Customary (General) International Law' (2000) <www.ila-hq.org/en/committees/index.cfm/cid/30>, which, due to personal unity, relies very much on Mendelson, *supra* n. 22. See on this also van Hoof, *supra* n. 6, at 85:

> The confusion and divergence of opinion which were said to prevail with respect to the doctrine of sources in general, reign supreme as far as customary international law is concerned. This is generally acknowledged and it has

> The theory of customary international law is one of the big mysteries of international law scholarship. Every student of international law knows what customary law is. And yet, nobody knows what it actually is.[75]

There is little agreement beyond the two-element theory,[76] as most recently confirmed by the International Law Commission,[77] although even that consensus is doubtful.[78] The two elements are inferred from the wording of Article 38(1) (b) of the STATUTE OF THE INTERNATIONAL COURT OF JUSTICE[79] and regarded as "the modern",[80] "most commonly cited",[81] and "most authoritative definition"[82] of "meta-custom"[83] "by a near-unanimous orthodoxy",[84] even if it represents "a real cliché".[85]

Some even *a priori* deny the value of customary international law as a true source of international law:[86] It has been pointed out that the grounds for its authority remain unclear[87] and formal procedures for its formation are

> become almost customary to start off a discussion of the nature of customary international law with some kind of lamentation signaling to the reader that he is about to embark upon an extremely intricate and complex subject.

75 Niels Petersen, Review of 'Brian D. Lepard, *Customary International Law. A New Theory with Practical Applications* (Cambridge: Cambridge University Press, 2010)', 21 *European Journal of International Law* (2010) 795.

76 See Kadens and Young, *supra* n. 185, Chapter 1, at 909; Koskenniemi, *From Apology to Utopia, supra* n. 2, Chapter 1, at 410; Simma and Verdross, *supra* n. 50, Chapter 1, at 346–347, § 551. See also American Law Institute, *supra* n. 9, at 30, §102, Reporter's Notes, para. 2: "No definition of customary law has received universal agreement [...]". For a systematic categorization of doctrinal views see Simma and Verdross, *ibid.*, with further references. See also Simma, *supra* n. 31, Chapter 1, at 32–34, with further analysis of these categorizations at 34–38. See on the disagreement with regard to non-treaty sources in general Bodansky, 'Prologue to a Theory of Non-Treaty Norms', *supra* n. 2, Chapter 1, at 121.

77 See Michael Wood, 'Second Report on Identification of Customary International Law', U.N. Doc. A/CN.4/672 (22 May 2014), at paras 3(a) and 21.

78 See *supra* n. 91, Chapter 1, for example.

79 See Michael P. Scharf, *Customary International Law in Times of Fundamental Change: Recognizing Grotian Moments* (Cambridge: Cambridge University Press, 2013) at 33.

80 *Ibid.*, at 32.

81 Guzman, *supra* n. 91, Chapter 1, at 123.

82 Cassese, *supra* n. 29, at 156. See also Guzman, *ibid.*, at 123.

83 See Tams, *supra* n. 87, Chapter 1, at 52–54.

84 Koskenniemi, *From Apology to Utopia, supra* n. 2, Chapter 1, at 410.

85 Luigi Condorelli, 'Customary International Law: The Yesterday, Today, and Tomorrow of General International Law', in Antonio Cassese (ed.), *Realizing Utopia. The Future of International Law* (Oxford: Oxford University Press, 2012) 148.

86 See, *e.g.*, Julio A. Barberis, 'La Coutume est-elle une Source de Droit International?', in *Le Droit International au Service de la Paix de la Justice et du Développement. Mélanges Michel Virally* (Paris: Éditions A. Pedone, 1991) 43–52.

87 See also Somek, *supra* n. 33, Chapter 1, at 171, citing Kammerhofer, *supra* n. 1, at 550, who discusses the theoretical issues related to customary international law as the *Grundnorm* of international law, cited in *supra* ns 65–66.

absent.[88] Those that accept it are unsure of its content.[89] One thing seems to be sure: "Customary international law is full of mysteries".[90]

As to the nature of customary international law, there exist, basically, two opposing positions: the voluntarists and the empiricists.[91] Countless nuances and attempts to reconcile these two or deconstruct one or the other are to be found throughout the literature. If the voluntarists are correct, customary international law is consensual law.

Before turning to those two opposing positions, it will be useful to recall the simple formula that every student of international law has memorized at one stage or other: Customary international law consists of state practice and *opinio iuris*. After all, it is also the starting point for any analysis under the empirical view.[92]

3 State Practice

The first, objective or "material"[93] element of customary international law is "general"[94] state practice, also referred to by its Latin term *usus* or *diurnitas* respective *diuturnitas*. It has been considered "the main *differentia specifica* of that kind of international law".[95]

This element has come under particular "attack" following the *Nicaragua* judgment of the International Court of Justice,[96] which puts an emphasis on the subjective element,[97] in particular by drawing on decisions of international organizations in determining customary international law.[98]

88 See Fastenrath, *supra* n. 1, at 318. See Somek, *ibid.*, at 171 and 173; Wolfke, *supra* n. 6, at 52.

89 See Wolfke, *ibid.*, at xiii.

90 Klabbers, *supra* n. 94, Chapter 1, at 179.

91 See *supra* n. 90, Chapter 1. Of course, there are a number of alternative explanations such as rational choice theory, for example. See *supra* n. 91, Chapter 1.

92 See Ago, *supra* n. 4, at 951:

> Un ordre juridique est une réalité objective dont l'existence se constate dans l'histoire et au regard de laquelle la tâche, que l'on a, est de la connaître, et non pas de la "fonder" sur des faits ou sur des principes idéaux. L'existence de l'ordre juridique international, en particulier, est une donnée qui ne peut se trouver démontrée qu'à la suite d'un examen scientifiquement objectif de la réalité empirique.

93 Koskenniemi, *supra* n. 72, Chapter 1, at 89.

94 See Cassese, *supra* n. 29, at 156.

95 Wolfke, *supra* n. 6, at 40–41.

96 Jan Klabbers characterizes *Nicaragua* as "the leading case on [...] the formation of customary international law", an unfortunate misnomer considering the dogmatic inconsistency of the argument made by the Court. See *id.*, *supra* n. 94, Chapter 1, at 188.

97 See on this *infra* n. 160 and accompanying text.

98 See *Case Concerning Military and Paramilitary Activities In and Against Nicaragua* (Nicaragua *v.* United States of America), Judgment of 27 June 1986

It is, supposedly, the sum of factual behavior of states, making the determination of customary international law an inductive, "upstream"[99] assessment. Thereby, what is referred to as state practice in the context of the formation of customary international law is, in the first instance, indistinguishable from generally legally insignificant behavior such as simple comity, *courtoisie*, diplomatic protocol, or friendship without any additional qualification.[100] It is simply any form of physical manifestation of the abstract entity of the state.

a What Constitutes State Practice?

In this sense, each and every act – or even omission – of a state may qualify as an instance of state practice.[101] As Jennings and Watts emphasize,

> practice of states [...] embraces not only their external conduct with each other but is also evidenced by such internal matters as their domestic legislation, judicial decisions, diplomatic dispatches, internal government memoranda, and ministerial statements in Parliaments and elsewhere.[102]

One of the problems associated with this is that, of course, not all of these documents may be publicly available.[103]

Still, authors have tried to demonstratively list examples to illustrate the vastness of possible sources for the determination of state practice. Dixon gives a number of generic categories as examples of state practice[104], such as:

> actual activity (acts and omissions), statements made in respect of concrete situations or disputes, statements of legal principle made in the abstract (such as those preceding the adoption of a resolution in the General Assembly), national legislation and the practice of international organisations.

(Merits), ICJ Reports 1986, p. 14, at 99–104, paras 188–195, and 105–108, paras 202–205. See Cannizzaro and Palchetti, *supra* n. 100, Chapter 1, at 3.

99 Pellet, *supra* n. 7, at 813, para. 211.

100 See also *infra* pp. 70 *et seq.*

101 For a critique of narrower views of what constitutes state practice, in particular of Anthony D'Amato, Karl Strupp, and Hugh Thirlway, see Akehurst, *supra* n. 50, Chapter 1, at 1–10.

102 See Jennings and Watts, *supra* n. 51, at 26, §10.

103 Akehurst, *supra* n. 50, at 13:

> Much of the evidence of State practice is hidden in unpublished archives. Consequently one can never prove a rule of customary law in an absolute manner but only in a relative manner – one can only prove that the majority of the evidence *available* supports the alleged rule.

Cf., however, Mendelson, *supra* n. 32, Chapter 1, at 195.

104 Dixon, *supra* n. 75, Chapter 1, at 31.

Brownlie points more specifically to

> diplomatic correspondence, policy statements, press releases, the opinions of official legal advisers, official manuals on legal questions, *e.g.* manuals of military law, executive decisions and practices, orders to naval forces etc., comments by governments on drafts produced by the International Law Commission, state legislation, international and national judicial decisions, recitals in treaties and other international instruments, a pattern of treaties in the same form, the practice of international organs, and resolutions relating to legal questions in the United Nations General Assembly

as "material sources of custom".[105]

Shaw lists "administrative acts, legislation, decisions of courts and activities on the international stage, for example treaty-making" and suggests to "read the newspapers, consult historical record, listen to what governmental authorities are saying and peruse the many official publications" as well as "memoirs of various past leaders, official manuals on legal questions, diplomatic interchanges and the opinions of national legal advisors".[106] Past the legal entity of the state itself, "one may note resolutions in the General Assembly, comments made by governments on drafts produced by the International Law Commission, decisions of the international judicial institutions, decisions of national courts, treaties and the general practice of international organisations".[107] Furthermore, Shaw lists a number of instances in which non-physical claims have constituted state practice.[108] So basically, one can assume that each and every activity (including the absence thereof) within the context of an official state function counts toward state practice. It is simply "what states actually do".[109] Categorizations or attempts at a taxative enumeration seem absent in awe of a sheer incomprehensible amount of eligible material.

The International Court of Justice itself has included "administrative acts or attitudes", "legislation", "acts of the judiciary" and "treaties".[110] In the *Jurisdictional Immunities* case, in order to determine the existence of immunity under customary international law, for example, it considered

> judgments of national courts faced with the question of whether a foreign State is immune, the legislation of those States which have enacted statutes dealing with immunity, the claims to immunity advanced by States before foreign courts and the statements made by States, first in the course of the extensive study of the subject by the International Law

105 Brownlie, *supra* n. 17, at 6–7.
106 Shaw, *supra* n. 88, Chapter 1, at 58.
107 *Ibid.*
108 *Ibid.*, at 59.
109 *Ibid.*, at 53.
110 See Pellet, *supra* n. 7, at 815–816, para. 217. For another list of examples drawn upon by the Court see Tams, *supra* n. 87, Chapter 1, at 67–68.

> Commission and then in the context of the adoption of the United Nations Convention.[111]

The International Law Commission, too, has arrived at a broad number of materials that may serve as evidence of state practice.[112] It is truly difficult to imagine anything produced within the periphery of a state organ – understood in the widest possible sense – that would not constitute evidence of state practice.[113]

b Three Characteristics of State Practice

In the absence of a taxative list of the physical manifestations of states, jurisprudence and doctrine have determined a number of characteristics that are relevant in assessing state practice: Scope, quality, and time.

I SCOPE

Following the number of states involved in the practice and, consequently, the geographical scope of its application, doctrine differentiates between "universal",[114] "general"[115] or "ordinary",[116] "particular",[117] "of a limited geographical

111 *Jurisdictional Immunities of the State* (Germany *v.* Italy; Greece intervening), Judgment of 3 February 2012, ICJ Reports 2012, p. 99, at 123, para. 55. See also the analysis undertaken by the Court throughout the following paragraphs.
112 See Report of the International Law Commission on Ways and Means for Making the Evidence of Customary International Law More Readily Available', *Yearbook of the International Law Commission* (1950-II), U.N. Doc. A/CN.4/Ser.A/1950, at 368–372, paras 33–78.
113 Cf. Wolfke, *supra* n. 6, at xv, fn. 6, arguing that state practice concerning dispute resolution is of little value, as "states as a rule use all possible arguments to this end". The issue, in particular with regard to international arbitration and in light of the relationship between party and counsel, is controversial.
114 See, *e.g.*, Dixon, *supra* n. 75, Chapter 1, at 32.
115 See *Delimitation of the Maritime Boundary in the Gulf of Maine Area* (Canada *v.* United States of America), Judgment of 12 October 1984 Given by the Chamber Constituted by the Order Made by the Court on 20 January 1982, ICJ Reports 1984, p. 246, at 300, para. 114; *Case Concerning Military and Paramilitary Activities In and Against Nicaragua* (Nicaragua *v.* United States of America), Judgment of 27 June 1986 (Merits), ICJ Reports 1986, p. 14, at 22, para. 23. This is either used synonymously with "universal", see, *inter alia*, Maarten Bos, 'The Identification of Custom in International Law', 25/3 *German Yearbook of International Law* (1982) 43; Thirlway, *supra* n. 8, at 106, or may also sometimes be used to indicate the existence of persistent objectors to the rule, as opposed to universal application, as in the teaching of the Section for International Law and International Relations of the Department of European, International and Comparative Law of the University of Vienna. See the passage on the persistent objector theory *infra* iii. The "Persistent Objector" Theory.
116 Shaw, *supra* n. 88, Chapter 1, at 65.
117 *Case Concerning Military and Paramilitary Activities In and Against Nicaragua* (Nicaragua *v.* United States of America), Judgment of 27 June 1986 (Merits), ICJ Reports 1986, p. 14, at 105, para. 199. See also Danilenko, *supra* n. 6, at 10;

scope",[118] "regional",[119] "local"[120] or "special",[121] and even "bilateral"[122] customary international law.

In order for universal or general customary international law, *i.e.* such as is binding upon all states, to emerge, practice needs to be "common to a significant number of states",[123] "generally [...] adopted",[124] or at least include the "States concerned".[125] "Regional" custom may even require all states involved to set state practice.[126] At the other end of the spectrum, Antonio Cassese held – in what may be deemed quite a cynical, though undoubtedly pragmatic, approach to legal theory – that universal participation in the formation of customary international law was never necessary, as

> is evidenced by the fact that no national or international court dealing with the question of whether a customary rule had taken shape on a certain matter has ever examined the views of all States of the world.[127]

However, this does not necessarily validate the view.

Josef L. Kunz, 'The Nature of Customary International Law', 47/4 *American Journal of International Law* (1953) 662.

118 Pellet, *supra* n. 7, at 829, para. 243.

119 Pellet, *ibid.*, at 829, para. 244; Shaw, *supra* n. 88, Chapter 1, at 65. See, for example, the *Colombian-Peruvian Asylum Case* (Colombia *v.* Peru), Judgment of 20 November 1950, ICJ Reports 1950, p. 266.

120 Brownlie, *supra* n. 17, at 11, who equalled it with "bilateral" customary international law; Dixon, *supra* n. 75, Chapter 1, at 32–34; Thirlway, *supra* n. 8, at 106–107, for whom it is synonymous with "special" custom, also explicitly including bilateral customary international law within the category.

121 D'Amato, *supra* n. 8, at 233–263; Guzman, *supra* n. 91, Chapter 1, at 159; Thirlway, *supra* n. 8, at 106–107.

122 See Danilenko, *supra* n. 6, at 10; Pellet, *supra* n. 7, at 831, para. 247. See, for example in this regard, the *Case Concerning Right of Passage over Indian Territory* (Portugal *v.* India), Judgment of 12 April 1960 (Merits), ICJ Reports 1960, p. 6. For an example of earlier practice see Wolfke, *supra* n. 6, at 12–13 and Peter Haggenmacher, 'La Doctrine des Deux Éléments du Droit Coutumier Dans la Pratique de la Cour Internationale', 90 *Revue Général du Droit International Public* (1986) 40–43 suggesting the example of *Free City of Danzig and International Labour Organization*, Advisory Opinion of 26 August 1930, PCIJ Series B – No. 18, p. 4. Cf., however, the issue concerning the legal personality of Danzig as of international character Karol Wolfke, *ibid.*, at 13, fn. 59.

123 Dixon, *supra* n. 75, Chapter 1, at 32.

124 *Fisheries Case* (United Kingdom *v.* Norway), Judgment of 18 December 1951, ICJ Reports 1951, p. 116, at 128.

125 *North Sea Continental Shelf Cases* (Federal Republic of Germany *v.* Denmark/ Federal Republic of Germany *v.* Netherlands), Judgment of 20 February 1969, ICJ Reports 1969, p. 3, at 44, para. 76. See on the difficulty of identifying the states "specially affected" Danilenko, *supra* n. 6, at 95–96.

126 See Danilenko, *ibid.*, at 94.

127 Cassese, *supra* n. 29, at 162.

Intermingling considerations of international relations theory, Shaw adds that "some correlation with power" is also part of the equation.[128] Along the lines of this notion, Charles de Visscher made the illustrative allegory of a gradually worn path:

> The slow growth of international custom has been compared to the gradual formation of a road across vacant land. To begin with, the tracks are many and uncertain, scarcely visible on the ground. Then most users, for some reason of common utility, follow the same line; a single path becomes clear, which in turn gives place to a road henceforth recognized as the only regular way, though it is impossible to say at what precise moment the latter change took place. [...] Among the users are always some who mark the soil more deeply with their footprints than others, either because of their weight, which is to say their power in this world, or because their interests bring them more frequently this way.[129]

Following this view, a select number of powerful states that are particularly affected by a certain issue could equally create customary international law that is universal in scope. One might only think of the state practice of the official – and maybe also unofficial – nuclear powers with regard to such issues.[130]

128 Shaw, *supra* n. 88, Chapter 1, at 57. See also Rosalyn Higgins, 'The Identity of International Law', in Cheng (ed.), *supra* n. 93, Chapter 1, at 43; Oscar Schachter, 'The Nature and Process of Legal Development in International Society', in Johnston and Macdonald (eds), *supra* n. 81, Chapter 1, at 751; de Visscher, *supra* n. 32, Chapter 1, at 155. One prominent example was the inability of non-capital-exporting states to effectively engage in a diverging compensation practice in cases of lawful expropriation in what was deemed the "new international economic order". See Scharf, *supra* n. 79, at 39–40. For an extensive study on the issue see Michael Byers, *Custom, Power and the Power of Rules: International Relations and Customary International Law* (Cambridge: Cambridge University Press, 2004).

129 De Visscher, *supra* n. 32, Chapter 1, at 155. This analogy seems to have been drawn from earlier works dealing with custom in municipal law. See Wolfke, *supra* n. 6, at 55.

130 A notion that has, of course, also been criticized, in particular in the context of newly independent states. Cf. Guha Roy, 'Is the Law of Responsibility of States for Injuries to Aliens a Part of Universal International Law?', 55 *American Journal of International Law* (1961) 881:

> But custom is limited in its operation to states which either were its birthplace or adopted it. [...] To argue from this semblance of universality of any branch of international law that it is really universal and as such must be treated as automatically binding on new members of the international community involves, in the writer's view, the assumption of an analogy between this community and a club. Today's international community is supposed in this argument to be merely an expanded version of the old, just like a club which does not necessarily cease to be the same old club because of an enlargement of its membership. This, like most analogies, seems superficial and misleading. A club is a community within a community and presupposes the existence of a larger community within which alone it can function. The club may have its own rules for the guidance of its members but these must be consistent with the laws of the larger community. The international

II QUALITY

With regard to the quality – or density – of practice, jurisprudence has held that state practice must be "constant and uniform"[131] or "both extensive and virtually uniform".[132] However, in making this determination, it is seemingly sufficient if there is "substantial, rather than complete, consistency".[133] This consistency is "built upon repetition".[134]

At the same time, the existence of conflicting state practice plays a role in determining "how much" of it is needed for the formation of a rule of customary international law.[135] It has also been suggested that the necessary quality of practice is relative to the corresponding *opinio iuris*.[136] The level of quality or density may also depend on the active or passive nature of a norm,

> community, on the other hand, was and is itself a community of communities and instead of itself functioning within a larger community, it has smaller communities of different types coexisting within it. A club may change its identity when structural or other changes, including a change of objectives, dictate the necessity or desirability of a new start. Whether there is a new start or not, the law of the larger community ensures its functioning according to its own rules.

Alexander Somek has called this an "oligarchic form of legislation". See Somek, supra n. 33, Chapter 1, at 173, brackets omitted.

131 *Colombian-Peruvian Asylum Case* (Colombia *v.* Peru), Judgment of 20 November 1950, ICJ Reports 1950, p. 266, at 276. See, interestingly, Dixon, *supra* n. 75, Chapter 1, at 31, who seems to find this phrase in the *Lotus* judgment. The present author has been unable to reproduce this result.

132 *North Sea Continental Shelf Cases* (Federal Republic of Germany *v.* Denmark/ Federal Republic of Germany *v.* Netherlands), Judgment of 20 February 1969, ICJ Reports 1969, p. 3, at 44, para. 74.

133 See Dixon, *supra* n. 75, Chapter 1, at 31. See *Fisheries Case* (United Kingdom *v.* Norway), Judgment of 18 December 1951, ICJ Reports 1951, p. 116, at 138:

> The Court considers that too much importance need not be attached to the few uncertainties or contradictions, real or apparent, which the United Kingdom Government claims to have discovered in Norwegian practice. They may be easily understood in the light of the variety of the facts and conditions prevailing in the long period which has elapsed since 1812, and are not such as to modify the conclusions reached by the Court.

134 Herman Meijers, 'How is International Law Made?', 9 *Netherlands Yearbook of International Law* (1978) 13. See also Gennady M. Danilenko, 'The Theory of International Customary Law', 31 *German Yearbook of International Law* (1988) 13. See, however, Akehurst, *supra* n. 50, Chapter 1, at 12–14.

135 See Akehurst, *supra* n. 50, Chapter 1, at 18:

> The number of States needed to create a rule of customary law varies according to the amount of practice which conflicts with the rule. A practice followed by a very small number of States can create a rule of customary law if there is no practice which conflicts with the rule.

136 See Frederic L. Kirgis, 'Custom on a Sliding Scale', 81/1 *American Journal of International Law* (1987) 149.

i.e. if the state is required to act or simply to refrain from taking action.[137] In other words: "Rules enhancing state sovereignty are often more easily established than rules limiting state sovereignty".[138]

In any case, according to the International Court of Justice in the *Asylum* case, the burden of proof lies with the party relying on the respective rule of customary international law:

> The Party which relies on a custom of this kind must prove that this custom is established in such a manner that it has become binding on the other Party. [...] [A] Government must prove that the rule invoked by it is in accordance with a constant and uniform usage practised by the States in question, and that this usage is the expression of a right appertaining to the State granting asylum and a duty incumbent on the territorial State. This follows from Article 38 of the Statute of the Court, which refers to international custom "as evidence of a general practice accepted as law".[139]

III TIME

Finally, the passage of time has a role to play in the analysis of state practice,[140] although it "is also not decisive".[141] The standard applied seems to be quite open and lax, however, so long as the practice is in itself clear and unequivocal enough, as the International Court of Justice held in the *North Sea Continental Shelf* cases:

> Although the passage of only a short period of time is not necessarily, or of itself, a bar to the formation of a new rule of customary international law on the basis of what was originally a purely conventional rule, an indispensable requirement would be that within the period in question, short though it might be, State practice, including that of States whose interests are specially affected, should have been both extensive and virtually uniform in the sense of the provision invoked; [...].[142]

137 See Dixon, *supra* n. 75, Chapter 1, at 32.
138 *Ibid.*, at 32.
139 *Colombian-Peruvian Asylum Case* (Colombia *v.* Peru), Judgment of 20 November 1950, ICJ Reports 1950, p. 266, at pp. 276–277. See Brownlie, *supra* n. 17, at 7 with further references to subsequent jurisprudence. See also the approach taken by the Permanent Court of International Justice in *The Case of the S.S. 'Lotus'* (France *v.* Turkey), Judgment of 7 September 1927, PCIJ Series A. – No. 10.
140 See Pellet, *supra* n. 7, at 817, para. 221. Some states used to assert certain time frames throughout which state practice would need to have taken place. See Scharf, *supra* n. 79, at 7 and 58.
141 Wolfke, *supra* n. 6, at 59.
142 *North Sea Continental Shelf Cases* (Federal Republic of Germany *v.* Denmark/ Federal Republic of Germany *v.* Netherlands), Judgment of 20 February 1969, ICJ Reports 1969, p. 3, at 44, para. 74. See Brownlie, *supra* n. 17, at 7.

Pronunciations such as these have opened the door to speculations as to the possibility of a complete absence of the time element in the formation of customary international law in the guise of "instant custom", for example.[143]

As nineteenth-century German jurist Georg Friedrich Puchta already pointed out, the term "practice"[144] implies the element of time.[145] Thus, nuanced approaches have arisen. In an alternative revival to the concept of "instant custom", Michael Scharf uses the term "Grotian Moments" to refer to an accelerated formation of customary international law that has "emerge[d] with unusual rapidity and acceptance",[146] "through acquiescence or endorsement in response to state acts".[147] For him, "a context of fundamental change" may serve as a "third factor" in identifying customary international law.[148]

143 This term was coined in 1965 by Bin Cheng in an article on space law in the *Indian Journal of International Law* referring to the principle of the peaceful use of outer space following the launch of Sputnik 1. See *id.*, 'United Nations Resolutions on Outer Space: "Instant" International Customary Law?', 5 *Indian Journal of International Law* (1965) 35–40. See also Wolfke, *supra* n. 6, at 60, who mentions the principle of sovereignty over airspace as having arisen "spontaneously at the outbreak of the First World War". Seemingly in agreement with Cheng on the possibility, Shaw, *supra* n. 88, Chapter 1, at 56, although he also points to jurisprudence as to the other temporal extreme. See *ibid.*, at 54, fn. 19, on the pronunciation by Judge Negulesco of the Permanent Court of International Justice. Cf. also Iain MacGibbon, 'Means for the Identification of International Law', in Cheng (ed.), *supra* n. 93, Chapter 1, at 18, fn. 35 and accompanying text; Pellet, *supra* n. 7, at 817, para. 221.

144 "Wiederholung" in German.

145 See Puchta, *Das Gewohnheitsrecht. Zweiter Theil* (Erlangen: Palm'sche Verlagsbuchhandlung, 1837) 104. However, he did allow for the absence of time in the case of tacit agreements:

> Kann der vorliegende Act als eine Beobachtung der ersten Art angesehen werden, als eine stillschweigende Willenserklärung, so beweist schon diese einmalige Beobachtung die Existenz des Rechtssatzes so vollkommen, wie eine ausdrückliche Erklärung. In diesem Fall ist also die gewöhnliche Meinung richtig [dass Gewohnheitsrecht aus nur einem Akt entstehen kann]. Hat aber der Act der Observanz jenen Character nicht, ist er also nur als eine Beobachtung der zweiten Art, als ein bloßes Zeugnis eines bestehenden Rechtssatzes zu betrachten, so gilt auch hier, was von der Erkenntnis des Gewohnheitsrechts anerkannt wird, daß aus einem einzelnen Fall der Uebung noch keineswegs auf das Daseyn einer ihr zu Grunde liegenden Regel geschlossen werden kann, daß dazu vielmehr eine wiederholte gleichmäßige Uebung gehört.

See *ibid.*, at 110. See also Kadens and Young, *supra* n. 185, Chapter 1, at 888–909; Koskenniemi, *From Apology to Utopia, supra* n. 2, Chapter 1, at 450.

146 Scharf, *supra* n. 79, at 5.

147 *Ibid.*, at 8, fn. 29. He sees the insistence on the element of practice as the main distinction between "Grotian Moments" and "instant custom". See *ibid.*, at 219–220.

148 *Ibid.*, at 211. He further holds:

> It can explain the rapid formation of customary rules in times of fundamental change, thereby imbuing those rules with greater authority. It can counsel

At the same time, the proposition that quite the opposite is the case, namely that "custom [...] is by definition backward looking and conservative",[149] that "[c]ustomary international law has developed slowly and unevenly, out of action and reaction in practice, rather than systematically or by major leaps",[150] and that "[c]ustomary law properly so-called is based upon the passage of a long period of time, and is accordingly both slow to develop and difficult to change"[151] still persists.

c Practice of International Organizations

As the formulation of Article 38(1)(b) of the STATUTE OF THE INTERNATIONAL COURT OF JUSTICE suggests, evidence of customary international law is primarily found in the acts of states.[152] However, the practice of international organizations has also been discussed as relevant for the formation of customary international law, although it has generally been held to bear relevance only for the body of law governing the relationship between international organizations and states.[153] This was also the position of the International Law Commission when it held that the "[r]ecords of the cumulating practice of international organizations may be regarded as evidence of customary international law with reference to States' relations to the organizations".[154] Of course, the practice of or within international organizations may play an even greater role in the debate on the subjective element of customary international law, *opinio iuris*.[155]

4 Opinio Iuris

The second, subjective or "psychological"[156] element of customary international law is *opinio iuris sive necessitatis* or *opinio iuris et necessitatis*,

> governments when to seek the path of a UN General Assembly resolution as a means of facilitating the formation of customary international law, and how to craft such a resolution to ensure that it is viewed as a capstone in the formation of such customary rules. It can in apt circumstances strengthen the case for litigants arguing the existence of a new customary international rule. And it can furnish international courts the confidence to recognize new rules of customary international law in appropriate cases despite a relative paucity and short duration of state practice.

See ibid., at 214–215.

149 Kadens and Young, *supra* n. 185, Chapter 1, at 909.

150 American Law Institute, *supra* n. 9, at 19.

151 Jennings, *supra* n. 93, Chapter 1, at 6.

152 See Jennings and Watts, *supra* n. 51, at 26, § 10.

153 See Pellet, *supra* n. 7, at 816–817, para. 219, and 828, para. 238; Shaw, *supra* n. 88, Chapter 1, at 59.

154 Report of the International Law Commission on Ways and Means for Making the Evidence of Customary International Law More Readily Available, *supra* n. 112, at 372, para. 78.

155 See the following elaborations, in particular p. 73 *et seq.*

156 Koskenniemi, *supra* n. 72, Chapter 1, at 89.

usually just *opinio iuris* for short. It takes a prominent position within a number of views on the formation of customary international law, both voluntarist and empiricist as well as in the jurisprudence of the International Court of Justice.

But this was not always the case: Early doctrine argued against the consideration of the subjective element in determining what is customary international law.[157] Both Paul Guggenheim and Hans Kelsen proposed customary international law formation without *opinio iuris*; both later revoked this view.[158] Yet even beyond these far away champions of legal scholarship, for a number of judges who delivered dissenting opinions in the *North Sea Continental Shelf* cases, the subjective element could in fact only be inferred from the practice or obvious necessity of the practice itself, as long as there was no evidence to the contrary.[159]

The main purpose of *opinio iuris* is to distinguish mere comity, *courtoisie*, or "friendship" between states from customary international law.[160] According to Shaw, it was first formulated with this purpose in mind by French jurist François Gény in his work "Méthode d'Interprétation et Sources en Droit Privé Positif" in 1899.[161] Its necessity was prominently determined by the Permanent Court of International Justice in the *Lotus* case,[162] paving the way towards the orthodox definition of customary international law.[163] As the International Court of Justice held in the *North Sea Continental Shelf* cases:

> Not only must the acts concerned amount to a settled practice, but they must also be such, or be carried out in such a way, as to be evidence of a

157 On such views see also Koskenniemi, *From Apology to Utopia, supra* n. 2, Chapter 1, at 411–414.

158 See Simma and Verdross, *supra* n. 50, Chapter 1, at 346, § 550 with the relevant references. See also Alston and Simma, *supra* n. 85, Chapter 1, at 88; Petersen, *supra* n. 141, Chapter 1, at 278.

159 See *North Sea Continental Shelf Cases* (Federal Republic of Germany *v.* Denmark/ Federal Republic of Germany *v.* Netherlands), Dissenting Opinion of Vice-President Koretsky, ICJ Reports 1969, p. 155, at 159; Dissenting Opinion of Judge Tanaka, *ibid.*, p. 172, at 177; Dissenting Opinion of Judge Lachs, *ibid.*, p. 219, at 232; Dissenting Opinion of Judge Sørenson, *ibid.*, p. 242, at 246–247. For further views of this sort expressed in the literature see Akehurst, *supra* n. 50, Chapter 1, at 32. See on a critique of this reasoning, however, only with regard to the *Asylum* case, D'Amato, *supra* n. 226, at 54–55.

160 See Akehurst, *supra* n. 50, Chapter 1, at 33–34; Brownlie, *supra* n. 17, at 8, who further lists "fairness" and "morality"; Danilenko, *supra* n. 6, at 99; Dixon, *supra* n. 75, Chapter 1, at 35; Jennings and Watts, *supra* n. 51, at 27, §10, who distinguish custom from "usage"; Wolfke, *supra* n. 6, at 40–41; Scharf, *supra* n. 79, at 48.

161 Shaw, *supra* n. 88, Chapter 1, at 53. See also Mendelson, *supra* n. 32, Chapter 1, at 194. See in more detail on Gény's contribution D'Amato, *supra* n. 8, at 48–49. Cf. Koskenniemi, *From Apology to Utopia, supra* n. 2, Chapter 1, at 415.

162 *The Case of the S.S. 'Lotus'* (France *v.* Turkey), Judgment of 7 September 1927, PCIJ Series A. – No. 10, p. 4, at 28.

163 See *supra* ns 80–82.

> belief that this practice is rendered obligatory by the existence of a rule of law requiring it. The need for such a belief, *i.e.* the existence of a subjective element, is implicit in the very notion of the *opinio juris sive necessitatis.* The States concerned must therefore feel that they are conforming to what amounts to a legal obligation. The frequency, or even habitual character of the acts is not in itself enough. There are many international acts, e.g., in the field of ceremonial and protocol, which are performed almost invariably, but which are motivated only by considerations of courtesy, convenience or tradition, and not by any sense of legal duty.[164]

When is the conviction legal and when does it arise from a sense of necessity? After all, something is not automatically legal, just because it is considered socially necessary.[165] Antonio Cassese takes a temporal view on this differentiation:

> Usually, a practice evolves among certain States under the impulse of economic, political, or military demands. At this stage the practice may thus be regarded as being imposed by social or economic or political needs (*opinio necessitatis*). If it does not encounter strong and consistent opposition from other States but is increasingly accepted, or acquiesced in, a customary rule gradually crystallizes. At this later stage it may be held that the practice is dictated by international law (*opinio juris*). In other words, now States begin to believe that they must conform to the practice not so much, or not only, out of economic, political, or military considerations, but because an international rule enjoins them to do so.[166]

a What Constitutes Opinio Iuris?

Similar to state practice, judges and authors have tried to determine a number of manifestations of the *opinio iuris* of states, once more in absence of a categorization or enumerative formula. In looking to these, it becomes quite clear that the borderline between the two elements of customary international law is fluid.

According to the *Nicaragua* judgment, *opinio iuris* may be derived from statements by state representatives, resolutions of international organizations, acts of ratification, or the simple acceptance of a text.[167] In the *Jurisdictional*

164 *North Sea Continental Shelf Cases* (Federal Republic of Germany *v.* Denmark/ Federal Republic of Germany *v.* Netherlands), Judgment of 20 February 1969, ICJ Reports 1969, p. 3, at 45, para. 77.

165 See Mendelson, *supra* n. 32, Chapter 1, at 197.

166 Cassese, *supra* n. 29, at 157.

167 *Case Concerning Military and Paramilitary Activities In and Against Nicaragua* (Nicaragua *v.* United States of America), Judgment of 27 June 1986 (Merits), ICJ Reports 1986, p. 14, at 100, para. 189; Jennings and Watts, *supra* n. 51, at 28, §10.

Immunities case, the International Court of Justice held with regard to immunity that

> [*o*]*pinio juris* in this context is reflected in particular in the assertion by States claiming immunity that international law accords them a right to such immunity from the jurisdiction of other States; in the acknowledgment, by States granting immunity, that international law imposes upon them an obligation to do so; and, conversely, in the assertion by States in other cases of a right to exercise jurisdiction over foreign States.[168]

For James Brierly (or Sir Humphrey Waldock for that matter), "opinion" may be derived from

> diplomatic correspondence; official instructions to diplomatists, consuls, naval and military commanders; acts of state legislation and decisions of state courts, which, we may presume, will not deliberately contravene any rule regarded as a rule of international law by the state; and opinions of law officers, especially when these are published, as they are in the United States.[169]

Malcolm Shaw argues that in addition to the factual existence of such statements, it is necessary that "the acting state will have to confirm" the view that these actually confer legality.[170] The will of a state must become "cognoscible".[171] Antonio Cassese breaks down the formula *opinio iuris sive necessitatis* into requiring either "the conviction that [...] practice reflects, or amounts to, law", or that it "is required by social, economic, or political exigencies".[172]

However, as Alain Pellet holds, *opinio iuris* is not to be equated with "an expression of will and is not easily grasped either legally or factually".[173] Similar to state practice,[174] much of what states deliberate is hidden from the public eye, leaving a limited amount of data for scholars to engage with.[175]

168 *Jurisdictional Immunities of the State* (Germany *v.* Italy; Greece intervening), Judgment of 3 February 2012, ICJ Reports 2012, p. 99, at 123, para. 55. See the analysis undertaken by the Court throughout the following paragraphs.
169 James Leslie Brierly, *The Law of Nations: An Introduction to the International Law of Peace*, Humphrey Waldock (ed.), 6th edn (Oxford: Clarendon Press, 1963) 61. For a more extensive analysis of what may or may not count see Mendelson, *supra* n. 22, at 198–209.
170 Shaw, *supra* n. 88, Chapter 1, at 63.
171 Meijers, *supra* n. 134, at 18.
172 Cassese, *supra* n. 29, at 156.
173 Pellet, *supra* n. 7, at 819, para. 224.
174 See *supra* n. 103.
175 See the remark by Georg Schwarzenberger:

> Nothing could be worse than the repetition of quotations from the very limited repertoire of diplomatic notes which are taken over from one textbook

b Implications of Opinio Iuris

Having discussed the possible manifestations of *opinio iuris*, it is still unclear what the legal character of these statements and expressions is. According to Koskenniemi, there are a variety of understandings of the concept present in jurisprudence and doctrine:

1 a collective (national, popular) unconscious;
2 tacit agreement;
3 the belief by a State that something is law;
4 the will by a State that something be law.

In addition, there is a fifth and a much stronger version of this view which grounds the primacy of psychology on the following claim:

5 "law cannot be dissociated from what States will or believe".[176]

Brierly required from states that *opinio iuris* at least meant "a feeling that, if the usage is departed from, some form of sanction will probably, or at any rate ought to, fall on the transgressor".[177] Mendelson characterized the element as a "claim".[178]

c Prominence of the Subjective Element

As has been pointed out, *opinio iuris* takes a prominent position within a number of views on the formation of customary international law. Two related issues, the idea that customary international law may derive from treaties, on the one hand, and from decisions of international organizations, in particular the General Assembly of the United Nations, on the other, have become theoretical debates in their own right.

I TREATIES AS CUSTOMARY INTERNATIONAL LAW

One of the big recurring questions and dogmatic problems in relation to the formation of customary international law has been the effect of the negotiation, signing, and ratification of treaties by states.[179] This was, in particular, fuelled

> into another and rarely supplemented by casual personal excursions of writers into the unknown wilderness of State papers.

See id., supra n. 122, at 35.

176 Koskenniemi, *supra* n. 72, Chapter 1, at 94. See also *id., From Apology to Utopia, supra* n. 2, Chapter 1, at 414.
177 Brierly, *supra* n. 169, at 59.
178 Mendelson, *supra* n. 32, Chapter 1, at 201.
179 For a concise overview of possible effects see Antonio Cassese, 'The Geneva Protocols of 1977 on the Humanitarian Law of Armed Conflict and Customary International Law', 3 *UCLA Pacific Basin Law Journal* (1984) 58–67.

by the International Court of Justice finding that customary international law could derive from a treaty provision "of a fundamentally normcreating character such as could be regarded as forming the basis of a general rule of law" in the *North Sea Continental Shelf Cases.*[180]

What we can, thereby, imagine is that universally accepted treaties such as the CHARTER OF THE UNITED NATIONS lead a parallel existence as customary international law, a "*Doppelganger*" or a reflection in a customary mirror,[181] whereby "it might be that, even without the passage of any considerable period of time, a very widespread and representative participation in the convention might suffice of itself, provided it included that of States whose interests were specially affected".[182]

In the *Libya-Malta Continental Shelf* case, the Court again held that multilateral treaties "may have an important role to play in recording and defining rules deriving from custom, or indeed in developing them".[183]

There has been extensive discussion on the possibility of parallel existence and cross-fertilization of customary international and treaty law,[184] in particular with a focus on the findings of the International Court of Justice in the *Nicaragua* case.[185] However, the inference of *opinio iuris* is problematic, in so far as the respective rule will primarily be followed as a treaty obligation with the consequence that states might not, thereby, contribute to the formation of customary international law.[186] The *opinio iuris* is simply indistinguishable from the treaty obligation.

Another approach is the inference of *opinio iuris* – or possibly even state practice, depending on one's view of the two elements – from signature or ratification behavior with regard to treaties.[187] This perspective is, however, also quite a paradox in that the creation of a treaty might in fact simultaneously

180 *North Sea Continental Shelf Cases* (Federal Republic of Germany *v.* Denmark/ Federal Republic of Germany *v.* Netherlands), Judgment of 20 February 1969, ICJ Reports 1969, p. 3, at 42, para. 72.

181 Abi-Saab, *supra* n. 8, at 45.

182 *North Sea Continental Shelf Cases* (Federal Republic of Germany *v.* Denmark/ Federal Republic of Germany *v.* Netherlands), Judgment of 20 February 1969, ICJ Reports 1969, p. 3, at 42, para. 73.

183 *Case Concerning the Continental Shelf* (Libyan Arab Jamahiriya *v.* Malta), Judgment of 3 June 1985, ICJ Reports 1985, p. 13, at 29–30, para. 27.

184 See, *inter alia*, D'Amato, *supra* n. 8, at 103–166; Danilenko, *supra* n. 6, at 137–146 and 156–162; Scharf, *supra* n. 79, at 43–45; Shaw, *supra* n. 88, Chapter 1, at 68–69. For a critical contemporary discussion of D'Amato see Thirlway, *supra* n. 13, at 81–84. See also, generally, Pellet, *supra* n. 7, at 849, para. 292 and accompanying references.

185 Referring to *Case Concerning Military and Paramilitary Activities In and Against Nicaragua* (Nicaragua *v.* United States of America), Judgment of 27 June 1986 (Merits), ICJ Reports 1986, p. 14, at 93–97, paras 174–182, see, *inter alia*, D'Amato, *supra* n. 125, at 101–105; Wladyslaw Czapliński, 'Sources of International Law in the Nicaragua Case', 38/1 *International and Comparative Law Quarterly* (1989) 152–156.

186 See also Thirlway, *supra* n. 13, at 90.

187 See Pellet, *supra* n. 7, at 821–823, para. 229, and 849, para. 292; Scharf, *supra* n. 79, at 43; Shaw, *supra* n. 88, Chapter 1, at 68.

support the assumption that there is no, or at least contrary, customary international law on the subject.[188] Why would states feel the need to accede to an existing multilateral treaty, if the obligations already existed under customary international law? Equally, this could lead to an "accession by way of custom"[189] for states that are not party to a treaty.[190]

In the case of bilateral treaties, the need for their creation may arise from the fact that, indeed, no parallel rule of customary international law exists. This is commonly held to be the case, for example, with regard to bilateral investment[191] and extradition treaties.[192] On the opposite side of the spectrum stands the idea that a number of treaties of similar content could be taken together to

188 See *The Mavrommatis Palestine Concessions* (Greece *v.* United Kingdom), Judgment of 30 August 1924, PCIJ Series A. – No. 2, p. 6, at 35. See Philip Alston and Ryan Goodman, *International Human Rights: The Successor to International Human Rights in Context: Law, Politics and Morals* (Oxford: Oxford University Press, 2013) 75; Koskenniemi, *supra* n. 72, Chapter 1, at 116–117; *id., From Apology to Utopia, supra* n. 2, Chapter 1, at 434–435; Pellet, *supra* n. 7, at 816, para. 218; Wolfke, *supra* n. 6, at 71. See also Scharf, *supra* n. 79, at 43.

189 Wolfke, *supra* n. 6, at 70.

190 As Judge Morelli held in his dissenting opinion in the *North Sea Continental Shelf Cases*:

> In connection with the Convention it may be observed that it was signed by the Federal Republic. This means that the Federal Republic participated in a technical operation which, to the extent of the Convention's avowed purpose of codification, consisted in the establishment of general international law. By its signature the Federal Republic expressed an opinion which, within the limits indicated above, may be qualified as an *opinio juris.* But it was a mere opinion and not a statement of will, which could only be expressed by ratification. For it is only by ratification that the States signatories to a Convention express their will either to accept new rules or, in the case of a codification convention, to recognize pre-existing rules as binding.

See *North Sea Continental Shelf Cases* (Federal Republic of Germany *v.* Denmark/ Federal Republic of Germany *v.* Netherlands), Dissenting Opinion of Judge Morelli, ICJ Reports 1969, p. 198, *ibid.*

191 See *Case Concerning Ahmadou Sadio Diallo* (Republic of Guinea *v.* Democratic Republic of the Congo), Judgment of 24 May 2007 (Preliminary Objections), ICJ Reports 2007, p. 582, at 615, para. 90:

> The fact invoked by Guinea that various international agreements, such as agreements for the promotion and protection of foreign investments and the Washington Convention, have established special legal régimes governing investment protection, or that provisions in this regard are commonly included in contracts entered into directly between States and foreign investors, is not sufficient to show that there has been a change in the customary rules of diplomatic protection; it could equally show the contrary.

192 See Bruno Simma and Stephan Wittich, 'Das Völkergewohnheitsrecht', in August Reinisch (ed.), *Österreichisches Handbuch des Völkerrechts. Band I – Textteil,* 5th edn (Vienna: Manz, 2013) 41, para. 190.

constitute *opinio iuris*.[193] Other scholars, such as Stephan Schill, have taken alternative views, speaking of the "multilateralization" of bilateral treaties, thereby avoiding the issue of customary international law altogether.[194]

Lifted from the level of black-letter argumentation alone, practice shows that not every treaty is endowed with the same level of legal authority. Myres McDougal pointed out this normative relativity: "Not all multilateral agreements, however deliberate and however much in accord or not in accord with customary law, make law. Many of them are illusions".[195]

II DECISIONS OF INTERNATIONAL ORGANIZATIONS

A second issue are decisions of international organizations, in particular the non-binding recommendations of the General Assembly of the United Nations.[196] They have been recurrently held to contribute to the formation of customary international law as expressions of *opinio iuris*, depending on how they were adopted.[197]

The lines here may be blurred between finding that the vote or acquiescence of a state is an expression of *opinio iuris*[198] and that the decision may function as *opinio iuris* as of itself, be it a recommendation by the General Assembly,[199]

193 See the approach taken by the tribunal in *Mondev International v. United States of America*, Award of 11 October 2002, ICSID Case No. ARB(AF)/99/2, para. 117. See Stephen M. Schwebel, 'Investor-State Disputes and the Development of International Law: The Influence of Bilateral Investment Treaties on Customary International Law', 98 *American Society of International Law Procedures* (2004) 29. See, generally, Wolfke, *supra* n. 6, at 71 with further references.

194 See Stephan W. Schill, *The Multilateralization of International Investment Law* (Cambridge: Cambridge University Press, 2009).

195 McDougal, *supra* n. 155, Chapter 1, at 23.

196 Not decisions within the ambit of Article 17 of the CHARTER OF THE UNITED NATIONS or questions relating to membership, which, of course, have binding force with respect to the organization and its members.

197 See, *e.g.*, *Legality of the Threat or Use of Nuclear Weapons*, Advisory Opinion of 8 July 1996, ICJ Reports 1996, p. 226, at 254–255, para. 70. See Cassese, *supra* n. 29, at 169; Pellet, *supra* n. 7, at 820–821, para. 228; Shaw, *supra* n. 88, Chapter 1, at 63. Cf., however, MacGibbon, *supra* n. 143, at 12–15. For an earlier critical assessment of this debate see Stephen M. Schwebel, 'The Legal Effect of Resolutions and Codes of Conduct of the United Nations', 7 *Forum Internationale* (1985) 1–16, reprinted in Stephen M. Schwebel (ed.), *Justice in International Law. Selected Writings of Stephen M. Schwebel* (Cambridge: Cambridge University Press, 1994) 499–513.

198 See Akehurst, *supra* n. 50, Chapter 1, at 11; Louis B. Sohn, '"Generally Accepted" International Rules', 61 *Washington Law Review* (1986) 1074. Notwithstanding, of course, any state may express its *opinio iuris* during the sessions of the General Assembly, just as it may do so at any other forum. See on the practice of assessing state conviction from voting behavior in the General Assembly also Koskenniemi, *supra* n. 72, Chapter 1, at 115–116.

199 See on this, generally, Pellet, *supra* n. 7, at 820–821, para. 228, and 828, paras 238–239, with further references. For an extensive analysis of the subject in favor of a larger role for General Assembly resolutions, but including extensive

a decision by the Security Council,[200] or the findings of independent treaty bodies such as the Human Rights Committee[201] or the International Law Commission.[202]

The first view does not cause too big a stir within the two-element theory. It is merely important to take into account the full context,[203] whether a state expressed itself in light of the recommendatory character of the resolution[204] or accepted or even supported a binding or non-binding decision as a mere political bargain – maybe it did not "mean it" at all.[205] These considerations

references to both sides of the literature, see Blaine Sloan, 'General Assembly Resolutions Revisited (Forty Years Later)', 58 *British Yearbook of International Law* (1987) *passim*. For another such analysis see Gaetano Arangio-Ruiz, 'The Normative Role of the General Assembly of the United Nations and the Declaration of Principles of Friendly Relations', 225 *Recueil des Cours de l'Académie de Droit International de La Haye* (1972-III) *passim*.

200 See on this Olivier Corten, 'La Participation du Conseil de Sécurité à l'Èlaboration, à la Cristallisation ou à la Consolidation de Régles Coutumières', 37/2 *Revue Belge de Droit International* (2004) 552–566 with further references.

201 See *Legal Consequences of the Construction of a Wall in the Occupied Palestinian Territory*, Advisory Opinion of 9 July 2004, ICJ Reports 2004, p. 136, at 179, para. 109. See also Pellet, *supra* n. 7, at 859–860, para. 318.

202 See *Case Concerning the Gabčíkovo-Nagymaros Dam* (Hungary *v.* Slovakia), Judgment of 25 September 1997, ICJ Reports 1997, p. 7, at 38–42, paras 47–54. See also Pellet, *ibid.*, at 823–824, para. 230.

203 See Koskenniemi, *From Apology to Utopia, supra* n. 2, Chapter 1, at 434–435; Oscar Schachter, 'Alf Ross Memorial Lecture: The Crisis of Legitimation in the United Nations', 50–51 *Nordisk Tidsskrift for International Ret* (1981–1982) 13. See also, on the view that General Assembly resolutions may simply be declaratory of existing law, Krzysztof Skubiszewski, 'Resolutions of the U.N. General Assembly and Evidence of Custom', in Alessandro Migliazza, Fausto Pocar, Pierluigi Lamberti Zanardi, and Piero Ziccardi (eds), *Le Droit International a l'Heure de sa Codification. Etudes en l'Honneur de Roberto Ago / Il Diritto Internazionale al Tempo Della sua Codificazione. Studi in Onore di Roberto Ago / International Law at the Time of its Codification. Essays in Honour of Roberto Ago* (Milan: Dott. A. Giuffré Editore, 1987) 519.

204 See MacGibbon, *supra* n. 143, at 23.

205 See Arangio-Ruiz, *supra* n. 199, at 457, with regard to the General Assembly:

> [N]o one witnessing the actual work of the United Nations escapes the perception that the activities of the Assembly are pervaded to an extreme by the urge of individual governments or groups of governments to get away from every session with as good an "image" as possible. This "image" factor is a very considerable driving force towards the proliferation of proposals, counter proposals and eventually resolutions. As everybody in the United Nations is convinced that recommendations are *per se* not mandatory, States tend to embellish their image by putting forward draft resolutions. Other States tend naturally to support such drafts. And potential or natural opponents are often reluctant to face the risk of tarnishing or spoiling their own image by opposing the proposal openly or by casting a negative vote.

led Stephen Schwebel to speak of a "fake consensus".[206] Maurice Mendelson remarked that "in United Nations practice, the adoption of a resolution 'by consensus' is simply a way of avoiding the expression of deep-seated disagreements".[207] One must look past the mere words to arrive at the actual *opinio iuris*, or, as Oscar Schachter wrote, "[a] strong dose of 'cynical acid' (in Justice Holmes' phrase) may be necessary to assess the actual expectations and conduct of states in relation to a resolution".[208]

Adding to this problem is the fact that expert committees, such as the International Law Commission, are often staffed with independent experts and scholars, whose opinions will sometimes correspond more with their academic track-record than with the position of the nominating state. Should these views still be attributed? The problem is similar to the question of whether arguments made by counsel during proceedings on behalf of a state should count;[209] it would go beyond the scope of this book to attempt an answer. It is only important to be aware of the pitfalls of taking into account decisions of international organizations at face value.

The second view, *i.e.* that the content of such a document may function as *opinio iuris* as of itself, is much more problematic. This is particularly so, if one goes as far as suggesting that non-binding recommendations, as of the General Assembly, may exert some legislative or operative effects;[210] to view them as "'quasi-legislative' activity".[211]

Judge Tanaka, in his separate opinion in the *South West Africa* cases argued that such was the case if accompanied by repetition of similar resolutions.[212] However, while this may sound convincing at first, it is a non-argument, as was shown quite pointedly by Iain MacGibbon:

> For the non-wrangler of tender years at least, a certain reluctance had to be overcome before acceptance was given to the proposition that however

206 Stephen M. Schwebel, 'The Effect of Resolutions of the U.N. General Assembly on Customary International Law', 73 *Proceedings of the American Society of International Law at its Annual Meeting* (1979) 308. See Scharf, *supra* n. 79, at 52.
207 Mendelson, *supra* n. 22, at 387.
208 Schachter, *supra* n. 203, at 14.
209 See also *supra* n. 113.
210 See, *e.g.*, S. James Anaya, 'Customary International Law', 92 *American Society of International Law Proceedings* (1998) 43; Higgins, *supra* n. 128, at 28 and 30–31; Skubiszewski, *supra* n. 203, at 143–156 *et passim*; Sloan, *supra* n. 199, *passim*; Oscar Schachter, 'The Twilight Existence of Nonbinding International Agreements', 71 *American Journal of International Law* (1977), 303–304; Weil, *supra* n. 35, Chapter 1, at 416–417. See further the possible interpretation of the *Tehran Hostages* case *infra* n. 8, Chapter 4 and accompanying text.
211 Oscar Schachter, 'Towards a Theory of International Obligation', in Stephen Schwebel (ed.), *The Effectiveness of International Decisions* (Leiden: Sijthoff, 1971) 11, reprinted in Koskenniemi (ed.), *supra* n. 2, Chapter 1, at 5.
212 See *South West Africa Cases* (Ethiopia *v.* South Africa; Liberia *v.* South Africa), Dissenting Opinion of Judge Tanaka, ICJ Reports 1966, p. 250, at 291–292. See on this also Schachter, *ibid.*, at 13 / 7.

> many times nothing was multiplied by the result was still nothing. The same inexorable result follows in the present context. Mere repetition works no magical change in the legal nature of a resolution. However many times a recommendation is multiplied it is still in the end of the day a recommendation and not a binding legal obligation.[213]

Of course, the broadness of academic opinions also allows for writers that would accept the omission of repetition under certain circumstances.[214]

However, these approaches are not necessarily dogmatically sound. When the Soviet Union expressed that it would "respect the principles enunciated in the draft declaration if it were unanimously adopted" with regard to what would later become the "Declaration of Legal Principles Governing the Activities of States in the Exploration and Use of Outer Space",[215] the better view, if one were to deduct a binding effect from this statement, would be to see it as a unilateral declaration, independent of the resolution itself.[216]

States themselves are not in consensus about the effect of General Assembly resolutions.[217] The better approach "in assessing their legal value" is, therefore, not to focus on "what *they* say, but what *the States* have had to say about them".[218] Of course, as was pointed out already, this correct appraisal might sometimes prove challenging to the observer.[219] However, the alternative view

213 MacGibbon, *supra* n. 143, at 17. See also Weil, *supra* n. 35, Chapter 1, at 417.

214 See, *e.g.*, Akehurst, *supra* n. 50, Chapter 1, at 14, fn. 4, asserting that sometimes "a single resolution, even if it is never repeated may sometimes create such a rule [...], provided that there is no practice contradicting the alleged rule", citing the dissenting opinion of Judge Tanaka in the *South West Africa Cases*, who actually says the opposite: "Of course, we cannot admit that individual resolutions, declarations, judgments, decisions, etc., have binding force upon the members of the organization". See *South West Africa Cases* (Ethiopia *v.* South Africa; Liberia *v.* South Africa), Dissenting Opinion of Judge Tanaka, ICJ Reports 1966, p. 250, at 292. See on this also MacGibbon, *supra* n. 143, at 17 with further references in fn. 32.

215 See Cheng, *supra* n. 143, at 34.

216 See also the emphasis on consensus taken in *Texaco v. Libyan Arab Republic*, Award on the Merits of 19 January 1977, 53 *International Law Reports* (1979) 422, at 487–488, para. 84, and 491–492, para. 87. Critical Schachter, *supra* n. 203, at 8.

217 Schwebel, *supra* n. 206, at 308:

> [T]he views of states are profoundly divided on the issues of the impact of General Assembly resolutions on the content of international law. It perhaps suggests that those states and scholars who have liberally construed the powers of the General Assembly and their effects on international law may find it necessary to reconsider their position, for it is hard to ascribe such powers to the General Assembly when leading members of that Assembly challenged them.

See also Scharf, *supra* n. 79, at 307–308.

218 Pellet, *supra* n. 7, at 825, para. 231.

219 See Scharf, *supra* n. 79, at 50–53.

simply omits the framework of international law, specifically the provisions of the CHARTER OF THE UNITED NATIONS, from the equation:

> It may be desirable that there should be an international legislature within or without the United Nations. But it cannot be contended that the Charter itself bound States members to accept such a law-making technique, and since no new source of law can, as we have noted, emerge *ex nihilo*, either amendment of the Charter or developments properly to be regarded as customary law are necessary to bring this about.[220]

In any case, substantive legislative powers of the General Assembly were expressly rejected at the San Francisco conference.[221] The fact that the General Assembly only has recommendatory powers was, after all, also a concession to the fact that a world legislature should not be composed of governments that are not necessarily representative of their peoples.[222] Its powers are "[c]rudely put [...] restricted to 'organizational' matters internal to the UN legal order".[223]

d Opinio Iuris *as Consent*

Voluntarists claim that customary international law is grounded in the consent of states.[224] Soviet international law doctrine, most prominently represented by Grigory Tunkin,[225] firmly upheld this view: "[T]he essence of the process of creating a norm of international law by means of custom consists of agreement between States, which in this case is tacit, and not clearly expressed".[226]

220 Thirlway, *supra* n. 13, at 79.
221 See Jorge Castañeda, *Legal Effects of United Nations Resolutions* (Columbia University Studies in International Organization, Number 6; New York: Columbia University Press, 1969) 2–3, also excluding the power of authentic interpretation, see fn. 2 at 196.
222 See Schwebel, *supra* n. 206, at 301.
223 Marko Divac Öberg, 'The Legal Effects of Resolutions of the UN Security Council and General Assembly in the Jurisprudence of the ICJ', 16/5 *European Journal of International Law* (2006), at 883.
224 For a brief overview of consensualist doctrine in the first half of the twentieth century including Anzilotti, Cavaglieri, Triepel, and Strupp, see Le Fur, *supra* n. 38, at 362–363. For a demonstration of problems relating to the consensualist view see I.M. Lobo de Souza, 'The Role of State Consent in the Customary Process', 44 *International and Comparative Law Quarterly* (1995) 521–539. For critiques of the voluntarist approach see Dupuy, *supra* n. 8, at 257–272; Mendelson, *supra* n. 32, Chapter 1, at 177–208; Mendelson, *supra* n. 22, at 253–267; Thirlway, *supra* n. 13, at 59.
225 See D'Amato, *supra* n. 8, at 188.
226 Grigory I. Tunkin, *Theory of International Law* (London: Wildy, Simmonds & Hill, 2003) 133. See also Danilenko, *supra* n. 134, at 13–14; *id., supra* n. 6, at 75–76, 118–119 *et passim*; Grigory I. Tunkin, 'Co-Existence and International Law', 95 *Recueil des Cours de l'Académie de Droit International de La Haye* (1958-III) 13–14.

However, while Soviet international law doctrine is a relic of history, voluntarism is still alive and well,[227] even if it has lost its once prominent foothold.

In particular, it is still argued with regard to regional or bilateral customary international law. Shaw writes that it requires an "acceptance of both (or all) parties to the rule".[228] Pellet finds that "unlike in the case of general custom, the *opinio juris* attached to them is of a consensualist kind".[229] Anthony D'Amato writes that "[s]pecial custom does indeed require stringent proof of consent or recognition of a practice on the part of the defendant state" as opposed to "general custom".[230] Furthermore, he argues that "we might think of treaties as a highly formal type of 'special custom', or indeed we might view special custom as an informal treaty".[231]

However, the nature of the dispute of the *Rights of Passage* case is more reminiscent of a servitude in domestic law than a tacit agreement. One might also think in analogy to the *North Sea Continental Shelf Cases*, in which the Court narrowed its look to the "States concerned".[232]

Both the Permanent Court of International Justice and the International Court of Justice have added to the confusion by pronouncing on the consensual character of customary international law. In the "unfortunate"[233] *Lotus* case, the Permanent Court held that:

> [i]nternational law governs relations between independent States. The rules of law binding upon States therefore emanate from their own free will as expressed in conventions or by usages generally accepted as expressing principles of law and established in order to regulate the relations between these co-existing independent communities or with a view to the achievement of common aims.[234]

227 For recent voluntarist views see José A. Cabranes, 'Customary International Law: What it is and What it is Not', 22 *Duke Journal of Comparative and International Law* (2011–2012) 148–149; Olufemi Elias, 'The Nature of the Subjective Element in Customary International Law', 44 *International and Comparative Law Quarterly* (1995) 502–516; Alexander Orakhelashvili, *Peremptory Norms in International Law* (Oxford: Oxford University Press, 2006) 32 with reference to Paul Guggenheim, 'La Validité et la Nullité des Actes Juridiques Internationaux', 74 *Recueil des Cours de l'Académie de Droit International de La Haye* (1949-I) 108; *id.*, *supra* n. 112, Chapter 1, *passim.* See also Watson, *supra* n. 56, Chapter 1, at 43, who argues that customary international law requires state practice and consent.

228 Shaw, *supra* n. 88, Chapter 1, at 66.

229 Pellet, *supra* n. 7, at 831, para. 246. He, however, acknowledges that this approach was not followed in the cases of the International Court of Justice dealing with regional and bilateral custom. See *ibid.*, at 831, para. 247.

230 D'Amato, *supra* n. 8, at 234.

231 *Ibid.*, at 250.

232 See *supra* n. 125.

233 Pellet, *supra* n. 7, at 819, para. 225.

234 *The Case of the S.S. 'Lotus'* (France *v.* Turkey), Judgment of 7 September 1927, PCIJ Series A. – No. 10, p. 4, at 18. See also Pellet, *supra* n. 7, at 819, para. 225.

To go even further, the dissenting opinion of Judge Weiss in the *Lotus* case spoke of the requirement of a "*consensus omnium*".[235] As Karol Wolfke pointed out with reference to the International Court of Justice,

> the way in which the Court has applied the element of acceptance of practice as an expression of law entirely confirms the supposition that this element has been considered as an element of the will of states, mainly in the form of presumed acquiescence in the practice, above all, on the part of those states against which the rule was to be applied.[236]

I HISTORICAL DEFINITION OF CUSTOMARY INTERNATIONAL LAW

What are the roots of this view of *opinio iuris* as consent? Most treatises on customary international law begin by stating that the voluntarist view used to prevail up until the early twentieth century, when the two-element theory found its way into the STATUTE OF THE PERMANENT COURT OF INTERNATIONAL JUSTICE; that until that time customary international law "ultimately rested on consent".[237] It has been held that the view goes as far back as Grotius and Vattel.[238]

Naturally, states, reluctant to acknowledge a source of law that could run contrary to their individual will, would favor the view as it is in line with a conception of absolute sovereignty[239] and, in the words of Robert Ago, the

235 *The Case of the S.S. 'Lotus'* (France *v.* Turkey), Judgment of 7 September 1927, Dissenting Opinion by M. Weiss, PCIJ Series A. – No. 10, p. 40, at 43–44. See Wolfke, *supra* n. 6, at 11.

236 Wolfke, *supra* n. 6, at 24

237 Cassese *supra* n. 29, at 153.

238 See Emer de Vattel, *Le Droit des Gens. Ou Principes de la Loi naturelle, appliqués à la Conduite et aux Affaires des Nations et des Souverains. Tome 1* (London, 1758) 7, § 25. See on this Verdross, *supra* n. 46, at 54, fn. 1. However, it may be contended that Grotius was not so clear in making this determination:

> Latius autem patens est ius Gentium, id est quod Gentium omnium aut multarum voluntate vim obligandi accepit. Multarum addidi, quia vix ullum [*sic*] ius reperitur extra ius naturale, quod ipsum quoque gentium dici solet, omnibus gentibus commune. Imo saepe in una parte orbis terrarum est ius gentium quod alibi non est, ut de captivitate ac postliminio suo loco dicemus. Probatur autem hoc ius gentium par modo quo ius non scriptum civile, suo continuo et testimonio peritorum. Est enim hoc ius, ut recte notar Dio Chrysostomus [...] repertum temporis et usus.

See Hugo Grotius, *De Iure Belli ac Pacis. Libri Tres. In Quibus Ius Naturae et Gentium: Item Iuris Publici Praecipua Explicantur* (Paris, 1625) 10, XIV.

239 See the following passage regarding the formation of customary international law by Härle, *supra* n. 62, at 10:

> Aus diesen Ausführungen geht deutlich hervor, [...] daß er [the author Louis Le Fur] einer gewohnheitsrechtlich allgemein entwickelten, von der Mehrheit

presence of custom as an autonomous form of law, independent of the will of the states has been considered a source of embarrassment to views preoccupied with establishing the omnipotence of these governments.[240] Koskenniemi associates the pull of voluntarism with an alleged turn towards positivism:

> Ever since the Grotian tradition became little more than an object of ritualistic invocation in keynote speeches at conferences of learned societies, international lawyers have had difficulty accounting for rules of international law that do not emanate from the consent of the states against which they are applied. [...] Once the idea of a natural law is discarded, it seems difficult to justify an obligation that is not voluntarily assumed.[241]

II THE HISTORICAL DEFINITION QUESTIONED

However, a brief sighting of the literature and jurisprudence of the period in question shows that the picture is not so uniform and clear.[242] Georg Friedrich Puchta's 1837 treatise on custom shows that he, indeed, differentiated between custom and tacit agreement.[243]

Antonio Cassese, in his textbook on international law, cites two cases to demonstrate the "traditional view",[244] the 1893 *Fur Seal Arbitration* and an 1825 US Supreme Court case on the prohibition of slavery. The most prominently cited passage in this regard is taken from the oral argument of Sir Charles Russell in the *Fur Seal Arbitration*:

> International law, properly so called, is only so much of the principles of morality and justice as the nations have agreed shall be part of those rules

> der Staatengemeinschaft anerkannten Norm, unter Umständen auch gegen einen dieser Rechtspraxis renitenten Staat effektive Normgeltung zugesteht. Man muß, das darf ruhig zugestanden werden, de lege ferenda diesem für den künftigen Rechtsfortschritt geradezu grundlegenden Prinzip, im Interesse auch der allgemeinen Rechtssicherheit und der Rechtssuniversalität, unbedingt beitreten. Leider sind aber die Staaten und mit ihnen die herrschende Lehre zu solchen Konzessionen noch nicht bereit und halten einstweilen noch mit aller Intransigenz an der absoluten Willenstheorie fest, die wiederum nur als Bestätigung der alles beherrschenden Souveränitätstheorie gelten soll.

240 See Ago, *supra* n. 4, at 936:

> La présence de la coutume comme forme autonome de droit, indépendante de la volonteé des gouvernements des différentes sociétés humaines, a toujours été une cause d'embarras pour les doctrines préoccupées d'établir la toute-puissance de ces gouvernements.

241 Koskenniemi, *supra* n. 36, Chapter 1, at 1946.
242 See *supra* n. 238.
243 See Puchta, *supra* n. 145, at 110.
244 Cassese, *supra* n. 29, at 154, fns 4–5.

> of conduct which shall govern their relations one with another. So far as they have by agreement incorporated into the rules which are to regulate their mutual arrangements, relations and conduct, and so far only, can there be said to be an incorporation of the rules of morality and of justice, as to which nations as well as men differ: so far and so far only can they be said to be incorporated into international law. In other words, international law, as there exists no superior external power to impose it, rests upon the principle of consent. In the words of Grotius, *Placuit ne gentibus?* is [*sic*] there the consent of nations? If there is not this consent of nations, then it is not international law: and I think it is very easy to illustrate that that must be so – that without that consent there cannot be said to be an *imprimatur*, which can give force and efficacy to international law. If it were not so, international law would be in a constant state of flux and uncertainty. [...] The law of nations incorporates many principles of ethics and of natural law; but only such as it is agreed shall be incorporated from part of that law. The phrase of Grotius, *placuit ne gentibus*, sums up the only possible and the only true idea of the law of nations; and when text-writers and theorists and diplomatists assert that such and such a usage is recognized by the law of nations, that such and such a usage is opposed to the law of nations, that such and such a right exists under the law of nations, in each case the criterion is not whether the rule so expressed, or the usage or the right so asserted, is humane, or is just, or is moral, the sole question is whether it has received the assent and consent of civilized nations: *placuitne gentibus?*[245]

To support his argument, Russell referred to the findings of the Lord Chief Justice of England, John Duke Coleridge, in the *Franconia* case. A closer look at that particular judgment shows, however, that what Russell invoked here was not as clear as he tried to convey in his oral argument. In fact, agreements as in treaties are seemingly considered distinct from a body of customary international law, and terminology is inconsistent throughout the judgment and within the references.[246]

For example, Chief Baron of the Exchequer, Sir Fitzroy Kelly, differentiated between "treaty, or express agreement" and "some uniform, general, and long-continued usage, evidenced by the actual exercise of such".[247] Judge Lord Chief Justice, Sir Alexander James Edmund Cockburn, held that "assent may be express, as by treaty or the acknowledged concurrence of governments, or may be implied from established usage".[248]

245 Oral Argument of Sir Charles Russell, Q.C.M.P., Her Britannic Majesty's Attorney-General, on Behalf of Great Britain in the *Fur Seal Arbitration*, printed in Vol. XIII, 8–10.

246 See *R v. Keyn* (1876) L.R. 2 Ex. D. 63 (Court for Crown Cases Reserved) *passim*.

247 See *ibid.*, at 151.

248 See *ibid.*, at 202.

Such statements show that, indeed, there was a sense of manifestations of the law that were not expressed through mutual agreement *sensu stricto*. Therefore, the *termini technici* of sources doctrine should not be taken at face value, when analyzing historical cases and the literature.[249]

III THE "PERSISTENT OBJECTOR" THEORY

In the *Anglo-Norwegian Fisheries* case, the International Court of Justice developed what doctrine has come to call the "persistent objector" theory,[250] thereby seemingly embracing the voluntarist view. In pronouncing on the applicability of a particular rule regarding coastline delimitation to Norway, the Court came to the conclusion that a state could immunize itself from customary international law if it had initially opposed the application of a particular norm and consequently upheld that position, as an "***initial and sustained*** objection".[251]

249 See also Robert Y. Jennings, 'What is International Law and How Do We Tell It When We See It?', in 37 *Schweizerisches Jahrbuch für Internationales Recht* (1981) 66, reprinted in Koskenniemi (ed.), *supra* n. 2, Chapter 1, at 34:

> For evidence of custom, Pitt Cobbett, in a good, popular case book of the period, lists "records of State action", and "Text-writers of Authority". As to what is now called the element of the *opinio juris sive necessitatis*, but was then frankly called consent, or assent, of States, there was no need to attempt to show that "the State in question" had assented to the rule; in the words of Professor Westlake's great text book of 1904, "it is enough to show that the general *consensus* of opinion within the limits of European civilization is in favour of the rule".

250 Dixon, *supra* n. 75, Chapter 1, at 32; Thirlway, *supra* n. 8, at 106–107. Thirlway points out that the same reasoning was already applied by the International Court of Justice in the *Colombian-Peruvian Asylum Case* (Colombia *v.* Peru), Judgment of 20 November 1950, ICJ Reports 1950, p. 266, at 277–278. Brownlie differentiated between the "persistent" and the "subsequent" objector, the latter actually applying to the treatment of the *Fisheries Case* by the International Court of Justice as a case of deviation from the "alleged rules", accompanied by acquiescence on the side of other states. It is not clear, however, how his nomenclature fits his dogmatic reasoning. See *id., Principles, supra* n. 17, at 11–12.

251 Dixon, *supra* n. 75, Chapter 1, at 33. See *Fisheries Case* (United Kingdom *v.* Norway), Judgment of 18 December 1951, ICJ Reports 1951, p. 116, at 131: "In any event the ten-mile rule would appear to be inapplicable as against Norway inasmuch as she has always opposed any attempt to apply it to the Norwegian coast". While this finding leaves open the problem of a subsequent objector violating an existing customary international law rule, other states could still acquiesce to such a violation. See Dixon, *supra* n. 75, Chapter 1, at 33 and 36. On this problem see also Gionata Piero Buzzini, 'Les Comportements Passifs des Etats et Leur Incidence sur la Réglementation de l'Emploi de la Force en Droit International Général', in Cannizzaro and Palchetti (eds), *supra* n. 67, Chapter 1, at 79–117, including a methodological study of the problems related to trying to ascertain prohibitive rules or the existence of rules that have been violated through

The "persistent objector" theory is problematic in a number of respects. First, it brings a voluntarist element into the two-element theory that does not properly fit within its basic structure.[252] Second, it reduces the universality of customary international law,[253] which does not *per se* require totality in the number of states participating in its formation:

> Custom is itself a matter of general rather than universal consent, so that a dissenting state cannot free itself by an act of will from the obligations imposed on it by a rule of customary law [...].[254]

The possibility of states dissociating themselves from an emerging rule would diminish the regulatory impact of customary international law as a whole and imply that "absence of agreement justifies exemption".[255] Interestingly enough, in the *North Sea Continental Shelf Cases*, while deliberating on reservations to treaties, the International Court of Justice itself seemingly ruled out the possibility of a "persistent objector":

> [F]or, speaking generally, it is a characteristic of purely conventional rules and obligations that, in regard to them, some faculty of making unilateral reservations may, within certain limits, be admitted; – whereas this cannot be so in the case of general or customary law rules and obligations which, by their very nature, must have equal force for all members of the international community, and cannot therefore be the subject of any right of unilateral exclusion exercisable at will by any one of them in its own favour. Consequently, it is to be expected that when, for whatever reason, rules or obligations of this order are embodied, or are intended to be reflected in certain provisions of a convention, such provisions will figure amongst those in respect of which a right of unilateral reservation is not conferred, or is excluded.[256]

In addition, the "persistent objector" theory seems to ignore the possibility of oral treaties, which would be a much more dogmatically coherent explanation for the phenomenon. Of course, states may object to a rule of customary international law, but this should rather be seen as evidence within the overall assessment of state practice and *opinio iuris*.

silence and abstentions; Corten, *supra* n. 199, Chapter 1, at 131–134; Shaw, *supra* n. 88, Chapter 1, at 63–65.

252 See also Danilenko, *supra* n. 6, at 42; Pellet, *supra* n. 7, at 819–820, paras 225–226.

253 Cf., *e.g.*, Scharf, *supra* n. 79, at 41, who speaks of the "voluntary nature of customary international law".

254 Jennings and Watts, *supra* n. 51, at 24–25. See also Koskenniemi, *From Apology to Utopia, supra* n. 2, Chapter 1, at 443.

255 Thirlway, *supra* n. 8, at 102.

256 *North Sea Continental Shelf Cases* (Federal Republic of Germany *v.* Denmark/ Federal Republic of Germany *v.* Netherlands), Judgment of 20 February 1969, ICJ Reports 1969, p. 3, at 39–40, para. 63.

Tomuschat, for one, has pointed out that the pronouncements in both the *Asylum* and the *Anglo-Norwegian Fisheries* cases were merely *obiter dicta*[257] and "[i]n reality, no such general recognition can be perceived";[258] state practice does not support the concept.

Still, it has become part of "[m]ainstream accounts of the principles governing the formation and application of rules of customary international law"[259] and "the principle of the persistent objector is firmly established in the orthodox doctrine on the sources of international law".[260] Even authors that reject the consensual view of custom have recognized the persistent objector theory without offering a coherent theoretical justification.[261] Some have even not shied away from the argument that the option of opting out favors the creation of new customary international law as the "persistent objectors" will not count towards inconsistent practice.[262]

IV *CONTRADICTIO IN SE*

The view that customary international law equates to a tacit agreement violates a number of general principles of law, in particular that of *ut res magis valeat quam pereat*. Article 38(1)(b) of the STATUTE OF THE INTERNATIONAL COURT OF JUSTICE would be devoid of meaning, a redundant repetition of Article 38(1)(a) of that same treaty which already includes silent agreements in its scope.

Further, the idea that customary international law may be universally applied, even though not all states participated in its formation or had not existed at the time,[263] would violate one of the more fundamental general principles of treaty law *pacta tertiis nec nocent nec prosunt* if understood as a tacit agreement. The voluntary formation of will by two parties cannot, generally, bind a third party.

It has also been pointed out that evidence of *opinio iuris* rarely contains expressions of consent in the contractual sense, making it "largely a matter of imputation".[264] Just because a state undertook a course of action due to its belief in an existing legal obligation does not equate this compliance with consent.

As Max Sørenson pointed out in his treatise on the sources of international law, there is a contradiction between the fact that only a select number of state representatives may bind a state at the level of treaty conclusion,[265] whereas

257 Tomuschat, *supra* n. 127, Chapter 1, at 286–287. See also Koskenniemi, *From Apology to Utopia*, *supra* n. 2, Chapter 1, at 443.
258 Tomuschat, *ibid.*, at 285. See also Stein, *supra* n. 122, Chapter 1, at 459–463.
259 Stein, *ibid.*, at 457. See also Koskenniemi, *From Apology to Utopia*, *supra* n. 2, Chapter 1, at 443.
260 Stein, *ibid.*, at 463.
261 See, *e.g.*, Wolfke, *supra* n. 6, at 66–67, citing further examples.
262 See Akehurst, *supra* n. 50, Chapter 1, at 26.
263 See Gihl, *supra* n. 75, Chapter 1, at 75.
264 See Fastenrath, *supra* n. 1, at 325.
265 See, nowadays, the enumeration in Article 7(2) VIENNA CONVENTION ON THE LAW OF TREATIES.

each and every organ of the state may contribute to the formation of customary international law.[266]

The originally Soviet argument that states will not follow a rule that has not been consented to[267] does not convince, as it fails to see the holistic nature of a legal system: "It is sufficient to the argument (and nearer to the reality) that consent is given to international law as a system rather than to each and every relationship contained in it [...]".[268]

States must accept and consent to the existence of customary international law as a concept, but not each and every rule thereof.

V QUASI-CONSENSUALITY OF *OPINIO IURIS*

Of course, it is clear that states take deliberate decisions to set practice. This implies a "quasi-consensual" element in customary international law. However, it is inherent in state practice, rather than *opinio iuris.* As Antonio Cassese writes, "[t]he main feature of custom is that normally it is not a deliberate lawmaking process. [...] The gradual birth of a new international rule is the side effect of State's conduct in international relations".[269]

Necessity, not consent, is what drives initial compliance: "The necessity of the order is thus the point of coincidence where politics and justice may meet and complete each other".[270]

As has been pointed out, if it were otherwise and customary international law a synonym for a silent treaty, the entire subject would become obsolete and could be discussed within the law of treaties under the heading of oral or silent agreements. That would also mean that quite a substantial number of international legal scholars spent their academic lives publishing under the wrong subject heading.

5 *Paradoxes of the Two-Element Theory*

One issue that has been withheld from the reader so far, is the paradox that is supposedly inherent in the two-element theory. Broken down to an abstract

266 Sørensen, *supra* n. 6, at 87–88.

267 See Danilenko, *supra* n. 134, at 11, citing Tunkin: "Within the international community, the creation of a legal rule requires agreement both as to the content of a rule of conduct and to the recognition of this rule as a legally binding norm of international law".

268 Louis Jaffe, *Judicial Aspects of Foreign Relations. In Particular of the Recognition of Foreign Powers* (Harvard Studies in Administrative Law, Vol. VI; Cambridge: Harvard University Press / Oxford University Press, 1933) 90.

269 Cassese, *supra* n. 29, at 156. Recalling that the subjective element is not just *opinio iuris* but also *necessitatis*, this view could be summed up in the words of Spinoza: "Der Wille kann nicht freie Ursache, sondern nur notwendige heißen". See Baruch de Spinoza, *Ethik* (Berlin Hofenberg, 2014) 32. See also the conclusion of Dupuy, *supra* n. 8, at 272.

270 De Visscher, *supra* n. 32, Chapter 1, at 144.

consideration of the formation of customary international law, the age-old causality dilemma of the chicken and the egg that is the determination of state practice and *opinio iuris* has worried scholars of international law for decades.

a Communis Error Facit Ius?

The first issue concerns the emergence of a new rule of customary international law that might conflict with an already existing one, what has been called the "Walking Dead View" of customary international law.[271] Under this "Freudian construct", each violation of an existing rule could either be the dawn of a new rule and equally be "just that – an unlawful act that does not really purport to establish a new rule".[272]

b Tautology

The second issue concerns the definition of the two-element theory itself: Customary international law consists of two elements, state practice and *opinio iuris*. Thereby, the latter subjective element entails a sense of legal obligation under which the practice occurred.

It even seems that the drafters themselves were unsure where to start, as the wording of Article 38(1)(b) of the STATUTE OF THE INTERNATIONAL COURT OF JUSTICE is drafted in a "clumsy way"[273] referring to "international custom, as evidence of a general practice accepted as law", whereas it should be worded the other way round or phrased as "evidenced by". Alain Pellet has called this fact "disconcerting", while at the same time "logical".[274] The assumption would be that a legal practitioner must find "a general practice accepted as law as evidence of international custom".[275] That is the essence of the two-element theory.

271 Bederman, *supra* n. 124, Chapter 1, at 35. Here, two general principles of law collide, *ex iniuria ius non oritur* and *rebus sic stantibus*. See also Koskenniemi, *supra* n. 72, Chapter 1, at 129.
272 Bederman, *ibid*., at 37. See also Enzo Cannizzaro, 'Customary International Law on the Use of Force: Inductive Approach vs. Value-Oriented Approach', in Cannizzaro and Palchetti (eds), *supra* n. 67, at 261.
273 Cheng, *supra* n. 81, Chapter 1, at 514.
274 Pellet, *supra* n. 7, at 813, para. 211.
275 See Danilenko, *supra* n. 134, at 10; *id., supra* n. 6, at 76; Gihl, *supra* n. 75, Chapter 1, at 76; Hans Kelsen, 'Théorie du Droit International Coutumier', I *Revue Internationale de la Théorie du Droit / Internationale Zeitschrift für Theorie des Rechts* (1939) 260; Koskenniemi, *supra* n. 72, Chapter 1, at 90, fn. 18; Simma and Verdross, *supra* n. 50, Chapter 1, at 348, § 552; Wolfke, *supra* n. 6, at 5–8, citing further critics of the draft of Article 38(1)(b) of the STATUTE OF THE INTERNATIONAL COURT OF JUSTICE; Sienho Yee, *Towards an International Law of Co-progressiveness, Part II. Membership, Leadership and Responsibility* (Leiden: Brill Nijhoff, 2014) 22.

The question is how a state can initiate a form of practice with the corresponding *opinio iuris* at a point in time, at which the rule does not yet exist.[276] What is clear is that there is a Faustian moment, a moment of collective choice, at which states are no longer free to fully deviate from the rule: "In the first we're free, in the second slaves to the act".[277]

In what Richard Falk has called "the most persuasive account of customary international law ever written",[278] Anthony D'Amato called the two-element theory "at worst a harmless tautology":[279]

> For if *we* can say that a state is acting in accordance with its conviction that it is acting in conformity with prevailing international law, then by implication we *already know* what that international law is.[280]

6 Schrödinger's Custom

Emphasis on these paradoxes seems artificial. As evident as the circularity may be, its criticism does not appreciate the dynamic character of customary international law formation that goes hand in hand with the day-to-day affairs of international relations.[281]

While it may be important to be aware of trends within a particular area of law in order to satisfy the rule of law and serve the expectations of its subjects, a concrete assessment will only be necessary whenever the argument that something constitutes customary international law is put forward. Like a snapshot photograph, customary international law is identified at a certain point in time, be it within judicial proceedings or in a scholarly publication:

> One way of dealing with this difficulty [the paradox of customary international law formation] is to ignore it. Often, the "consumer" of legal rules does not need to know when the fruit ripened, but simply whether it is

276 See Somek, *supra* n. 33, at 172:

> *Opinio iuris* asserts that something has already become law without its own contribution even though something can only become law by virtue of being endorsed by it. *Opinio iuris* is hence mistaken not only about what the law is, but also about its own constitutive role. It is perplexingly self-effacing.

See also Kammerhofer, *supra* n. 1, at 534–535.

277 See Johann Wolfgang von Goethe, *Faust. Eine Tragödie* (Tübingen: J.G. Cotta'sche Buchhandlung, 1808) 90: "Das erste steht uns frey, beym zweyten sind wir Knechte". English taken from the 2003 eBook translation by Anthony S. Klein, available at www.poetryintranslation.com/.

278 Richard Falk, 'Foreword' to D'Amato, *supra* n. 8, at viii.

279 See also Dixon, *supra* n. 75, Chapter 1, at 35.

280 D'Amato, *supra* n. 8, at 73. For an earlier critique along similar lines see Kelsen, *supra* n. 275, at 263–265. See also Danilenko, *supra* n. 6, at 81 and 100–102.

281 See Shaw, *supra* n. 88, Chapter 1, at 62. He concedes, however, that such "[c]hange is rarely smooth but rather spasmodic".

ripe when he comes to eat it, or is still too hard or sour to eat. Indeed (to change the metaphor), to ask a follower of fashion at what point exactly something became the mode is in a sense to miss the point of informal rule-systems.[282]

The moment, in which it becomes clear that new customary international law has formed, may be illustrated by the famous thought experiment of the Austrian physicist Erwin Schrödinger.[283] In his (for animal lovers luckily only theoretical) experimental set-up, a cat is placed in a steel chamber together with a vial of deadly acid that is released the moment an atom from a piece of radioactive material decays. However, it is equally probable that the radioactive material does not decay. Without an observer, there is no knowing whether the atom has decayed. Until that point in time, both the living and the dead cat must be assumed to exist. They are "mixed or smeared" together.[284]

What Schrödinger intended as an illustration of the paradox between reality and theoretical quantum-mechanics may easily be transposed to the problem of customary international law formation. Until an observer is introduced, it is unclear how many states have already set state practice and *opinio iuris* regarding a particular rule; whether there is a breach or a new norm has emerged. The observer in this case may be the judiciary, legal counsel, or a "highly qualified publicist" who will help determine the respective rule.

The formation of customary international law is in constant flux. The paradox that a customary international law rule must first be broken in order for a new norm to emerge follows the Linnaean urge of scholars to sort and categorize their surroundings. But this approach does not do justice to the

282 Mendelson, *supra* n. 32, Chapter 1, at 203.

283 This analogy was first formulated by the author as a helpful illustration of the paradoxical formation of customary international law for law school students in the textbook co-authored with Melanie Fink and Ralph Janik, *Völkerrecht verstehen* (Vienna: Facultas, 2015) 49. Contrary to what some students believe, this is a tribute to Austrian physicist Erwin Schrödinger and not to the TV-series *The Big Bang Theory*.

284 See Erwin Schrödinger, 'Die gegenwärtige Situation in der Quantenmechanik', 23/49 *Die Naturwissenschaften* (1935) 812:

> Man kann auch ganz burleske Fälle konstruieren. Eine Katze wird in eine Stahlkammer gesperrt, zusammen mit folgender Höllenmaschine (die man gegen den direkten Zugriff der Katze sichern muß): in einem Geigerschen Zählrohr befindet sich eine winzige Menge radioaktiver Substanz, *so* wenig, daß im Lauf einer Stunde *vielleicht* eines von den Atomen zerfällt, ebenso wahrscheinlich aber auch keines; geschieht es, so spricht das Zählrohr an und betätigt über ein Relais ein Hämmerchen, das ein Kölbchen mit Blausäure zertrümmert. Hat man dieses ganze System eine Stunde lang sich selbst überlassen, so wird man sich sagen, daß die Katze noch lebt, *wenn* inzwischen kein Atom zerfallen ist. Die ψ-Funktion des ganzen Systems würde das so zum Ausdruck bringen, daß in ihr die lebende und die tote Katze (s. v. v.) zu gleichen Teilen gemischt oder verschmiert sind.

dynamic nature of a set of norms that is largely dependent upon the interaction of states. Following the metaphor of "Schrödinger's custom", until an observer needs to determine what the particular customary rule is in a certain moment in time, customary international law is "mixed or smeared".

However, this should not be mistaken with the identification of an exact point in time, at which a particular norm of customary international law has formed. As Maurice Mendelson has pointedly remarked,

> it makes no more sense to ask a member of a customary law society "Exactly how many of you have to participate in such-and-such a practice for it to become law" than it would to approach a group of skinheads in the centre of The Hague and ask them, "How many of you had to start wearing a particular type of trousers for it to become the fashion – and, indeed, *de rigeur* – for members of your group?" [...] The customary process is in fact a continuous one, which does not stop when the rule has emerged, even if one could identify that exact moment. To illustrate the point, I would like to introduce a simile [...]. My simile is the building of a house. It is often not easy or even possible to say exactly when a house has been created. Clearly, it is not when the first foundation stone is laid. But it is not when the last lick of paint has been added either. It is problematic at exactly what point we could say "This is a house". Do we have to wait for the roof to go on, for the windows to be put in, or for all of the utilities to be installed? So it is with customary international law.[285]

Rather than the point of formation, the observer will "take a still photograph, so to speak, of the state of the (customary) law at a given moment",[286] the *lex lata*. After all, the relevant question in practice will be the application of a certain rule to a particular set of circumstances, rather than a historic narrative of how a rule has formed.[287] This process is simply a manifestation of the dynamic character of international relations: "In international relations more than elsewhere, the fact precedes its classification".[288]

7 The Man on the Clapham Omnibus

Of course, as has been the meta-theme of this book, international legal scholarship today is driven, to a large extent, by the wish to promote a certain legal policy or lobby an agenda. The need is, therefore, not just to overcome a theoretical paradox, but to reconsider the process of the identification of international law – as it is, not "as you like it".

285 Mendelson, *supra* n. 22, at 173–175. See also *ibid.*, at 284.
286 *Ibid.*, at 253.
287 See also Scelle, *supra* n. 10, at 400: "Mais la source suppose une nappe souterraine, parfois inconnue ou mal connue, dont l'existence est pourtant indiscutable, puisque les sources sans elle n'existeraient pas".
288 De Visscher, *supra* n. 32, Chapter 1, at 153.

As opposed to the preceding analogy, this issue concerns the integrity and quality of assessment of state practice and *opinio iuris*. Having introduced an observer to identify what is customary international law at a certain point in time, the question is: What do we imagine this observer should look like? Obviously, it cannot be a lobbyist or policy-maker, nor an idealist international lawyer.

So should it be a judicial robot, mechanically processing an empirical algorithm? While this idea of an objective assessment seems attractive *a prima vista*, it is hard to see how this would deliver equitable results; more likely, such a sterile approach to law identification – which ultimately relies on the interaction of states as basic data – might result in a "Bizarro World" picture of international law.

While the finding that the prohibition against torture is not warranted through customary international law may be hard to accept, yet plausible, the fact that states torture with the conviction that they have a legitimate basis for doing so – one must only think of the "ticking time bomb" scenario[289] – should not create a permissive rule allowing torture. The analysis requires an underlying human corrective. It is in the same sense that Andreas Paulus and Bruno Simma speak of the need for an "enlightened positivism".[290]

Instead, it would seem fitting to rely on the proverbial man on the Clapham omnibus. This reasonable "extra-terrestrial observer" is neither an idealist, nor a cynic, neither a revisionist, nor an innovator. He is as little driven by a particular national interest, as by the ideal of the international community as a *civitas maxima*.

Admittedly, this is a "you know it, when you see it" approach, but in combination with the identification of customary international law restricted to a certain point in time it will surely allow for a more grounded assessment of the body of customary international law than any elaborate game theory model or natural law based impulse.

Occam's razor will easily help in the identification of state practice and *opinio iuris*. Such a common-sense appreciation of the obvious will lead to a more honest assessment of what states consider to be the law, to assess the legal *status quo*.[291]

8 *Practice of the International Court of Justice*

Having recapitulated the basic issues regarding the two-element theory as well as some related questions, such as the effect of treaties and decisions of international organizations or the paradoxes of formation, one cannot ignore the fact that, indeed, much emphasis has been laid on what "the wise old men",[292]

289 See on this, *e.g.*, the case of *Gäfgen v. Germany*, Grand Chamber, Judgment of 1 June 2010, Application No. 22978/05.
290 Paulus and Simma, *supra* n. 34, Chapter 1, at 307.
291 See Paust, *supra* n. 78, Chapter 1, at 149–150.
292 Mendelson, *supra* n. 22, at 167.

to use a less flattering characterization of the judges of the International Court of Justice, have had to say on the formation of customary international law.

This moniker from the seminal lecture on customary international law by Maurice Mendelson at The Hague Academy of International Law has not been chosen here to unnecessarily insult or provoke, let alone portray the International Court of Justice as a "men's only club", but to illustrate that the decisions of the International Court of Justice are lastly dependent on a select group of international legal scholars, be it of great renown, that come together to deliberate on what are basically diplomatic disputes with a select number of core legal issues; diplomacy in legal clothing. Of course, this circumstance also influences their decision-making. As Richard Falk writes in his foreword to Anthony D'Amato's *The Concept of Custom in International Law*:

> Third-party decision-makers, for instance, courts, are influenced by many factors in determining whether or not to validate a claim that an action constitutes a customary norm of international law. These factors include the reasonableness of the claim, the effectiveness of its assertion, past practice, the quantity and quality of protest, the overall attitude of the international community, and the compatibility of the claim with prevailing ideas of justice.[293]

Each of the 15 judges have published widely in the field and, aside from the holding itself, now have the opportunity to pack the decisions with *obiter dicta* reflecting their respective views on international law. They are equally affected by and part of the phenomena described in the introductory chapter of this book.

However, as their role as judges of the Court endows their opinions with great authority that constantly perpetuates itself through reliance on former decisions,[294] notwithstanding Article 59 of the STATUTE OF THE INTERNATIONAL COURT OF JUSTICE,[295] it is worth dwelling on the issue for a moment. After all, the International Court of Justice has become a *de facto* legislature,[296] at least for the scholars who wait for it to toss them another legal *dictum*. Of course, this cannot be the place here for a comprehensive appraisal of the

293 Falk, *supra* n. 278, at ix.

294 See American Law Institute, *supra* n. 9, at 37, §103, Comment b, pointing out that there is great reliance on past decisions. Karol Wolfke speaks of a "fetishization of precedent in that law" and of Article 38(1)(d) of the STATUTE OF THE INTERNATIONAL COURT OF JUSTICE as an "acquiescence in a degree of influence on law-creation" in this regard. See Wolfke, *supra* n. 6, at 74–75.

295 See on this also Watson, 'Normativity and Reality', *supra* n. 97, Chapter 1, at 226.

296 Of course, it should be the other way around. See Somek, *supra* n. 106, Chapter 1, at 424: "The validity of a norm, however, does not turn on whether a judge believes it to be valid. On the contrary, once the validity of a norm has been established it has to be recognized by a judge". See, generally, on the International Court of Justice as a law-maker Danilenko, *supra* n. 6, at 253–265.

jurisprudence of the International Court of Justice with regard to customary international law; but some elaboration on its general approach is in order.

The International Court of Justice has failed to embark on any serious analysis of state practice and *opinio iuris*,[297] while at the same time confirming its validity.[298] Thereby, it rules "quasi *ex cathedra*",[299] in the words of Karl Zemanek a luxury only available to international courts and tribunals.[300] Stefan Talmon holds that "[m]ethodology is probably not the strong point of the International Court of Justice".[301]

One of the most prominent decisions in this regard was passed down in the *Nicaragua* case. Here, the International Court of Justice, while reiterating the necessity of state practice and *opinio iuris*,[302] relied solely on the element of *opinio iuris* in determining the prohibition of the use of force under customary international law.[303] Thereby, it relied on General Assembly resolutions, in particular the Friendly Relations Declaration,[304] as a means of determining the

297 Similar to the scholarship that will be presented in the two case examples in Chapter 4. See, most prominently, *North Sea Continental Shelf Cases* (Federal Republic of Germany *v.* Denmark/Federal Republic of Germany *v.* Netherlands), Judgment of 20 February 1969, ICJ Reports 1969, p. 3.

298 See *North Sea Continental Shelf Cases* (Federal Republic of Germany *v.* Denmark/ Federal Republic of Germany *v.* Netherlands), Judgment of 20 February 1969, ICJ Reports 1969, p. 3, at 44, para. 77.

299 Tomuschat, *supra* n. 127, Chapter 1, at 259. See also Koskenniemi, *From Apology to Utopia, supra* n. 2, Chapter 1, at 396.

300 See Zemanek, *supra* n. 37, Chapter 1, at 898: "Doch nur internationale Gerichte – insbesondere der Internationale Gerichtshof – können sich mit apodiktischen Behauptungen des Bestandes von Gewohnheitsrecht begnügen". However, he does concede that the *Tadić* decision of the ICTY constitutes an actual effort to establish state practice and *opinio iuris*. See *ibid*., at 900. For such a domestic decision attempting to comprehensively survey state practice and *opinio iuris* see Hathaway, *supra* n. 33, Chapter 1, at 33, fn. 59. Cf. also the approach of the ICJ in the *Jurisdictional Immunities of the State* (Germany *v.* Italy; Greece intervening), Judgment of 3 February 2012, ICJ Reports 2012, p. 99, at 123, para. 55 *et seq*.

301 Talmon, *supra* n. 73, at 418.

302 *Case Concerning Military and Paramilitary Activities In and Against Nicaragua* (Nicaragua *v.* United States of America), Judgment of 27 June 1986 (Merits), ICJ Reports 1986, p. 14, at 97–98, paras 183-184. Meron comments that this "emphasis on the need to establish the existence of practice was more in the nature of a verbal protestation than a serious inquiry into the presence of the necessary elements of customary law". Meron, *supra* n. 82, Chapter 1, at 110.

303 See *Case Concerning Military and Paramilitary Activities In and Against Nicaragua* (Nicaragua *v.* United States of America), Judgment of 27 June 1986 (Merits), ICJ Reports 1986, p. 14, at 98–106, paras 187–201. See on this also Danilenko, *supra* n. 6, at 93–94; Pellet, *supra* n. 7, at 814, para. 214; Tomuschat, *supra* n. 7, Chapter 1, at 259.

304 See General Assembly Resolution. 2625 (XXV), 'Declaration on Principles of International Law Concerning Friendly Relations and Co-operation Among States in Accordance with the Charter of the United Nations', U.N. Doc. A/RES/25/ 2625 (24 October 1970).

legal *status quo.*[305] It paid mere "lip-service to a traditional doctrine and to the letter of Art. 38 of the ICJ Statute".[306] Listing a number of prominent documents is not sufficient to establish *opinio iuris.*[307] There is no such thing as proof by example.

As Theodor Meron has pointed out, the *Nicaragua* case is merely the culmination of a longer process of decreasing detail with which state practice and *opinio iuris* were analyzed by the Court.[308] Both the International Court of Justice and its *de facto* predecessor institution, the Permanent Court of International Justice, held it sufficient to proclaim the existence of state practice or *opinio iuris* without referring to them, let alone setting out to prove their existence:[309] "Over the years, the ICJ has pulled a number of customary international law 'rabbits' out of its hat".[310] Cases in which both courts have referred to *opinio iuris* have even been singled out as a "'strict scrutiny' approach to *opinio iuris*",[311] as opposed to what Stefan Talmon simply calls the method of "assertion".[312]

A number of other instances saw the Court confirming a "legal *status quo*" that runs parallel to, rather than intersecting, the realities of state practice and *opinio iuris.* In the *Nicaragua* case,[313] the *Oil Platforms* case,[314] the *Wall* advisory opinion,[315]

305 *Case Concerning Military and Paramilitary Activities In and Against Nicaragua* (Nicaragua *v.* United States of America), Judgment of 27 June 1986 (Merits), ICJ Reports 1986, p. 14, on the Friendly Relations Declaration, in particular at 99–100, para. 188, at 101, para. 191, and at 106, para. 202; invocations of other General Assembly resolutions, *e.g.*, at 103, para. 195, on armed attack, or at 107, para. 203, on non-intervention.
306 Palmisano, *supra* n. 103, Chapter 1, at 207.
307 See Zemanek, *supra* n. 37, Chapter 1, at 900.
308 See Meron, *supra* n. 82, Chapter 1, at 108–113. For an enumeration of instances in which the International Court of Justice pronounced rules as customary international law, mostly without any form of further verification, see Wolfke, *supra* n. 6, at 25–29.
309 See Pellet, *supra* n. 7, at 815, para. 216, and 826–827, paras 235–236 with further references. With regard to the Permanent Court of International Justice see also Sørensen, *supra* n. 6, at 84: "La Cour n'a jamais dans sa pratique attaché une importance décisive aux termes de la stipulation [of Article 38]".
310 Talmon, *supra* n. 73, at 434.
311 Fidler, *supra* n. 74, Chapter 1, at 206. See also Brownlie, *supra* n. 17, at 8–10.
312 See Talmon, *supra* n. 73, at 434 and 437–440.
313 *Case Concerning Military and Paramilitary Activities In and Against Nicaragua* (Nicaragua *v.* United States of America), Judgment of 27 June 1986 (Merits), ICJ Reports 1986, p. 14, at 103–104, para. 195. See also Scharf, *supra* n. 79, at 183.
314 *Case Concerning Oil Platforms* (Islamic Republic of Iran *v.* United States of America), Judgment of 6 November 2003, ICJ Reports 2003, p. 161, at 195–196, para. 72.
315 *Legal Consequences of the Construction of a Wall in the Occupied Palestinian Territory,* Advisory Opinion of 9 July 2004, ICJ Reports 2004, p. 136, at 194, para. 139, avoiding the general issue by basing its decision on a distinction between occurrences within the territory of a state from those outside of it.

and the Ugandan *Armed Activities* case,[316] the International Court of Justice positioned itself unfavorable to the possibility of self-defence against non-state actors[317] which had just recently been at the forefront of the discourse in the context of the "Bush doctrine"[318] and which not only the "most highly qualified publicists" endorse,[319] including a number of individual judges of the International Court of Justice,[320] but which also represents constant state practice by states concerned[321] as well as the position of the Security Council of the United Nations.[322]

An "extra-terrestrial observer" should assume that the judgments of the International Court of Justice play a significant role in identifying the legal *status quo*.[323] However, they are seemingly engaged in creating an "international common law".[324] One can now simply assume that something constitutes customary international law by relying on the Court. However, even if a large number of academics and practitioners may have been trained in the common law tradition and have been socialized within its confines, international law is not a genuine common law system, even though it is, admittedly,

316 *Case Concerning Armed Activities on the Territory of the Congo* (Democratic Republic of the Congo *v.* Uganda), Judgment of 19 December 2005, ICJ Reports 2005, p. 168, at pp. 222–223, paras 146–147.

317 See Scharf, *supra* n. 79, at 185 and 216.

318 See on this Scharf, *supra* n. 79, at 183–210.

319 See, *inter alia*, Ian Johnstone, 'The Plea of "Necessity" in International Legal Discourse: Humanitarian Intervention and Counter-terrorism', 43 *Columbia Journal of Transnational Law* (2004–2005) 370–372; Hanspeter Neuhold, 'Das Gewalt- und Interventionsverbot', in Reinisch (ed.), *supra* n. 192, at 428, para. 1686; Ruth Wedgwood, 'The ICJ Advisory Opinion on the Israeli Security Fence and the Limits of Self-Defense', 99 *American Journal of International Law* (2005) 58 and 61.

320 See also *Case Concerning Armed Activities on the Territory of the Congo* (Democratic Republic of the Congo *v.* Uganda), Separate Opinion of Judge Kooijmans, ICJ Reports 2005, p. 306 at 313–315, paras 25–32, and the Separate Opinion of Judge Simma, ICJ Reports 2005, p. 334, at 335–338, paras 5–15; *Legal Consequences of the Construction of a Wall in the Occupied Palestinian Territory*, Separate Opinion of Judge Higgins, ICJ Reports 2004, p. 136, at 207, para. 33, and Separate Opinion of Judge Kooijmans, ICJ Reports 2004, p. 219, at 229–230, para. 35.

321 In particular the United States and Israel as well as most recently France with regard to the so-called Islamic State. See also Scharf, *supra* n. 79, at 204–205, citing the practice of Colombia, Ethiopia, Kenya, Russia, Turkey, and the United States together with further references to literature on each instance.

322 See Security Council Resolution 1373, 'Threats to International Peace and Security Caused by Terrorist Acts', U.N. Doc. S/RES/1373 (28 September 2001); Security Council Resolution 1368, 'Threats to International Peace and Security Caused by Terrorist Acts', U.N. Doc. S/RES/1368 (12 September 2001).

323 See, *inter alia*, Cassese, *supra* n. 29, at 160.

324 See William Burnham, *Introduction to the Law and Legal System of the United States* (St. Paul: West, 2011) 327 on the role of common law judges in determining the nature of provisions of the Constitution of the US: "[C]ommon law judges are especially comfortable with judicial law-making".

coming more strongly under its influence.[325] Others have characterized this phenomenon as a "gradual drift into naturalism" by the Court.[326]

Through its stance on the formation of customary international law and, of course, due to its apparent legal authority in doing so, the International Court of Justice has broadly facilitated scholarship turning a blind eye on authoritative proof of state practice and *opinio iuris*. In Alain Pellet's pointed metaphor: "the chrysalis is transformed into [a] butterfly [*sic*] through a process which remains partly mysterious but leads to a globally acceptable result".[327] In expectance of a dogmatically sound assessment of the legal *status quo*, this approach is, of course, hardly tenable. It is a mere "'bootstrap' argument".[328]

Scholarship has willingly embraced this approach, arguing that the International Court of Justice should "bring the process of crystallisation of customary law to a swift conclusion";[329] what Michael Scharf has called supplying the "authoritative gloss".[330] For Martin Dixon, the Court plays a role in "accelerat[ing] the creation of customary law by confirming trends in state practice and by 'discovering' the necessary *opinio juris*".[331] It has even been observed that the International Court of Justice is participating in the mandate of the International Law Commission,[332] *i.e.* "encouraging the progressive development of international law and its codification". However, as the Court itself held in the *South West Africa Cases*: "As is implied by the opening phrase of Article 38, paragraph 1, of its Statute, the Court is not a legislative body. Its duty is to apply the law as it finds it, not to make it".[333]

325 See Colin B. Picker, 'International Law's Mixed Heritage: A Common/Civil Law Jurisdiction', 41 *Vanderbilt Journal of Transnational Law* (2008) 1102 *et passim*.
326 Rubin, *supra* n. 198, Chapter 1, at 192.
327 Pellet, *supra* n. 7, at 828, para. 240. This phenomenon is not restricted to the International Court of Justice or other tribunals under international law. See, *e.g.*, Justice Scalia's dissenting opinion in *Roper v. Simmons* before the US Supreme Court on its methodology:

> Today's opinion provides a perfect example of why judges are ill equipped to make the type of legislative judgments the Court insists on making here. To support its opinion that States should be prohibited from imposing the death penalty on anyone who committed murder before age 18, the Court looks to scientific and sociological studies, picking and choosing those that support its position. It never explains why those particular studies are methodologically sound, none was ever entered into evidence or tested in an adversarial proceeding. [...] In other words, all the Court has done today, to borrow from another context, is to look over the heads of the crowd and pick out its friends.

See *Roper v. Simmons*, at 616–617 respective 1222.
328 Thirlway, *supra* n. 13, at 43.
329 Dixon, *supra* n. 75, Chapter 1, at 45.
330 Scharf, *supra* n. 79, at 218.
331 Dixon, *supra* n. 75, Chapter 1, at 45.
332 See Pellet, *supra* n. 7, at 866, para. 331.
333 *South West Africa Cases* (Ethiopia *v.* South Africa; Liberia *v.* South Africa), Judgment of 18 July 1966 (Second Phase), ICJ Reports 1966, p. 6, at 48, para. 89.

In the *Gulf of Maine* case the International Court of Justice emphasized an inductive approach, painting a rather "conservative" picture, as opposed to its usual take on the subject:

> A body of detailed rules is not to be looked for in customary international law which in fact comprises a limited set of norms for ensuring the co-existence and vital co-operation of the members of the international community, together with a set of customary rules whose presence in the *opinio juris* of States can be tested by induction based on the analysis of a sufficiently extensive and convincing practice, and not by deduction from preconceived ideas.[334]

Again, in the *Nuclear Weapons* advisory opinion, the International Court of Justice almost apologetically showed that it knew better:

> It is clear that the Court cannot legislate [...]. Rather its task is to engage in its normal judicial function of ascertaining the existence or otherwise of legal principles and rules applicable to the threat or use of nuclear weapons. The contention that the giving of an answer to the question posed would require the Court to legislate is based on a supposition that the present *corpus juris* is devoid of relevant rules in this matter. The Court could not accede to this argument; it states the existing law and does not legislate. This is so even if, in stating and applying the law, the Court necessarily has to specify its scope and sometimes note its general trend.[335]

It is unclear, therefore, why it does not practice restraint in determining the legal *status quo*. As Alfred Rubin pointed out in the context of the *Nuclear Tests* case:[336]

See Pellet, *supra* n. 7, at 752, para. 65. See also the *Fisheries Jurisdiction Case* (United Kingdom of Great Britain and Northern Ireland *v.* Iceland), Judgment of 25 July 1974 (Merits), ICJ Reports 1974, p. 3, at pp. 23–24, para. 53: "In the circumstances, the Court, as a court of law, cannot render judgment *sub specie legis ferendae*, or anticipate the law before the legislator has laid it down". See Scharf, *supra* n. 79, at 47. This position goes back to the original drafting of Article 38 of the STATUTE OF THE INTERNATIONAL COURT OF JUSTICE in the context of its predecessor, the Permanent Court of International Justice. See Sørensen, *supra* n. 6, at 32.

334 *Delimitation of the Maritime Boundary in the Gulf of Maine Area* (Canada *v.* United States of America), Judgment of 12 October 1984 Given by the Chamber Constituted by the Order Made by the Court on 20 January 1982, ICJ Reports 1984, p. 246, at 299, para. 111. See, however, Talmon, *supra* n. 73, at 418, who argues that the use of the wording "can be" suggests that the Court also considers the deductive method as a valid alternative.

335 *Legality of the Threat or Use of Nuclear Weapons*, Advisory Opinion of 8 July 1996, ICJ Reports 1996, p. 226, at 237, para. 18. See also Scharf, *supra* n. 297, at 47.

336 *Nuclear Tests Case* (New Zealand *v.* France), Judgment of 20 December 1974, ICJ Reports 1974, p. 457.

> The loss has been not to international law as a moral, sociological and otherwise persuasive force in world politics, but to the tribunal; the perversion of the substantive positive law by its highest tribunal has led to a loss of authority by that tribunal and a general mistrust of the positive law and its enforcement mechanisms.[337]

9 *"Modern" Approaches to the Formation of Custom*

Aside from the practice of the International Court of Justice, doctrine has proposed a number of approaches to the formation of customary international law that abandon the restraints of Article 38(1)(b) of the STATUTE OF THE INTERNATIONAL COURT OF JUSTICE altogether. Increasingly, international practice and scholarship have relied on what has been called a "value-oriented approach" which does not look at state practice and *opinio iuris* but rather "take[s] into account the emerging values and interests of individual states as well as those of the international community as a whole".[338] Louis Sohn writes:

> that the methods of developing new rules of customary international law have greatly changed since the Second World War. These changes have not been imposed on states by any external authority; they are the result of a voluntary acceptance by states of the need to adapt the methods of law-creation to the needs of the rapidly growing and changing world community. Any prior restrictions on the law-creating process were self-made, and they can be changed by the very method that established them in the first place.[339]

Anthea Roberts distinguishes here between the inductively attained "traditional custom" of the two-element theory and deductive "modern custom".[340] Therein, she also includes the approaches favoring the element of *opinio iuris* through consideration of treaties[341] and decisions of international organizations.[342] Philip Alston and Bruno Simma speak of "a product grown in the hothouse of parliamentary diplomacy and all too often 'sold' as customary law before actually having stood the test of time":[343] "This new, radical customary

337 Rubin, *supra* n. 198, Chapter 1, at 195.
338 Cannizzaro, *supra* n. 272, at 248. For an account of this development see also Kennedy, *supra* n. 56, Chapter 1, at 232–239.
339 Sohn, *supra* n. 198, at 1079.
340 See Roberts, *supra* n. 73, Chapter 1, at 758. See also the article by Gunning, *supra* n. 113, Chapter 1. Roberts presents a conciliatory approach she calls the "reflective interpretive approach", which piggy-backs "modern custom" on the dogmatic legitimacy of "traditional custom". See *ibid.*, at 788–791 *et passim*. For further references see William Thomas Worster, 'The Inductive and Deductive Methods in Customary International Law Analysis', 45 *Georgia Journal of International Law* (2013–2014) 449–450, fn. 8.
341 See on this *supra* pp. 74 *et seq.*
342 See on this *supra* pp. 77 *et seq.*
343 Alston and Simma, *supra* n. 85, Chapter 1, at 89.

law has lost the element of retrospection; if its protagonists look back at the past it is a look back in anger, full of impatience with the imperfections and gaps of the old rules".[344]

As Koskenniemi writes in the introduction to his volume, *Sources of International Law*:

> In practice, "custom" has become a generic category for practically all binding non-treaty standards. This is in line with agnosticism about natural principles and general principles as it seems sometimes simply too difficult to argue about such principles within the conventions of legal rhetoric and proof. "Custom" seems both more legitimate in origin and more tangible in application – even if the various standards thus classified as "custom" cannot easily be fitted within the standard theory about the emergence and ascertainment of customary law.[345]

Fidler finds three different perspectives in international legal scholarship on customary international law; first, the "dinosaur perspective" that customary international law is out-dated and a "legal fossil",[346] second, the contrary "dynamo perspective" that customary international law is still "a vital part of modern international law" and "critical to tackling the new circumstances of international relations and to making progress towards a better world",[347] and, third, the "dangerous perspective" that believes that customary international law is prone to "legal and political abuse" and "has been abused at the international and national levels":[348]

> The chief complaint of the dangerous perspective at the level of international law is that the CIL process has been transformed from a conservative, limited international legal process into the international legal equivalent of a wish list for Santa Claus. The number of so-called rules of CIL in today's international law is staggering.[349]

This is indeed a problem. International legal scholarship today is often driven by the wish to promote a certain legal policy or lobby an agenda. With such motivation usually comes a particular view of the functioning of the global community, hand in hand: "Much of the confusion that haunts CIL stems

344 *Ibid.*, at 90.
345 Koskenniemi, 'Introduction', *supra* n. 2, Chapter 1, at xxi.
346 See Fidler, *supra* n. 74, Chapter 1, at 216–220.
347 *Ibid.*, at 220–224. Further attributes include customary international law "as a progressive, innovative force in contemporary international relations" and as "the 'common law' of mankind because it, and sometimes only it, can accommodate, or create a debate about, urgent concerns of justice and equity in international politics".
348 *Ibid.*, at 224–231. He further equates these three views with rationalism, revolutionism, and realism. See *ibid.*, at 232–234.
349 *Ibid.*, at 224.

from the fact that participants in the debate often fail to make explicit their assumptions about international relations".[350]

10 Assessment

The conflict here is not between "consent and justice-based explanations",[351] but between inductive empiricism and the two. Neither the voluntarist view nor any of the "modern" approaches to customary international law dogmatically convince. Both run counter to the general principle of law *ut res magis valeat quam pereat* if one accepts the catalogue of manifestations of international law in Article 38(1) of the STATUTE OF THE INTERNATIONAL COURT OF JUSTICE as an expression of state consensus. While a quasi-consensual element pervades customary international law, it cannot simply be equated to a tacit or oral agreement. Equally, as the common saying "hard cases make bad law" illustrates, it cannot be a credible approach to view the formation of customary international law as a railroad switch, dependent on the subject matter.

Of course, it may seem difficult to assess the practice and *opinio iuris* of around 200 legal entities of complex structure and different levels of transparency. Equally, some subject areas may simply produce less state practice or *opinio iuris* than others. The view that the assessment of the two elements should take place on a sliding scale seems appealing here.[352] But this should not lead to a result-oriented assessment of what is essentially an empirical exercise. Sometimes, there might just not be enough, or even too much contrary state practice; all the governmental statements in the world will not make it customary international law. In any case, an assessment must be made.

Considering the number of unpaid interns and junior level associates in law offices around the world, it cannot be too much to expect an analysis, whether practice is "generally [...] adopted",[353] at least by the "States concerned",[354] if a party to a proceeding – or a scholar for that matter – wants to base its claim on customary international law.[355] Applying the analogy of "Schrödinger's custom", this is not an impossible effort, in particular if one takes into account the capacity of scholars for repetitive publications.[356]

350 *Ibid.*, at 148.
351 Koskenniemi, *supra* n. 73, Chapter 1, at 52 / 21.
352 See Kirgis, *supra* n. 136, at 149. See Worster, *supra* n. 340, at 451 with further references in fn. 14.
353 *Fisheries Case* (United Kingdom *v.* Norway), Judgment of 18 December 1951, ICJ Reports 1951, p. 116, at 128.
354 *North Sea Continental Shelf Cases* (Federal Republic of Germany *v.* Denmark/ Federal Republic of Germany *v.* Netherlands), Judgment of 20 February 1969, ICJ Reports 1969, p. 3, at 44, para. 76. See on the difficulty of identifying the states "specially affected" Danilenko, *supra* n. 6, at 95–96.
355 For a possible methodological guideline see Worster, *supra* n. 340, at 480–519.
356 See Joseph Weiler, 'On My Way Out – Advice to Young Scholars II: Career Strategy and the Publication Trap', *EJIL: Talk!* (18 February 2016) <www.ejiltalk.org/on-my-way-out-advice-to-young-scholars-ii-career-strategy-and-the-publication-trap/>.

Only following such a sound assessment can customary international law resume its proper place within the manifestations of international law:

> What makes international custom authoritative is that it consists of the resultants of divergent state vectors (acts, restraints) and thus brings out what the legal system considers a resolution of the underlying state interests.[357]

There is still a role to play for customary international law if understood through the two-element theory. It is a manifestation of international law that does not directly spring from the "will" or "consent" of states but reflects their perpetual international relations. Customary international law properly understood does not constitute an "international agreement". States do not voluntarily form a will at the international level but consciously or unconsciously influence its creation through their actions. This also means that custom might not have the same capacity for self-restrictive regulation of conduct as treaties do.

C General Principles of Law

Included within the list of Article 38(1) of the Statute of the International Court of Justice to preclude the possibility of a *non liquet* situation,[358] the "enigmatic"[359] general principles of law "recognized by civilized nations"[360] present a particularly confusing case due both to terminological unclarity[361] and disagreement as to their nature and formal identification.[362] As has been pointed out, it has even been called into question whether they stand on an equal footing with the other two sources of international law.[363] On the other hand, they have been deemed, in the words of Max Sørensen, the cement that assures the cohesion of international law with the domestic legal orders.[364]

357 D'Amato, *supra* n. 124, Chapter 1, at 102.

358 See Pellet, *supra* n. 7, at 832, para. 250; Shaw, *supra* n. 88, Chapter 1, at 69–70; Simma and Verdross, *supra* n. 50, Chapter 1, at 387, § 601; Thirlway, *supra* n. 8, at 108.

359 Jennings, *supra* n. 249, at 71 / 39.

360 See on the concept of "civilization" in international law, generally, Yadh Ben Achour, *Le Rôle des Civilisations dans le Système International (Droit et Relations Internationales)* (Collection de Droit Internationales, Vol. 50; Bruxelles: Editions Bruylant / Editions de l'Université des Bruxelles, 2003).

361 See Danilenko, *supra* n. 6, at 8–10. For an early analysis of the different meanings of "general principles of international law" see Sørensen, *supra* n. 6, at 112–122. See also Wolfke, *supra* n. 6, at 8 in this regard.

362 See Jennings and Watts, *supra* n. 51, at 36, §12 and fn. 1 with extensive references. See Pellet, *supra* n. 7, at 852, para. 300.

363 See *supra* pp. 54 *et seq*.

364 Sørensen, *supra* n. 46, at 16, speaking of "le ciment qui assure la cohésion du droit international avec les ordres juridiques nationaux et qui permet de concevoir

Probably one of the most important applications of general principles of law is the incorporation of the consideration of good faith in the relation between states.[365]

1 Terminology

Terminologically, one must differentiate between the terms "general principles of law" in the sense of Article 38(1) of the Statute of the International Court of Justice, "general principles" or simply "principles" of varying meaning, and, finally, "general principles of international law".[366] Koskenniemi distinguishes at least four different meanings of the term "principle":

> 1 Standards common to all (or most) national legal systems. Especially Western scholars have regarded that Article 38(1)(c) refers to such [...].
> 2 Standards of international law proper, generated through State practice [...].
> 3 Certain basic (or "fundamental") standards of international law. These would cover at least the *jus cogens* principles from which no derogations are allowable [...].
> 4 Standards of natural law, applicable in inter-State relations.[367]

Neither the International Court of Justice nor the Permanent Court of International Justice have been very helpful in this regard. For example, in the *Lotus* case, the latter held that "the words 'principles of international law', as ordinarily used, can only mean international law as it is applied between all nations belonging to the community of States".[368]

Similarly, in the *Gulf of Maine* case, the International Court of Justice made the pronouncement that:

> the association of the terms "rules" and "principles" is no more than the use of a dual expression to convey one and the same idea, since in this context "principles" clearly means principles of law, that is, it also includes rules of international law in whose case the use of the term

tous les phénomènes juridiques de l'humanité sous un aspect unite". In the words of *The Big Lebowski*, they are the rug that "really tied the room together".

365 See Jennings and Watts, *supra* n. 51, at 38, §12; Pellet, *supra* n. 7, at 836, para. 206.

366 For a historical appraisal of recourse to such principles see Vladimir-Djuro Degan, 'General Principles of Law (A Source of General International Law)', 3 *Finnish Yearbook of International Law* (1992) 7–58.

367 Koskenniemi, 'General Principles', *supra* n. 49, at 363–364.

368 *The Case of the S.S. 'Lotus'* (France *v.* Turkey), Judgment of 7 September 1927, PCIJ Series A. – No. 10, p. 4, at 16.

> "principles" may be justified because of their more general and more fundamental character.[369]

There has been no decision in which either of these bodies has explicitly based its reasoning on general principles of law.[370] However, the International Court of Justice has referred to the existence of such principles and applied them without making an explicit subsumption under the manifestations listed in Article 38(1) of its STATUTE.[371]

The Soviet interpretation of Article 38(1)(c) of the STATUTE OF THE INTERNATIONAL COURT OF JUSTICE had viewed it as encompassing merely general principles of international law:[372]

> [T]he question arises whether in contemporary conditions of the existence of States not only with different but also with opposed socio-economic systems there can exist normative principles common to socialist law and to bourgeois law. One must say very definitely that normative principles which would be common to the two opposed systems of law, socialist and bourgeois, do not exist.[373]

General principles of international law, rather than being specific rules in and as of themselves, usually refer to "bundles of rights",[374] which are again grounded in treaty or custom.[375] Cassese defines them as

> sweeping and loose standards of conduct that can be deduced from treaty and customary rules by extracting and generalizing some of their most

369 *Delimitation of the Maritime Boundary in the Gulf of Maine Area* (Canada *v.* United States of America), Judgment of 12 October 1984 Given by the Chamber Constituted by the Order Made by the Court on 20 January 1982, ICJ Reports 1984, p. 246, at 289–290, para. 79.

370 See *supra* ns 45–46.

371 See *supra* ns 49–50. For a detailed analysis of judicial and state practice see Danilenko, *supra* n. 6, at 178 and 181–186.

372 See Dixon, *supra* n. 75, Chapter 1, at 41; Shaw, *supra* n. 88, Chapter 1, at 70 on the writings of Grigory Tunkin.

373 Tunkin, *Theory*, *supra* n. 226, at 217.

374 Dixon, *supra* n. 75, Chapter 1, at 42.

375 See *ibid.*, at 43. Ian Brownlie gives a very broad definition of "general principles of international law":

> The rubric may refer to rules of customary law, to general principles of law as in Article 38(1)(c), or to logical propositions resulting from judicial reasoning on the basis of existing international law and municipal analogies. [...] In many cases these principles are to be traced to state practice. However, they are primarily abstractions from a mass of rules and have been so long and so generally accepted as to be no longer *directly* connected with state practice. In a few cases the principle concerned, though useful, is unlikely to appear in ordinary state practice.

See *id.*, *supra* n. 17, at 19.

significant common points. They do not make up a source proper. Most of them primarily serve the purpose of filling possible gaps or of making a particular construction prevail at any time when two or more interpretations are possible.[376]

He further differentiates two kinds of "general principles of international law":

> At present, in the world community, *two distinct classes of general principles* may be relied upon. First, there are general principles of international law, namely those principles which can be inferred or extracted by way of induction and generalization from conventional and customary rules of international law. Some of these principles have been restated by States in international instruments designed to set out the fundamental standards of behaviour that should govern the relations among members of the international community [...]. Second, there are principles that are peculiar to a particular branch of international law (the law of the sea, humanitarian law, the law of State responsibility, etc.). These principles are general legal standards overarching the whole body of law governing a specific area.[377]

Alan Boyle also speaks of "soft law general principles" as policy goals impacting on "interpretation, application, and development of other rules of law".[378]

2 Identification

As to the nature and formal identification of general principles of law, there are a variety of approaches that can be broadly divided into a comparative law approach, on the one hand, and a natural law approach, on the other. The latter view was originally championed by the Belgian representative, Baron Descamps, in the Advisory Committee of Jurists, which drafted the original wording of what would later become Article 38(1)(c) of the STATUTE OF THE INTERNATIONAL COURT OF JUSTICE, whereas the United States representative Elihu Root and United Kingdom representative Lord Phillimore emphasized the former position.[379] So while one end of the spectrum views general

376 Cassese, *supra* n. 29, at 188.

377 *Ibid.*, at 189, fn. 3.

378 See Alan Boyle, 'Soft Law in International Law-Making', in Malcolm D. Evans (ed.), *International Law* (Oxford: Oxford University Press, 2010) 132–134.

379 On the original drafting process of the STATUTE OF THE PERMANENT COURT OF INTERNATIONAL JUSTICE and the discussion on the scope of general principles of law within the Advisory Committee of Jurists see Maarten Bos, 'The Recognized Manifestations of International Law. A New Theory of "Sources"', 20 *German Yearbook of International Law* (1977), at 33–40; Brownlie, *supra* n. 17, at 16; Cassese, *supra* n. 29, at 190–191; Pellet, *supra* n. 7, at 832–833, paras 250–252; Sørensen, *supra* n. 46, at 17–18. For an early overview of diverging doctrinal approaches see Sørensen, *supra* n. 6, at 123–136; Béla Vitanyi, 'Les Positions de la Doctrine Concernant le Sens de la Notion de Principes Généraux de Droit

principles of law as common rules and principles derived (through a variety of different methods) from the world's (domestic) legal systems,[380] the other extreme views general principles as a means for natural law theory[381] to enter the body of international law.[382]

Of course, there are a number of nuances to each of these views.[383] Schachter identifies five different approaches to the content and scope of general principles of law:

1 The principles of municipal law "recognized by civilized nations".
2 General principles of law "derived from the specific nature of the international community".
3 Principles "intrinsic to the idea of law and basic to all legal systems".
4 Principles "valid through all kinds of societies in relationships of hierarchy and co-ordination".

Reconnus par les Nations Civilisées', 86 *Revue Générale de Droit International Public* (1982) 85–102.

380 See, *inter alia*, Brierly, *supra* n. 169, at 62–63; Cassese, *supra* n. 29, at 191–192, arguing that this view was merely codified by Article 38(1)(c) of the STATUTE OF THE INTERNATIONAL COURT OF JUSTICE, as it was already applied by international tribunals prior to 1921; Bin Cheng, *General Principles of Law as Applied by International Courts and Tribunals* (Cambridge: Cambridge University Press, 1953); Dixon, *supra* n. 75, Chapter 1, at 41; Gihl, *supra* n. 75, Chapter 1, at 85–87; Härle, *supra* n. 62 *et seq.*; Jennings and Watts, *supra* n. 51, at 36–37, §12; Hersch Lauterpacht, *Private Law Sources and Analogies of International Law. With Special Reference to International Arbitration* (London: Longmans, Green and Co., 1927) *passim*, however, see also Hersch Lauterpacht, 'Règles Générales du Droit de la Paix', 64 *Recueil des Cours de l'Académie de Droit International de La Haye* (1937-IV) 164; Pellet, *supra* n. 7, at 783, paras 137–139, and 834, para. 254; Jean Spiropoulos, *Die allgemeinen Rechtsgrundsätze im Völkerrecht. Eine Auslegung von Art. 38 3 des Statuts des ständigen Internationalen Gerichtshofs* (Aus dem Institut für internationales Recht an der Universität Kiel. Erste Reihe. Vorträge und Einzelschriften 7; Kiel: Verlag des Instituts für internationales Recht an der Universität Kiel, 1928) *passim*. See further on this view Vitanyi, *ibid.*, at 103–110. Furthermore, seemingly in favor, Meron, *supra* n. 82, Chapter 1, at 88. For a critical view see Jennings, *supra* n. 249, at 71–72 / 40–41. For a conciliatory view see Simma and Verdross, *supra* n. 50, Chapter 1, at 383–384, § 601.

381 For a brief introduction to the distinction and synthesis between natural law and positivism in early legal thought and philosophy see Rubin, *supra* n. 198, Chapter 1, at 6–18.

382 Most prominently Austrian scholar Alfred Verdross in his works, *inter alia*, 'Les Principes Généraux du Droit Comme Source du Droit de Gens', in Appleton (ed.), *supra* n. 10, at 383–388. See on this also Sørensen, *supra* n. 6, at 133–136. See also Verdross' contemporaries Le Fur, *supra* n. 38, at 368–370, and Charles de Visscher, 'Contribution à l'Étude des Sources du Droit International', in Appleton (ed.), *supra* n. 10, 395–396. Cf., however, the more critical Scelle, *supra* n. 10, at 423–426. See also Alston and Simma, *supra* n. 85, Chapter 1, at 102.

383 For example, Arnold Duncan McNair sees them primarily in the work of tribunals and writers. See *id.*, 'The General Principles of Law Recognized by Civilized Nations', 33 *British Yearbook of International Law* (1957) 15.

5 Principles of justice founded on "the very nature of man as a rational and social being".[384]

However, whereas points (1) and (3) can easily be subsumed under the comparative law approach, point (2) seems more reminiscent of what has been referred to as "general principles" or simply "principles" to refer to such defining features of international law as sovereignty, reciprocity, and effectivity.[385] Points (4) and (5) pertain to the natural law approach.[386] For the purpose of the present analysis, it is sufficient to consider general principles of law against the dualist generalization of comparative and natural law.

One view may also be as just seeing Article 38(1)(c) as descriptive of rules originating from either treaty or custom.[387] The majority of scholars, however, argue for a "pre-existing legal validity" of such norms that does "not need to be validated by either custom or treaty to have legal effect".[388] It could just as easily be argued that the opposite is suggested by the introductory clause of Article 38(1) of the STATUTE OF THE INTERNATIONAL COURT OF JUSTICE "in accordance with international law".[389]

a Comparative Law

Of the two views, that of a comparative analysis of general principles *in foro domestico*, as claimed by Elihu Root and Lord Phillimore, seems to be the prevailing interpretation,[390] be it through mere incorporation of procedural or administrative rules[391] – including the notion of equity[392] – or even substantive norms of international law.[393]

384 Schachter, *supra* n. 6, Chapter 1, at 50. For more on these views see *ibid.*, at 50–55, with further references.
385 See *ibid.*, at 50–54.
386 See *ibid.*, at 54–55.
387 See on this Vitanyi, *supra* n. 379, at 50–85. See Dixon, *supra* n. 75, Chapter 1, at 41.
388 See, for example, Dixon, *supra* n. 75, Chapter 1, at 41; Pellet, *supra* n. 7, at 835, para. 258, and 850, para. 296. See, however, the comment by Lord Phillimore in the drafting committee that "it was through custom that general principles came to be recognised". See Permanent Court of International Justice, *supra* n. 46, at 334.
389 See Wolfke, *supra* n. 6, at 106.
390 See *supra* n. 380. See Danilenko, *supra* n. 6, at 177; Vitanyi, *supra* n. 379, at 113; Zemanek, *supra* n. 99, Chapter 1, at 402. See, in agreement with this view, American Law Institute, *supra* n. 9, at 28, §102, Comment l and 34, §102, Reporter's Notes, para. 7.
391 For examples see Brownlie, *supra* n. 17, at 17–18; Dixon, *supra* n. 75, Chapter 1, at 41; Pellet, *supra* n. 7, Chapter 1, at 836, para. 260; Shaw, *supra* n. 88, Chapter 1, at 71–75.
392 See Brownlie, *supra* n. 17, at 25–26; Dixon, *supra* n. 75, Chapter 1, at 42; Shaw, *supra* n. 88, Chapter 1, at 75–77.
393 See, *e.g.*, *International Status of South-West Africa*, Advisory Opinion of 11 July 1950, Separate Opinion by Sir Arnold McNair, ICJ Reports 1950, p. 146, at

The wording of Article 21(1)(c) ROME STATUTE, "general principles of law derived by the Court from national laws of legal systems of the world including, as appropriate, the national laws of States that would normally exercise jurisdiction over the crime, provided that those principles are not inconsistent with this Statute and with international law and internationally recognized norms and standards", seems to favor the comparative law approach,[394] if one were to acknowledge it as a form of subsequent appraisal of Article 38(1)(c) of the STATUTE OF THE INTERNATIONAL COURT OF JUSTICE.

However, similarly to the practice of the Permanent Court of International Justice and the International Court of Justice with regard to customary international law, it is hard to find any serious attempt at establishing that a general principle of law is in fact recognized within the principal legal systems of the world.[395]

Some have argued that general principles of law may be viewed as customary international law without the element of state practice.[396] However, this goes past

148–153. For further examples see Brownlie, *supra* n. 17, at 17–18; Dixon, *supra* n. 75, Chapter 1, at 41; Shaw, *supra* n. 88, Chapter 1, at 78. For an extensive, though not exclusive, enumeration of general principles of law see the – outdated but still standard – treatise on the topic by Cheng, *supra* n. 380, *passim*. For an equally seminal account see also Lauterpacht, 'Private Law Sources and Analogies of International Law', *supra* n. 380, Parts II and III. Note that both of these works, of course, also list a broad range of procedural and administrative general principles.

394 See Cassese, *supra* n. 29, at 193; Thirlway, *supra* n. 8, at 109, fn. 37.

395 See Sørensen, *supra* n. 46, at 18:

> On a fait observer, que dans les nombreux cas où cette méthode a été employé on cherche en vain, dans les avis des juges s'est assuré que le principe invoqué était effectivement un principe reconnu par les nations civilisées. Dans les divers cas, les textes des décisions laissent l'impression que le juge s'est basé sur son intuition, probablement inspirée par le ou les systèmes juridiques aves lesquels il était familier.

396 See, *e.g.*, Petersen, *supra* n. 141, Chapter 1, at 292:

> In order to rationalize the legal discourse, the requirement "as recognized by civilized nations" has been introduced. Only those natural law principles that have been widely recognized by the international community as such should enter into legal discourse. The recognition requirement thus already shows that general principles do not necessarily have to be derived from natural law maxims. They rather refer to the implicit consensus of the international community. They are thus distinct from customary international law insofar as they do not require the proof of state practice. The existence of an opinio juris is thus sufficient to establish general principles. This implicit state consensus can be identified by referring to not directly binding declarations of a considerable part of the international community. Such expressions of an opinio juris may be found in resolutions of the U.N. General Assembly or declarations of other representative international bodies and organs. Further, the preambles of multilateral treaties, which are not directly legally binding, may indicate the existence of general principles.

both the considerations within the Committee of Jurists and any credible reading of the wording of Article 38(1) of the STATUTE OF THE INTERNATIONAL COURT OF JUSTICE. If one chose to understand general principles of law in such a way, Article 38(1)(b) would, in effect, become obsolete, which is not a desirable outcome under the interpretative principle *ut res magis valeat quam pereat.*

b Natural Law

On the other side of the spectrum stands the view represented by Baron Descamps, which was later promoted by Alfred Verdross.[397] It was also embraced by Judge Tanaka in his dissenting opinion to the *South West Africa Cases.*[398]

However, it has been held that even if such natural law principles should apply, they would "have to be 'legalized' by their incorporation into the legal systems of States".[399] As Robert Jennings points out, "the intention of Root's formulation of para. (c) was to limit discretion of Judges, lest they be tempted to impose subjective notions of justice".[400]

3 Excursus: "Civilized Nations"

The subordinate clause "recognized by civilized nations"[401] is particularly controversial.[402] The common consensus seems to be that it has since become "irrelevant and can be ignored",[403] "is nowadays entirely devoid of any particular meaning",[404] or is at least now "out of place"[405] and "inappropriate".[406] In Dixon's assessment "possibly this was meant to exclude consideration of 'primitive' or 'underdeveloped' legal systems, rather than being a reference to the economic or political status of different countries".[407] Sørenson writes that with the establishment of the United Nations as a universal organization, this distinction has become irrelevant.[408] However, it must not necessarily be

397 See *supra* n. 382.
398 See *South West Africa Cases* (Ethiopia *v.* South Africa; Liberia *v.* South Africa), Dissenting Opinion of Judge Tanaka, ICJ Reports 1966, p. 250, at 294–300; Schachter, *supra* n. 211, at 13 / 7.
399 Pellet, *supra* n. 7, at 835, para. 257.
400 Jennings, *supra* n. 249, at 71 / 39. See with regard to this also Sørensen, *supra* n. 6, at 33.
401 Article 38(1)(c) of the STATUTE OF THE INTERNATIONAL COURT OF JUSTICE.
402 See the particularly fervent criticism of Judge Ammoun in his separate opinion, *North Sea Continental Shelf Cases* (Federal Republic of Germany *v.* Denmark/ Federal Republic of Germany *v.* Netherlands), Separate Opinion of Judge Fouad Ammoun, ICJ Reports 1969, p. 101, at 133–135, para. 33. See also Danilenko, *supra* n. 6, at 177; Vitanyi, *supra* n. 379, at 54–55.
403 Dixon, *supra* n. 75, Chapter 1, at 40.
404 Pellet, *supra* n. 7, at 836–837, para. 261.
405 Thirlway, *supra* n. 8, at 109.
406 Yee, *supra* n. 275, at 23.
407 Dixon, *supra* n. 75, Chapter 1, at 40.
408 See Sørensen, *supra* n. 46, at 20.

viewed as a relic of the idea of colonial superiority. Maarten Bos points out that the term may simply be seen as an expression of "idealism which animated Baron Descamps".[409] Instead of feeling snubbed by the term, one could breathe life into it and see it as a normative safeguard.[410]

4 Assessment

It is really quite impossible to come up with a definitive assessment of general principles of law. As opposed to what Ian Brownlie had to say about *ius cogens*, that "the vehicle does not often leave the garage",[411] they leave the garage quite a lot. But neither the Permanent Court of International Justice nor the International Court of Justice have been willing to stick a label on such instances. The terminological difficulties could just as easily lead to the

409 Bos, *supra* n. 379, at 42.

410 See Ernst-Ulrich Petersmann, 'Constitutionalism and International Adjudication: How to Constitutionalize the U.N. Dispute Settlement System?', 31 *New York University Journal of International Law and Politics* (1998–1999) 785, arguing that the International Court of Justice should apply "the general principles of international law in light of the human rights jurisprudence of international human rights courts and the U.N. human rights bodies". See also Tomuschat, *supra* n. 127, Chapter 1, at 319:

> What matters are the principles recognized by all those States that seek to abide by standards of civilization respecting human dignity. In sum, the qualification "civilized" is an essential screening element which permits distinctions between States, departing from formalistic reliance on sovereign equality. Unfortunately, it is a fact of life that a State machinery, usurped by a gang of unscrupulous politicians, can turn into an instrument of crime, both internally and externally. According to the law as it stands, even such a State does not forfeit automatically all of its rights under international law. But its legal régime and practice must be left out of consideration in determining the foundations of the international community, translated into legal substance by Article 38 (1) (c) of the ICJ Statute. It is therefore utterly wrong to state that under the auspices of the Charter of the United Nations every State must be acknowledged as a civilized nation.

The subordinate clause could function, for example, to bar rules such as deriving from Islamic *sharia* law that entail cruel, inhuman or degrading punishment, or gross gender inequality from evolving into general principles at the international level. As Max Sørenson points out, general principles may naturally also derive from this body of law. See *id., supra* n. 46, at 22. With regard to the same issue in connection with the similar Article 21(1)(c) of the ROME STATUTE see Beham, *supra* n. 160, Chapter 1, at 359–361. For the wording of Article 21(1)(c) of the ROME STATUTE see *supra* n. 380. Vladimir-Djuro Degan has suggested that the subordinate clause "civilized nations" could be applied as a bar in contexts such as the historical example of a state embracing a national-socialist legal system. See *id., supra* n. 366, at 55–56.

411 See Ian Brownlie, 'Discussion', in Antonio Cassese and Joseph H. H. Weiler (eds), *Change and Stability in International Law Making* (European University Institute, Series A; Berlin Walter de Gruyter, 1988) 110.

assumption that the courts were referring to some other manifestations of international law.

Scholarly appraisals have been equally discouraging about the general principles of law, considering them subsidiary to both treaties and customary international law, mere gap fillers to prevent *non liquet* situations. Others have denied their existence as an autonomous source of international law.

Even if they are looked upon favorably, what kind of manifestation of law should we see in them? Those arrived at through a comparative assessment of the major legal systems of the world or those derived from natural law? In light of the above elaborations, the mainstream view seems to be that they are drawn from the *forum domesticum*. Resort to general principles for the minimum standards of equity and procedure present within the principal legal systems of the world seems credible, while it is hard to imagine how general principles could represent a dignified substitute as a basis of obligation for other substantive rules of international law. Surely, the principle of good faith can be seen as an uncontroversial example of a general principle of law.

3 Morality and State Interest

Having conveyed an understanding of the non-treaty sources of international law, it is now time to discuss whether they might, indeed, be suitable vehicles for the pursuit of normative projects. After all, are the practice and *opinio iuris* of a state or its domestic legal regime not inherently connected to its interests? If that is the case, the question turns to whether legal rules based on moral concepts, creating "altruistic obligations", will likely manifest themselves in these non-treaty sources.

A Defining Morality and Legality

1 Morality

Before determining whether legality and morality coincide, one must first answer the following question: What do we mean by the term "morality"? *The Stanford Encyclopedia of Philosophy* defines it as being used either:

> 1 descriptively to refer to some codes of conduct put forward by a society or, a. some other group, such as a religion, or b. accepted by an individual for her own behavior, or
> 2 normatively to refer to a code of conduct that, given specified conditions, would be put forward by all rational persons.[1]

It is, of course, the latter definition that human rights scholars think of, when they talk of human rights as an expression of universal values as put forward in the "Vienna Declaration and Programme of Action" of 1993,[2] and which underlies ideas such as "humanitarian intervention" or the "responsibility to protect".[3] Morality is the determination of what is right and proper, the search

1 Bernard Gert, 'The Definition of Morality', in: Edward N. Zalta (ed.), *The Stanford Encyclopedia of Philosophy* (Fall 2012 Edition) <http://plato.stanford.edu/archives/fall2012/entries/morality-definition/>.
2 See *supra* n. 147, Chapter 1.
3 See Venzke and von Bernstorff, *supra* n. 38, Chapter 1, at para. 2.

for good – or it may be defined, in the sense of "critical morality", as "propositions asserted as objective truth".[4]

The first of the above definitions is more appealing to cultural relativists.[5] The possibility of a descriptive use of the term entails that morality may indeed differ from society to society, "the morality of a social group".[6] Such "conventional morality" simply "consists of propositions supported by social consensus".[7] While this definition is not useful for the purpose of the present argument, it should be kept in mind to understand such issues as related to the aspiration of universal application of treaties as an argument for the existence of customary international human rights law.[8] Linguistic nuances in reservations or interpretative declarations, ever so small as they might be, differ between states.[9]

In addition, morality may be distinguished as to its application in international relations theory. Here, morality may also, more generally, mean the overall assessment of ethical decision-making. For example, the school of realism considers "prudence – the weighing of the consequences of alternative political actions – to be the supreme virtue in politics".[10]

Throughout this book, the term morality is and has been used in its normative sense, the determination of what is right and proper, the search for good.[11]

2 *Legality*

It cannot be the place here to repeat and mull over philosophical foundations of law from Aristotle to Marx or the multitude of theories of compliance with regard to international law.[12] For the present purpose, it will be sufficient to hold that "legality" relates to the observance of what is formally "law". According to the definition of the *Concise Oxford English Dictionary*, "law" is "a rule or system of rules recognized by a country or community as regulating the actions of its members and enforced by the imposition of penalties", "something regarded as having binding force or effect". More inclusive definitions, such as that of Steven Shavell, describe "law" as "the rules that are

4 George P. Fletcher, 'Law and Morality: A Kantian Perspective', 87/3 *Columbia Law Review* (1987) 533.
5 See *supra* n. 149, Chapter 1. See on this also Roberts, *supra* n. 73, Chapter 1, at 762.
6 Neil Cooper, 'Two Concepts of Morality', 41/155 *Philosophy* (1966) 19. See further *ibid. et seq.*
7 Fletcher, *supra* n. 4, at 533.
8 See Kadens and Young, *supra* n. 185, Chapter 1, at 910.
9 See *supra* ns 160–161, Chapter 1, and pp. 74 *et seq.*
10 Morgenthau and Thompson, *supra* n. 64, Chapter 2, at 12.
11 See on this also Steven Shavell, 'Law Versus Morality as Regulators of Conduct', 4/2 *American Law and Economics Review* (2002) 231.
12 For an overview of the latter see Burgstaller, *supra* n. 108, Chapter 1.

determined and enforced by the state and that are intended to channel behavior and resolve certain adverse events".[13]

The functioning of the international legal system illustrates, however, that any differentiation between morality and legality attached to the aspect of enforceability can only insufficiently grasp the entire scope of the issue whether morality, those actions that are right and proper, corresponds with legality, that which is binding in the sense of a unified – Aquinian – "moral law".

3 Two Planes

When John Austin considered international law as "positive international morality", he did so only to distinguish it from "actual" law in that it lacks enforcement by "a given sovereign to a person or persons in a state of subjection to its author",[14] not to claim that "international legality" corresponded with an "international morality" in the sense of the above differentiation between the two planes.

Kant held that all rules contain two elements: first, an obligation making the intended act objectively necessary and secondly, an inner motivation – a "*Triebfeder*" – to follow such a rule.[15] Thereby, he differentiated between two possible kinds of rules: The rule, which makes an act an obligation and where, at the same time, that obligation constitutes the motivation to follow it, is "ethical" ("*ethisch*").[16] The rule, however, which makes an act an obligation but does not comprise the motivation to follow it or might even allow for a motivation other than the idea of the obligation itself, is "juridical" ("*juridisch*").[17] Compliance with the former kind of rules is what Kant called "morality", "*Moralität (Sittlichkeit)*".[18] Compliance with the latter kind of rules is what he called "legality", "*Legalität (Gesetzmäßigkeit)*".

In the latter case, the idea that the rule is binding may in itself constitute sufficient motivation for compliance.[19] Morality by itself, however, only creates an inner obligation for an actor.[20] Hence, the differentiation between the two planes springs from the respective inner motivation for compliance.[21] In this

13 Shavell, *supra* n. 11, at 229.
14 See John Austin, *The Province of Jurisprudence Determined* (London: John Murray, 1832) 207–224.
15 See Immanuel Kant, *Die Metaphysik der Sitten. Erster Theil. Metaphysische Anfangsgründe der Rechtslehre*, 2nd edn (Königsberg: Friedrich Nicolovius, 1798) XIII-XIV.
16 *Ibid.*, at XIV.
17 *Ibid.*, at XIV–XV.
18 *Ibid.*, at XV.
19 *Ibid.*, at XVI.
20 *Ibid.*, at XVII–XVIII. See also Ulrich Fastenrath, *Lücken im Völkerrecht. Zu Rechtscharakter, Quellen, Systemzusammenhang, Methodenlehre und Funktionen des Völkerrechts* (Schriften zum Völkerrecht, Band 93; Berlin: Duncker & Humblot, 1991) 46.
21 See Fastenrath, *ibid.*, at 153.

understanding, "individual moral intuitions" cannot "replace a formal approach to legality".[22] In order for a moral obligation to become externally applicable, it must be cast into positive legal form.

Hans Kelsen viewed morality and legality as stemming from two – to use his own terminology – individual "sources", two different "oughts",[23] or "two different realms of normative thought",[24] a fact that has often been overlooked,[25] purposely or not.

In the sphere of international law, this would mean that a "moral law" must manifest itself as either treaty, customary international law, or general principle of law for it to constitute – for lack of a better term but illustrating quite clearly the two distinctive planes – "legal law".[26] As David Kennedy argues,

> [n]orms are legally binding which fit within one of a series of doctrinally elaborated categories, not when a persuasive argument about political interest or theoretical coherence can be made for their observance.[27]

"Real international law" is the sum of obligations based either in treaty or non-treaty law.[28] Thereby, moral concepts may indeed become international law, once they have morphed into either a treaty provision, a rule of customary international law, or a general principle of law. Unless this process can be inductively demonstrated, these moral concepts remain what they inherently are: ethical proclamations.[29]

This differentiation between morality and legality, *i.e.* normative and prescriptive rules, familiar to any practitioner of domestic law, also explicitly found its appreciation in contemporary international law (for the differentiation was already present in the works of Francisco Suárez and Hugo Grotius[30]) through the *South West Africa Cases* before the International Court of Justice:

> Throughout this case it has been suggested, directly or indirectly, that humanitarian considerations are sufficient in themselves to generate legal rights and obligations, and that the Court can and should proceed accordingly. The Court does not think so. It is a court of law, and can take account of moral principles only in so far as these are given a sufficient

22 Venzke and von Bernstorff, *supra* n. 38, Chapter 1, at para. 5.
23 Kelsen, *supra* n. 5, Chapter 2, at 107.
24 See Fletcher, *supra* n. 4 at 543.
25 See *ibid.*
26 See *supra* pp. 52 *et seq.*
27 David Kennedy, 'The Sources of International Law', 2/1 *American University International Law Review* (1987) 88.
28 See Funck-Brentano and Sorel, *supra* n. 3, Chapter 1, at 3.
29 See Georg Schwarzenberger, *Civitas Maxima?* (Recht und Staat in Geschichte und Gegenwart, Vols 413/414; Tübingen: J.C.B. Mohr [Paul Siebeck], 1973) 21.
30 See Fastenrath, *supra* n. 20, at 20.

> expression in legal form. Law exists, it is said, to serve a social need; but precisely for that reason it can do so only through and within the limits of its own discipline. Otherwise, it is not a legal service that would be rendered.
>
> Humanitarian considerations may constitute the inspirational basis for rules of law, just as, for instance, the preambular parts of the United Nations Charter constitute the moral and political basis for the specific legal provisions thereafter set out. Such considerations do not, however, in themselves amount to rules of law. All States are interested – have an interest – in such matters. But the existence of an "interest" does not of itself entail that this interest is specifically juridical in character.[31]

Somewhat surprisingly, in light of the normative turn,[32] this view still remains part of the canon of standard international law textbooks,[33] even though the case is controversially discussed for a variety of other reasons.[34]

The distinction between the two planes of morality and legality needs to be kept in mind when seeking to identify the legal *status quo* in international law, particularly with regard to its non-treaty sources. There might be "no Rubicon between morality and law in the real world of affairs" but "there is a fairly well-defined swampy area that should be shown on the map as dangerous".[35] Amidst the rushes lie moral concepts.

4 Moral Concepts

The term "moral concepts" has been chosen to refer to ideas, not necessarily rules, that are grounded in the sphere of morality; what is considered right and proper, as opposed to what is merely "legal". Of course, moral concepts may be or become legal, granted they have passed through either one of the processes of formation of international law. What distinguishes these ideas in the transposition into law, is that the primary motivation to do so is the urge to do good. Oftentimes, they appear in the form of normative projects of an epistemic community such as, here, international lawyers.

31 *South West Africa Cases* (Ethiopia *v.* South Africa; Liberia *v.* South Africa), Judgment of 18 July 1966 (Second Phase), ICJ Reports 1966, p. 6, at 34, paras 49–50. This differentiation was not even disputed by the large number of separate and dissenting opinions to the judgment. See, in particular, the explicit acknowledgement of the existence of such a distinction in the Dissenting Opinion of Vice-President Wellington Koo, ICJ Reports 1966, p. 216, at 228, and the Dissenting Opinion of Judge Jessup, ICJ Reports 1966, p. 325, at 441.

32 See *supra* n. 66, Chapter 1, and accompanying text.

33 See, *e.g.*, Dixon, *supra* n. 75, Chapter 1, at 5 and 342.

34 See, *inter alia*, Victor Kattan, 'Decolonizing the International Court of Justice: The Experience of Judge Sir Muhammad Zafrulla Khan in the South West Africa Cases', 4 *Asian Journal of International* (2014) 1-46.

35 Rubin, *supra* n. 198, Chapter 1, at 192.

a Human Rights

Human rights serve as an archetypical example of moral concepts. For one, they are unquestionably related to ideas of natural law,[36] *a priori* evident from rational deduction,[37] not originally positive law but values which may and should be made positive law,[38] universally applicable,[39] "closely allied with ethics and morality",[40] and proposed to arise from the "conscience" of the international community.[41]

These attributes are what make such a strong case for the *droits-de-l'hommistes*, the "human rightists", as Alain Pellet called the "lobbyist" fraction of human rights scholars.[42] However, these attributes will also apply to a number of other ideas in international law that trace their roots to natural law. The difference is, however, that international human rights are based on a primarily altruistic impulse.[43] "Pure" international human rights law is not necessarily paired with other state interests or reciprocal pay-offs. The whole idea behind the concept is that states concede power to the individual by shielding the latter's rights from their own purview.

b Altruism

The *Concise Oxford English Dictionary* defines "altruism" as either "selfless concern for the well-being of others" or, in the behavioral sense, which seems even more relevant to the present argument, as "behaviour of an animal that benefits another at its own expense". This is exactly what the animal we call "state" does with regard to human rights. It limits its own power for the

36 See Dixon, *supra* n. 75, Chapter 1, at 341.

37 See Kant's categorical imperative, *e.g.*, in §7 of his *Critic der practischen Vernunft*, 2nd edn (Riga: Johann Friedrich Hartknoch, 1792) 54, or Cicero's *vera lex*. See Marcus Tullius Cicero, *De Re Publica. Tertius Liber*, 33.

38 See Christian M. Stadler, 'Rechtsethische Aspekte des Internationalen Militäreinsatzes', in Erich Reiter (ed.), *Der Krieg um das Kosovo 1998/99* (Mainz: v. Hase & Koehler, 2000) 183.

39 See Alston and Goodman, *supra* n. 188, Chapter 2, at 145 and as opposed to cultural relativism at 351 *et seq.*

40 Shaw, *supra* n. 88, Chapter 1, at 195.

41 See General Assembly Resolution 217/A (III), 'Universal Declaration of Human Rights', U.N. Doc. A/RES/3/217A (10 December 1948), Preamble. See also, with regard to the emergence of *ius cogens*, Cassese, *supra* n. 29, Chapter 2, at 160–161, with regard to the Martens Clause; Thomas Weatherall, *Jus Cogens. International Law and Social Contract* (Cambridge: Cambridge University Press, 2015).

42 See, *supra* ns 157–158, Chapter 1.

43 Of course, the proto-human rights field of diplomatic protection and, in further development, investment treaty law inherently carry altruistic elements or, at least, effects that benefit the individual (or corporation). The same applies to humanitarian law. Aside from other political and economic interests of the state in such affairs, there are individuals and investors that benefit from the legal processes by receiving diplomatic protection or compensation.

benefit of the individual. Hence, it is fair to speak of human rights not just as moral concepts but as altruistic obligations.

Therefore, while the protection of human rights may seem a more desirable and noble normative endeavor than not interfering with the inviolability of the premises of a diplomatic mission,[44] in the terminology of Joseph Raz, the latter exclusionary reason, by matter of reciprocity, complies with the "first-order reason" of the state. That is not always necessarily the case with moral concepts.

c Sovereignty

Many "first generation" human rights – freedom of association, freedom of speech, protection of privacy, and protection of property, just to name a few – aim to restrict the state in its ability to take action, whereas economic, social, and cultural rights even require some form of affirmative action from states.[45] What interests would states have in practising self-restraint or indulging their citizens? In international human rights law, the concern goes beyond even this state-citizen relationship. After all, "the international protection of human rights necessarily implies a limitation of sovereignty".[46]

The disparity of underlying interests is most visible, where broad concessions have been made, as in the case of the EUROPEAN CONVENTION OF HUMAN RIGHTS. A number of member states of the Council of Europe continue to express dissatisfaction with the jurisprudence of the European Court of Human Rights[47]

44 Prominent examples of this rule being upheld in a balancing situation include, *inter alia*, the diplomatic asylum of Julian Assange in the Ecuadorian embassy in London in 2012, the shooting of Yvonne Fletcher from the Libyan embassy in London in 1984, or the diplomatic asylum of Víctor Raúl Haya de la Torre in the Colombian embassy in Lima in 1948. For the latter see *Colombian-Peruvian Asylum Case* (Colombia *v.* Peru), Judgment of 20 November 1950, ICJ Reports 1950, p. 266, *passim*. The most prominent exception is the Tehran hostage situation of 1979–1981. See *Case Concerning United States Diplomatic and Consular Staff in Tehran* (United States of America *v.* Iran), Judgment of 24 May 1980, ICJ Reports 1980, p. 3.

45 See Hélène Ruiz Fabri, 'Human Rights and State Sovereignty: Have the Boundaries Been Significantly Redrawn?' in Alston and MacDonald (eds), *supra* n. 174, Chapter 1, at 38.

46 *Ibid.*, at 40.

47 See, most recently, on the attitude of the government of the United Kingdom, Philippe Sands, 'The Government is Playing a Dangerous Game Trying to Scrap the Human Rights Act', *The Guardian* (21 October 2015) <www.theguardian.com/commentisfree/2015/oct/21/government-human-rights-act-legal-europe-uk>; Jessica Elgot, 'British Judges not Bound by European Court of Human Rights, Says Leveson', *The Guardian* (24 May 2015) <www.theguardian.com/law/2015/may/24/british-courts-echr-leveson>; and, generally, Jon Henley, 'Why is the European Court of Human Rights Hated by the UK Right?', *The Guardian* (22 December 2013) <www.theguardian.com/law/2013/dec/22/britain-european- court-human-rights>. See Pierre-Henri Imbert, 'L'Utilisation des Droits de l'Homme Dans les Relations Internationales', in Société Française pour le Droit International (ed.),

and have refused to execute its judgments,[48] although they are undoubtedly under a legal treaty obligation to do so. Still, it is not law derived from a sense of self-interest or reciprocal compliance;[49] and the reasons for discomfort are not the treaty obligations alone but their dynamic interpretation by the European Court.

Of course, states may also show similar behavior towards other areas of law, such as immunities or economic barriers. However, the character of these legal obligations is a different one, as more often than not, again following Joseph Raz, the "first-order reason" for compliance will correspond with the exclusionary rule.[50]

B State Interest

This leads to the follow-up question: What are these supposed state interests?[51] As political scientist Joseph Frankel wrote in his seminal work on the subject, "no agreement can be reached about its ultimate meaning",[52] but an approximation will hopefully be possible. In any case, irrespective thereof, it is undoubtedly an important factor in the decision-making of political stakeholders,[53] best reflected in the anecdotal quotes of Charles De Gaulle and Henry Kissinger that their respective states had "no friends" but "only interests".

1 States

Every student of international law knows that the "primary subjects"[54] of international law and "by far the most important legal persons"[55] consist of a permanent population, a defined territory, and a government.[56] In addition,

Colloque de Strasbourg. La Protection des Droits de l'Homme et l'Évolution du Droit International (Paris: Éditions A. Pedone, 1998) 283.

48 For example, Turkey. See Tulay Karadeniz and Ece Toksabay, 'Turkey to Ignore Court Order to pay Compensation to Cyprus', *Reuters* (13 May 2014) <www.reuters.com/article/us-turkey-cyprus-davutoglu-idUSBREA4C0AX20140513>.

49 Fabri, *supra* n. 45, at 64. Cf., however, also *ibid*., at 71. See also *supra* pp. 26 *et seq*.

50 See *supra* n. 194, Chapter 1, and accompanying text.

51 It is understood here in the abstract sense of the term, as opposed to specific interests of a state within a specific constellation as it is used, *e.g*., in the analysis of "permanent interests" by Georg Schwarzenberger, *Power Politics: A Study of World Society*, 3rd edn (London: Stevens & Sons, 1964) 44–51. It goes without saying that it is not restricted to mere legal interest either. For a general caveat on the use and usefulness of the term "state interest" see Simma, *supra* n. 9, Chapter 1, at 75–77.

52 Frankel, *supra* n. 91, Chapter 1, at 15.

53 See *ibid*., at 18.

54 Cassese, *supra* n. 29, Chapter 2, at 71.

55 Shaw, *supra* n. 88, Chapter 1, at 143.

56 See Article 1 of the CONVENTION ON THE RIGHTS AND DUTIES OF STATES (1933). See also Brownlie, *supra* n. 17, Chapter 2, at 70–71; Dixon, *supra* n. 75, Chapter 1, at 115; Jennings and Watts, *supra* n. 51, Chapter 2, at 120, § 33;

Article 1 of the MONTEVIDEO CONVENTION requires that these entities possess the "capacity to enter into relations with the other states".[57]

This catalogue inherently contains the banal assumption that state and government are not identical, and states may even continue to exist under international law irrespective of an effective government.[58] At the same time, this complicates any further study of the matter, as it is the government that acts on behalf of the state. To a large extent, therefore, the state will be perceived through the acts and omissions of the respective government, its state officials, and so forth. The abstract entity of the state does not "act" out of its own capacity.

However, while states require individuals to take action on their behalf, these "do not act on their own account but as State officials, as the tools of the structures to which they belong",[59] a view that is further reflected in the rules of attribution in the International Law Commission's Articles on State Responsibility.[60] The state organs are limited by the framework that is the respective state, even if this is little more than the collectivity of individual decisions. Its economy, social structure, and cultural heritage will largely determine what is opportune.

Still, the definition of the state is tainted by the fact that individuals act on its behalf. The way it is externally perceived is shaped by its successive governments. Yet this is little different from the way that multi- or transnational corporations such as Walmart, Royal Dutch Shell, or ExxonMobil are perceived against the background of a change in the board of directors. Only in extreme situations such as a revolution, is it likely that states entirely change their character on the initiative of a government or other persons or groups of persons exercising authority. States, as all other juridical persons, are legal fictions to express the idea that individuals may come together to create an entity that pursues goals not necessarily representing their own and vice-versa.

Shaw, *supra* n. 88, Chapter 1, at 144. See for further elaborations Jennings and Watts, *ibid.*, at 121–122, § 34; Hans Kelsen, 'Recognition in International Law: Theoretical Observations', 35/4 *American Journal of International Law* (1941) 607–608. See also American Law Institute, *supra* n. 9, Chapter 2, at 72, §201:

> State Defined. Under international law, a state is an entity that has a defined territory and a permanent population, under the control of its own government, and that engages in, or has the capacity to engage in, formal relations with other such entities.

57 CONVENTION ON THE RIGHTS AND DUTIES OF STATES (1933). It has also been pointed out that compliance with human rights is not part of the catalogue of formal criteria used to identify what a state is, although this seems obvious as this would fall more within the sphere of the acting government than what makes the abstract entity that is the state. See, *e.g.*, Irene Etzersdorfer and Ralph Janik, *Staat, Krieg und Schutzverantwortung. Militärische Interventionen im Namen fundamentaler Menschenrechte aus staatstheoretischer und völkerrechtlicher Perspektive* (Vienna: Facultas, 2016) 61.

58 See Brownlie, *supra* n. 17, Chapter 2, at 71; Dixon, *supra* n. 76, Chapter 1, at 116.

59 Cassese, *supra* n. 29, Chapter 2, at 4.

60 See the Draft Articles on Responsibility of States for Internationally Wrongful Acts, *supra* n. 77, Chapter 1.

Therefore, it is important to differentiate between the state, its organs, and its population in making any determinations as to its character. Brierly defined the state exactly along these lines as "a system of relations which men establish among themselves as a means of securing certain objects, of which the most fundamental is a system of order within which their activities can be carried on". At the same time, he cautioned that the state "should not be confused with the whole community of persons living on its territory", as "it is only one among a multitude of other institutions, such as churches and corporations, which a community established for securing different objects".[61]

2 Interest

In the introduction to his standard textbook on international law, Cassese wrote that states

> are legal entities, aggregates of human beings dominated by an apparatus that wields authority over them. Their general goals are quite distinct from the goals of each individual or group.[62]

The term "interest" derives from the Latin *interesse*, which carries the meaning "to differ" or "to make a difference". The interest is something that makes a difference to someone – or, if speaking of a juridical entity, something.[63]

Some writers have gone as far as to argue that states are not capable of holding such interests, "as if artificial entities could have discernible motivations".[64] However, this position overlooks the idea of statehood as represented through the collective of individual organs.

Just as what makes a difference for an individual does not necessarily make a difference for a corporation, it does not necessarily make a difference for a state.[65] Each entity, the natural as well as the juridical person, carries distinct goals and purposes. Some may correlate, some may differ. It is the nature of the actor that determines the interest.

While an educated humanist may naturally align with what is morally opportune, states are abstract entities to which human rights are what "corporate social responsibility" is to the corporation. Such programs may be

61 Brierly, *supra* n. 169, Chapter 2, at 126.

62 Cassese, *supra* n. 29, Chapter 2, at 3. Contrary Jennings and Watts, *supra* n. 51, Chapter 2, at 51–52, § 17, stating that "the duties and rights of states are only the duties and rights of the people who compose them".

63 Of course, in discussing these issues, one is always confronted with the problem of anthropomorphization of states. See Frankel, *supra* n. 91, Chapter 1, at 115: "More generally, the tendency to personalize the state and to compare its goals and needs with those of the individuals, if pushed too far, inevitably leads to confusion".

64 D'Amato, *supra* n. 8, Chapter 2, at 271.

65 Kritsiotis sarcastically refers to this construction of states as "corporate Hobbesian offspring". See Dino Kritsiotis, 'Reappraising Policy Objections to Humanitarian Intervention', 19 *Michigan Journal of International Law* (1997–1998) 1034.

implemented, as many practical examples show, but one certainly does not arrive at the concept of "corporate social responsibility" by an inductive analysis of a corporation.[66]

3 Interests of States

The expression "state interest" or "national interest", as it is sometimes found in the literature, confers the idea that there must be a common set of factors that are important to the existence of the abstract entity of the state. As it is mostly states that create international law, state interests are also determinative to this process. The idea that law formation is governed by the interplay of these interests is not new. Carl Schmitt already argued that public international law in the nineteenth century rested less on ideas of sovereignty and rather on a selection of specific state interests.[67] So what are these interests?

a Survival of the State

As has been pointed out, the state as an actor in international law and, generally, in international relations is tainted by the fact that individuals act on its behalf. Its organs or other persons or groups of persons exercise governmental authority that results in state practice. In turn, these acts are limited by the framework of the economy, social structure, and cultural heritage of a state. Thus, states may weigh their interests differently and in accordance with additional factors such as ideology, be it liberal democracy, socialism, or some pan-territorial or ethnic component.[68]

What then are the lowest common denominating factors that determine how states will act? Gerhard Hafner identified five traditional areas of state interest: "the protection of statehood, territorial integrity, sovereignty, security and economic wealth".[69] Nicholas Onuf speaks, after Hobbes, of "standing, security, and wealth".[70]

66 See Shavell, *supra* n. 11, at 242–243.
67 See Carl Schmitt, *Der Begriff des Politischen. Text von 1932 mit einem Vorwort und drei Corollarien* (Berlin: Duncker & Humblot, 1963) 115.
68 What Yadh Ben Achour calls "civilisation", giving the state "its cohesive spiritual power, its ideology" [translation by the present author]. See *id., supra* n. 360, Chapter 2, at 19.
69 Hafner, *supra* n. 75, Chapter 1, at 29. He goes on:

> Under the traditional perspective, international law generated by states had to reflect a behaviour of states that was deemed to be reasonable. Such reasonable state conduct was expected to be motivated by the intention of maximising power, comparable with the REM hypothesis, *i.e.*, the conduct of a rational, egoistic and maximising man.

See *ibid.*
70 Onuf, *supra* n. 44, Chapter 1, at 258–279.

Undoubtedly, Austria, China, and Israel each have a different understanding of statehood, territorial integrity, and national security. For sure, they rely on different models to accumulate economic wealth. Each has a particular conception of its "standing". However, these differences in ideology that stem from historical developments and the resulting economic, social, and cultural structures do not change the common parameters.

Following the areas of state interest pointed out by Hafner, these can be generalized as two principal considerations: first, national security, comprising the protection of statehood, territorial integrity, as well as sovereignty, and, second, a functioning economy. Recalling the definition of what constitutes a state, these "traditional" interests are inextricably linked to its "survival".[71]

In a sense, to anthropomorphize states once more, this "survival instinct" feature is not so different from that of individuals. The latter are equally interested in escaping the Hobbesian *bellum omnium contra omnes* before all else. The social contract that allows for this escape wants to be upheld. Thereby, state interest is equated with the survival of the state. It stands at the heart of international relations.[72]

The issue – and, thereby, an answer to the main question of this book – is whether this state interest and the survival of the state comprise moral considerations concerning the well-being of individuals. Do moral concepts fall within the scope of state interest?

b Democratization and State Interest

The primary structural argument that has been made to place the interests of the individual and, thereby, moral concepts within the ambit of state interest, has been the alleged world-wide democratization of states.[73] Supposedly, by electing its government, the individual and its respective interests are directly represented by the state. However, this argument – while attractive to any educated humanist – does not hold closer scrutiny for two reasons:

71 See *supra* p. 121–122. See also Frankel, *supra* n. 91, Chapter 1, at 131–132; Onuf, *ibid.*, at 278. See on this notion in jurisprudence also *Legality of the Threat or Use of Nuclear Weapons*, Advisory Opinion of 8 July 1996, ICJ Reports 1996, p. 226, at 263, paras 96–97.

72 See also Martin Wight, 'Why is There no International Theory?', 2 *International Relations* (1960) 48: "International theory is the theory of survival". See on this notion also *Legality of the Threat or Use of Nuclear Weapons*, Advisory Opinion of 8 July 1996, ICJ Reports 1996, p. 226, at 263, paras 96–97.

73 See, *e.g.*, Hafner, *supra* n. 75, Chapter 1, at 28–29 and 36. See also D'Amato, *supra* n. 124, Chapter 1, at 104, referencing himself in fn. 13:

> Human rights interests, for example, have worked a revolutionary change upon many of the classic rules of international law as a result of the realization by states in their international practice that they have a deep interest in the way other states treat their own citizens.

First, it overlooks the fact that even in democracies, the ruling classes are mostly composed of a select elite. It is not guaranteed that they carry the same interests as a "regular" individual or, should they have promised to share them, that they will represent these interests throughout their term of office. Again, if they indeed choose to do so, the underlying interest could simply be re-election.

Second, the argument that democratization exists as a universal phenomenon does not stand to empirical scrutiny. In fact, contrary to common perception, the opposite is the case. The NGO Freedom House found in its 2015 report that there was an "overall drop in freedom for the ninth consecutive year" and "the number of countries with improvements hit its lowest point since the nine-year erosion began".[74] The extent of this development away from democratization is even more blatant when put into relation with the low number of improvements in overall democratic standards.[75]

Even in regions more attracted to the idea of electoral democracy, there is no uniform practice but rather a case-by-case basis attitude as to how far democratic values are implemented.[76] Joshua Kurlantzick, in a 2013 Foreign Policy article, observed that "as European democracy falters, old-fashioned coups are returning elsewhere". In particular, military coups, which "had become rare by the late 1990s" started to surge "between 2006 and 2012" and "where the military did not launch an outright coup, it still managed to restore its power as a central actor in political life".[77] To illustrate his point, he lists the state practice of 14 states throughout the span of seven years. Rather than aim for more democratic governance, "[i]t seems [...] that this new global middle is choosing stability over all else".[78]

Hence, there is, at least currently, no empirical evidence to support what has been called "liberal millenarianism", a term coined by Susan Marks to refer to interpretations of international law that flourished throughout the 1990s and early 2000s, alleging an element of democratic legitimacy in international law.[79]

74 Freedom House, 'Freedom in the World 2015. Discarding Democracy: Return to the Iron Fist' (2015) <https://freedomhouse.org/report/freedom-world/freedom-world-2015>.

75 See Freedom House, 'Freedom in the World 2015. Discarding Democracy: Return to the Iron Fist. Highlights From Freedom House's Annual Report on Political Rights and Civil Liberties' (2015), at 4 <https://freedomhouse.org/sites/default/files/01152015_FIW_2015_final.pdf>.

76 See David Wippman, 'Defending Democracy Through Foreign Intervention', 19 *Houston Journal of International Law* (1997) 666, fn. 51 and accompanying text. See also, generally, Markus P. Beham and Ralph R.A. Janik, 'A "Responsibility to Democratise"? The "Responsibility to Protect" in Light of Regime Change and the "Pro-Democratic" Intervention Discourse', in Richard Barnes and Vassilis Tzevelekos (eds), *Beyond Responsibility to Protect. Generating Change in International Law* (Cambridge: Intersentia, 2016) 63.

77 Joshua Kurlantzik, 'Opening Gambit: One Step Forward, Two Steps Back', *Foreign Policy* (March/April 2013) 21.

78 *Ibid.*

79 See Susan Marks, 'The "Emerging Norm": Conceptualizing "Democratic Governance"', 91 *American Society of International Law Proceedings* (1997) 373. For

Such evidence could arise, but the structural argument can simply not be verified at this point in time. It ignores the pluralism among states and the global authoritarian pull of the later millennial years.

As Euro- or "Western"-centric as the democratization argument may seem with regard to a comprehensive assessment of states, it is an equal fallacy to propose that the idea is restricted to this tradition. However, the ideology of democracy is not an inherent building block of international law.[80] It has been held that the international system as a whole "is structured so as to preclude the ideal of political equality", in particular as "citizens of strong states that are internally democratic at least have a theoretical equality of opportunity to prevail in getting their states to promote their external policy preferences", whereas those of "weak states [...] are restricted in their ability to influence global decision-making".[81] As James Crawford concluded in his seminal article on the subject, international law is "deeply undemocratic, or at least [...] capable of operating in a deeply undemocratic way".[82]

In addition to these structural considerations, it is questionable whether the protection of human rights abroad weighs as heavily as does the interest of citizens in their own personal well-being, even in states with a long-standing democratic tradition. Empirical survey data seems to suggest that international human rights protection is located at the end of the spectrum of interests of individuals, when weighed with opposing considerations of national security, for example.[83] This is equally true for governments.[84] Vice versa, Jack Donnelly even raised doubts about whether the urge towards the enjoyment of human rights is even a determinative factor in the failure of undemocratic governments, seeking the cause more in the economic collapse of such regimes.[85]

an overview of existing propositions of democracy as a value under international law see also Beham and Janik, *supra* n. 76, at 59–62.

80 See Weil, *supra* n. 35, Chapter 1, at 420: "But ideological neutrality is also necessary to guarantee the coexistence of heterogeneous entities in a pluralistic society. Both religious and ideological neutrality are inherent in the basic concept of international law".

81 Andrew Strauss, 'International Law as Democratic Law', 103 *American Society of International Law Proceedings* (2009) 389.

82 James Crawford, 'Democracy and International Law', 64 *British Yearbook of International Law* (1993) 123–125 (the article also appeared in an updated form as 'Democracy and the Body of International Law', in Gregory H. Fox and Brad R. Roth (eds), *Democratic Governance and International Law* (Cambridge: Cambridge University Press, 2000) 91–120, there at 116–117).

83 See with regard to the United States Sam McFarland and Melissa Mathews, 'Who Cares About Human Rights?', 26/3 *Political Psychology* (2005) 366–367. See also Anthony D'Amato, 'Human Rights as Part of Customary International Law: A Plea for a Change of Paradigms', 25 *Georgia Journal of International Law* (1995/1996) 80.

84 See William F. Schulz, 'Spread the Word. Organizing the Grassroots to End Atrocity Crimes', in Richard H. Cooper and Juliette Voïnov Kohler (eds), *Responsibility to Protect. The Global Moral Compact for the 21st Century* (New York: Palgrave Macmillan, 2009) 156.

85 See Donnelly, *supra* n. 41, Chapter 1, at 611.

c Pressure Upon States

The argument has also been made that "states have to include [NGOs] in their foreign policy analysis and respect their interests in the process of creating norms of international law" as a result of "the power exercised by them through the use of media and similar means".[86] However, these are means to an end:[87] The survival of states and, in this case, governments.

Hence, governments will likely set acts in the name of a state that aim at preventing civil unrest or cultivating a happy electorate. But these are, if one must call them so, "subsidiary interests" that do not necessarily show what states will do, when competing core interests of survival arise. In such cases, states will usually resort to "Realpolitik".[88] They will, generally, not compromise on their interests out of altruistic motives – in this case *vis-à-vis* states – or out of concern for public opinion.[89]

This could most recently be witnessed in the Russian decision to annex Crimea on 18 March 2014,[90] the Hungarian position in the refugee crisis as of 2015,[91] or the execution of a prominent *shi'ite* leader by Saudi Arabia at its mass execution of 2 January 2016.[92] Going even further, the Chinese view, as identified by the EU, is that raising human rights violations is simply an instrument for the destabilization of governments and a violation of the principle of non-intervention.[93]

As Efraim Halevy, former chief of Mossad, predicted in 2006 against the background of the post-9/11 global order and terrorist threat:

> The upshot of this will be that the very fundamentals of conventional international law will be swept away by the dictates of basic national survival. Governments and their senior executive officials will take action, the like of which has rarely ever been dreamed of in the past. Preemption will not

86 See Hafner, *supra* n. 75, Chapter 1, at 35. See also Paulus and Simma, *supra* n. 34, Chapter 1, at 306; Paust, *supra* n. 78, Chapter 1, at 160–161.
87 See also *infra* ns 121–122 and accompanying text.
88 See Imbert, *supra* n. 47, at 283. See also Frankel, *supra* n. 91, Chapter 1, at 154–155.
89 See Frankel, *ibid.*, at 152.
90 See Adrian Croft and Aleksandar Vasovic, 'U.S. EU set Sanctions as Putin Recognises Crimea "Sovereignty"', *Reuters* (18 March 2014) <http://in.reuters.com/article/ukraine-crisis-crimea-referendum-idINDEEA2G00620140318>.
91 See Ivana Sekularac and Krisztina Than, 'Hungary Shuts EU Border, Taking Migrant Crisis Into its own Hands', *Reuters* (16 September 2015) <http://uk.reuters.com/article/uk-europe-migrants-hungary-idUKKCN0RE2DS20150916>.
92 See Angus McDowall, 'Shi'ite Cleric Among 47 Executed in Saudi Arabia, Stirring Anger in Region', *Reuters* (2 January 2016) <www.reuters.com/article/saudi-security-idUSKBN0UG03F20160103>.
93 See European Parliament, Directorate-General for External Policies, Policy Department, 'China's Foreign Policy and External Relations' (July 2015) 8, 21, 43, and 47, para. 13 <www.europarl.europa.eu/RegData/etudes/STUD/2015/549057/EXPO_STU(2015)549057_EN.pdf>.

await U.N. Security Council resolutions or relatively long-term creations of international coalitions. I predict that there will be a concentration of measures, sometimes complementary and at other times independent, tailored to deal with a rapidly evolving situation. Legislation will create an entirely fresh set of ground rules to deal with challenges. Executive authority will be empowered to take action as seldom before. International law or custom will either bend to the change or be circumvented as necessity demands.[94]

d Interests in the International Community

Of course, state interest is not a one-way street. Interests of other states must be taken into account at some level, in particular in an international relations reality that has become dominated by a universal international organization that is the United Nations.[95] This is a necessity of the discourse within which international relations take place:[96]

> International law is essentially the product of State interests. Even in this era of globalization, it remains under the long shadow of the Westphalian paradigm founded on State sovereignty. Progress, however, has been achieved as States' interests and the values that their societies embrace have converged, demanding greater conformity by States to certain human aspirations. Spurred by economic globalization, States' international cooperation has increased substantially. In some areas, it has given rise to collective decision-making processes.[97]

There is a certain impetus of morality that may determine action in the case of mass extermination of a civilian population or allow restraints on warfare, for example.[98] But this altruistic impulse seems, in most cases, too weak to spur any form of meaningful intervention.[99] As Michael Walzer observed, the

94 Efraim Halevy, *Man in the Shadows. Inside the Middle East Crisis with a Man who led the Mossad* (London: Phoenix, 2007) 267–268.

95 See also *supra* n. 113, Chapter 1.

96 See Frankel, *supra* n. 91, Chapter 1, at 151. However, he also points out that the "successes of the United Nations have been on issues remote from the immediately vital interests of its members such as the concord on Antarctica or outer space". See *ibid.*, at 152. This, of course, fails to see the bigger picture of coordination that happens within the framework of the United Nations.

97 M. Cherif Bassiouni, 'Revisiting the Architecture of Crimes Against Humanity. Almost a Century in the Making, with Gaps and Ambiguities Remaining – the Need for a Specialized Convention', in Leila Nadya Sadat (ed.), *Forging a Convention for Crimes Against Humanity* (New York: Cambridge University Press, 2011) 43.

98 See Morgenthau and Thompson, *supra* n. 64, Chapter 2, at 249–260; Hans J. Morgenthau, 'The Twilight of International Morality', 58/2 *Ethics* (1948) 82.

99 See *supra* n. 196, Chapter 1.

> global community is pluralist in character, a community of nations, not of humanity, and the rights recognized within it have been minimal and largely negative, designed to protect the integrity of nations and to regulate their commercial and military transactions.[100]

The constitutionalist or Kantian argument still stands strong within international legal scholarship, spurred by Wolffian ideas of a *civitas maxima*.[101] Its moral superiority is, after all, compelling. However, it is not based on a sound assessment of the legal *status quo*. As Alexander Somek pointedly remarks, this "constitutionalizing perspective on public international law is also supposed to create a wow-effect":

> Positive-sounding norms have the power to create, in and of themselves, more observance, just like good-looking people are likely to be more successful in life. What we get, in the final event, is the fetish-character of public international law and the regression of legal science.[102]

Furthermore, the constitutionalist argument does not stand empirical scrutiny. Just as states will bulldoze over public image considerations, whenever their survival interests are at stake, states will limit their activism with regard to *ius cogens* and *erga omnes* obligations to situations, in which their own interests are concerned.[103]

In addition, it has been pointed out that "supranationalism" is favored mostly by states that are too weak to engage in international power politics.[104] While this view is, of course, debatable, it is certainly true that Austria is particularly active in promoting cooperation in international organizations and a normative rule of law,[105] whereas other, more powerful states are not. In this regard, one might also mention the "Small Five" initiative of Costa Rica, Jordan, Liechtenstein, Singapore, and Switzerland that presented a draft

100 Michael Walzer, 'The Moral Standing of States: A Response to Four Critics', 9/3 *Philosophy and Public Affairs* (1980) 226–227.

101 For such a Wolffian *civitas maxima* view of the international community see M. Cherif Bassiouni, 'Advancing the Responsibility to Protect Through International Criminal Justice', in Cooper and Kohler (eds), *supra* n. 84, at 36–37.

102 Somek, *supra* n. 66, Chapter 1, at 578.

103 See Cassese, *supra* n. 29, Chapter 2, at 210.

104 See Frankel, *supra* n. 91, Chapter 1, at 154.

105 See, *e.g.*, the statement by the Austrian representative to the 67th session of the General Assembly:

> [W]e would like to stress that our efforts to promote the rule of law do not serve an abstract goal, but the protection of the rights and interests of individuals. Austria, also in its role as coordinator of the Group of Friends of the Rule of Law, will continue to give utmost priority to this subject.

Reproduced in Markus P. Beham and Gerhard Hafner, 'Austrian Diplomatic and Parliamentary Practice in International Law / Österreichische Diplomatische und Parlamentarische Praxis zum Internationalen Recht', 17 *Austrian Review of International and European Law* (2012) 461.

General Assembly resolution aimed at Security Council reform.[106] Unsurprisingly, it was decided to withdraw the draft resolution soon after, in order to avoid further political scuffles.[107] The powerful states – in this case the veto powers of the Security Council – were less interested in reform.

e Concessions in the Literature

These elaborations are, contrary to common perception, not the minority view. Already in the second paragraph of the first chapter of his ground-breaking treatise *Le Droit des Gens*, Emer de Vattel – by nature a proponent of natural law[108] – addressed the present question by holding that each nation or state has its own specific affairs and interests.[109] He also proposed that these would be mostly present and direct in the relation between states as opposed to more noble, more general, or less direct interests.[110] The instance, in which states would not grant what he refers to as "les Offices de l'humanité",[111] namely what states owe to each other through reciprocity, were merely disorderly passions, particular interests, and misunderstanding.[112] Yet he also conceded that practice shows how states strengthen and enrich themselves at the cost of others.[113]

Immanuel Kant, one of those authors most championed for the cause of lofty values, pointed out that the well-being of the state – the "*Heil des Staates*" – does not necessarily correspond with the well-being or happiness of its respective citizens.[114]

Though one could easily point towards the year of publication of Vattel's or Kant's treatises and argue that such ideas no longer apply to the relationship between states, their findings have been reaffirmed within the literature up until this day: Jean D'Aspremont, for example, holds that "[e]ven liberals and constitutionalists agree that States first strive to promote their own interests" and that "they naturally act to maximize the interest of their constituency given their perception of the interests of other States and the distribution of State power".[115] Martti Koskenniemi has called reference to this fact a "truism,

106 See Costa Rica, Jordan, Liechtenstein, Singapore, and Switzerland: Revised Draft Resolution, 'Enhancing the accountability, transparency and effectiveness of the Security Council', U.N. Doc. A/66/L.42/Rev.2 (15 May 2012).

107 See United Nations, Meetings Coverage and Press Releases, 'Switzerland Withdraws Draft Resolution in General Assembly Aimed at Improving Security Council's Working Methods to Avoid "Politically Complex" Wrangling' (16 May 2012) <www.un.org/press/en/2012/ga11234.doc.htm>.

108 See Rubin, *supra* n. 198, Chapter 1, at 45–48.

109 De Vattel, *supra* n. 238, Chapter 2, at 1, § 2.

110 *Ibid.*, at 265, § 12.

111 *Ibid.*, at 257, § 2.

112 *Ibid.*, at 267–268, § 16 [misprinted as § 17].

113 *Ibid.*, at 268, § 16 [misprinted as § 17].

114 Kant, *supra* n. 15, at 202.

115 Jean D'Aspremont, 'The Foundations of the International Legal Order', 18 *Finnish Yearbook of International Law* (2007) 228.

present since Vattel".[116] Finally, Richard Steinberg convincingly shows how different schools of international legal thought and international relations theory resorted to realism whenever they dealt with states.[117]

According to Malcolm Shaw, the motivation behind an act of a state lies within the way in which "it perceives its interests", which again depends upon "the power and role of the state and its international standing".[118] When Martin Dixon writes in his introductory textbook on international law that "[i]t is true of all legal systems that vital interests of its subjects may prevail over the dictates of the law",[119] this sentence can be read either way, depending on whether one assumes that individuals are the subjects of international law. Even Gerhard Hafner, who takes a position that emphasizes the role of the individual in international law, concedes that states take all the weight in this balance of interests when he writes that "the reflection of the – nevertheless increasing – individual-oriented interests in norms of international law still depends on the will of states".[120]

4 Assessment

Notwithstanding these considerations of state interest, there are many reasons for states to observe altruistic inclinations: preventing civil unrest, cultivating a happy electorate,[121] attracting investment and highly skilled labor, securing development aid, gaining admission to an international organization – the list goes on.[122] But these are the means, not the end in itself.[123]

If the structural argument that the democratization of states has moved the individual to the centre of international relations is met by the overall experience that states will favor self-interest over communitarian or humanistic ideals, even under pressure from NGOs and the press, it may simply be the case that moral concepts do not play into the equation. The educated humanist may disagree, but "what is true for individuals is not necessarily true for states".[124]

In the competition of "first-order reasons", to borrow Joseph Raz's terminology,[125] those related to the survival of the states will, naturally, prevail. In

116 Martti Koskenniemi, 'The Place of Law in Collective Security', in Martti Koskenniemi (ed.), *The Politics of International Law* (Oxford: Hart Publishing, 2011) 91.
117 See Richard H. Steinberg, 'Wanted – Dead or Alive: Realism in International Law', in Jeffrey L. Dunoff and Mark A. Pollack (eds), *Interdisciplinary Perspectives on International Law and International Relations* (Cambridge: Cambridge University Press, 2013) *passim*.
118 Shaw, *supra* n. 88, Chapter 1, at 56.
119 Dixon, *supra* n. 75, Chapter 1, at 14.
120 Hafner, *supra* n. 75, Chapter 1, at 28–29 and 39.
121 See on these two considerations *vis-à-vis* foreign policy interests Frankel, *supra* n. 91, Chapter 1, at 132.
122 See Goldsmith and Posner, *supra* n. 40, Chapter 1, at 109–119.
123 See Imbert, *supra* n. 47, at 283.
124 Goldsmith and Posner, *supra* n. 40, Chapter 1, at 190.
125 See Joseph Raz, *supra* n. 194, Chapter 1, at 34.

absence of an exclusionary rule, a state will balance these interests in accordance with their respective "strength" or "weight".[126] A ready example is the primacy that states accord to national security considerations over basic citizen's rights in the face of terrorism.[127] Even within the CHARTER OF THE UNITED NATIONS, human rights play a secondary role to peace and security.[128]

While the literature may concede the primacy of states' interests, too little attention has been given to the interplay of this "truism" and the formation of the sources of international law, in particular customary international law and general principles of law. It is obvious that parties bring their interests to the table, when negotiating a treaty. It is less obvious, however, what the above findings imply when moral concepts are sought in state practice and *opinio iuris* or by derivation from the domestic legal systems of states.

126 See Henry S. Richardson, 'Moral Reasoning', in Edward N. Zalta (ed.), *The Stanford Encyclopedia of Philosophy* (Winter 2014 Edition) <http://plato.stanford.edu/archives/win2014/entries/reasoning-moral>.

127 See also with regard to the balancing of interests of democratic states between ending human rights abuses abroad and the risk of their own citizens, McFarland and Mathews, *supra* n. 83, at 365 *et passim*.

128 See Murphy, *supra* n. 192, Chapter 1, at 70 and 81–82.

4 Doctrine and Indeterminacy

A Human Rights as Non-Treaty Law: Doctrine

1 Prelude: Human Rights and the United Nations

Although there are a number of precursors to the protection of the individual in international law,[1] human rights as a subject of international law only really made the stage with the creation of the United Nations, primarily as a response to the traumas of World War II.[2] Specific references towards human rights within the CHARTER OF THE UNITED NATIONS are contained in the preamble as well as Articles 1(3) concerning the purpose of the United Nations and 55(c) concerning international economic and social cooperation.[3]

One approach to the validity of human rights as positive international law, propagated in particular by Louis Sohn,[4] the "quintessential charterist",[5] and

1 See Fabri, *supra* n. 45, Chapter 3, at 38, fn. 20; Shaw, *supra* n. 88, Chapter 1, at 197–198; Rhona K.M. Smith, *Textbook on International Human Rights,* 5th edn (Oxford: Oxford University Press, 2012) 5–22.

2 See Dixon, *supra* n. 75, Chapter 1, at 344; Shaw, *ibid.*, at 198–199; Smith, *ibid.*, at 22–23 and Chapter 3 *passim.*

3 CHARTER OF THE UNITED NATIONS, Preamble, Arts. 1(3) and 55(c). For more on these as a direct source of human rights see Oscar Schachter, 'International Law Implications of U.S. Human Rights Policies', 24 *New York Law School Law Review* (1978–1979) *passim.* Mention of human rights is also made with regard to the competences and objectives of the General Assembly, the Economic and Social Council as well as the International Trusteeship System. See the CHARTER OF THE UNITED NATIONS, Articles 13(1)(b), 62(2), 68, and 76(c).

4 See, *e.g.*, Louis B. Sohn, 'The Human Rights Law of the Charter', 12 *Texas International Law Journal* (1977) 133; *id.*, 'John A. Sibley Lecture. The Shaping of International Law', 8/1 *Georgia Journal of International and Comparative Law* (1978) 14–25; *id.*, 'The New International Law: Protection of the Rights of Individuals Rather Than States', 32 *American University Law Review* (1982–1983) 17; *id., supra* n. 198, Chapter 2, at 1074. Critically, however, Eric Lane, 'Human Rights Within the World Legal Order: A Reply to Sohn and McDougal', 10 *Hofstra Law Review* (1981–1982) *passim; id.*, 'Mass Killing by Governments: Lawful in the World Legal Order?', 12 *New York University Journal of International Law and Politics* (1970–1980) 257–259. See also Meron, *supra* n. 82, Chapter 1, at 82–85.

5 Lane, 'Human Rights', *ibid.*, at 750.

embraced by the Carter administration of the United States,[6] is to see the various General Assembly resolutions such as the "Universal Declaration of Human Rights" as interpretative instruments of the CHARTER OF THE UNITED NATIONS.[7] The International Court of Justice itself implicitly adopted this approach in the *Tehran Hostages* case:

> Wrongfully to deprive human beings of their freedom and to subject them to physical constraint in conditions of hardship is in itself manifestly incompatible with the principles of the Charter of the United Nations, as well as with the fundamental principles enunciated in the Universal Declaration of Human Rights.[8]

Depending on one's interpretation and understanding of the verb "enunciate", one might even go as far as suggesting that the International Court of Justice grants independent legal value to the "Universal Declaration of Human Rights". The ordinary meaning, according to the *Concise Oxford English Dictionary*, however, is to "say or pronounce clearly" or to "set out precisely or definitely",[9] thus supporting a reading along the lines of the interpretative theory.[10]

6 See Alston and Simma, *supra* n. 85, Chapter 1, at 100; Schachter, *supra* n. 3, at 63–65 *et passim*. Cf. also, critically, Eric Lane, 'Demanding Human Rights: A Change in the World Legal Order', 6/2 *Hofstra Law Review* (1978) 286–295. See also *Filártiga v. Peña-Irala*, at paras 24–26, referring to the "Universal Declaration of Human Rights" as evidence and definition of customary international law.

7 See also Smith, *supra* n. 1, at 39. Critically, however, Watson, *supra* n. 148, Chapter 1, at 62.

8 *Case Concerning United States Diplomatic and Consular Staff in Tehran* (United States of America *v.* Iran), Judgment of 24 May 1980, ICJ Reports 1980, p. 3, at 43, para. 91. See Meron, *supra* n. 82, Chapter 1, at 83, in particular fn. 8.

9 See the entry "enunciate" in the *Concise Oxford English Dictionary*.

10 In a memorandum on the 'Use of the Terms "Declaration" and "Recommendation"' the Office of Legal Affairs held:

> In United Nations practice, a "declaration" is a formal and solemn instrument, suitable for rare occasions when principles of great and lasting importance are being enunciated, such as the Declaration on Human Rights. A recommendation is less formal. 4. Apart from this distinction just indicated, there is probably no difference between a "recommendation" or a "declaration" in United Nations practice as far as strict legal principle is concerned. A "declaration" or a "recommendation" is adopted by resolution of a United Nations organ. As such it cannot be made binding upon Member States, in the sense that a treaty or convention is binding upon the parties to it, purely by the device of terming it a "declaration" rather than a "recommendation". However, in view of the greater solemnity and significance of a "declaration", it may be considered to impart, on behalf of the organ adopting it, a strong expectation that Members of the international community will abide by it. Consequently, in so far as the expectation is gradually justified by State practice, a declaration may by custom become recognized as laying down rules binding upon States. 5. In conclusion, it may be said that in United Nations practice, a "declaration" is a solemn

While it cannot be the place here to expand on this theme, it does not seem dogmatically convincing to assert that the preambular passages of the CHARTER OF THE UNITED NATIONS create individual rights.[11] However, the spirit of this claim perfectly points the way from hortatory provisions contained in international instruments to what has become non-treaty human rights law. Instead of aiming for a sound assessment of the legal *status quo*, the discussion has moved to a reconsideration of methodology: If the outcome of the analysis is not the validity of human rights, something must be wrong with the analysis.

2 Human Rights as Customary International Law

The majority of textbooks on public international law or human rights tell the attentive reader that – if not all, then at least the most "fundamental"[12] – human rights represent customary international law[13] or even *ius cogens.*[14] While some authors matter-of-factly make the statement without further reference or cite "highly qualified publicists", others refer to (usually numerous random or few very prominent) domestic[15] and international court

> instrument resorted to only in very rare cases relating to matters of major and lasting importance where maximum compliance is expected.

See Commission on Human Rights, 18th Session, 'Use of the Terms "Declaration" and "Recommendation"', Memorandum by the Office of Legal Affairs, U.N. Doc. E/CN.4/L.610 (2 April 1962), paras 3–4.

11 See on the value of these instruments further *supra* pp. 77 *et seq.* Cf Lane, 'Human Rights', *supra* n. 4, *passim*; Lane, 'Mass Killing by Governments', *supra* n. 4, at 254.

12 There is, of course, no common definition of what "fundamental" means in most circumstances, but as Shaw holds, *e.g.*, it "would certainly include the prohibition of torture, genocide and slavery and the principle of non-discrimination". Shaw, *supra* n. 88, Chapter 1, at 201. On the use of the terms "*erga omnes*", "peremptory", "essential", "inderogeable", and "intransgressible" see Pellet, *supra* n. 7, Chapter 2, at 825–826, fn. 651. See also Koji Teraya, 'Emerging Hierarchy in International Human Rights and Beyond: From the Perspective of Non-derogable Rights', 12/5 *European Journal of International Law* (2001) 921.

13 It is impossible to give a comprehensive list, but see the references *supra* n. 150, Chapter 1, and given throughout the following passages. See also the list of customary international human rights law recognized by the International Court of Justice given by Ahmed and de Jesús Butler, *supra* n. 27, Chapter 1, at 779.

14 See on this also *supra* n. 184, Chapter 1, and accompanying text. On judicial practice in this regard see Ahmed and de Jesús Butler, *ibid.*, at 779–781.

15 Of course, while convincing at first sight, this does not by itself support the determination that something is customary international law under international law. See American Law Institute, *supra* n. 9, Chapter 2, at 19:

> A determination of international law by the Supreme Court of the United States resolves the matter for purposes of the law of the United States; it is not conclusive as to what international law is for other states, and perhaps not even as to what it is for the United States in its relations with other countries.

cases.[16] The "Universal Declaration of Human Rights" of 1948, although a General Assembly resolution by nature,[17] is also widely considered as an expression of customary international law or even *ius cogens*.[18] International treaties as evidence of customary international law[19] and other alternative methodological approaches such as a move from consent to consensus and development of norms through multilateral negotiation are resorted to.[20] The attempts at substantiating the proposition that human rights constitute customary international law – without doing so – are legion.

Of course, authors inevitably support their statements by referencing the state of the art through authoritative publications: "Almost no one actually 'finds' custom. Instead, arbitrators, academics and counsel typically refer to other sources that supposedly have already 'found' custom".[21] This book is no

16 See, *e.g.*, as a *pars pro toto* Shaw, *supra* n. 88, Chapter 1, at 201, referring to the *Restatement of the Law (Third), supra* n. 9, Chapter 2, the domestic *Filártiga* case, Theodor Meron's *Human Rights and Humanitarian Norms as Customary International Law, supra* n. 82, Chapter 1, and Vol. 25 of the *Georgia Journal of International Law* – the latter journal hardly serves as an unequivocal determination of human rights as customary international law, but rather as one of the more important contributions to the debate on all sides of the spectrum. See *ibid.*, at 201, fn. 58. See also Cassese, *supra* n. 29, Chapter 2, at 203, arguing that the prohibition of racial discrimination and torture are rules of customary international law, endowed with *ius cogens* status even. For the former proposition he cites the *Restatement of the Law (Third), supra* n. 9, Chapter 2, as a source, for the latter to the *Furundžija* case of the ICTY and to the domestic *Pinochet* case. See *ibid.*, fns 6 and 7.

17 Although the hyperbole as to its status has led to it even being mistaken for a treaty. See, *e.g.*, Jost Dülffer, 'The United Nations and the Origins of the Genocide Convention 1946–1948', in Eckart Conze and Christoph Safferling (eds), *The Genocide Convention Sixty Years After its Adoption* (The Hague: T.M.C. Asser Press, 2010) 57.

18 See, *inter alia*, Lillich, *supra* n. 68, Chapter 1, at 1–10 with further references; Rehman, *supra* n. 21, Chapter 1, at 80–82; Naomi Roht-Arriaza, 'State Responsibility to Investigate and Prosecute Grave Human Rights Violations in International Law', 78/2 *California Law Review* (1990) 492; Fabri, *supra* n. 45, Chapter 2, at 44 and 46–47; Schachter, *supra* n. 3, at 68. For further references and detailed commentary see Hurst Hannum, 'The Status of the Universal Declaration of Human Rights in National and International Law', *Georgia Journal of International and Comparative Law* (1995–1996) 323–351 *et passim*. Critically, however, *e.g.*, Thirlway, *supra* n. 13, Chapter 2, at 10–11. On the general underlying issues of such an assumption see *supra* pp. 77 *et seq.*

19 See, *inter alia*, Richard R. Baxter, 'Multilateral Treaties as Evidence of Customary International Law', 41 *British Yearbook of International Law* (1965–1966) 286; Meron, *supra* n. 82, Chapter 1, at 92–93; Roht-Arriaza, *ibid.*, at 490–492; Arthur M. Weisburd, 'The Effect of Treaties and Other Formal International Acts on the Customary Law of Human Rights', 25/1 *Georgia Journal of International Law* (1995–1996) 109–111. See on this also, generally, *supra* pp. 74 *et seq.*

20 Anaya, *supra* n. 210, Chapter 2, at 42–43.

21 See Anthea Roberts, 'Custom, Public Law and the Human Rights Analogy', *EJIL: Talk!* (14 August 2013) <www.ejiltalk.org/custom-public-law-and-the-human-rights-analogy/>.

exception in resorting to what others have written before. What matters, however, is the underlying motive for doing so:

> [W]riters about international law invariably cite each other as supporting "authority"; they really have to do so, because the reigning culture of the subject requires of writers, especially young writers still making a career, that they show they have read widely in this ocean of publications and the approved way to demonstrate this is by learned footnotes. [...] The consequence of this punishing academic culture is, in international law in particular, that for many propositions which are in truth proposals *de lege ferenda*, there can be made to appear a great mass of "authority". One can by this method of mutual citation "research" an imposing array of authority for many a juridically questionable proposition.[22]

If references provide a short-cut for making an assertion that would take too much effort and space in regard to an otherwise unrelated question, fine. After all, that is the whole point of the academic exercise of footnoting and citation. In light of the sheer scope of publications in the international legal discourse, it would hardly prove feasible to start off each contribution with an original and minute substantiation of each proposition. Yet, if the references are circular or simply serve as a veil behind which there is no final reference to make the claim, it is simply an elaborate deception of the reader.

James Hathaway analyzed a number of "senior publicists" from the UK and the USA to determine which rights they found to constitute customary international law, arriving at

> freedom from (1) systemic racial discrimination; (2) genocide; (3) slavery; (4) extrajudicial execution or enforced disappearance; (5) torture, cruel inhuman, or degrading treatment; (6) prolonged arbitrary detention; and (7) serious unfairness in criminal prosecution.[23]

This list resembles the *Restatement of the Law (Third)*,[24] which now presents a perfect dead-end reference for anyone seeking to assert one of the above rights as customary international law. It has the air of an official publication of one of the most powerful, if not the most powerful, state in the world, even though it is at most a work of the "most highly qualified publicists".[25] Still, it is eagerly resorted to for any claim of custom.

To take the example of a casebook of international law,[26] where the prohibition of slavery and servitude is portrayed as constituting part of customary

22 Jennings, *supra* n. 3, Chapter 1, at 333–334.
23 Hathaway, *supra* n. 33, Chapter 1, at 36.
24 See American Law Institute, *supra* n. 9, Chapter 2, at §702.
25 See Article 38(1)(c) of the Statute of the International Court of Justice.
26 One would think that a casebook involves an engagement with actual sources, not with scholarly works.

international law, simply by resorting to *Restatement of the Law (Third)*:[27] This is either ill-informed – for there is the possibility that the editors assume that the authors of the *Restatement of the Law (Third)* undertook an in-depth probe into state practice and *opinio iuris* and simply did not cite it – or simply a way of adding authoritative gloss to an otherwise simple statement. Who would doubt the moral power of the prohibition? It must be legal!

There are various more elaborate ways of convincing the reader that customary international human rights law must be true, as through critical stances introduced by entry phrases such as "[d]espite the indisputable existence of customary human rights law" while at the same time only including favorable references and omitting critical ones.[28] Others invite the reader to trust them and understand that any scholarly enquiry into state practice or *opinio iuris* would just be far too burdensome in light of the voluminous amount of evidence.[29] Of course, no kind-hearted reader could expect the author to embark on such an onerous quest.

These are some of the rhetorical "tricks" that academia has up its sleeve. How about the legal ones? Oscar Schachter sums up the arguments for claiming that human rights are customary international law as follows:

- human rights provisions in many national constitutions and laws;
- frequent references in United Nations resolutions and declarations to the "duty" of all States to observe faithfully the Universal Declaration of Human Rights;
- resolutions of the United Nations and other international bodies condemning specific human rights violations as violative of international law;
- statements by national officials criticizing other States for serious human rights violations;

27 Melissa Castan and Sarah Joseph, *The International Covenant on Civil and Political Rights: Cases, Materials, and Commentary*, 3rd edn (Oxford: Oxford University Press, 2013) 330, 10.02, fn. 1.

28 See Brian D. Lepard, 'International Law and Human Rights', in Thomas Cushman (ed.), *Handbook of Human Rights* (Oxon: Routledge, 2012) 587–588, citing to Humphrey (see *infra* n. 29), Meron (see *supra* n. 82, Chapter 1), the *Restatement of the Law (Third)* (see *supra* n. 9, Chapter 2), and a number of US cases.

29 See John P. Humphrey, 'The Universal Declaration of Human Rights: Its History, Impact and Juridical Character', in Bertram G. Ramcharan (ed.), *Human Rights: Thirty Years After the Universal Declaration. Commemorative Volume on the Occasion of the Thirtieth Anniversary of the Universal Declaration of Human Rights* (The Hague: Martinus Nijhoff, 1979) 28–29:

> Not only has [the Universal Declaration of Human Rights] become an international standard by which the conduct of governments is judged both within and outside the United Nations (it has been invoked so many times that it would require a major effort of research simply to list them); [...].

- a dictum of the International Court of Justice that obligations *erga omnes* in international law include those derived "from the principles and rules concerning the basic rights of the human person" (*Barcelona Traction* Judgment, 1970);
- some decisions in various national courts that refer to the Universal Declaration as a source of standards for judicial decision.[30]

He goes on to concede that "[n]one of the foregoing items of 'evidence' of custom conform to the traditional criteria".[31] How do scholars deal with this fact? A probe into the literature shows that there is no need for that. The *Restatement of the Law (Third)*, unsurprisingly, follows the ideas laid out by Schachter.[32] Irrespective of the chosen argument, the above approaches have become the "mainstream", methodology the accessory after the fact. The following reasons listed for the necessity of a "Convention on Crimes Against Humanity" illustrate this process:

> [A]n international convention would increase pressure on governments that commit crimes against humanity because they would be violating international law that will become *jus cogens*. The convention would develop into customary international law.[33]

a The Pull of the Mainstream

In an iconic book review of Theodor Meron's *Human Rights and Humanitarian Norms as Customary International Law*, Martti Koskenniemi speaks in this context of the "pull of the mainstream". On this, Alfred Rubin adds:

> Theodor Meron occupies a position in the mainstream of scholarship and diplomatic action. This makes it difficult to say whether his approach follows from the mainstream or creates part of it.[34]

Of course, this is not necessarily a flattering determination. Usually, the term "mainstream" "is meant to describe either a dominant group of professionals

30 Schachter, *supra* n. 6, Chapter 1, at 336. For a recent overview of approaches to the determination of human rights as customary international law see Noora Arajärvi, *The Changing Nature of Customary International Law: Methods of Interpreting the Concept of Custom in International Criminal Tribunals* (Oxon: Routledge, 2014) 30–33.
31 Schachter, *supra* n. 6, Chapter 1, at 336.
32 See American Law Institute, *supra* n. 9, Chapter 2, at §701.
33 Gregory H. Stanton, 'Why the World Needs an International Convention on Crimes Against Humanity', in Leila Nadya Sadat (ed.), *Forging a Convention for Crimes Against Humanity* (New York: Cambridge University Press, 2011) 357.
34 Alfred P. Rubin, Review of Theodor Meron, *Human Rights and Humanitarian Norms as Customary Law* (Oxford: Clarendon Press, 1989), 31/2 *Harvard Journal of International Law* (1990) 685.

that adhere to an orthodox reading of the law or a dominant type of argumentation that is shaped by the reliance on orthodox methods and concepts".[35]

Hence, the mainstream is usually conservative and uncontroversial by definition, the opposite of *avant-garde*. In human rights scholarship, however, the mainstream appears normative and progressive. While Meron presents his study as "clarifying the status of international human rights and humanitarian norms in public international law", in particular "by examining the sources, evidence, and process of the creation of such rights",[36] he presents a stereotypical example of this unorthodox, progressive "mainstream":

> Throughout the book one has the impression that whenever Meron states that some humanitarian or human rights principle is a part of customary law, the conclusion does not really follow from the arguments, but instead existed in Meron's head even as the arguments were chosen. [...] Might it not be that the certainty we have of the illegality of genocide, or of torture, or of depriving ethnic wholes the right of self-determination, is *by itself sufficient reason* to include those norms in international law?[37]

Hence, Meron's book can serve as an illustrative *pars pro toto* for pointing out a number of phenomena of this human rights "mainstream".

The book was – and still is – highly influential and critically acclaimed. It has been called a "well-researched, carefully documented book",[38] a "very instructive and admirably presented work whose arguments are supported by a wealth of references",[39] and, ironically, "a model for those who wish to argue successfully that a particular right has attained the status of a customary right"[40] as well as a "practical tool for the invocation of human rights law in international courts";[41] ironic, seeing as the book is such a prime example of

35 D'Aspremont, *supra* n. 202, Chapter 1, at 6–7.

36 Meron, *supra* n. 82, Chapter 1, at 1.

37 Koskenniemi, *supra* n. 36, Chapter 1, at 1952. As polemical as this assessment might be, Meron indeed opens himself to criticism, when he builds up his arguments by beginning with phrases such as "I believe" and "I consider". See, *e.g.*, Meron, *supra* n. 82, Chapter 1, at 34–35.

38 Ranee K.L. Panjabi, Review of Theodor Meron, *Human Rights and Humanitarian Norms as Customary Law* (Oxford: Clarendon Press, 1989)International Law Journal *(1989–1990) 381.*

39 Marco Sassòli, Review of Theodor Meron, *Human Rights and Humanitarian Norms as Customary Law* (Oxford: Clarendon Press, 1989), 29/273 *International Review of the Red Cross* (1989) 603.

40 Hilmy Ismail, Review of Theodor Meron, *Human Rights and Humanitarian Norms as Customary Law* (Oxford: Clarendon Press, 1989), XI/1 *Boston College Third World Law Journal* (1991) 401.

41 Hal Edelman, Review of Theodor Meron, *Human Rights and Humanitarian Norms as Customary Law* (Oxford: Clarendon Press, 1989)o;, 4 *Harvard Human Rights Journal* (1991) 241.

"human rightism". However, one review did point out that "while Meron is very cautious about the methodology for obtaining the status of a right, he is less so when declaring which rights now stand as customary norms".[42] Still, it took the deconstructive perspectives of Koskenniemi and Rubin to put the finger on what Meron is actually doing in his book.[43]

Meron's methodology moves between unsubstantiated assertions, self-referentiality,[44] and misconceptions of the sources of international law. To take but a few examples: With regard to the "basic prohibition of torture", no reference is given at all when Meron determines its status as customary international law and even *ius cogens.*[45] His assessment that the "principal provisions" of the International Convention on the Elimination of All Forms of Racial Discrimination constitute customary international law is misleadingly substantiated by a self-reference.[46] As to the prohibition of genocide, he comments that the 1948 Convention on the Prevention and Punishment of the Crime of Genocide was "largely codificatory" of customary international law.[47] In fact,

42 Panjabi, *supra* n. 38, at 385.

43 It should be mentioned, however, that Koskenniemi himself capitulates before positivist sources doctrine:

> But it is also, and more fundamentally, useless because we do not wish to condone anything that states may do or say, and because it is really our certainty that genocide or torture is illegal that allows us to understand state behaviour and to accept or reject its legal message, not state behaviour itself that allows us to understand that these practices are prohibited by law. It seems to me that if we are uncertain of the latter fact, then there is really little in this world we can feel confident about.

See *id., supra* n. 36, Chapter 1, at 1952. See also Niels Petersen, *Demokratie als teleologisches Prinzip. Zur Legitimität von Staatsgewalt im Völkerrecht* (Max-Planck-Institut für ausländisches öffentliches Recht und Völkerrecht, Beiträge zum ausländischen öffentlichen Recht und Völkerrecht, Vol. 204; Berlin: Springer, 2009) 66. See also *ibid., supra* n. 141, Chapter 1, at 284.

44 See on the deficiencies of self-referentiality Watson, *supra* n. 40, Chapter 1, at 636–637.

45 See Meron, *supra* n. 82, Chapter 1, at 23.

46 Meron, *supra* n. 82, Chapter 1, at 21, fn. 54, referring to Theodor Meron, *Human Rights Law-Making in the United Nations: A Critique of Instruments and Process* (Oxford: Clarendon Press, 1986) 194. However, this only contains the following passage relevant to racial discrimination concerning the draft version of the *Restatement of the Law (Third)*: "Even apart from apartheid, there is little disagreement with the overall prohibition of racial discrimination, but the consensus narrows as one moves from the general principle to specific manifestations of discrimination".

47 Meron, *supra* n. 82, Chapter 1, at 91 and 110–111. Indeed, the International Court of Justice in its *Reservations* advisory opinion stated:

> The origins and character of that Convention, the objects pursued by the General Assembly and the contracting parties, the relations which exist between the provisions of the Convention, inter se, and between those provisions and these objects, furnish elements of interpretation of the will of the General Assembly and the

the concept of outlawing acts committed against one's own citizens, particularly outside the context of armed conflict, was a quite novel and somewhat controversial idea at the time, as evidenced by the NUREMBERG CHARTER.[48] So, again the reference is misleading, if one would not *arguendo* attribute the preceding General Assembly Resolution 96(I)[49] as having created customary international law.[50] When in doubt, Meron refers to the *Restatement of the Law (Third)*.[51]

> parties. The origins of the Convention show that it was the intention of the United Nations to condemn and punish genocide as "a crime under international law" involving a denial of the right of existence of entire human groups, a denial which shocks the conscience of mankind and results in great losses to humanity, and which is contrary to moral law and to the spirit and aims of the United Nations (Resolution 96 (1) of the General Assembly, December 11th 1946). The first consequence arising from this conception is that the principles underlying the Convention are principles which are recognized by civilized nations as binding on States, even without any conventional obligation. A second consequence is the universal character both of the condemnation of genocide and of the Co-operation required "in order to liberate mankind from such an odious scourge" (Preamble to the Convention). The Genocide Convention was therefore intended by the General Assembly and by the contracting parties to be definitely universal in scope.

Reservations to the Convention on the Prevention and Punishment of the Crime of Genocide, Advisory Opinion of 28 May 1951, ICJ Reports 1951, p. 15, at 23. It is hard to see, however, how Meron sees this as supportive of his argument. An ordinary reading conveys the impression that the universal character is acknowledged by the International Court of Justice at the moment of the creation of the Convention. On the other hand, Meron is in the good company of the ICTY, which held in *Krstic*:

> The Convention on the Prevention and Punishment of the Crime of Genocide [...], adopted on 9 December 1948, whose provisions Article 4 adopts *verbatim*, constitutes the main reference source in this respect. Although the Convention was adopted during the same period that the term "genocide" itself was coined, the Convention has been viewed as codifying a norm of international law long recognised and which case-law would soon elevate to the level of a peremptory norm of general international law (*jus cogens*).

Prosecutor v. Radislav Krstic, Trial Chamber, Judgement of 2 August 2001, Case No. IT-98-33-T, para. 541.

48 CHARTER OF THE INTERNATIONAL MILITARY TRIBUNAL, London, 8 August 1945. See on this also D'Amato, *supra* n. 83, Chapter 3, at 47–48 and 76. Meron, however, explicitly refers to the NUREMBERG CHARTER for practice of the international crime of genocide. See Meron, *supra* n. 82, Chapter 1, at 111, fn. 93.

49 General Assembly Resolution 96(I), 'The Crime of Genocide', U.N. Doc. A/RES/96(I) (11 December 1946).

50 See Markus P. Beham, 'Genocide and Crimes Against Humanity: Siamese Twins or Separated at Birth?', in *id.* and Marija Wakounig (eds), *Mind and Memory in Discourse. Critical Concepts and Constructions* (Vienna: LIT Verlag, 2014) 185–188 on the development of the concept with particular regard to the definition of crimes against humanity within the NUREMBERG CHARTER. For an earlier detailed description of the development of the concept prior to 1945 see Egon Schwelb, 'Crimes Against Humanity', 23 *British Yearbook of International Law* (1946) 179–188.

51 Meron, *supra* n. 82, Chapter 1, *passim*.

The style of writing is nothing short of excellent and the book is an overly enjoyable read. Just like the Pied Piper, he leads the reader towards a view of customary international human rights law that seems utterly convincing on the surface. Even customary international law "conservatives" are served to satisfaction, when he emphasizes the two-element theory, as he points out that "[e]mpiric studies of state practice are [...] of the highest importance in establishing whether a particular right has matured into customary law".[52] Equally, he is a sharp critic of misconceptions of the sources of international law in other writers:

> Tendencies, apparent in various fields of international law, to impose treaty norms on non-parties in the guise of general international law or customary law, even in the absence of state practice dehors the treaty, have been examined and censured by Professor Weil.[53] Such trends have been especially strong in the human rights field, where they have focused not only on treaties but also on declarations and resolutions adopted by the United Nations and other international organizations. States parties to human rights instruments and supporters of declarations and the universality of human rights by attempting to assure concordant behaviour by non-parties to the instruments concerned and by states which have not supported the adoption of the declarations and resolutions. But this approach generates tension between the important human rights values advocated by states parties to human rights instruments and the sovereignty of non-parties. The credibility of international human rights therefore requires that attempts to extend their universality utilize irreproachable legal methods.[54]

As one reviewer remarked, Meron "is always very prudent in putting forward his views and is careful to point out counter-evidence and opposite trends, thus making his propositions all the more convincing".[55] So far, so good. However, he fails to practice what he preaches. He lures the reader into the "tarpit trap" of conservative, orthodox doctrine only to strike back with normative and progressive mainstream.

His favored method throughout the book seems to be criticism of a certain opinion or approach, only to then matter-of-factly use identical methodology later on in the text when and where it suits him. For example, he critically discusses views attributing legal value to the consensus arrived at during the drafting process of international conventions and resolutions, calling it a "controversial method".[56] Later on, in another passage he writes:

52 *Ibid.*, at 94.
53 Referring to Weil, *supra* n. 35, Chapter 1, at 434–439.
54 Meron, *supra* n. 82, Chapter 1, at 81.
55 Sassòli, *supra* n. 39, Chapter 1, at 603.
56 See Meron, *supra* n. 82, Chapter 1, at 85–88. On this method see, generally, *infra* pp. 74 *et seq.*

> Through acceptance of norms stated in human rights instruments by states, especially non-parties, human rights treaties have generated new customary rules of international law. New human rights instruments have been adopted that already embody certain customary rules. The repetition of certain norms in many human rights instruments is in itself an important articulation of law.[57]

He lures the reader into trusting his critical view of the debate, only to pave the road down the same argumentative path he criticized a moment before. Dotted throughout his book, Meron shines a light on his flexible understanding of legal methodology in the formation of customary international law, placing all cards on the table at times:

> As with other widely ratified treaties, if states parties comply with the Geneva Conventions in actual practice, verbally affirm their vital normative value, and accept them in *opinio juris*, both states and tribunals will be reluctant to advance or to accept the argument that the law of Geneva is solely, or even primarily, conventional. Such observance by the parties will eventually lead, *in the perception of governments and scholars, to the blurring of the distinction* between norms of the Conventions that are already recognized as customary law and other humanitarian provisions of the Conventions that have not yet achieved that status.[58]

On another occasion, he turns full-on "human rightist" and openly advocates "blurring" sources doctrine altogether, in order to promote non-treaty human rights law:

> Human rights lawyers should play an important role in promoting Article 38(1)(c) as a route for the passage of international human rights norms into general international law. As in other fields of international law,[59] the distinction between international customary law mentioned in Article 38 (1)(b) and general principles of law *will eventually become blurred*.[60]

57 Meron, *ibid.*, at 92. See also Rubin, *supra* n. 34, at 689.
58 Meron, *supra* n. 82, Chapter 1, at 62 [emphasis added by the present author].
59 Towards which he fails to point the reader.
60 Meron, *supra* n. 82, Chapter 1, at 88–89 [emphasis added by the present author]. For a more recent repetition of Meron's view see Payam Akhavan, 'The Universal Repression of Crimes Against Humanity Before National Jurisdictions', in Leila Nadya Sadat (ed.), *Forging a Convention for Crimes Against Humanity* (New York: Cambridge University Press, 2011) 36:

> It is recognized that the tendency to equate *opinio juris* with State practice with respect to human rights norms blurs the distinction between customary law and general principles as different sources of international law. In this respect, it is noted that the status of crimes against humanity as part of *jus cogens* may be derived from either source.

Finally, the natural lawyer is fully revealed, when Meron writes that "[t]he fact that the content of a norm reflects important considerations of humanity should promote its acceptance as customary law".[61] He also refers to the Human Rights Committee's findings with regard to Article 10 International Covenant on Civil and Political Rights that there must exist rights "of universal application which cannot depend entirely on material resources".[62]

With regard to rules that are habitually breached by states, such as the prohibition of torture, Meron holds that "[t]heir endurance as legal norms,

61 *Ibid.*, at 35. This view was also expressed by Antonio Cassese with regard to the Martens Clause:

> In consequence [of the Martens Clause] it is logically admissible to infer (and is borne out of practice) that the requirement of State *practice* may not need to apply to the formation of a principle or a rule based on the laws of humanity or the dictates of public conscience. Or, at least, this requirement may not be so high as in the case of principles and rules having a different underpinning or rationale. In other words, when it comes to proof of the emergence of a principle or general rule reflecting the laws of humanity (or the dictates of public conscience), as a result of the impact of the Martens Clause on international law the requirement of *usus* may be less stringent than in other cases where the principle or rule may have emerged as a result of economic, political, or military demands. By the same token, the requirement of *opinio juris* or *opinio necessitatis* may take on special prominence. As a result, the expression of legal views by a number of States and other international subjects about the binding value of a principle or a rule, or the social and moral need for its observance by States, may be held to be conducive to the formation of a principle or a customary rule, even when there is no widespread and consistent State practice, or even no practice at all, to back up those legal views. Thus, arguably the Martens Clause (in its present legal dimension) loosens, in the limited area of humanitarian law, the requirements prescribed for *usus*, while at the same time elevating *opinio* (*juris* or *necessitatis*) to a rank higher than that normally admitted.

See *id.*, *supra* n. 29, Chapter 2, at 160–161. Cassese did concede, however, that practice does not support such an interpretation. See *ibid.* The proposition was also prominently adapted by the court in the *Paquete Habana* and *Lola*:

> This review of the precedents and authorities on the subject appears to us abundantly to demonstrate that at the present day, by the general consent of the civilized nations of the world, and independently of any express treaty or other public act, it is an established rule of international law, founded on considerations of humanity to a poor and industrious order of men, and of the mutual convenience of belligerent states, that coast fishing vessels, with their implements and supplies, cargoes and crews, unarmed and honestly pursuing their peaceful calling of catching and bringing in fresh fish, are exempt from capture as prize of war.

See Jennings, *supra* n. 249, Chapter 2, at 65 / 33.

62 See Meron, *supra* n. 82, Chapter 1, at 96, citing to Human Rights Committee, 16th Session, 'General Comment No. 9: Article 10 (Humane Treatment of Persons Deprived of Their Liberty)', 30 May 1982.

despite frequent breaches, can also be explained by a deeply felt belief in the norms' importance".[63] Such fervor may have served a college student in 1968, but it will probably not serve the international community in creating a credible rule of law. While Meron acknowledges that "states normally shield themselves with self-serving justifications, calculated to minimize international censure of their course of action", he identifies an urge of the international community in the stability of customary international law:

> Why should states challenge a rule head on, if less provocative conduct would better serve them? Of course, because of its legitimate interest in safeguarding the stability of customary law, the international community tends to view violations as mere episodic breaches which do not directly challenge the binding character of a recognized norm.[64]

But if this is true – which it is, though in a more cynical sense than Meron probably intended – then the customary international law is identified – if not for rhetoric purposes – for the mere sake of doing so. It becomes an academic self-purpose, devoid of any legal relevance: customary international law and "customary international law".

This probably does not bother Meron too much, seeing as any norm ultimately undergoes the metamorphosis of a butterfly, from the caterpillar of scholarly writing to the chrysalis of customary international law to, finally, the beautiful butterfly of *ius cogens*:[65]

> [C]onsensus that the Geneva Conventions are declaratory of customary international law would strengthen the moral claim of the international community for their observance by emphasizing their humanitarian underpinnings and deep roots in tradition and community values. Such consensus might also represent a step in a process that begins with the crystallization of a contractual norm into a principle of customary law and culminates in its elevation to *jus cogens* status.[66]

Here, he is in the good company of the International Court of Justice, which has determined "elementary considerations of humanity, even more exacting in peace than in war" as among "general and well-recognized principles" applicable even in the absence of a treaty.[67] It does not, however, provide for any proof in either state practice or *opinio iuris* of states where such a principle exists, as pointed out by Meron himself:[68]

63 Meron, *ibid.*, at 58.
64 *Ibid.*, at 60. See in this regard also Henkin, *supra* n. 108, Chapter 1, at 69–70.
65 See Pellet, *supra* n. 327, Chapter 2.
66 *Ibid.*, at 8–9.
67 *The Corfu Channel Case* (United Kingdom of Great Britain and Northern Ireland *v.* Albania), Judgment of 9 April 1949 (Merits), ICJ Reports 1949, p. 4, at 22.
68 See Meron, *supra* n. 82, Chapter 1, at 109.

> The teleological desire to solidify the humanizing content of the humanitarian norms clearly affects the judicial attitude underlying the "legislative" character of the judicial process. Given the scarcity of actual practice, it may well be that tribunals have been guided, and may continue to be guided, by the degree to which certain acts are offensive to human dignity. The more heinous the act, the more willing the tribunal will be to assume that it violates not only a moral principle of humanity but also a positive norm of customary law.[69]

b A Phenomenon of "United States Scholarship"?

One argument of European scholars in particular, to shield themselves from deconstruction, has been that academics from the United States are more likely to regress to such cross- and self-referentiality to establish customary international human rights law due to the poor ratification behavior of the United States regarding human rights treaties.[70] The argument is tempting, in particular, as the works of Meron taken together with the *Restatement of the Law (Third)* provide such great textbook examples. However, the claim cannot be substantiated by empirical evidence.

First, the United States has ratified a number of important international human rights treaties, including the CONVENTION ON THE PREVENTION AND PUNISHMENT OF THE CRIME OF GENOCIDE, the INTERNATIONAL COVENANT ON CIVIL AND POLITICAL RIGHTS, as well as two of the seven "core conventions", the INTERNATIONAL CONVENTION ON THE ELIMINATION OF ALL FORMS OF RACIAL DISCRIMINATION and the CONVENTION AGAINST TORTURE AND OTHER CRUEL, INHUMAN OR DEGRADING TREATMENT OR PUNISHMENT.

In addition, the United States signed another three of these "core conventions", the CONVENTION ON THE ELIMINATION OF ALL FORMS OF DISCRIMINATION AGAINST WOMEN, the CONVENTION ON THE RIGHTS OF THE CHILD, and the CONVENTION ON THE RIGHTS OF PERSONS WITH DISABILITIES, arguably obligating the United States not to defeat the object and purpose of these treaties prior to their subjective entry into force.[71]

Second, "human rightism" is a broader phenomenon than just the United States, also existent in European human rights scholarship, irrespective of the common or civil law tradition, as will be shown.

c "European Scholarship"

The following examples are a random selection of works from both the common law and the civil law tradition. Starting off with Manfred Nowak, to

69 Meron, *supra* n. 82, Chapter 1, at 42.
70 See, *e.g.*, Alston and Simma, *supra* n. 85, Chapter 1, at 83 and 87. The argument was also made by Manfred Nowak during a presentation of the main argument of the present book at the Round Table of the Section for International Law and International Relations of the University of Vienna on 20 January 2016.
71 See Article 18 of the VIENNA CONVENTION ON THE LAW OF TREATIES.

take one of the most eminent European human rights scholars,[72] he is often nuanced in his determinations, making clear that certain rights have only been referred to as customary international law or *ius cogens* in the literature.[73] On other occasions, however, he draws *ius cogens* from the "universal character" and "deeply rooted acceptance by the international community", whereby he relies on other scholarly articles "with further references" in the footnotes.[74]

In his commentary on the INTERNATIONAL COVENANT ON CIVIL AND POLITICAL RIGHTS, with regard to the prohibition of torture, he first cites Yoram Dinstein, who supposedly provides further references to the extent that this human right constitutes *ius cogens*. Dinstein provides only a single reference to an article by Michael O'Boyle on the *Ireland v. United Kingdom* case before the European Court of Human Rights[75] with the following passage referring to *ius cogens*:

> Accepting that Article 3 has its counterpart in the Universal Declaration of Human Rights, the UN Covenant on Civil and Political Rights, the Inter-American Convention on Human Rights; the UN Declaration on Torture, Inhuman and Degrading Treatment; Common Article 3 of the Geneva Convention; and that it has probably become part of customary international law, it would appear to be a norm of international law accepted and recognized by the international community of states as a whole as required by Article 53 of the Vienna Convention.[76]

The fact that the prohibition of torture has "probably become part of customary international law" in the words of O'Boyle,[77] suddenly transforms through the medium of Dinstein to "an integral part of customary international law" that "may have even have acquired the lineament of a peremptory norm"[78] which, finally, "justifies the view that torture is prohibited by customary international law and even ranks as *jus cogens* under international law, pursuant to Art. 53 of the VCLT" in the words of Manfred Nowak.[79] The

72 And someone who supports the proposition. See *supra* n. 70.

73 See, *e.g.*, with regard to the right to life Manfred Nowak, *U.N. Covenant on Civil and Political Rights. CCPR Commentary*, 2nd edn (Kehl: N.P. Engel, 2005) 122, para. 1.

74 See, *e.g.*, *ibid.*, at 157–158, para. 1, fn. 2 with regard to the prohibition of torture or 197, para. 7, fn. 13 with regard to the prohibition of slavery.

75 Yoram Dinstein, 'The Right to Life, Physical Integrity, and Liberty', in Louis Henkin, *The International Bill of Rights: The Covenant on Civil and Political Rights* (New York: Columbia University Press, 1981) 122, fn. 56.

76 Michael O'Boyle, 'Torture and Emergency Powers Under the European Convention on Human Rights: Ireland v. the United Kingdom', 71 *American Journal of International Law* (1977) 687.

77 See *ibid.*

78 Dinstein, *supra* n. 75, 122.

79 Nowak, *supra* n. 73, at 157–158, para. 1

caterpillar spins its customary pupa before emerging as a *ius cogens* Goliath Birdwing butterfly.

In addition to Dinstein, Nowak references himself, two US-scholars, Richard Lillich and Rosalyn Higgins, and, lastly, the article by Philip Alston and Bruno Simma in the *Australian Yearbook of International Law* that actually concedes that there is no customary international human rights law, but that recourse must be taken to the general principles of law.[80]

Others are more frank about their approach. In a lecture at The Hague Academy, emphasizing the omission of a footnote, Christian Tomuschat simply holds that "[e]quality of human beings, protection of human life and physical integrity, freedom from torture and slavery are without any doubt propositions that need no additional confirmation through practice and *opinio iuris*".[81]

The entry on *ius cogens* in the *Max Planck Encyclopedia of International Law* holds that "fundamental human rights form part of *ius cogens*, although details may be open to doubt".[82] It would be more representative of the legal *status quo* and sources doctrine to state that its basics are open to doubt.[83] In another German standard textbook of international law any supporting reference for the prohibition of slavery is omitted.[84]

In the commentary on the CONVENTION RELATING TO THE STATUS OF REFUGEES, the authors hold that "it is rightly assumed that the [...] prohibition of torture enjoys status of customary international law, even *jus cogens*".[85] Thereby, they rely on the *Furundžija* case of the ICTY and a reference within the commentary within the footnote.[86] The passage within the commentary, however, only discusses the issue of *non-refoulement*, not the customary international law or *ius cogens* status of the prohibition of torture.[87] The *Furundžija*

80 See *ibid.*, at 157–158, para. 1, fn. 2. For the relevant passages of the article by Alston and Simma see *id., supra* n. 85, Chapter 1, at 99–100 and 102.

81 Tomuschat, *supra* n. 127, Chapter 1, at 303.

82 Jochen A. Frowein, 'Ius Cogens', in *Max Planck Encyclopedia of Public International Law* <http://opil.ouplaw.com/view/10.1093/law:epil/9780199231690/law-9780199231690-e1437?rskey=uLHVY9&result=8&prd=EPIL>, at para. 8.

83 See, *e.g.*, Anthony D'Amato, 'It's a Bird, It's a Plane, It's Jus Cogens!', 6/1 *Connecticut Journal of International Law* (1990–1991) 1–6.

84 See Kay Hailbronner and Marcel Kau, 'Der Staat und der Einzelne als Völkerrechtssubjekte', in Wolfgang Graf Vitzthum (ed.), *Völkerrecht,* 5th edn (Berlin: De Gruyter, 2010) 227, para. 232.

85 Philipp Wennholz and Andreas Zimmermann, 'Article 33, para. 2 (Prohibition of Expulsion to Return ("*Refoulement*")/Défense d'Expulsion et de Refoulement)', in Andreas Zimmermann (ed.), *The 1951 Convention Relating to the Status of Refugees and its 1967 Protocol. A Commentary* (Oxford: Oxford University Press, 2011) 1411, para. 64.

86 *Ibid.*, fn. 76.

87 See Martina Caroni, Lukas Heim, and Walter Kälin, 'Article 33, para. 1 (Prohibition of Expulsion to Return ("*Refoulement*")/Défense d'Expulsion et de Refoulement)', in Zimmermann (ed.), *supra* n. 85, at 1345, para. 32.

case itself draws upon treaties,[88] broad ratification of the GENEVA CONVENTIONS,[89] the fact that no state has claimed it may torture in armed conflict,[90] and the finding of the International Court of Justice in the *Nicaragua* case concerning the customary international law validity of the obligations under common Article 3 of the GENEVA CONVENTIONS.[91] It is needless to say that the International Court of Justice did not substantiate its findings that the standards contained therein constituted "elementary considerations of humanity".[92] Nowhere in the commentary or the two decisions is the paradox of contrary practice even mentioned.

In a commonly used English textbook of international human rights law by Javaid Rehman, one reads that "customary law represents the essential basis upon which modern human regime [*sic*] is grounded"[93] and that "it can be argued that a majority of the provisions of the [Universal Declaration of Human Rights] now represent customary international law".[94] The author concedes that

> there is a debate about the legal value and content of a number of rights, in particular of economic, social and cultural rights. Thus, questions have been raised about the legal and juridical value of such rights as the right to rest and leisure, the right to a decent standard of living, and the right to participate in the cultural life of the community.[95]

Only two paragraphs later, when discussing a possible *ius cogens* status of the "Universal Declaration of Human Rights" even, he also mentions "the right to seek asylum (Article 14) and the various facets of the right to freedom of thought, conscience and religion (Article 18)".[96] In making his original determination as to the customary international law status of the "Universal Declaration of Human Rights", he cites three authors, Hans-Joachim Heintze, Sarah Joseph, and Louis Sohn.

Heintze himself only states that "most of the international lawyers support the opinion that its principles are customary international law".[97] His reference guides to Humphrey, who has already been mentioned before with regard to

88 See *Prosecutor v. Anton Furundžija*, Trial Chamber, Judgement of 10 December 1998, Case No. IT-95–17/1-T, at 52–53, para. 137.
89 See *ibid.*, at 53, para. 137.
90 *Ibid.*
91 *Ibid.*
92 See *Case Concerning Military and Paramilitary Activities In and Against Nicaragua* (Nicaragua *v.* United States of America), Judgment of 27 June 1986 (Merits), ICJ Reports 1986, p. 14, at 114, para. 218.
93 Rehman, *supra* n. 21, Chapter 1, at 23.
94 *Ibid.*, at 80. On this discussion see, generally, also the references given by Ahmed and de Jesús Butler, *supra* n. 27, Chapter 1, at 778, fn. 39.
95 Rehman, *ibid.*, at 82.
96 *Ibid.*
97 Hans-Joachim Heintze, 'The UN Convention and the Network of the International Human Rights Protection by the UN', in Michael Freeman and Philip

the "Universal Declaration of Human Rights".[98] Joseph calls the view "the more radical end of the spectrum of arguments" and quotes the *Restatement of the Law (Third)* and the same article by Sohn that Rehman cites. Sohn, in turn, does not bother to give any references when making bold assessments of the nature of "soft law" human rights instruments:

> It has been argued, in particular, that most of these documents are "soft law", or even "normes sauvages", rather than "hard law". According to this view, these documents contain no more than mere guidelines, which states need not follow. Furthermore, there are no effective means of implementing the documents, and violators go unpunished. The better view is that these documents have become a part of international customary law and, as such, are binding on all states.[99]

Sohn manages to skip the question of formation of international law by taking a "creationist" view of customary international human rights law: "These documents do not create new rights; they recognize them".[100] It is almost a paradoxical step that he then sees the need to refer to any such notions as consensus with regard to a particular treaty, when going one step further:

> Although the line between codification and development of international law is a thin one, the consensus on virtually all provisions of the Covenant on Civil and Political Rights is so widespread that they can be considered part of the law of mankind, a *jus cogens* for all.[101]

With regard to the prohibition of torture, Rehman holds that it constitutes both "international customary law" and "a norm of *jus cogens*, a norm from which no derogation is permissible".[102] He cites another author[103] who finds

> that the best evidence for a customary rule of international law is to be found in what states say they think the rule is (*opinio iuris*), and what they say they are doing (or not doing) in terms of that rule. The fact is that a large number of the governments that proclaim their adherence to the prohibition of torture and their compliance with it, actually commit acts of torture in the dark and secret reaches of their power. But this no more undermines the validity of the prohibition than the covert activities of

Veerman (eds), *The Ideologies of Children's Rights* (International Studies in Human Rights, Vol. 23; Dordrecht: Martinus Nijhoff, 1992) 72.

98 See Rehman, *supra* n. 21, Chapter 1, at 82, fn. 6, citing to Humphrey, *supra* n. 29.

99 Sohn, *supra* n. 4, at 12.

100 See *ibid.*, at 32.

101 *Ibid.*

102 Rehman, *supra* n. 21, Chapter 1, at 810.

103 Nigel Rodley, *The Treatment of Prisoners Under International Law*, 2nd edn (Oxford: Clarendon Press, 1999) 74.

> secret services invalidate international law rules on non-intervention against state sovereignty.[104]

Similar to Meron, the author of the textbook reads his references with an eye to what the result of the analysis should be.[105] Thereby, he either misrepresents the sources or cites other authors that, in turn, engage in self-referentiality or similar misassertion.

In a casebook on the International Covenant on Civil and Political Rights, the reader is informed that, "[a]s discussed below, self-determination is also a peremptory norm of general international law (*jus cogens*), admitting no derogation and taking priority even in the event of a conflict with norms of a lesser state".[106] Unfortunately the idea is never discussed "below". The reference is simply omitted.

These subjectively selected examples from both the civil law and the common law tradition of "European scholarship" make clear that the phenomenon is not restricted to the United States alone. It is universal.

d A Cursory Look at Torture

As this random probe into scholarly appraisal shows, the prohibition of torture seems to be considered one of the most uncontroversial cases. Of course, no person of sane mental constitution would postulate that torture is permissible. However, the question is whether the prohibition of torture and the right to freedom from torture are protected under customary international law, not whether an educated humanist would condone it.

For one, the Convention Against Torture and Other Cruel, Inhuman or Degrading Treatment or Punishment currently boasts 162 parties.[107] These states are bound by the treaty, in particular the prohibition of torture under Article 1 – which excludes "pain or suffering arising only from, inherent in or incidental to lawful sanctions" – in combination with Articles 2 to 5 and the prohibition against cruel, inhuman, or degrading treatment under Article 16.

Under the logic of the *North Sea Continental Shelf Cases*, one might be tempted to speak of these core provisions as of "fundamentally normcreating character such as could be regarded as forming the basis of a general rule of law".[108] What it comes down to in this regard, however, is the (interpretation of the) definition of torture, the scope of the lawful sanctions clause, and the reservations of states

104 *Ibid.*, at 67.
105 See *supra* n. 37.
106 David Kinley, Jacqueline Mowbray, and Ben Saul, *The International Covenant on Economic, Social and Cultural Rights: Commentary, Cases, and Materials* (Oxford: Oxford University Press, 2014) 14.
107 A large step from the situation in the early 1990s. See Weisburd, *supra* n. 19, at 128–129.
108 *North Sea Continental Shelf Cases* (Federal Republic of Germany *v.* Denmark/ Federal Republic of Germany *v.* Netherlands), Judgment of 20 February 1969, ICJ Reports 1969, p. 3, at 42, para. 72.

parties.[109] In any case, as has been pointed out already, the approach of deriving customary international law from treaties alone is paradoxical and problematic.[110] In addition, ratification behavior, domestic implementation, and compliance do not necessarily correlate in the case of torture.[111]

According to Amnesty International, out of 160 states analyzed, 131 committed torture or otherwise "ill-treated" individuals in 2014.[112] That amounts to approximately 82% of those 160 states.[113] Put in relation to the 193 member states of the United Nations, this means that at least two thirds of these either torture or "ill-treat" members of their population, although this figure does not differentiate between a pattern or policy of torture in these states and isolated, single acts. At the same time, one must also consider that the statistics only include the number of known violations, whereas torture usually "takes place in the shadows".[114] Even democratic states fail to uphold the prohibition, in particular in the face of terrorism and violent protest.[115] Academic assessment seems blind to this empirical evidence:

> To the extent that there is a consensus, for example, on the right not to be tortured, the international community can be seen as willing to act upon that right independently of some affirmative act of state consent.[116]

Still, it is prohibited in most national laws and constitutions of the world;[117] domestic laws are also considered as evidence of state

109 See *supra* n. 160, Chapter 1.

110 See *supra* pp. 74 *et seq.*

111 See Adam S. Chilton and Mila Versteeg, 'The Failure of Constitutional Torture Prohibitions', 44/2 *Journal of Legal Studies* (2015) 418 *et passim* with further references to empirical data. See generally on the weak correlation between human rights treaty ratification and the human rights situation within states Linda Camp Keith, 'The United Nations International Covenant on Civil and Political Rights: Does it Make a Difference in Human Rights Behavior?', 36/1 *Journal of Peace Research* (1999) 103–105 and 112–113; Todd Landman, 'Measuring Human Rights: Principle, Practice, and Policy', 26/4 *Human Rights Quarterly* (2004), 914–915; Eric Neumayer, 'Do International Human Rights Treaties Improve Respect for Human Rights?', 49/6 *Journal of Conflict Resolution* (2005) 932–951; Weisburd, *supra* n. 19, 135. For further empirical studies see the references given by Todd Landman, *ibid.*, at 908, fn. 5.

112 See also Chilton and Versteeg, *ibid.*, at 418.

113 See Amnesty International, 'Human Rights Facts and Figures for 2014' (25 February 2015) <www.amnesty.org/en/latest/news/2015/02/annual-report-201415-facts-and-figures/>.

114 Amnesty International, 'Torture in 2014. 30 Years of Broken Promises' (May 2014), at 10 <www.amnestyusa.org/sites/default/files/act400042014en.pdf>.

115 See Chilton and Versteeg, *supra* n. 111, at 418.

116 Anaya, *supra* n. 210, Chapter 2, at 43.

117 Supposedly, as of 2011, 84% of the world's constitutions prohibited torture. See Chilton and Versteeg, *supra* n. 111, at 420. For an early appraisal see the appendix to M. Cherif Bassiouni and Daniel Derby, 'An Appraisal of Torture in International Law and Practice: The Need for an International Convention for the

practice.[118] States habitually condemn violations of the prohibition against torture. Yet the argument that these prohibitions and state condemnation of violations constitutes practice is not correct, as the expression of disapproval is not related to "the subject of the putative customary norm".[119] The actual requirement is a "concrete performance or self-restraining *in regard to* the matter said to acquire binding force".[120] In any case, the empirical data shows that torture and mistreatment of individuals by states are still widespread enough to suggest their scale would even stretch the *Nicaragua* approach.[121] How then arrive at a customary international law for prohibition of torture?

e Assessment

If Meron does not manage throughout his book to provide for evidence of customary international law in any dogmatically convincing fashion, then it seems that he is at least in good company of a large number of international legal practitioners and scholars – including the International Court of Justice – that have engaged in such appraisal of human rights.[122] Statements seem sufficient proof. Thorough evaluations of customary international law are scarce.

Prevention and Suppression of Torture', 48/3–4 *Revue Internationale de Droit Pénal* (1977) at 139–211, compiled by Spencer Landsman. Out of a pool of 158 states, he finds 45 constitutions that specifically prohibit torture and 36 that prohibit cruel and unusual or inhuman or degrading punishment. See *ibid.*, at 208–209. At the same time, he finds 98 constitutions that "provide for exceptional powers under which torture might not be prohibited". See *ibid.*, at 210.

118 See, *e.g.*, Meron, *supra* n. 82, Chapter 1, at 93–94.

119 See Hathaway, *supra* n. 33, Chapter 1, at 35. See also Alston and Simma, *supra* n. 85, Chapter 1, at 99. See also Chinkin, *supra* n. 86, Chapter 1, at 112: "For evident policy reasons – the desire not to deny the existence of a rule of customary international law prohibiting torture – custom may be asserted by reference to states' words rather than the reality of their actions".

120 Hathaway, *supra* n. 33, Chapter 1, at 35.

121 See *supra* n. 100, Chapter 1, and accompanying text.

122 On a side note, the following transcript of a discussion between Ambassador Helmut Tichy, Legal Adviser of the Austrian Foreign Ministry, and Karl Zemanek at a Round Table event of the Section of International Law and International Relations on 23 October 2013 nicely illustrates the conflict between the dogmatic approach to source doctrine and diplomatic practice:

Zemanek: "What is disturbing to an academic is the levity with which diplomats throw about notions like customary or subsequent practice. The answer is, they would have to be verified".

Tichy: "You can do that".

Zemanek: "Yeah, not with a statement".

Tichy: "You don't apply …"

Zemanek: "You, you cannot prove customary international law with an academic statement, that is impossible. That requires inductive work with state practice of many, many states and it has never been done – but, of course, you are in the very good company of the International Court of Justice, [which] does the same, and it simply says that's customary international law, and then, of course,

Karl Zemanek once remarked on this: "I have never encountered such an article in my entire academic life".[123]

Possibly, the reason is the seemingly onerous, at best tedious task of assessing state practice and *opinio iuris* of around 200 entities, or at least the 193 member states of the United Nations. Of course, this problem is not one restricted to customary international human rights law alone, but customary international law in general.

Maybe scholars are just caught in between wanting to say customary international human rights law exists and having to face the reality that they do not know how. Indeed, it has been conceded by some that the determination of human rights as customary international law is controversial.[124] In 1977, the International Law Commission issued a comment emphasizing that the larger portion of human rights norms remain largely and solely treaty obligations.[125] Arthur Weisburd argues that the fact that states tend to opt out of enforcement procedures under human rights treaties, when given the option, speaks against the existence of an international responsibility for human rights violations.[126] Still, the rhetoric of customary human rights law is honored the world over, by state representatives, the treaty bodies of international organizations, and human rights activists. Yet not by reality.

Unfortunately, scholars have so far failed to reconcile customary international law and human rights or embrace the inherent friction. Instead, they

> since it is a court it is, and since you are the highest authority on international law in the foreign ministry, of course, what you say it is. But there is no proof".

Round Table, 'OSINT (Open Source Intelligence) Through Embassies in Austria. Is That Lawful?', Vienna, 23 October 2013 [video recording of the event on file with the author].

123 Comment by Karl Zemanek at the Joint-Meeting of the International Law Departments of Budapest and Vienna University, Vienna, 29 April 2013. Meron, in his book, manages to name two, when he speaks of "empiric studies of state practice". See Meron, *supra* n. 82, Chapter 1, at 94, fn. 35.

124 See, *e.g.*, August Reinisch, 'Developing Human Rights and Humanitarian Law Accountability of the Security Council for the Imposition of Economic Sanctions', 95/4 *American Journal of International Law* (2001) 859, who, however, also states that some human rights may "qualify as customary rules" and that "strong and convincing arguments may be made for considering [...] some basic human rights, as having attained the status of nonderogable, peremptory norms in the sense of *jus cogens* obligations" at 860 with reference only to an International Law Commission report referring to humanitarian law and the article by Theodor Meron, 'On a Hierarchy of International Human Rights', 80 *American Journal of International Law* (1986), which provides discussion but lacks further evidence beyond the *Restatement of the Law (Third)*. Reinisch goes on to deal with a number of human rights without going into discussion on their status as customary international law; see *ibid.*, at 861–863. See also Schachter, *supra* n. 6, Chapter 1, at 336.

125 See the Draft Articles on State Responsibility with Commentaries, U.N. Doc. A/CN.4/Ser.A/1977/Add.1 (Part 2), *Yearbook of the International Law Commission* (1977-II), at 46, para. 46.

126 Weisburd, *supra* n. 19, at 135.

have chosen to approach the subject by engaging in unsubstantiated assertions, self-referentiality, and misconception of the sources of international law.

3 Human Rights as General Principles of Law

Human rights as general principles of law gained broad attention as a way out of the dilemma of customary international human rights law through an article by Bruno Simma and Philip Alston published in the 1992 *Australian Yearbook of International Law.*[127] Theodor Meron, in his *Human Rights and Humanitarian Norms as Customary Law*, had already taken into account the possibility of resorting to general principles, concluding:

> As human rights norms come to be reflected in national law, the general principles of law (Article 38(1)(c) of the Statue of the ICJ) will and should increasingly become one of the principal methods for the maturation of human rights and humanitarian norms standards into the mainstream of international law.[128]

There are two ways in which it would be possible to incorporate human rights into the body of international law through general principles of law, irrespective of the difficulties associated with this source as such.[129] First, their presence *in foro domestico* could be taken to elevate them to the level of international law as general principles of law. Second, their origin in natural law could be taken to induce their existence *a priori* as general principles of law.

a Following the Comparative Law Approach

The comparative law approach asserts that human rights may be drawn from the *forum domesticum*, be it from constitutions or "regular" domestic law:

> Here, one does indeed encounter principles which are recognized by all domestic systems, such as respect for human life, prohibition of torture and banning of slavery. These principles are today recognized by all nations, notwithstanding the fact that time and again formal pledges are forgotten and breached.[130]

Louis Henkin spoke of "constitutional" and "non-conventional" law in arguing that human rights have "drawn on (and in turn permeated) once-excluded sources, the domestic constitutional systems of states".[131] However, as has already

127 See Alston and Simma, *supra* n. 85, Chapter 1, at 82–108.
128 Meron, *supra* n. 82, Chapter 1, at 247. See, generally, *ibid.*, at 88–89.
129 See *supra* pp. 104 *et seq.*
130 Tomuschat, *supra* n. 128, at 315.
131 See Louis Henkin, 'Sibley Lecture, March 1994. Human Rights and State "Sovereignty"', 25/1 *Georgia Journal of International and Comparative Law* (1995–1996) 39.

been shown with regard to customary international law, constitutional protection does not necessarily correlate with compliance,[132] which may also have to do with the relativity in understanding of rules from one legal system to another, not taking into account the additional problems brought about by language and cultural nuances. How easily can the terms "life", "liberty", or "torture" be understood within the domestic laws of the principal legal systems of the world?

b Following the Natural Law Approach

Alston and Simma, through their 1992 article, emerged as the two main proponents of this idea of non-descriptive, normative general principles of law that gets by entirely without resort to practice: "International law has grown to encompass the protection of the human person spontaneously rather than out of a habit; in the development of human rights law principles have always preceded practice".[133]

In particular, they invoke case law of the International Court of Justice to support their position,[134] which is a convenient reference, as the International Court of Justice in each case simply postulated the existence of rights without delving into their respective origin.[135] In another article by Bruno Simma and Andreas Paulus, general principles of law become equal to customary international law *hors* state practice: "Increasingly, general principles of international law establish themselves from the top down, as it were; that is, not by deduction from domestic law but by proclamation in international fora".[136]

The idea itself, however, was not entirely novel at the publication date of Alston's and Simma's acclaimed article. It had already surfaced with regard to the question of racial discrimination in the dissenting opinion of Judge Tanaka in the *South West Africa Cases.* It is worth reproducing here in length the passages, in which he elaborates on his interpretation of the "general principles of law" of Article 38(1)(c) of the Statute of the International Court of Justice:

> To restrict the meaning to private law principles or principles of procedural law seems from the viewpoint of literal interpretation untenable. [...] In short, they may include what can be considered as "juridical truth". [...] The uniformity of national laws on the protection of human rights is not derived [...] from considerations of expediency by the legislative organs or from the creative power of the custom of a community, but it already exists in spite of its more-or-less vague form. This is of nature *jus naturale* [*sic*] in roman law. [...] The existence of human rights does not depend on the will of a State; neither internally on its law or any other legislative measure, nor internationally on treaty or custom, in which the express or tacit will of a State

132 See *supra* pp. 153 *et seq.*
133 Alston and Simma, *supra* n. 85, Chapter 1, at 107.
134 See *ibid.*, at 104–106.
135 See *supra* ns 122, Chapter 3; 13; 67–69; 92; and 122.
136 Paulus and Simma, *supra* n. 34, Chapter 1, at 307.

> constitutes the essential element.[137] A State or States are not capable of creating human rights by law or by convention; they can only confirm their existence and give them protection. The role of the State is no more than declaratory. [...] [I]t is undeniable that in Article 38, paragraph 1 (c), some natural law elements are inherent. It extends the concept of the source of international law beyond the limit of legal positivism according to which, the States being bound only by their own will, international law is nothing but the law of the consent and auto-limitation of the State. But this viewpoint, we believe, was clearly overruled by Article 38, paragraph 1 (c), by the fact that this provision does not require the consent of States as a condition of the recognition of the general principles. [...] From this kind of source international law could have the foundation of its validity extended beyond the will of States, that is to say, into the sphere of natural law and assume an aspect of its supra-national and supra-positive character.[138]

Oscar Schachter also embraced the idea of general principles of law as a gateway for natural law in 1978.[139]

This view of Alston, Schachter, Simma, and Tanaka was, however, sharply criticized by Alain Pellet – and rightly so, in light of the general principle of law *ut res magis valeat quam pereat*[140] – for representing a sort of "customary international law light".[141]

137 Here, Tanaka refers to the *Reservations* advisory opinion, which he may be reading too narrowly. The wording there is "even without any conventional obligation". This does not *per definitionem* exclude customary international law or general principles of law. See *Reservations to the Convention on the Prevention and Punishment of the Crime of Genocide*, Advisory Opinion of 28 May 1951, ICJ Reports 1951, p. 15, at 23.

138 *South West Africa Cases* (Ethiopia *v.* South Africa; Liberia *v.* South Africa), Dissenting Opinion of Judge Tanaka, ICJ Reports 1966, p. 250, at pp. 294–298.

139 Schachter, *supra* n. 3, at 68.

140 See *supra* n. 396, Chapter 2 and accompanying text.

141 See Pellet, *supra* n. 148, Chapter 1, at 7:

> [T]he problem remains and our authors turn, perhaps too lightly, towards the famous "third source" of international law, the "general principles of law recognised by civilized nations", mentioned in Article 38 of the Statute of the International Court of Justice. But they do not hesitate to profoundly modify the very nature of these principles which, as is generally accepted, must be recognised in foro domestico (by the domestic systems of all the States of which they constitute the common basis) and transposable at international level [*sic*]. But that does not suit our friends who know very well that the freedom of expression or of association, for example, not to mention the right to a fair trial, are far from being guaranteed by the laws of very many States (since it seems that all States must be considered to be "civilised" ...). Thus, these authors hold that the principles in question are sufficiently anchored in positive law by the opinio juris of which they are declared to be the object, hiding, if need be, behind the authority of the International Court of Justice. We have come full circle: our authors have, in this way, reinvented a custom without practice, or general principles of law without the recognition of domestic systems.

A further proponent of the natural law approach, although by way of introducing the additional category of "principles", is Augusto Trindade. In his understanding of international law, these underlie the legal system *a priori*: "If there are no principles, there is no legal system at all. [...] Without general principles, there is no legal system at all".[142]

Louis Henkin also takes this approach, which he calls "constitutional" and "non-conventional" human rights, arguing that "[c]onceptually, it may have sneaked into the law on the back of another idea, '*ius cogens*'".[143]

c Assessment

Although, at first glance, a superficial view might lead to the assumption that torture is prohibited as a general principle of law based upon a comparative legal assessment, this does not take into account relativist considerations that ultimately narrow the prohibition to an empty shell. The problem is that just because the constitutions of a large number of states outlaw torture, this does not mean that the term "torture" is equally understood. It would be absurd to postulate that the freedom of speech, freedom of the press, and freedom of association constituted customary international law on the grounds that Article 125 of the CONSTITUTION OF THE UNION OF SOCIALIST SOVIET REPUBLICS of 5 December 1936 guaranteed them: "Constitutions with human rights provisions that are little more than window-dressing can hardly be cited as significant evidence of practice or 'general principles' of law".[144]

As Lord McNair already held in the *South-West Africa* advisory opinion in 1950:

> The way in which international law borrows from this source is not by means of importing private law institutions "lock, stock and barrel", ready-made and fully-equipped with a set of rules.[145]

Alston and Simma themselves concede that general principles of law do not set out as the most promising candidate for human rights as a non-treaty source of international law.[146] However, they still set out to change this perspective on the general principles of law. Yet until today, "it does not seem that their position has influenced decision-makers".[147]

142 Augusto A. Cançado Trindade, 'General Principles of Law as a Source of International Law', Original Lecture, Sources of Law, United Nations Audiovisual Library of International Law <http://untreaty.un.org/cod/avl/ls/Cancado-Trindade_IL_video_3.html>.
143 See Henkin, *supra* n. 131, 38.
144 Schachter, *supra* n. 6, Chapter 1, at 336.
145 *International Status of South-West Africa*, Separate Opinion of Sir Arnold McNair, ICJ Reports 1950, p. 146, at 148.
146 See Alston and Simma, *supra* n. 85, Chapter 1, at 107: "Admittedly, general principles have not fared too well as a source of international law, mainly due to their natural law flavor and the uncertainties surrounding the ways in which they are to be established and applied".
147 Chinkin, *supra* n. 86, Chapter 1, at 115. For a more contemporaneous appraisal see O'Connell, *supra* n. 67, Chapter 1, at 18.

4 *Preliminary Conclusion*

The main question of this book is whether non-treaty sources are suitable manifestations for normative projects. The distinction between morality and legality is all too often forgotten or, at least, ignored, wilfully or not. Human rights, if they are to exist as (enforceable) rules of international law, must find themselves in either treaty, custom, or general principle of law. In addition to this, moral concepts are distinct from many other areas of international law, in that compliance is based on an altruistic impulse rather than reciprocal relations between states.

Assuming that the acts of state are determined by their respective interests, the underlying motor of reciprocal behavior, this raises the question whether these also encompass an urge for altruism. However, an empirical and structural analysis shows that core consideration related to the survival of the state prevail. These common parameters are national security and a functioning economy. While other factors may play into the equation, they are subsidiary at the most. This is immediately confirmed by a cursory look at state practice. Whenever such subsidiary interests as human rights come into play, they are often means traceable to ulterior ends.

While recognizing these deficiencies, the debate on customary international human rights law has refrained from satisfactorily addressing the issues at either the abstract or the substantive level. Rather, it engages in repetitive self-referentiality, unsubstantiated assertions, and a general misconception of the sources of international law. A high-level empirical analysis of the prohibition of torture under international law perfectly illustrates this deficiency. Scholars have failed to reconcile human rights and customary international law.

The alternative view that human rights would better be conceived as general principles of law has gained little momentum. Apart from the general confusion surrounding this source, both schools of thought on its formation face difficulties when it comes to the identification of human rights. First, their presence *in foro domestico* cannot be proven at face value, taking into account the relativity of what may initially be perceived as one and the same legal concept. "Torture" in the United States is not "torture" in Saudi Arabia. Second, general principles derived from natural law face the hurdle of convincing which plane they are currently on, morality or legality. In addition, the distinction between Article 38(1)(b) and (c) of the STATUTE OF THE INTERNATIONAL COURT OF JUSTICE would be driven *ad absurdum* by simply viewing general principles of law as customary international law *hors* state practice. This would also violate the general principle of law *ut res magis valeat quam pereat.*

What the discourse needs, is an honest assessment of the legal *status quo*. To do this, it is essential that the spheres of morality and legality are clearly distinguished and scholars take a more dogmatic approach based on a positivist understanding of the non-treaty sources of international law:

> What is to be done? That depends on what result is sought. If the advancement of particular values, like human rights, then a recognition that those "values" may be implicit in the legal order but are not enforced by its positive

> institutions could result in a better direction of effort than the current hectoring approach. [...] Indeed, the more the current scene is contemplated, the more clear it becomes that the greatest inhibitions on the use of law to support the order, stability and rationality on which we all depend for economic development and military and political security are the misapprehensions on both sides of the scales: The argument on one side that the law is futile because it rests on idealism in a harsh world, and on the other that the law is futile because it does not embody our highest humanitarian ideals.[148]

The alternative is long-term damage to the credibility of international law and the international human rights regime by failing to meet the legitimate expectations of its subjects and observers; the "meta-effects" of the ivory tower.

B Humanitarian Use of Force: Indeterminacy

The following pages turn to the second example of a normative project of non-treaty law, humanitarian exceptions to the prohibition of the use of force. While human rights served as the best test object to contrast moral concepts with survival interests of the state (and, largely, the disregard of this fact in doctrine), these allow for the discussion of moral concepts in relation to the determinacy of state practice.

The argument is made with regard to two related, yet distinct concepts: Humanitarian intervention theory and the so-called responsibility to protect. Peter Hilpold characterizes them as "two concepts intimately related and yet so far apart".[149] While the "responsibility to protect" is ultimately a development of the former and could, thus, be discussed within its ambit, they will be treated separately to best reflect the individual debates on both ideas.

1 Prohibition of the Threat or Use of Force

Following the devastating course of World War II, the future member states of the newly established United Nations finally introduced a general prohibition of the use as well as the threat of force in Article 2(4) of the Charter of the United Nations.[150] Since then, the international law on the use of force is more or less exclusively governed by the paradigm shift brought about by this provision, which – following the literature and pronouncements by judicial bodies,[151] even if not always mirrored by state practice – constitutes customary

148 Rubin, *supra* n. 198, Chapter 1, at 196.

149 Peter Hilpold, '"And With Success Comes Pardon Hand in Hand": Some Essential Features of R2P and Humanitarian Intervention Drawn From History of International Law' (2014) 1 <http://papers.ssrn.com/sol3/papers.cfm?abstract_id=2413184&download=yes>.

150 See Thomas M. Franck, *Recourse to Force: State Actions Against Threats and Armed Attacks* (Cambridge: Cambridge University Press, 2002) 1.

151 See, prominently, the findings of the International Court of Justice in the *Case Concerning Military and Paramilitary Activities in and Against Nicaragua*

international law[152] and *ius cogens*,[153] even if critical voices have, in part, remained.[154]

(Nicaragua *v.* United States of America), Judgment of 27 June 1986 (Merits), ICJ Reports 1986, p. 14, at 98–106, paras 185–201.

152 See, exemplary for the literature, Dixon, *supra* n. 75, Chapter 1, at 312; Shaw, *supra* n. 88, Chapter 1, at 814. For an early appraisal pointing out that this is likely also the case for non-members of the United Nations, see Arnold Duncan McNair, *The Law of Treaties* (Oxford.: Oxford University Press, 1961) 217. Some even argue such a status prior to the existence of the CHARTER OF THE UNITED NATIONS. See, *e.g.*, *Case Concerning Military and Paramilitary Activities In and Against Nicaragua* (Nicaragua *v.* United States of America), Separate Opinion of President Nagendra Singh, ICJ Reports 1986, p. 151, at 152. See Czapliński, *supra* n. 185, Chapter 2, at 158 with further references in fn. 30. Cf., however, for a more cautious stance Cassese, *supra* n. 29, Chapter 2, at 55.

153 See, *e.g.*, Alston and Simma, *supra* n. 85, Chapter 1, at 103; Olivier Corten, *The Law Against War: The Prohibition on the Use of Force in Contemporary International Law* (French Studies in International Law, Vol. 4; Oxford: Hart Publishing, 2010) 201–213; Frowein, *supra* n. 82; Jennings and Watts, *supra* n. 51, Chapter 1, at 7–8, § 2, and 416, § 126; Nigel Rodley, 'Humanitarian Intervention', in Marc Weller (ed.), *The Oxford Handbook of the Use of Force in International Law* (Oxford: Oxford University Press, 2015) 779; Schachter, *supra* n. 157, at 648; Shaw, *supra* n. 88, Chapter 1, at 89; Simma and Verdross, *supra* n. 50, Chapter 1, at 75, § 96; Bruno Simma, 'NATO, the UN and the Use of Force', 10 *European Journal of International Law* (1999) 3. See also Brownlie, *supra* n. 17, Chapter 2, *passim*; André De Hoogh, '*Jus Cogens* and the Use of Armed Force', in Weller (ed.), *ibid.*, at 1164; Francesco Francioni, 'Balancing the Prohibition of Force With the Need to Protect Human Rights: A Methodological Approach', in Cannizzaro and Palchetti (eds), *supra* n. 67, Chapter 1, at 271 with further references in fn. 5; Gray, *supra* n. 100, Chapter 1, at 30. This is also the position of the United States as reflected in the *Restatement of the Law (Third)*, see American Law Institute, *supra* n. 9, Chapter 2, at 28, §102, Comment k. Interestingly, the International Court of Justice is often attributed as having embraced this notion in the *Nicaragua* case (see, *e.g.*, Alston and MacDonald, *supra* n. 174, Chapter 1, at 7, fn. 19; Zemanek, *supra* n. 162, Chapter 1, at 1106). However, in the often cited p. 100, para. 190, the International Court of Justice merely quotes the position of the International Law Commission on the subject:

> The International Law Commission, in the course of its work on the codification of the law of treaties, expressed the view that "the law of the Charter concerning the prohibition of the use of force in itself constitutes a conspicuous example of a rule in international law having the character of *jus cogens*" (paragraph (1) of the commentary of the Commission to Article 50 of its draft Articles on the Law of Treaties, *ILC Yearbook*, 1966–11, p. 247).

Case Concerning Military and Paramilitary Activities In and Against Nicaragua (Nicaragua *v.* United States of America), Judgment of 27 June 1986 (Merits), ICJ Reports 1986, p. 14. See on this fact also Pellet, *supra* n. 7, Chapter 2, fn. 650; Dina Shelton, 'International Law and "Relative Normativity"', in Malcolm D. Evans (ed.), *International Law,* 4th edn (Oxford: Oxford University Press, 2014) 145.

154 See, *e.g.*, Christian Stadler, 'Zur Aktualität der Theorie vom "Gerechten Krieg". Rechtsethische Überlegungen zur Weltfriedensbotschaft des Hl. Vaters vom Jänner 2000', *Ethica. Jahrbuch des Instituts für Religion und Frieden* (2000) 84,

At face value, the provision seems fairly inclusive. A purely textual reading prohibits the use of force in all circumstances, even if not directed towards the territory of a state itself ("or political independence"). The catch-all phrase "or in any other manner inconsistent with the Purposes of the United Nations" suggests that the use of force may not even be opportune if it is not even directed against a particular state (against non-state actors or in areas that are not part of any state territory such as the high seas or the moon, for example).

The voices emphasizing the pivotal importance of Article 2(4) of the CHARTER OF THE UNITED NATIONS are countless. James Leslie Brierly went as far as to call it "the corner-stone of the Charter system",[155] a notion later picked up by the International Court of Justice in its 2005 *Armed Activities* case.[156] Oscar Schachter has referred to it as "a key principle of the minimum world public order essential for peace and security".[157] Christine Gray calls Article 2(4) of the CHARTER OF THE UNITED NATIONS "[t]he starting point for any examination of the law" on the subject.[158]

who speaks of a "halbherzig-rhetorische Ächtung durch Normierung eines potjomkinschen Gewaltverbots der UNO" in light of prevailing high numbers of civilian casualties; Zemanek, *supra* n. 37, Chapter 1, at 902; *id., supra* n. 162, Chapter 1, at 1106, that the frequency of violations has kept the International Law Commission itself from pronouncing on its status as a norm. Cf., however, *Case Concerning Military and Paramilitary Activities In and Against Nicaragua* (Nicaragua *v.* United States of America), Judgment of 27 June 1986 (Merits), ICJ Reports 1986, p. 14. See on such critical views also O'Connell, *supra* n. 67, Chapter 1, at 11 with further references in fn. 7; Gray, *supra* n. 100, Chapter 1, at 4 with further references in fns 16 and 17. Furthermore, there are a number of interpretations such as the so-called Reagan doctrine, which interpret the prohibition of the use of force as applying only where an element of reciprocity exists. See Jeane J. Kirkpatrick, 'Law and Reciprocity', 78 *Proceedings of the American Society of International Law at its Annual Meeting* (1984) 67–68. See also David J. Scheffer, 'Introduction: The Great Debate of the 1980s', in Allan Gerson, Louis Henkin, Stanley Hoffmarin, Jeane J. Kirkpatrick, William D. Rogers, and David J. Scheffer (eds), *Right v. Might. International Law and the Use of Force*, 2nd edn (New York: Council of Foreign Relations Press, 1991) 2. See further the recent revealing comments by the former Legal Adviser for the US Department of State, John B. Bellinger III: "Many European governments really are sticklers on international law rules on the use of force, particularly after the Iraq war. [...] This may look a lot more justifiable, but they nonetheless feel the obligation to have a legal basis". See Somini Segupta, 'A Host of Possible Objections to Expanded Airstrikes in Syria', *New York Times* (17 September 2014) <www.nytimes.com/2014/09/18/world/middleeast/a-host-of-possible-objections-to-expanded-airstrikes.html?ref=world&_r=0>.

155 Brierly, *supra* n. 169, Chapter 2, at 414.

156 See *Case Concerning Armed Activities on the Territory of the Congo* (Democratic Republic of the Congo *v.* Uganda), Judgment of 19 December 2005, ICJ Reports 2005, p. 168, at 223, para. 148.

157 Oscar Schachter, 'The Legality of Pro-Democratic Invasion', 78/3 *American Journal of International Law* (1984) 646.

158 Gray, *supra* n. 100, Chapter 1, at 6.

The CHARTER OF THE UNITED NATIONS even breaks with the general principle of law of *pacta tertiis nec nocent nec prosunt* in connection with the regulation of the use of force and includes non-member states within the scope of application of Article 2(4) of the CHARTER.[159] Equally, the protection from the threat or use of force is not restricted to member states of the United Nations through the text.

There exist two important exceptions to the prohibition of the threat or use of force within the CHARTER itself: use of force for the purpose of self-defence and measures of collective security.[160] The possible implications of Article 107 of the CHARTER OF THE UNITED NATIONS – one of two "enemy state clauses" of the CHARTER – are not dealt with here, as this provision may now safely be seen as obsolete.[161]

a First Exception: Self-defence

The first exception, self-defence, is traceable as a notion as far back in "Western" philosophy as Cicero,[162] if not even further,[163] and is considered firmly grounded in customary international law.[164] Although the CHARTER OF

159 See Article 2(6) of the CHARTER OF THE UNITED NATIONS: "The Organization shall ensure that states which are not Members of the United Nations act in accordance with these Principles so far as may be necessary for the maintenance of international peace and security". See also Hanspeter Neuhold, *Internationale Konflikte – Verbotene und erlaubte Mittel ihrer Austragung. Versuche einer transdisziplinären Betrachtung der Grundsätze des Gewalt- und Interventionsverbots sowie der friedlichen Streitbeilegung im Lichte der UN-Prinzipiendeklaration 1970 und der modernen Sozialwissenschaft* (Forschungen aus Staat und Recht 37; Vienna: Springer-Verlag, 1977) 71; Shaw, *supra* n. 88, Chapter 1, at 815.

160 Antonio Cassese lists Article 53 of the CHARTER OF THE UNITED NATIONS, which concerns the use of regional arrangements, as a separate exception. See *id., supra* n. 29, Chapter 2, at 56. This provision is, however, to be seen in combination with the Chapter VII powers of the Security Council and may, thus, be subsumed under collective security.

161 See Ian Brownlie, *International Law and the Use of Force by States* (Oxford: Clarendon Press, 1963) 336–337; Cassese, *supra* n. 29, Chapter 2, at 56; Dixon, *supra* n. 75, Chapter 1, at 313. Article 107 of the CHARTER OF THE UNITED NATIONS reads:

> Nothing in the present Charter shall invalidate or preclude action, in relation to any state which during the Second World War has been an enemy of any signatory to the present Charter, taken or authorized as a result of that war by the Governments having responsibility for such action.

Arguably, member states could use force against Germany or Japan, for example, notwithstanding the obligation contained in Article 2(4) of the CHARTER OF THE UNITED NATIONS. See Hans Kelsen, *The Law of the United Nations: A Critical Analysis of its Fundamental Problems* (London: Stevens & Sons, 1950) 805-815. Cf., however, *ibid.*, at 120–121.

162 See Cicero, *supra* n. 37, Chapter 3, 35.

163 See Stephen C. Neff, *War and the Law of Nations: A General History* (Cambridge: Cambridge University Press, 2005) 38.

164 See, with an extensive analysis of state practice, Brownlie, *supra* n. 161, at 113 and 264–275, who comes to the conclusion that the wording of Article 51 of the

THE UNITED NATIONS itself references a pre-existing – "inherent" – right of self-defence, the relevant provisions and procedures are detailed in Article 51 of the CHARTER OF THE UNITED NATIONS.[165]

b Second Exception: Collective Security

The second exception to the prohibition of the threat or use of force are measures taken under the system of collective security, commonly referred to as "Chapter VII", in accordance with the chapter number of the CHARTER OF THE UNITED NATIONS containing the relevant provisions. The power to authorize such measures of collective security rests with the Security Council of the United Nations[166] and the member states of the United Nations have agreed to accept and carry out these measures.[167] The Security Council "has a discretion both in deciding when to act (Article 39) and how to act (Articles 40, 41 an 42 of the Charter)".[168]

CHARTER OF THE UNITED NATIONS simultaneously lays down the provision as it existed under customary international law in 1945. See also, *inter alia*, Jennings and Watts, *supra* n. 51, Chapter 2, at 417–418, § 127; Shaw, *supra* n. 88, Chapter 1, at 1131. See further the findings by the International Court of Justice in the *Case Concerning Military and Paramilitary Activities In and Against Nicaragua* (Nicaragua *v.* United States of America), Judgment of 27 June 1986 (Merits), ICJ Reports 1986, p. 14, 94–97, paras 176–181, and 102–103, para. 193.

165 See also Gray, *supra* n. 100, Chapter 1, at 6:

> Irrespective of whether the UN Charter is seen as a revolutionary departure from existing customary international law on the use of force or as a codification of rules that had already undergone a major shift in the twentieth century, the Charter system was a marked departure from that of the League of Nations, and the language of Articles 2(4) and 51 provides a new terminology and the first expression of the basic rules in their modern form.

166 See Article 24 of the CHARTER OF THE UNITED NATIONS. The parties to the CHARTER specifically agree that "in carrying out its duties under [the primary] responsibility [for the maintenance of international peace and security] the Security Council acts on their behalf". See Richard B. Bilder, 'The Implications of Kosovo for International Human Rights Law', in Alston and MacDonald (eds), *supra* n. 174, Chapter 1, at 149; Olivier Corten, 'Human Rights and Collective Security: Is There an Emerging Right of Humanitarian Intervention?', in *ibid.*, at 87–88.

167 See Article 25 of the CHARTER OF THE UNITED NATIONS. See also *supra* n. 166. Indeed, by way of Article 103 of the CHARTER, the Security Council may arguably override other obligations of member states. See *Questions of Interpretation and Application of the 1971 Montreal Convention Arising From the Aerial Incident at Lockerbie* (Libyan Arab Jamahiriya *v.* United Kingdom), Request for the Indication of Provisional Measures, Order of 14 April 1992, ICJ Reports 1992, p. 3, at 15, paras 39–42. Contrary, Öberg, *supra* n. 223, Chapter 2, at 884.

168 Erika de Wet, *The Chapter VII Powers of the United Nations Security Council* (Oxford: Hart Publishing, 2004) 133, outlining the arguments both in favor of and against a broad discretion of the Security Council in this regard with further references throughout the chapter. See also Ian Brownlie, 'The Decisions of Political Organs of the United Nations and the Rule of Law', in Ronald St. John Macdonald (ed.), *Essays*

In what Michael Byers and Simon Chesterman have deemed the "Humpty Dumpty school of interpretation",[169] even though it has been argued that the Security Council does not carry a "*Kompetenz-Kompetenz*",[170] there are *de facto* no legal restrictions to its actions.[171] This is mainly due to the fact that even if there were, these would be "*de facto* 'non-justiciable'".[172] As August Reinisch has pointed out, the CHARTER OF THE UNITED NATIONS "carefully avoids language that would clearly oblige the Security Council to strictly follow the law when carrying out its policing function"[173] and that "[t]he text of the UN Charter remains 'indeterminate' in this respect".[174] He further holds that its powers concerning international peace and security are "virtually unlimited".[175] In Hans Kelsen's words, "[t]he purpose of the enforcement action under Article 39 is not: to maintain or restore the law, but to maintain, or restore the peace, which is not necessarily identical with the law".[176]

Hence, the Security Council has a broad discretion in deciding if, when, and how such measures will be taken.[177] This should not lead to the conclusion, however, that moral considerations once applied allow for an ensuing threat or use of force in such situations, let alone a legal obligation of the international community to act. It merely means that "domestic affairs" are an invalid "shield" against the application of international measures, as it is up to the Security Council to decide what constitutes such a "domestic affair".

in Honour of Wang Tieya (Dordrecht: Martinus Nijhoff, 1994) 96. Morgenthau calls these provisions the "heart of the United Nations system of law enforcement". See *id.* and Thompson, *supra* n. 64, Chapter 2, at 320.

169 Michael Byers and Simon Chesterman, '"You, the People": Pro-democratic Intervention in International Law', in Gregory H. Fox and Brad R. Roth (eds), *Democratic Governance and International Law* (Cambridge: Cambridge University Press, 2000) 283.

170 See Nico Krisch, 'General Framework', in Daniel-Erasmus Khan, Georg Nolte, Andreas Paulus, and Bruno Simma (eds), *The Charter of the United Nations. A Commentary. Volume II* (Oxford: Oxford University Press, 2012) 1256, para. 38.

171 See, *inter alia*, David L. Bosco, *Five to Rule Them All: The UN Security Council and the Making of the Modern World* (Oxford: Oxford University Press, 2009) 3–4: "There are almost no limits to the body's authority". On the framework within which the Security Council should act *de iure* see Krisch, *ibid.*, at 1263, paras 40–52.

172 De Wet, *supra* n. 168, at 138.

173 August Reinisch, 'Value Conflicts Within the United Nations Security Council', 14 *Austrian Review of International Law* (2009) 41.

174 *Ibid.*, at 54.

175 *Ibid.*, at 60. See further on this issue Aristoteles Constantinides, *Νομικοί Περιορισμοί και Δικαστικός Έλεγχος του Συμβουλίου Ασφαλείας των Ηνωμένων Εθνών* [*Legal Restrictions and Judicial Control of the Security Council of the United Nations*] (Athens: Εκδόσεις Σάκκουλα, 2004); Evelyne Lagrange, 'Le Conseil de Sécurité des Nations Unies Peut-il Violer le Droit International', 37/2 *Revue Belge de Droit International* (2004) 568–591.

176 Kelsen, *supra* n. 161, at 294.

177 See *supra* n. 168 and accompanying text.

2 Non-intervention

For the sake of inclusiveness, one must also mention the principle of non-intervention[178] when discussing Article 2(4) of the CHARTER OF THE UNITED NATIONS. After all, any use of force against a state necessarily means an act that collides with the principle of sovereignty. This "favorite norm of small powers",[179] is "one of the most strongly affirmed [principles] in international law, in classical doctrine at least".[180] Not only does it go "hand in hand" with the prohibition of the threat or use of force,[181] it is a logical consequence of the principle of sovereign equality of states enshrined in Article 2(1) of the CHARTER OF THE UNITED NATIONS.[182] Already Article 8 of the MONTEVIDEO CONVENTION stipulates that "[n]o state has the right to intervene in the internal or external affairs of another".[183] The principle further found entry into the CHARTER OF THE UNITED NATIONS through the inclusion of the rule of non-intervention in the domestic affairs of states through the United Nations in Article 2(7) of the CHARTER OF THE UNITED NATIONS.

Generally, "intervention" has been held to include any interference with the "political, economic, social and cultural systems" of a state or in "its foreign policy".[184] It must be "forcible or dictatorial, or otherwise coercive, in effect depriving the state intervened against of control over the matter in question".[185] As is the case with the prohibition of the use or threat of force, the principle of non-intervention is considered a rule of customary international law.[186]

178 For a recent concise overview of the principle of non-intervention in public international law with further references see Karin Traunmüller, *Völkerrechtliche Fragen im Zusammenhang mit der Einbürgerung von Personen mit Wohnsitz im Ausland am Beispiel der Gesetzgebung der Russischen Föderation* (Doctoral Thesis at the University of Vienna, 2014) 362–364. For a more comprehensive appraisal see Kritsiotis, *supra* n. 65, Chapter 3, at 1008–1013 with extensive references.
179 Henkin, *supra* n. 108, Chapter 1, at 198.
180 Fabri, *supra* n. 45, Chapter 3, at 1008.
181 See Scharf, *supra* n. 79, Chapter 2, at 158. See also Jennings and Watts, *supra* n. 51, Chapter 2, at 428–429, § 128; Shaw, *supra* n. 88, Chapter 1, at 832.
182 Article 2(1) of the CHARTER OF THE UNITED NATIONS: "The Organization is based on the principle of the sovereign equality of all its Members".
183 Article 8 of the CONVENTION ON THE RIGHTS AND DUTIES OF STATES.
184 Jennings and Watts, *supra* n. 51, Chapter 2, at 431, § 129.
185 *Ibid.*, at 432, § 129. On this emphasis on the element of coercion in the earlier versions of Oppenheim's treatise see Ralph Janik, 'Das Interventionsverbot im Zeitalter der Demokratie: Zwischen Obsoleszenz und (Wieder-)Auferstehung', in Andrea Bockley, Ursula Kriebaum, and August Reinisch (eds), *Nichtstaatliche Akteure und Interventionsverbot. Beiträge zum 39. Österreichischen Völkerrechtstag 2014 in Klosterneuburg* (Völkerrecht, Europarecht und Internationales, Vol. 20; Frankfurt am Main: Peter Lang, 2015) 112 with further references as to its reception. See also *ibid.*, at 114 concerning the definition within the *Nicaragua* case. See also, generally, the definition by Simma and Verdross, *supra* n. 50, Chapter 1, at 300, § 490.
186 See Jennings and Watts, *ibid.*, at 429, § 128; Shaw, *supra* n. 88, Chapter 1, at 832 with further references. See further the findings by the International Court of Justice in the *Case Concerning Military and Paramilitary Activities In and*

However, theory and practice have shown that the principle of non-intervention bears much relevance with regard to the use of force, in particular when it comes to measures taken by the Security Council under its Chapter VII powers.[187] Internal situations without relevant cross-border effects have been deemed a "threat to the peace" on numerous occasions,[188] including situations in which the main issue seems to have been the violation of human rights.[189] Furthermore, the development of international criminal law, human rights protection, and the concept of international liability have long lifted or at least have the capacity to break through the shield of "domestic jurisdiction", when it comes to the internal affairs of states. Hélène Ruiz Fabri writes that, generally, "from the perspective of international law, there exist no affairs that are necessarily internal by nature".[190]

While the principle of non-intervention and Article 2(7) of the CHARTER OF THE UNITED NATIONS set out to bar involvement by states as well as the United Nations in the domestic affairs of any other state, the intellectual evolution of human rights and humanitarian concerns perceived as issues concerning the international community as a whole threatens that the principle will become an argument of rhetorical value only.

3 Changing the Rules of Force

The prohibition of the threat or use of force is regulated by the CHARTER OF THE UNITED NATIONS in such an inclusive fashion that one might be tempted to speak of a "self-contained regime".[191] It is hardly possible to think about the use of force outside of this framework. Unless one would rely on the "permissive" interpretation of an existing body of customary international law regarding the use of force that continues to validly co-exist alongside,[192]

Against Nicaragua (Nicaragua *v.* United States of America), Judgment of 27 June 1986 (Merits), ICJ Reports 1986, p. 14, 106–110, paras 202–209.

187 See also Article 2(7) of the CHARTER OF THE UNITED NATIONS, stating that "this principle shall not prejudice the application of enforcement measures under Chapter VII".

188 See with regard to this practice Niko Krisch, 'Article 39', in Khan, Nolte, Paulus, and Simma (eds), *supra* n. 170, at 1282, para. 19. See also Scharf, *supra* n. 79, Chapter 2, at 158–159; Shaw, *supra* n. 88, Chapter 1, at 898–900.

189 See Corten, *supra* n. 166, at 87; Murphy, *supra* n. 192, Chapter 1, at 283–288; Zemanek, *supra* n. 196, Chapter 1, at 2. On human rights as a concern for the international community see Brownlie, *supra* n. 17, Chapter 2, at 295; Cassese, *supra* n. 29, Chapter 2, at 54; Dixon, *supra* n. 75, Chapter 2, at 343; Fabri, *supra* n. 45, Chapter 3, at 37 and 42.

190 Fabri, *supra* n. 45, Chapter 3, at 36.

191 See *Case Concerning United States Diplomatic and Consular Staff in Tehran* (United States of America *v.* Iran), Judgment of 24 May 1980, ICJ Reports 1980, p. 3, at 40, para. 86.

192 See Ian Brownlie, 'Thoughts on Kind-Hearted Gunmen', in Richard B. Lillich (ed.), *Humanitarian Intervention and the United Nations* (Charlottesville: University Press of Virginia, 1973) 141; Dixon, *supra* n. 75, Chapter 1, at 312–315; Gray, *supra* n. 100, Chapter 1, at 31–33. This view has only been relied on

deviation from the United Nations system will never take precedence, in accordance with Article 103 of the CHARTER OF THE UNITED NATIONS.

Still, this does not mean that it should not be possible for any superseding provision in form of either a *lex posterior* or a *lex specialis* to derogate from this body of law. Member states of the United Nations could collude with each other to debunk the system envisioned by the CHARTER. If a sufficient number conspired together to recognize and accept this derogation as a novel peremptory system,[193] not even its *ius cogens* status could save the prohibition of the threat or use of force of the CHARTER OF THE UNITED NATIONS.[194]

Article 103 of the CHARTER OF THE UNITED NATIONS secures the framework on the use of force.[195] Yet, a positivist, textual reading of the "supremacy" or "primacy of the Charter"[196] allows for an interpretation through which non-treaty law could modify the current legal framework to develop new instruments to end atrocities.[197] However, it is arguable that Article 103 of the CHARTER OF THE UNITED NATIONS elevates the provisions

by states twice since 1945: By the UK before the International Court of Justice in the *Corfu Channel Case* and by Israel in 1976 concerning Operation Entebbe. See Brownlie, *supra* n. 161, at 266; Dixon, *supra* n. 75, Chapter 1, at 313–315; Gray, *supra* n. 100, Chapter 1, at 31–33. For some of the rare examples in the literature see Derek W. Bowett, *Self-Defence in International Law* (Manchester: Manchester University Press, 1958) 150–152; Michael Reisman and Myres S. McDougal, 'Humanitarian Intervention to Protect the Ibos', in Richard B. Lillich (ed.), *ibid.*, at 172.

193 See Article 53 of the VIENNA CONVENTION ON THE LAW OF TREATIES, "a norm accepted and recognized by the international community of States".

194 Cf., however, Article 41 VIENNA CONVENTION ON THE LAW OF TREATIES.

195 See Ronald St. Macdonald, 'The Charter of the United Nations as a World Constitution', in Michael N. Schmitt (ed.), *International Law Across the Spectrum of Conflict: Essays in Honour of Professor L.C. Green on the Occasion of his Eightieth Birthday* (International Law Studies, Vol. 75; Newport: Naval War College, 2000) 272–273:

> Article 2.6, together with Article 103, represents the strongest suggestion that the Charter of the United Nations may be seen as a constitutional charter or at least as proof of the universal vocation of the organization itself. […] Article 103, even more forcefully, assigns the Charter a quasi-constitutional relevance by giving it priority over any other treaty obligation that conflicts with the Charter.

See also Simma, *supra* n. 153, at 4–5.

196 See, *e.g.*, Dixon, *supra* n. 75, Chapter 1, at 76. The function has also been compared to the relationship between federal and state law in domestic legal orders. See the statement by the representative of Uruguay, Mr. Oribe, to the 6th Committee at its 18th session regarding the law of treaties UNGAOR, 18th Session, 6th Committee, 792nd Meeting, U.N. Doc. A/C.6/SR.792 (14 October 1963), at 58, para. 23.

197 Of course, this also requires an understanding of customary international law as a non-consensual source which was discussed in Chapter 2.

of the CHARTER to peremptory norms, if only for the member states of the United Nations.[198] This is, generally, held to be the case with regard to

198 See the archetypical definition of *ius cogens* in Article 53 of the VIENNA CONVENTION ON THE LAW OF TREATIES:

> [A] peremptory norm of general international law is a norm accepted and recognized by the international community of States as a whole as a norm from which no derogation is permitted and which can be modified only by a subsequent norm of general international law having the same character.

See in this regard also the statement by the representative of the Netherlands, Mr. Tammes, to the 6th Committee at its 18th session regarding the law of treaties:

> The question of *jus cogens*, dealt with in draft article 37, was not one of classical international law. In an era when the use of force in international relations had been almost unrestricted and when international law had barely begun to recognize human rights, international public order had been the vaguest of concepts. The Agreement concerning the Sudeten German Territory, signed at Munich on 29 September 1938, was one of the few examples of treaties which had come to be regarded as contrary to international public order. The Commission had taken an important step by recognizing the existence of peremptory norms of general international law. The Charter of the United Nations embodies several incontrovertible norms of public international law, such as the prohibition of the use of force in international relations and the obligation to respect fundamental human rights, and Article 103 made those norms peremptory so far as the Member States were concerned. Thus the Charter, as a quasi-universal law-making instrument, had made the idea of jus cogens very much a reality of international law.

See UNGAOR, 6th Committee, 781st Meeting, U.N. Doc. A/C.6/SR.781 (30 September 1963), at 9, para. 2. See also the statement by the representative of the United Arab Republic, Mr. El-Erian:

> The International Law Commission had been right to recognize the existence of rules having the character of jus cogens in Article 37 of its draft. As the representative of the Netherlands had said at the 781st meeting, the United Nations Charter contained several incontestable norms of international public law, and Article 103 of the Charter made those norms obligatory, at any rate for Member States. As a quasi-universal set of norms, the Charter had thus helped considerably to make the idea of jus cogens an international reality. As long ago as 1927, in the case of the S.S. Lotus, Judge J.B. Moore had stated in his dissenting opinion that piracy was in its jurisdictional aspects sui generis and that a pirate was treated as an outlaw, as the enemy of all mankind – hostis humani generis. The origin of the notion of jus cogens went back to the prohibition of certain actions in international law, and the recognition of that notion by the International Law Commission marked the transition from classical international law to the modern law of the United Nations.

See UNGAOR, 18th Session, 6th Committee, 791st Meeting, U.N. Doc. A/C.6/SR.791 (14 October 1963), at 51, para. 16. See further the statements by the representative of Morocco, Mr. Benjelloun, to the 6th Committee, UNGAOR, 18th Session, 6th Committee, 792nd Meeting, U.N. Doc. A/C.6/

prohibition of the use or threat of force.[199] Notwithstanding, a new right would simply have to bear at least equal quality.[200]

SR.792 (14 October 1963), at 57, para. 17, and the representative of Cyprus, Mr. Rossides, UNGAOR, 20th Session, 6th Committee, 892nd Meeting, U.N. Doc. A/C.6/SR.892 (7 December 1965), at 319, para. 19. See in the literature also Robert Kolb, *Théorie du Ius Cogens International* (Paris: Presses Universitaires de France, 2001) 131–134; *id.*, 'L'Article 103 de la Charte des Nations Unies', 367 *Recueil des Cours de l'Académie de Droit International de La Haye* (2013) 86–96; Schwarzenberger, *supra* n. 121, Chapter 1, at 112; Simma and Verdross, *supra* n. 50, Chapter 1, at 75, § 94; Simma, *supra* n. 153, at 5. Contrary Wolfram Karl, *Vertrag und spätere Praxis im Völkerrecht. Zum Einfluß der Praxis auf Inhalt und Bestand völkerrechtlicher Verträge* (Berlin: Springer, 1983) 70, fn. 325:

> Deswegen [because of Article 103 of the CHARTER OF THE UNITED NATIONS] ist die Satzung aber noch nicht *ius cogens*. Ein augenscheinlicher Unterschied liegt z.B. darin, daß Art. 53 WVK im Zusammenhalt mit Art. 44 ergibt, daß der *ius cogens*-widrige Vertrag zur Gänze dahinfällt, während die Rechtsfolgen des Art. 103 SVN nur in einem, überdies auch bloß vorübergehenden, Zurückdrängen des mit der Satzung kollidierenden Vertrags bestehen.

However, while the argument is dogmatically spot-on, the result is essentially the same. The provision in conflict with the obligation under the CHARTER OF THE UNITED NATIONS is inapplicable until the amendment or extinction of the CHARTER, neither of which can be expected within the near future. Thus, it seems fair to speak of the obligations under the CHARTER as "peremptory norms" at least, if not *ius cogens sensu stricto*. See Johann Leiß and Andreas Paulus, 'Article 103', in Khan, Nolte, Paulus, and Simma (eds), *supra* n. 170, at 2136, para. 79. See also Michel Virally, 'Réflexions sur le "jus cogens"', 12 *Annuaire Français de Droit International* (1966) 26, who argues that Article 103 of the CHARTER OF THE UNITED NATIONS merely establishes a hierarchy, whereas *ius cogens* voids the contrary norm. Of course, *ius cogens* also creates a hierarchy. To differentiate between a procedural and a substantial hierarchy in this regard may be as dogmatically correct as it is artificial. The outcome remains in effect the same. Wolfram Karl argues, however, that the CHARTER is higher ranking due to the provision of Article 30(1) VIENNA CONVENTION ON THE LAW OF TREATIES:

> Höherrangig im derogatorischen Sinn ist auch die *Satzung der Vereinten Nationen*. Grundlage für diese Feststellung ist nicht sosehr die Vorrangregel des Art. 103 SVN selbst als vielmehr Art. 30 Abs. 1 WVK. Schon Art. 103 SVN bestimmt zwar, daß im Fall eines Widerspruchs zwischen den sich aus der Satzung ergebenden Mitgliederpflichten und Verpflichtungen aus irgendeinem anderen internationalen Abkommen den Satzungverpflichtungen der Vorrang gebührt. Darin unterscheidet er sich aber nicht wesentlich von anderen Derogationsverboten in Verträgen, welche keine Höherrangigkeit nach sich ziehen. Ausschlaggebend ist jedoch der in Art. 30 Abs. 1 WVK enthaltene Vorbehalt zugunsten Art. 103 SVN, womit dieser Fall der gewöhnlichen Behandlung von Vertragskonflikten entzogen und indirekt im Sinne einer Höherrangigkeit der Satzung geregelt wird.

See *ibid.*, at 70.

199 See *supra* n. 153.

200 See Corten, *supra* n. 166, at 87–88, at 135; Zemanek, *supra* n. 197, Chapter 1, at 73.

That Article 108 of the CHARTER OF THE UNITED NATIONS has been of so little practical relevance, should not create the impression that there have not been any informal developments[201] throughout the history of the organization, such as the possibility of an abstention in the voting procedure of Article 27(3) of the CHARTER OF THE UNITED NATIONS,[202] the replacement of Taiwan and the USSR by China and the Russian Federation respectively,[203] or, most prominently in the public eye, peace-keeping.[204] The "blue helmet" has become the ultimate figurehead of United Nations activity and the term "Chapter Six and a Half",[205] which may first have been coined by former UN Secretary-General Dag Hammarskjöld,[206] is emblematic of the possibility of informal developments outside the framework of the CHARTER OF THE UNITED NATIONS.

Another instance is Article 43 of the CHARTER OF THE UNITED NATIONS, which envisions the creation of a kind of standing military force in order for the Security Council to fulfil its responsibilities under Article 24 of the CHARTER OF THE UNITED NATIONS. However, no such agreement has ever been negotiated by the Security Council. Much rather, in light of the Korean War and a chance blunder by the Soviet representative to the Security Council,[207] a *modus operandi* was established that has prevailed until today, by which measures of armed force are effectively led and coordinated by the respective "willing" member states of a military coalition.[208]

Should these informal developments be called "customary international law"? With regard to the amendment of Security Council voting procedure, Cassese spoke of a "customary modification" and called the voting procedure a "customary process".[209] It has even been argued that

> far from supplanting customary law, and reducing its field of operation to a minimum, the codifying of great tracts of international law will, on account of

201 For an extensive elaboration of informal development and derogation of treaties through customary international law and subsequent practice see Karl, *supra* n. 198.

202 Georg Witschel, 'Article 108', in Khan, Nolte, Paulus, and Simma (eds), *supra* n. 170, at 2205, para. 10.

203 See *ibid.*, at 2205, para. 10.

204 On the early origins of peace-keeping see Cassese, *supra* n. 29, Chapter 2, at 343–344; Shaw, *supra* n. 88, Chapter 2, at 890–891. For further examples of progressive development see Wolfke, *supra* n. 6, Chapter 2, at 79–83.

205 See Shaw, *supra* n. 88, Chapter 1, at 890.

206 *Ibid.*, at 890, fn. 105.

207 For a contemporary appraisal of United Nations practice with regard to the situation in Korea see Hans Kelsen, *Recent Trends in the Law of the United Nations: A Supplement to 'The Law of the United Nations'* (London: Stevens & Sons, 1951) 927–949 and 953–990.

208 See Cassese, *supra* n. 29, Chapter 2, at 350, who argues that a "*customary* rule has evolved in the international community which is also operative within the UN legal system, in that it broadens the scope of Chapter VII of the Charter". See also *ibid.*, at 339–340 and 346–347; Dixon, *supra* n. 75, Chapter 1, at 330–331; Shaw, *supra* n. 88, Chapter 1, at 909–910; Simma, *supra* n. 153, at 4.

209 Cassese, *supra* n. 29, Chapter 2, at 166.

> the practical and political difficulties of amending multilateral treaties, whether codifying or otherwise, give over the development of international law almost entirely into the hands of custom, operating upon and beyond the codifying treaties.[210]

Such informal amendments of the CHARTER OF THE UNITED NATIONS have also been referred to as "dynamic interpretations" or "*de facto* modification of the Charter":[211] "The Charter is, as often stated, a living instrument. It is, like every constitutional instrument, continuously interpreted, molded and adapted to meet the interests of the parties".[212]

The possibility of such amendments has since been confirmed by the International Court of Justice in the *Namibia* advisory opinion with regard to the Security Council voting procedure, whereby the International Court of Justice seemed to frame it as an act of interpretation of the CHARTER.[213] In any case, all these instances have in common that they are grounded in the acceptance of states of that particular practice of the organization.

For present argument, it is important insofar as it shows that there is not just the formal possibility through a restrictive interpretation of Article 103 of the CHARTER OF THE UNITED NATIONS of amending the provisions of the CHARTER through customary international law, but that there is also historic precedent, including with regard to the use of force.

4 Humanitarian Intervention Theory

While the preceding pages have already dealt with the concept of "intervention", which is usually restricted to the use of force in the context of humanitarian intervention theory, "humanitarian" cannot be equated with "human" directly, as in the sense of human rights. Rather, "humanitarian" has been defined as "concerned with the condition of man, considered solely as a human being without regard to the value which he represents as a military, political, professional or other unit".[214] This definition implicitly conveys the context in which the term becomes relevant here: armed conflict.

210 Thirlway, *supra* n. 8, Chapter 2, at 146.

211 See Nico J. Schrijver, 'The Future of the Charter of the United Nations', 10 *Max Planck Yearbook of United Nations Law* (2006) 13.

212 Schachter, *supra* n. 6, Chapter 1, at 118–119.

213 See *Legal Consequences for States of the Continued Presence of South Africa in Namibia (South West Africa) notwithstanding Security Council Resolution 276 (1970)*, Advisory Opinion of 21 June 1971, ICJ Reports 1971, p. 16, at 22, para. 22. As Michael Akehurst points out, some refer to it as an "amendment", whereas the *Namibia* opinion refers to is as an "interpretation". See *id.*, 'The Hierarchy of the Sources of International Law', 47 *British Yearbook of International Law* (1974–1975) 278.

214 Jean S. Pictet (ed.), *The Geneva Conventions of 12 August 1949. Commentary. Volume I. Geneva Convention for the Amelioration of the Condition of the Wounded*

Humanitarian intervention theory deals with the use of force to end atrocities abroad. Its development is usually categorized into two separate stages, distinguished in accordance with state practice: nineteenth-century humanitarian intervention and "modern" humanitarian intervention.[215]

a Nineteenth-Century "Humanitarian" Intervention

Throughout the nineteenth century, the use or threat of force was considered a legitimate means of protecting citizens and their property (or that of states) abroad.[216] As opposed to "modern" humanitarian intervention theory, the nineteenth-century model can be seen as the more extreme variant of diplomatic protection, aimed at protecting ethnic and religious minorities and kin.[217]

It is highly questionable, whether states were primarily driven by their humanitarian considerations during these instances.[218] These "expeditions" were frequently aimed at furthering political or diplomatic interests of the intervening state.[219] In addition, the idea of humanitarian concern for the affairs of foreign citizens was already sharply criticized by its contemporaries, most prominently John Stuart Mill.[220]

and Sick in Armed Forces in the Field (Geneva: International Committee of the Red Cross, 1952) 108, Article 9.

215 See Brownlie, *supra* n. 17, Chapter 2, at 742.

216 See Shaw, *supra* n. 88, Chapter 1, at 829. For a general overview of nineteenth-century practice see Franck and Rodley, *supra* n. 192, Chapter 1, at 279–285; Reisman and McDougal, *supra* n. 192, at 178–183; Murphy, *supra* n. 192, Chapter 1, at 33–64.

217 See Richard B. Lillich, 'Forcible Self-Help Under International Law', 62 *International Law Studies Series. US Naval War College* (1980) 134:

> For instance, the phrase was always stated that if the treatment of a state to its nationals shocks the conscience of mankind, as did the treatment of the Jews in Russia and various Christians in Turkey during the last century, then generally the great powers would mount some kind of expedition that would intervene and attempt to bring an end to what they deemed to be a shocking violation of human rights.

See also Rodley, *supra* n. 153, at 775.

218 See Etzersdorfer and Janik, *supra* n. 57, Chapter 3, at 187; Franck and Rodley, *supra* n. 192, Chapter 1, at 279; Murphy, *supra* n. 192, Chapter 1, at 63; Rodley, *supra* n. 153, at 780. Cf. Hafner, *supra* n. 75, Chapter 1, at 36, who connects these actions with the democratic development of intervening states.

219 See Brownlie, *supra* n. 17, Chapter 2, at 742, giving the United States' invasion of Cuba in 1898 as an example for state practice using humanitarian concerns as a pretext for imperial interests; Cassese, *supra* n. 29, Chapter 2, at 299.

220 See Thomas M. Franck, 'The Emerging Right to Democratic Governance', 86/1 *American Journal of International Law* (1992) 82: "John Stuart Mill once observed that the moral fiber of a nation is weakened if the intervention of outsiders spares its people the trouble of liberating themselves". See also Karsten Nowrot and Emily W. Schabacker, 'The Use of Force to Restore Democracy:

b "Modern" Humanitarian Intervention

Today, humanitarian intervention is usually understood as the application of armed force on humanitarian grounds in the absence of a situation of self-defence or a Security Council mandate.[221] Alternatively, it is understood either as a right or justification or a duty[222] – or simply a political term for that matter.[223] Sean Murphy, in his seminal treatise on the topic that captures the discourse prior to Kosovo,[224] uses the following working definition, reflecting the change of paradigms from classic, nineteenth century to "modern" humanitarian intervention theory:

> Humanitarian intervention is the threat or use of force by a state, group of states, or international organization primarily for the purpose of protecting the nationals of the target state from widespread deprivations of internationally recognized rights.[225]

The focus has, thus, shifted from the protection of nationals and ethnic or religious kin to the protection of "nationals of the target state".[226]

Numerous examples of supposed state practice for "purely humanitarian" intervention[227] have been considered in the literature: Belgium and the United States in the Congo in 1964, the United States in the Dominican Republic in 1965, India in Bangladesh (then Eastern Pakistan) in 1971, Syria in Lebanon in 1976, Tanzania in Uganda in 1979, Vietnam in Cambodia in 1978, the Soviet Union in Afghanistan in 1979, France in the Central African Empire in 1979, the United States in Grenada in 1983 and in Panama in 1989, France, the United Kingdom, and the United States in Iraq in 1991, ECOMOG in Liberia and Sierra Leone between 1989 and 1999, and NATO in the Federal Republic of Yugoslavia in 1999:[228]

International Legal Implications of the ECOWAS Intervention in Sierra Leone', 14 *American University International Law Review* (1998–1999) 410.

221 For a first overview of the general literature on this subject see, *inter alia*, the references given by Brownlie, *supra* n. 17, Chapter 2, at 742, fn. 38; Shaw, *supra* n. 88, Chapter 1, at 838, fn. 194.

222 See Alston and MacDonald, *supra* n. 174, Chapter 1, at 7.

223 See Katharina Wodarz, *Gewaltverbot, Menschenrechtsschutz und Selbstbestimmungsrecht im Kosovo-Konflikt* (Schriften zum Staats und Völkerrecht, Vol. 95; Frankfurt am Main: Peter Lang, 2002) 64.

224 See also the excellent bibliography provided by Murphy, *supra* n. 192, Chapter 1, at 399–418. For an earlier overview of the literature see Reisman and McDougal, *supra* n. 192, at 168–178.

225 Murphy, *supra* n. 192, Chapter 1, at 12.

226 For a later example of the nineteenth-century approach, see Lane, 'Mass Killing by Governments', *supra* n. 4, at 244–245.

227 See Franck, *supra* n. 150, Chapter 9 (of Franck's book).

228 See, *inter alia*, Franck, *ibid.*, at 139–173; Rodley, *supra* n. 153, at 781–787; Murphy, *supra* n. 192, Chapter 1, at 83–115. For a more critical perspective on

> In assessing these incidents, the initial line of inquiry is whether the intervening state's primary reason for intervening was to prevent the severe and widespread deprivation of human rights. If this cannot be said, then the intervention is not evidence of a belief by the intervening state that a right of unilateral humanitarian intervention exists under the UN Charter.[229]

However, it seems that none of these are fully devoid of ulterior motives.[230] Indeed, as Michael Walzer holds in his seminal treatise on the subject of armed conflict:

> I have not found any [clear examples of what is called "humanitarian intervention"], but only mixed cases where the humanitarian motive is one among several. States don't send their soldiers into other states, it seems, only in order to save lives. The lives of foreigners don't weigh that heavily in the scales of domestic decision-making. So we shall have to consider the moral significance of mixed motives. It is not necessarily an argument against humanitarian intervention that it is, at best, partially humanitarian, but it is a reason to be skeptical and to look closely at the other parts.[231]

c Kosovo

NATO's Operation Allied Force against the Federal Republic of Yugoslavia in 1999 has become the benchmark for "modern" humanitarian intervention theory,[232] "regarded by some as pointing to a genuine paradigm shift at the level not just of international relations but also of international law itself".[233] Notwithstanding the absence of a Security Council resolution, NATO forces commenced the bombing of targets throughout the Federal Republic of Yugoslavia.[234]

the precedents of humanitarian intervention theory see Franck and Rodley, *supra* n. 192, Chapter 1, at 285–289; Zemanek, *supra* n. 99, Chapter 1, at 414–417.

229 Murphy, *supra* n. 192, Chapter 1, at 85. See also *ibid.*, at 143.

230 See with regard to Uganda and Vietnam Lane, 'Mass Killing by Governments', *supra* n. 4, at 241–242. With regard to Kosovo see *infra* ns 254–255.

231 Walzer, *supra* n. 200, Chapter 1, at 102.

232 See Alston and MacDonald, *supra* n. 174, Chapter 1, at 7; Ryan Goodman, 'Humanitarian Intervention and Pretexts for War', 100 *American Journal of International Law* (2006) 108; Hilpold, *supra* n. 192, Chapter 1, at 437; Tesón, *supra* n. 205, Chapter 1, at 42.

233 Corten, *supra* n. 166, at 108.

234 For a concise recapitulation of the activities at the level of international relations and the United Nations in particular see Antonio Cassese, 'A Follow-up: Forcible Humanitarian Countermeasures and Opinio Necessitatis', 10/4 *European Journal of International Law* (1999) 792–796; Ian Johnstone, 'The Plea of "Necessity" in International Legal Discourse: Humanitarian Intervention and Counter-terrorism', 43 *Columbia Journal of Transnational Law* (2004–2005) 362–366; Hilpold, *supra* n. 192, Chapter 1, at 438–442 and 459–462; Simma, *supra* n. 153, at 6–14.

Did this represent an act of state practice accompanied with *opinio iuris* of such weight to create customary international humanitarian intervention law? Michael Scharf and Paul Williams quote an interesting passage by the acting legal adviser of the US Department of State, Michael Matheson on the issue:

> About six months before the actual conflict, at the time when NATO was considering giving an order to threaten the use of force, the political community of NATO got together and had a discussion about what the basis of such threat of force would be. At the end of the discussion, it was clear that there was no common agreement on what might be the justification. There were some NATO members who were prepared to base it on a new doctrine of humanitarian intervention; but most members of the NATO Council were reluctant to adopt a relatively open-ended new doctrine. So at the end of that week, the NATO political community said, here is a list of all of the important reasons why it is necessary for us to threaten the use of force. And at the bottom, it said that under these unique circumstances, we think such actions would be legitimate. There was deliberate evasion of making a "legal" assertion. And this same process occurred in the U.S. Government. There were some who wanted to articulate that humanitarian intervention in [*sic*] now the basis for U.S. action. There was another theory from the Department of Defense, which wanted to adopt sort of an expanded idea of self-defense based on the general interest of the United States in the region; but on reflection, nobody was really prepared to throw all the eggs into either of those baskets. So we ended up with a formulation similar to that of NATO, where we listed all of the reasons why we were taking action and, in the end, mumbled something about its being justifiable and legitimate but not a precedent. So in a sense, it was something less than a definitive legal rationale – although it probably was taken by large parts of the public community as something like that.[235]

In Scharf's terminology,[236] the 1999 NATO intervention did not fulfil its potential to represent a "Grotian Moment".[237] Contrary, Murphy held that any "positivist analysis must consider the precedential value of Kosovo as a law-shaping incident":[238]

235 Michael P. Scharf and Paul R. Williams, *Shaping Foreign Policy in Times of Crisis: The Role of International Law and the State Department Legal Adviser* (Cambridge: Cambridge University Press 2010) 124–125. See also Scharf, *supra* n. 79, Chapter 2, at 172–173.

236 See *supra* n. 147, Chapter 2.

237 Scharf, *supra* n. 79, Chapter 2, at 181.

238 Sean D. Murphy, 'The Intervention in Kosovo: A Law-shaping Incident?', 94 *American Society of International Law Proceedings* (2000) 303.

> In short, for positivists baldly to claim that the intervention in Kosovo was unlawful rings hollow given the global reaction, and those who persist in calling it unlawful risk becoming irrelevant voices in the wilderness. Moreover, for positivists to assert that regardless of the legality of this incident, the old rules remain unchanged, also rings hollow.[239]

Most legal analysis or synthesis of the debate, either in favor or against a humanitarian exception to the prohibition of the use of force, has focused on either of the following: government and international organization statements and their underlying lines of argument; the problems of definition or case by case application, *i.e.* who decides when to intervene and when not; general operative concerns as the *ius humanum in bello* as a precondition to a *ius ad bellum humanitarium.*[240] Rarely, if at all, was the dogmatic issue of law formation scrutinised in the context of intervention.[241] As Brownlie points out, "the partisans of humanitarian intervention either ignore the conditions for the formation of new principles of customary law or, on occasion, propose that the requirement of *opinio juris* be relaxed".[242]

Some simply argue that both legality and illegality may be legitimately argued.[243] While the spectrum within the academic debate ranges from violation of international law to an existing right of humanitarian intervention, Operation Allied Force was ultimately deemed "illegal but legitimate" in the 2000 "Goldstone Report".[244] Simma finds that "there do occur 'hard cases' in which terrible dilemmas must be faced, and imperative political and moral considerations may appear to leave no choice but to act outside the law".[245] Then US Secretary of State at the time, Madeleine Albright, called it a "unique situation *sui generis* in the region of the Balkans".[246] One

239 *Ibid.*, at 303.

240 See Bilder, *ibid.*, at 153–159; Jochen A. Frowein, 'Der Schutz des Menschen ist zentral. Der Krieg in Kosovo und die völkerrechtliche Regelung der Gewaltanwendung', *Neue Zürcher Zeitung* (17 July 1999) 62; Christian Stadler, 'Internationales Recht – Völkerrecht und humanitäre Intervention', in Edwin R. Micewski, Brigitte Sob, and Wolfgang Schober (eds), *Ethik und internationale Politik/Ethics and International Politics* (Schriftenreihe der Landesverteidigungsakademie; Vienna: Literas – Universitätsverlag, 2001) 30–31; Wodarz, *supra* n. 223, at 145–150.

241 See Dixon, *supra* n. 75, Chapter 1, at 325.

242 Brownlie, *supra* n. 17, Chapter 1, at 745.

243 Hurd, *supra* n. 240, at 308.

244 Independent International Commission on Kosovo, *The Kosovo Report. Conflict. International Report. Lessons Learned* (Oxford: Oxford University Press, 2000) 4. Cf, also *ibid.*, at 186 and 289. For a critique of this approach see Anthea Roberts, 'Legality Verses Legitimacy: Can Uses of Force be Illegal but Justified?', in Alston and MacDonald (eds), *supra* n. 174, Chapter 1, at 184–213.

245 Simma, *supra* n. 153, at 22.

246 US Department of State, Secretary of State Madeleine K. Albright, Press Conference with Russian Foreign Minister Igor Ivanov, Singapore, 26 July 1999 <http://1997-2001.state.gov/www/statements/1999/990726b.html>.

author went as far as to herald the return of natural law.[247] Of course, from the rule of law perspective, these determinations are utterly unsatisfactory.

Scholars have held it a "significant feature"[248] of the NATO campaign that "there were no strategic or material interests of NATO nations in Kosovo".[249] Retrospective analysis has shown, however, that humanitarian concerns were not the only underlying interest. As Brownlie points out,

> beginning in October 1998, the threats of force were linked directly to a collateral political agenda, that is, the acceptance by Yugoslavia of various *political* "demands" concerning the status of Kosovo, these "demands" being presented under threat of a massive bombing campaign.[250]

Additionally, it has been regarded as "significant that the situation was unfolding just five years after the UN failed to take action to halt genocide in Rwanda".[251]

d Assessment

The Charter of the United Nations can neither be explicitly read to allow for humanitarian intervention,[252] nor has there been any subsequent practice to confirm a change. The International Court of Justice, in the *Nicaragua* case, clearly spoke out against the existence of a right of unilateral humanitarian intervention.[253] Drawing a line back to the genocide of the

247 See, *e.g.*, Rudolf Weiler, 'Krieg und Frieden in der VR-Ethik', *Ethica. Jahrbuch des Instituts für Religion und Frieden* (2000) 177.

248 Scharf, *supra* n. 79, Chapter 2, at 161.

249 Tesón, *supra* n. 205, Chapter 1, at 43. See also Murphy, *supra* n. 995, at 302.

250 Brownlie, *supra* n. 17, Chapter 2, at 743.

251 Scharf, *supra* n. 79, Chapter 2, at 157.

252 See Murphy, *supra* n. 192, Chapter 1, at 75.

253 See *Case Concerning Military and Paramilitary Activities In and Against Nicaragua* (Nicaragua *v.* United States of America), Judgment of 27 June 1986 (Merits), ICJ Reports 1986, p. 14, at 134–135, para. 268:

> [W]hile the United States might form its own appraisal of the situation as to respect for human rights in Nicaragua, the use of force could not be the appropriate method to monitor or ensure such respect. With regard to the steps actually taken, the protection of human rights, a strictly humanitarian objective, cannot be compatible with the mining of ports, the destruction of oil installations, or again with the training, arming and equipping of the *contras*. The Court concludes that the argument derived from the preservation of human rights in Nicaragua cannot afford a legal justification for the conduct of the United States, and cannot in any event be reconciled with the legal strategy of the respondent State, which is based on the right of collective self-defence.

See Goodman, *supra* n. 232, at 111; Murphy, *supra* n. 192, Chapter 1, at 129. See also *The Corfu Channel Case* (United Kingdom of Great Britain and Northern

Armenians in the Ottoman Empire, Jay Winter asks and immediately answers whether

> anyone [can] advocate selective intervention after the risk of genocide is established without opening the floodgates to unilateral military action of a more undifferentiated kind? No one has a clear answer to this question today, and no one had one in 1915.[254]

State practice is erratic[255] or, possibly, reduced to singular instances[256] and underlined by a myriad of underlying interests with varying expressions of *opinio iuris.*[257] It is, thus, no coincidence that accounts of humanitarian intervention educate the reader more about historical incidents than on the status of the law. Franck writes that "law [...] does not thrive when its implementation produces *reductio ad absurdum*: when it grossly offends most persons' common moral sense of what is *right*".[258] At the same time, the rule of law does not thrive, when the law is derived from a "common moral sense", dependent on the contemporaneous public sentiment. As Martin Dixon holds,

> should it be true that a right of humanitarian intervention is in the making, we must remember that for the international lawyer who believes in a

Ireland *v.* Albania), Judgment of 9 April 1949 (Merits), ICJ Reports 149, p. 4, at 35. See on this Franck and Rodley, *supra* n. 192, Chapter 1, at 303; Zemanek, *supra* n. 196, Chapter 1, at 5.

254 Jay Winter, 'Introduction: Witness to Genocide', in Jay Winter (ed.), *America and the Armenian Genocide of 1915* (Cambridge: Cambridge University Press, 2013) 3.

255 See Dixon, *supra* n. 75, Chapter 1, at 324; Zemanek, *supra* n. 196, Chapter 1, at 8. Critically, however, Franck, *supra* n. 150, at 189:

> Actions taken in assertion of humanitarian purpose should be judged primarily by whether other remedies had been exhausted, and whether the crisis was averted or assuaged by the intervenor, with the least possible collateral damage. But it is no argument that states willing to intervene in Kosovo may not be equally willing to intervene in Chechnya or Tibet. Such inconstancy [*sic*] demonstrates little but states' sensible tactical realism. The ultimate test of a humanitarian intervention's legitimacy is whether it results in significantly more good than harm, not whether there has been a consistent pattern of such interventions whenever and wherever humanitarian crises have arisen.

For a more differentiated view see Kritsiotis, *supra* n. 65, Chapter 3, at 1037–1039.

256 See Cassese, *supra* n. 234, at 796–797.

257 See, in particular, on reactions to the NATO operation in Kosovo, Brownlie, *supra* n. 17, Chapter 2, at 743–744, and Goodman, *supra* n. 232, at 112, fn. 26 and accompanying text. For an attempt at distilling customary international law at face value see Arthur M. Weisburd, 'Consistency, Universality, and the Customary Law of Interstate Force', in Cannizzaro and Palchetti (eds), *supra* n. 67, Chapter 1, at 31–77.

258 Thomas M. Franck, *Recourse to Force. State Actions Against Threats and Armed Attacks* (Cambridge: Cambridge University Press, 2002) 178.

> theory of the "sources" of international law, such a right can exist only if it is based in treaty or found in state practice supported by adequate *opinio juris*. There is no moralistic magic that can manufacture the right simply because it ought to exist.[259]

Similarly, Olivier Corten, holds:

> Technically, the consecration of a "right of humanitarian intervention" could only emerge from three equally difficult paths: Formal amendment of the UN Charter, authentic interpretation of the Charter, or the establishment of a new customary rule which would supplant the principles of the Charter.[260]

Thus, if customary international law were to be proven, the proverbial "man on the Clapham omnibus" would have to find sufficient state practice and *opinio iuris*. In addition to the question of state interest, humanitarian intervention suffers from the fact that the humanitarian motive may simply not be discernible. State practice and even statements are indeterminate, as the Kosovo example shows.

An alternative would be to simply focus on official governmental statements for the identification of *opinio iuris*. However, if the analysis is restricted to the arguments and rhetoric of states, as has been suggested by a number of authors,[261] the German annexation of Bohemia and Moravia in 1938[262] or the intervention of the Soviet Union in Hungary in 1956 and in Czechoslovakia in 1968[263] could even be rationalized as instances of humanitarian intervention. This extreme example shows the necessity of a common-sense assessment of the legal *status quo* through application of sound legal methodology. The International Court of Justice itself has distinguished between international rhetoric and *opinio iuris*.[264]

259 Dixon, *supra* n. 75, Chapter 1, at 325.
260 Corten, *supra* n. 166, at 134.
261 See, *e.g.*, Corten, *ibid.*, at 88, Chapter 1: "The 'humanitarian' part need not be exclusive, but must be an essential aspect of the justification put forward by those intervening. The criterion thus refers to the justificatory discourse rather than the true reasons for military action [...]".
262 See also Brownlie, *supra* n. 192, at 143; Franck and Rodley, *supra* n. 192, Chapter 1, at 284; Goodman, *supra* n. 232, at 113; Koskenniemi, *supra* n. 66, Chapter 1, at 167.
263 See also Franck and Rodley, *supra* n. 192, Chapter 1, at 278 and 285–286.
264 See *Case Concerning Military and Paramilitary Activities In and Against Nicaragua* (Nicaragua *v.* United States of America), Judgment of 27 June 1986 (Merits), ICJ Reports 1986, p. 14, at 109, para. 207:

> In fact however the Court finds that States have not justified their conduct by reference to a new right of intervention or a new exception to the principle of its prohibition. The United States authorities have on some occasions clearly stated their grounds for intervening in the affairs of a foreign State for reasons connected with, for example, the domestic policies of that country, its ideology, the level of its armaments, or the direction of its foreign policy. But these

However, the view persists that such a foundation in positive international law is unnecessary[265] or that it would be best to simply acquiesce in violations.[266] Thomas Franck has argued that "it is not necessary to insist that humanitarian intervention has become legal"; consequences are not to be expected.[267] In Myres McDougal's words, it is simply enough "for influential people to assert in a very loud voice that it is law".[268]

Alternatively, Antonio Cassese points to *opinio necessitatis* as a possible benchmark for assessing customary international law in the case of humanitarian intervention.[269] While this seems a more convincing proposition than the identification of customary international law by resorting to natural law or *opinio iuris* derived from state rhetoric, Cassese himself emphasized the differentiation between *opinio iuris* and *opinio necessitatis*, with the latter standing at the beginning of the development towards a new customary international law before becoming *opinio iuris* if it "does not encounter strong and consistent opposition from other States but is increasingly accepted, or acquiesced in".[270]

In Kosovo, this was clearly not the case. The fact that no Security Council mandate existed is in and of itself indicative of strong and consistent opposition. Cassese writes that "a limited number of countries" protested and criticized Operation Allied Force. However, this "limited number of countries" included two permanent members of the Security Council, Russia and China, as well as two states that took part in the operation, Germany and Belgium.[271]

5 *The "Responsibility to Protect"*

Following the ebb of humanitarian intervention debate in the wake of the 'Goldstone Report', the concept marvellously resurfaced as a new idea: the "responsibility to protect", oftentimes abbreviated as "RtoP" or "R2P".[272] It

were statements of international policy, and not an assertion of rules of existing international law.

265 See Roland Rich, 'Bringing Democracy into International Law', 12/3 *Journal of Democracy* (2001) 25: "The best response to those who object to 'new' rights is that broadening the subject matter may be the most effective way to ensure the widest adherence to all human rights norms".

266 See Schachter, *supra* n. 6, Chapter 1, at 126: "It would be better to acquiesce in a violation that is considered necessary and desirable in the particular circumstances than to adopt a principle that would open a wide gap in the barrier against unilateral use of force".

267 Franck, *supra* n. 262, at 191.

268 See *supra* n. 154, Chapter 1.

269 Cassese, *supra* n. 234, at 797–798.

270 See *supra* n. 166, Chapter 2, and accompanying text.

271 Cassese, *supra* n. 234, at 798.

272 For an overview of the discourse see Jean-Marc Thouvenin, 'Genèse de l'Idée de Responsabilité de Protéger', in Société Française Pour le Droit International (ed.), *Colloque de Nanterre. La Responsabilité de Protéger* (Paris: Éditions Pedone, 2008) 21–38.

was – at least for a while – arguably "all the rage in UN circles",[273] although some simply found it a rebranding of the humanitarian intervention debate.[274] The words changed and allowed for the reconsideration of a discourse that had run into a dead-end.[275] The "responsibility to protect" is, thus, a prime example of Koskenniemi's *dictum* that "[w]ords are politics".[276]

At the same time, the parameters changed and the idea of humanitarian intervention was stripped of its post-colonial underpinnings through omission of the word "intervention".[277] It was remodelled into a responsibility.[278] The dilemma of humanitarian intervention and state sovereignty would be overcome since the opposing "two sovereign foundations of modern discourse; state and man" could now "supposedly live side by side".[279] The concept "constitutes a synthesis" between "the protection of civilians (human rights law, humanitarian law, international criminal law, and refugee law)" and "the law on the use of force".[280]

273 José E. Alvarez, 'The Schizophrenias of R2P', in Alston and MacDonald (eds), *supra* n. 174, Chapter 1, at 275.

274 See William Schabas, *Unimaginable Atrocities: Justice, Politics, and Rights at the War Crimes Tribunals* (Oxford: Oxford University Press, 2012) 117.

275 See critically, however, *ibid.*, at 283–284.

276 Koskenniemi, *supra* n. 191, Chapter 1, at 395.

277 See Thouvenin, *supra* n. 276, at 23:

> Dans "intervention humanitaire", le premier mot, "intervention", tonne aux oreilles des juristes comme un coup de canon, suggérant les abus de la politique de la canonnière que la célèbre convention Drago-Porter a entendu partiellement interdire à compter de 1907.

See also Anne Orford, *Reading Humanitarian Intervention: Human Rights and the Use of Force in International Law* (Cambridge: Cambridge University Press, 2003) *passim*; Zemanek, *supra* n. 195, Chapter 1, at 4.

278 For the origins of this concept see Francis M. Deng, Sadikiel Kimaro, Terrence Lyons, Donald Rothchild, and I. William Zartman, *Sovereignty as Responsibility: Conflict Management in Africa* (Washington: The Brookings Institution, 1996). See also Alvarez, *supra* n. 277, at 275; Alex J. Bellamy, 'The Responsibility to Protect and the Problem of Military Intervention', 84/4 *International Affairs* (2008) 618–620; *id.*, 'Realizing the Responsibility to Protect', 10 *International Studies Perspectives* (2009) 111; Anne Peters, 'The Responsibility to Protect: Spelling out the Hard Legal Consequences for the UN Security Council and its Members', in Ulrich Fastenrath, Rudolf Geiger, Daniel-Erasmus Khan, Andreas Paulus, Sabine von Schorlemer, and Christoph Vedder (eds), *From Bilateralism to Community Interest: Essays in Honour of Judge Bruno Simma* (Oxford: Oxford University Press, 2011) 299. See also on the importance of responsibility within this discourse Christian Stadler, 'Military Ethics as Part of a General System of Ethics', in Edwin R. Micewski (ed.), *Civil-Military Aspects of Military Ethics (Volume 1)* (Vienna: National Defense Academy Printing Office, 2003) 6–7.

279 Helle Malmvig, 'The Reproduction of Sovereignties. Between Man and State During Practices of Intervention', 36 *Cooperation and Conflict* (2001) 266.

280 Peters, *supra* n. 282, at 297.

The report published by the International Commission on Intervention and State Sovereignty in 2001[281] pictured atrocity prevention not as intervention into the domestic affairs of states, but as part of the package deal that is state sovereignty.[282] At the same time, the underlying concerns were the same.[283] How should the international community react to atrocities, in particular in the absence of a Security Council mandate?

While the original report by the International Commission was "intentionally ambiguous"[284] on the subject of Security Council authorization,[285] all following definitions[286] have dropped this controversial aspect.[287] The working definition[288] of the "responsibility to protect" is that of the wording adopted by the UN General Assembly in the prominently cited points 138 and 139 of its 2005 "World Summit Outcome" document.[289] It draws up a

281 On the institution of this commission see Bellamy, 'The Responsibility to Protect', *supra* n. 282, at 620.
282 See International Commission on Intervention and State Sovereignty, *The Responsibility to Protect* (Ottawa: International Development Research Centre, 2001) 9, paras 1.39–1.41, and 15–18, paras 2.24–2.33.
283 See Bellamy, 'Realizing the Responsibility to Protect', *supra* n. 282, at 118.
284 Scharf, *supra* n. 79, Chapter 2, at 168.
285 International Commission on Intervention and State Sovereignty, *The Responsibility to Protect* (Ottawa: International Development Research Centre, 2001) 53, para. 6.28.
286 See High-level Panel on Threats, Challenges and Change, A More Secure World: Our Shared Responsibility (2004); Secretary General's Report, In Larger Freedom: Towards Development, Security and Human Rights for All (2005).
287 See Bellamy, 'The Responsibility to Protect', *supra* n. 282, at 638.
288 See *ibid.*, at 622.
289 General Assembly Resolution 60/1, '2005 World Summit Outcome', U.N. Doc. A/RES/60/1 (24 October 2005):

> 138. Each individual State has the responsibility to protect its populations from genocide, war crimes, ethnic cleansing and crimes against humanity. This responsibility entails the prevention of such crimes, including their incitement, through appropriate and necessary means. We accept that responsibility and will act in accordance with it. The international community should, as appropriate, encourage and help States to exercise this responsibility and support the United Nations in establishing an early warning capability. 139. The international community, through the United Nations, also has the responsibility to use appropriate diplomatic, humanitarian and other peaceful means, in accordance with Chapters VI and VIII of the Charter, to help to protect populations from genocide, war crimes, ethnic cleansing and crimes against humanity. In this context, we are prepared to take collective action, in a timely and decisive manner, through the Security Council, in accordance with the Charter, including Chapter VII, on a case-by-case basis and in cooperation with relevant regional organizations as appropriate, should peaceful means be inadequate and national authorities are manifestly failing to protect their populations from genocide, war crimes, ethnic cleansing and crimes against humanity. We stress the need for the General Assembly to continue consideration of the responsibility to protect populations from genocide, war crimes, ethnic cleansing and crimes against humanity and its implications, bearing in mind the principles of

three-prong concept, at the end of which stands action by the international community. In addition, it cleverly links the concept to international criminal law, listing "genocide, war crimes, ethnic cleansing and crimes against humanity" as triggers for intervention, while keeping it more political than legal through the inclusion of "ethnic cleansing", not itself a category under the Rome Statute.

"R2P" has since become a brand of its own. While a myriad of conferences, events, monographs, edited volumes, journals, articles, and reports had sprung up since the International Commission Report,[290] making the concept an academic success story,[291] its impact on the body of international law has been modest at best.[292] There is still little consensus as to what the content or legal value of the concept should be.[293] As José Alvarez writes, "it means too many things to too many different people".[294] It was not until the intervention in Libya that the responsibility gained further momentum.

> the Charter and international law. We also intend to commit ourselves, as necessary and appropriate, to helping States build capacity to protect their populations from genocide, war crimes, ethnic cleansing and crimes against humanity and to assisting those which are under stress before crises and conflicts break out.

290 See Alex J. Bellamy, 'The Responsibility to Protect – Five Years On', 24/2 *Ethics and International Affairs* (2010) 143–144; Edward C. Luck, 'The Responsibility to Protect: Growing Pains or Early Promise?', 24/4 *Ethics and International Affairs* (2010) 349.

291 See Thomas G. Weiss, 'RtoP Alive and Well after Libya', 25/3 *Ethics and International Affairs* (2011) 287: "With the exception of Raphael Lemkin's efforts on behalf of the 1948 Genocide Convention, no idea has moved faster in the international normative arena than 'the responsibility to protect' [...]". See also Bellamy, 'The Responsibility to Protect', *supra* n. 282, at 615–617. Although he lists more examples of rhetorical use of the concept than anything else.

292 See, *e.g.*, the 2008 op-ed by Madeleine K. Albright, 'The End of Intervention', *The New York Times* (11 June 2008):

> And despite recent efforts to enshrine the doctrine of a "responsibility to protect" in international law, the concept of humanitarian intervention has lost momentum. The global conscience is not asleep, but after the turbulence of recent years, it is profoundly confused. Some governments will oppose any exceptions to the principle of sovereignty because they fear criticism of their own policies. Others will defend the sanctity of sovereignty unless and until they again have confidence in the judgment of those proposing exceptions. <www.nytimes.com/2008/06/11/opinion/11albright.html?_r=0>

293 See the conflicting statements and references given by Peters, *supra* n. 282, at 300–303, as well as her own position at 304. See also Bellamy, *supra* n. 294, at 144; Irmgard Marboe, 'The Responsibility to Protect', in Karolina M. Januszewski, Tina Hofstätter, and Manfred Nowak (eds), *All Human Rights for All. Vienna Manual on Human Rights* (Vienna: Intersentia / Neuer Wissenschaftlicher Verlag, 2012) 503.

294 Alvarez, *supra* n. 277, at 277.

a Libya

The Operation Unified Protector in Libya is for the "responsibility to protect" what Kosovo was for humanitarian intervention theory. It has been considered "a model intervention".[295] Scholarship immediately embraced the Security Council mandate, Resolutions 1970 and 1973,[296] as an instance of state practice and there were sufficient statements to feed the idea.[297]

President Obama enigmatically pronounced that "when our interests and values are at stake, we have a responsibility to act".[298] Following the granting of "enhanced observer" status to the European Union within the General Assembly, EU Council President Herman Van Rompuy specifically referred to the "responsibility to protect" in his address at the 66th General Debate on 22 September 2011, arguing that "[t]he principle of 'responsibility to protect' was put into action – with perseverance and success" in Libya.[299] However, rather than the protection of civilians, Libya ultimately became a symbol for regime change above all else.[300]

b Assessment

As opposed to Kosovo, the intervention in Libya cannot contribute to the humanitarian exceptions debate *per se*, as it was already based on an "exclusionary reason", the Security Council mandate. Any additional "first-order reasons" are irrelevant.

295 Ivo H. Daalder, and James G. Stavridis, 'NATO's Victory in Libya. The Right Way to Run an Intervention', 91 *Foreign Affairs* (2012) 2.

296 Security Council Resolution 1970, 'Peace and Security in Africa', U.N. Doc. S/RES/1970 (26 February 2011); Security Council Resolution 1973, 'Libya', U.N. Doc. S/RES/1973 (17 March 2011).

297 See, *e.g.*, Alex J. Bellamy, 'Libya and the Responsibility to Protect: The Exception and the Norm', 25/3 *Ethics and International Affairs* (2011) 262; Manfred Nowak, 'Responsibility to Protect: Is International Law Moving from Hobbes to Locke?', in Gerhard Hafner, Franz Matscher, and Kirsten Schmalenbach (eds), *Völkerrecht und die Dynamik der Menschenrechte. Liber Amicorum Wolfram Karl* (Vienna: Facultas.wuv, 2012) 364.

298 Administration of Barack Obama, 2011, Address to the Nation on the Situation in Libya, 28 March 2011 <www.whitehouse.gov/the-press-office/2011/03/28/remarks-president-address-nation-libya>.

299 Herman Van Rompuy, Address to the 66th United Nations General Assembly General Debate, 22 September 2011, EUCO 78/11.

300 See Ralph Janik, 'China, Russia, and the Failure of the Responsibility to Protect in Syria: Does the Fear of Regime Change Offer a Serviceable Explanation?', 58/1 *Studia Universitatis Babeş-Bolyai. Studia Europaea* (2013) 70–72; James Pattison, 'The Ethics of Humanitarian Intervention in Libya', 25/3 *Ethics and International Affairs* (2011) 273–274.

The argument that the General Assembly, the Secretary-General,[301] and the Security Council[302] have endorsed the concept, and that the latter has referred to it, when authorizing collective security measures[303] fails to take into account the fact that it still comes down to Chapter VII of the Charter of the United Nations.[304] Of course, the General Assembly would like to see itself at an empowered vantage point, reaffirming its "role in the process of standard-setting and the codification of international law",[305] but this does not change the legal value of a General Assembly resolution. There is no added value to the prohibition of the use of force.

Scholarship was quick to offer alternative ideas such as an obligation of the Security Council to take action,[306] at least through discussion of appropriate measures,[307] the necessity of giving justifications for a veto,[308] the possibility of a veto constituting an abuse of rights with varying consequences,[309] or even a supposed "responsibility not to veto".[310] Such proposals are as bold as they are bound to fail. Other approaches consider the "responsibility to protect" a norm, but define the term "norm" as non-binding.[311]

The "responsibility to protect", in particular its adoption in the "World Summit Outcome" document should be seen as indicative of its status as a policy proposal. The reference to "ethnic cleansing", which is not an established category under international criminal law (as opposed to genocide,

301 See, *inter alia*, the annual reports by Secretary-General Ban Ki-moon since 2009, available at the Office of the Special Adviser on the Prevention of Genocide, Documents, Publications <www.un.org/en/preventgenocide/adviser/documents.shtml>.

302 Security Council Resolution 1674, 'Protection of Civilians in Armed Conflict', U.N. Doc. S/RES/1674 (28 April 2006); Security Council Resolution 1706, 'Sudan', U.N. Doc. S/RES/1706 (31 August 2006). See also Bellamy, 'Realizing the Responsibility to Protect', *supra* n. 282, at 113–116.

303 See, *e.g.*, Scharf, *supra* n. 79, Chapter 2, at 157.

304 See Simon Chesterman, '"Leading From Behind": The Responsibility to Protect, the Obama Doctrine, and Humanitarian Intervention After Libya', 25/3 *Ethics and International Affairs* (2011) 279–280.

305 General Assembly Resolution 60/1, '2005 World Summit Outcome', U.N. Doc. A/RES/60/1 (24 October 2005), at para. 149.

306 See Peters, *supra* n. 282, at 307–310.

307 See Andreas Zimmermann, 'The Obligation to Prevent Genocide: Towards a General Responsibility to Protect?' in Fastenrath, Geiger, Khan, Paulus, von Schorlemer, and Vedder (eds), *supra* n. 282, at 638-643.

308 See Peters, *supra* n. 282, at 323–324.

309 See *ibid.*, at 317–319.

310 See Ariela Blätter and Paul D. Williams, 'The Responsibility not to Veto', 3/3 *Global Responsibility to Protect* (2011) 319–320; Nowak, *supra* n. 301, at 365–366. See also Zimmermann, *ibid.*, at 644. Contrary Wodarz, *supra* n. 223, at 102–103. See also the draft resolution of the "Small Five" Costa Rica, Jordan, Liechtenstein, Singapore and Switzerland: Revised Draft Resolution, 'Improving the Working Methods of the Security Council', U.N. Doc. A/60/L.49 (17 March 2006), para. 14.

311 See Alex J. Bellamy, 'The Responsibility to Protect Turns Ten', 29/2 *Ethics and International Affairs* (2015) 162.

crimes against humanity, and war crimes), is further indicative of the political rather than legal character of the "responsibility to protect". While the debate was briefly revived, the legal status stands where it left off: "unlawful but legitimate"[312] – whenever it is opportune. However, that the debate continued against the background of a non-existent Security Council mandate, emphasizes once more the power of "[p]ositive-sounding norms".[313]

6 Preliminary Conclusion

Can there be such a thing as "customary international humanitarian intervention law" or a "customary international responsibility to protect"? That a state would act exclusively upon a moral maxim might be appealing both to governmental representatives, activists, and scholars, but it blinds the eye to the high economic and political costs of military action. These factors all weigh into the determination of state practice and *opinio iuris*, if one does not decide to rest the argument "on some moral high ground or on the sole basis of some fundamental humanitarian presumption or ideal".[314] In addition, the moral ambiguity with respect to almost unavoidable "collateral" damage taints that noble motive.[315] Outside the mind of an international law scholar or human rights activist, there is no such thing as a scalpel-cut intervention.

Although the rhetoric of states and international organizations may often invoke humanitarian grounds or even "responsibility to protect"-language, it should prove a difficult exercise to find any instance of military intervention since the end of World War II, in which not a single alternate interest was present on behalf of the intervening side. As Karl Zemanek once commented, the only responsibility he could see looking at the intervention in Libya in 2011 was the "R2POI – the responsibility to protect the oil industry".[316] The take-away from this somewhat cynical remark is that there is no such thing as a monocausal use of armed force by states. More often than not, even if there is no pure economic interest, the underlying motive is political, rather than humanitarian, as is shown by the fluidity between humanitarian and democratic intervention discourse:[317]

> Humanitarian intervention draws its powerful appeal from the revolutionary discourse of human rights, which promises liberation from tyranny

312 See *supra* n. 248.
313 See Somek, *supra* n. 66, Chapter 1, at 578.
314 Kritsiotis, *supra* n. 65, Chapter 3, at 1049.
315 For a discussion of these costs see recently Benjamin A. Valentino, 'The True Costs of Humanitarian Intervention: The Hard Truth About a Noble Notion', 90/6 *Foreign Affairs* (November/December 2011).
316 Christopher Michaelsen, 'The Responsibility-to-Protect Doctrine after Libya and Syria: Yesterday's Concept for Yesterday's Problems?', Round Table at the Section for International Law and International Relations at the University of Vienna, 4 June 2013.
317 See Beham and Janik, *supra* n. 76, Chapter 3, *passim*.

> and a future built on something other than militarised and technocratic state interests.[318]

Empirical evidence that the interest is always weaker in protecting foreign nationals, as opposed to one's own kin, is equally valid for humanitarian use of force,[319] as "[p]eople are only concerned, unfortunately, when they have some interest in it themselves, and the interest, of course, is generally based upon their own nationals".[320]

These findings, in turn, reaffirm the cliché that hard cases – and all cases involving military force are hard cases – simply make bad law:

> [I]nstability borders on confusion and disorder in periods of generalized high political tension such as ours. It strips international relations of the regularities necessary to the development and continuity of law. It impedes the consolidation of practices and their evolution into customary rules.[321]

Furthermore, a lawyer can only grasp the facts at hand. The true character of events is often only revealed in retrospect. Archives and historians are the enemy of the progressive development of international law.

Irrespective of these deficiencies, the existence of an almost universally ratified treaty, the CHARTER OF THE UNITED NATIONS, suggests that state practice and *opinio iuris* would have to be overwhelming:

> [I]n a situation where an almost universally ratified treaty provides rules that prohibit the unilateral use of force except in self-defense, the amount of State practice and evidence of *opinio juris* necessary to change any rule of customary international law existing parallel to those treaty rules – and thus, arguably, the treaty rules themselves – would have to be substantial, widespread, and more or less consistent, so as to overcome the resistance to change inherent in the treaty (as a set of established, legally binding obligations backed up by the principle of *pacta sunt servanda*) and in its ratifications (as individual instances of State practice and evidence of *opinio juris* for the purposes of customary international law).[322]

Rather than aiding and alleviating the available mechanisms for swift action, international utopianism slows them down by ignoring competing state interests. Success ultimately rests on a lack of conflict among the veto powers.[323]

318 Orford, *supra* n. 281, at 34.
319 See *supra* n. 83, Chapter 3.
320 Lillich, *supra* n. 217, at 137.
321 De Visscher, *supra* n. 32, Chapter 1, at 140. See with regard to the Kosovo case also Simma, *supra* n. 153, at 14 and 22.
322 Byers and Chesterman, *supra* n. 169, at 266.
323 See Hans J. Morgenthau, *In Defense of the National Interest: A Critical Examination of American Foreign Policy. With a New Introduction by Kenneth W. Thompson* (Washington, D.C.: University Press of America, 1982) 101–102.

Of course, this is not to say that states should be completely disinterested, when resorting to force on humanitarian grounds,[324] only that it is not possible to determine their *opinio iuris* for the purpose of establishing customary international law. This is particularly true in light of the erratic and equivocal nature of the accompanying practice. Alternative mechanisms must be found that have the potential of escaping the circular character of the humanitarian intervention and "responsibility to protect" debate. To put it in existentialist terms:

> [...] c'est que le lâche se fait lâche, que le héros se fait héros; il y a toujours une possibilité pour le lâche de ne plus être lâche, et pout le héros de cesser d'être un héros. Ce qui compte, c'est l'engagement total, et ce ne'est pas un cas particulier, une action particulière, qui vous engagent totalement.[325]

Dead-end debate, no heroes.

324 See on this issue Antoine Rougier, 'La Théorie de l'Intervention d'Humanité', XVII *Revue Générale de Droit International Public* (1910) 502–503. See Murphy, *supra* n. 192, Chapter 1, at 323. See also, for a more recent appraisal, Kritsiotis, *supra* n. 65, Chapter 3, at 1034–1039.

325 Jean-Paul Sartre, *L'Existentialisme est un Humanisme* (Collection Pensées; Paris: Éditions Nagel, 1946) 61–62. See also Michael Walzer, 'The Politics of Rescue', 61/1 *Social Research* (1995) 66.

5 Conclusion

The present analysis has been a long journey in terms of questions raised and issues touched upon. Starting with an essayist portrayal of the main question and its underlying arguments, it has led through the formation of customary international law and general principles of law, the relationship between morality and legality, to the debate on human rights as well as humanitarian exceptions to the use of force and atrocity prevention. The hope is that at least a few inspirations, if not answers, could be offered along the way.

Not shunning the vulnerability of clear language[1] and the dangers of the black letter,[2] the two conclusions drawn from the analysis of state interest and the sources of international, non-treaty law, seem to be as follows:

First, neither human rights, nor humanitarian exceptions or obligations in connection with the regulation of the use of force are likely to be found in customary international law by a genuine analysis of state practice and *opinio iuris*. By nature of its purpose, a state is not altruistically motivated. Even in cases, in which state practice would be available, it is not possible to discern any specific motivation from other underlying interests. The element of state interest naturally stands in the way of concluding that either human rights or obligations or exceptions to the prohibition of the threat or use of force constitute customary international law. Irrespective thereof, doctrine has hardly made an effort.

Second, general principles of law do not offer a valid alternative, unless they are construed as importing natural law into the catalogue of Article 38(1) of the Statute of the International Court of Justice. General principles of law identified *in foro domestico* can only lead to a relativist approach to human rights.

1 Habitually, proponents of legal theory, in particular critical legal studies, and philosophy of law shroud their statements in nested sentences and technical jargon borrowed from the political and social sciences, linguistically immunizing themselves from any form of argumentative attack. See on this issue, generally and humorously, Karl R. Popper, 'Wider die großen Worte. Ein Plädoyer für intellektuelle Redlichkeit', *Zeit Online* <www.zeit.de/1971/39/wider-die-grossen-worte>, originally published in 39 *Die Zeit* (14 September 1971). See also D'Aspremont, *supra* n. 44, Chapter 1, at 589–590 and 593–594.

2 As the Roman jurist Iavolenus Priscus remarked: "Omnis definitio in iure civili periculosa est; parum est enim, ut non subverti posset".

Even if the opposite were the case, the gravitational pull of general principles of law towards compliance is so low and the controversy as to their true nature still unresolved, making it hard to see in them a dignified substitute for the validity of human rights norms, as has been suggested by some, let alone as a basis for exceptions or obligations in connection with the regulation of the use of force.

Analogous to the age-old question, whether criminal law may serve as a deterrent,[3] which has never been empirically proven,[4] a possible international responsibility concerning human rights or the possibility of intervention to prevent violation of human rights could prevent states from abusing their sphere of domestic affairs. However, as Albert Camus recalls, in his famous essay 'Réflexions sur la Guillotine', thieves were most active during the hanging of their less lucky colleagues, an example often cited by abolitionists to criticize the notion of deterrence through the death penalty.[5] If this is the case for alleged deterrents based in positive law, there is little hope that much positive will come from an illusory non-treaty human rights law or humanitarian intervention and "responsibility to protect" debate.

Irrespective thereof, scholars may continue to assert that something represents a manifestation of international law by shifting the methodology, but it is doubtful that an academic fragmentation of sources doctrine will contribute to the credibility of international law: "Most of the non-treaty law of today is not at all like this [...]. The time has surely come to recognize boldly that it is not custom at all, and never was".[6]

The positions taken in this book, of course, raise a multitude of questions for further debate. Yet, if it has been somewhat possible to raise the appeal of analytical honesty and show the benefits of emphasizing positive law and legal methodology for the sake of credibility of the discipline, the book has served its purpose. One need not be a full-fledged positivist or realist to appreciate the capacity of sound legal reasoning to reconstruct a foundation for normative change that gets by without illusions.

To paraphrase Nobel laureate Saul Bellow: "There is a great deal of intelligence among the scholars of international law that needs to be invested in finding ways to bring about normative change. However, the need for disillusion is deep".[7]

3 See, *e.g.*, Bassiouni, *supra* n. 101, Chapter 3, at 33. Gareth Evans, 'The Responsibility to Protect. From an Idea to an International Norm', in Cooper and Kohler (eds), *supra* n. 84, Chapter 3, at 26.

4 See Donald Bloxham and Devin O. Pendas, 'Punishment as Prevention? The Politics of Punishing Génocidaires', in Donald Bloxham and A. Dirk Moses (eds), *The Oxford Handbook of Genocide Studies* (Oxford: Oxford University Press, 2010) 628 and 633.

5 Albert Camus, 'Réflexions sur la Guillotine', in Albert Camus and Arthur Koestler, *Réflexions sur la Peine Capitale* (Paris: Calmann-Lévy, 1957) 119–170: "On peut lire dans Koestler qu'à l'époque où les voleurs à la tire étaient exécutés en Angleterre, d'autres voleurs exerçaient leurs talents dans la foule qui entourait l'échafaud où l'on pend ait leur confrère".

6 Jennings, *supra* n. 93, Chapter 1, at 6.

7 See Saul Bellow, *To Jerusalem and Back: A Personal Account* (London: The Alison Press / Secker & Warburg, 1976) 127.

Bibliography

All works are listed in alphabetical order of the author and within that in chronological order of publication for easier reference. Where no author data was available, mostly in the case of newspaper articles, the work has been listed by its publication medium; where it is not usual to cite the authors or editors, as in the case of dictionaries, the work has been listed by its title.

A Books

Achour, Yadh Ben, *Le Rôle des Civilisations dans le Système International (Droit et Relations Internationales)* (Collection de Droit Internationales, Vol. 50; Bruxelles: Editions Bruylant / Editions de l'Université des Bruxelles, 2003)

Alston, Philip, and Ryan Goodman, *International Human Rights: The Successor to International Human Rights in Context: Law, Politics and Morals* (Oxford: Oxford University Press, 2013)

American Law Institute, *Restatement of the Law (Third): The Foreign Relations of the United States* (St. Paul: American Law Institute Publishers, 1987)

American Society for International Law (ed.), *International Law: 100 Ways it Shapes our Lives* <www.asil.org/sites/default/files/100%20Ways%20Booklet_2011.pdf>

Arajärvi, Noora, *The Changing Nature of Customary International Law: Methods of Interpreting the Concept of Custom in International Criminal Tribunals* (Oxon: Routledge, 2014)

Austin, John, *The Province of Jurisprudence Determined* (London: John Murray, 1832)

Beham, Markus, Melanie Fink, and Ralph Janik, *Völkerrecht verstehen* (Vienna: Facultas, 2015)

Bellow, Saul, *To Jerusalem and Back: A Personal Account* (London: The Alison Press / Secker & Warburg, 1976)

Benedek, Wolfgang, and Matthias C. Kettemann, *Freedom of Expression and the Internet* (Strasburg: Council of Europe Publishing, 2014)

Birnie, Patricia, Alan Boyle, and Catherine Redgwell, *International Law and the Environment*, 3rd edn (Oxford: Oxford University Press, 2009)

Bosco, David L., *Five to Rule Them All: The UN Security Council and the Making of the Modern World* (Oxford: Oxford University Press, 2009)

Bowett, Derek W., *Self-Defence in International Law* (Manchester: Manchester University Press, 1958)

Brierly, James Leslie, *The Outlook for International Law* (Oxford: Clarendon Press, 1944)

Brierly, James Leslie, *The Law of Nations: An Introduction to the International Law of Peace*, Humphrey Waldock (ed.), 6th edn (Oxford: Clarendon Press, 1963)

Brownlie, Ian, *International Law and the Use of Force by States* (Oxford: Clarendon Press, 1963)

Brownlie, Ian, *Principles of Public International Law*, 7th edn (Oxford: Oxford University Press, 2008)

Burgstaller, Markus, *Theories of Compliance with International Law* (Leiden: Martinus Nijhoff, 2005)

Burnham, William, *Introduction to the Law and Legal System of the United States* (St. Paul: West, 2011)

Byers, Michael, *Custom, Power and the Power of Rules: International Relations and Customary International Law* (Cambridge: Cambridge University Press, 2004)

Cassese, Antonio, *International Law*, 2nd edn (Oxford: Oxford University Press, 2005)

Cassese, Antonio, *Five Masters of International Law. Conversations with R-J Dupuy, E Jiménez de Aréchaga, R Jennings, L Henkin and O Schachter* (Oxford: Hart Publishing, 2011)

Castan, Melissa, and Sarah Joseph, *The International Covenant on Civil and Political Rights: Cases, Materials, and Commentary*, 3rd edn (Oxford: Oxford University Press, 2013)

Castañeda, Jorge, *Legal Effects of United Nations Resolutions* (Columbia University Studies in International Organization, Number 6; New York: Columbia University Press, 1969)

Cheng, Bin, *General Principles of Law as Applied by International Courts and Tribunals* (Cambridge: Cambridge University Press, 1953)

Chomsky, Noam, *9–11* (New York: Seven Stories Press, 2001)

Cicero, Marcus Tullius, *De Re Publica*. Tertius Liber

Constantinides, Aristoteles, *Νομικοί Περιορισμοί και Δικαστικός Έλεγχος του Συμβουλίου Ασφαλείας των Ηνωμένων Εθνών* [*Legal Restrictions and Judicial Control of the Security Council of the United Nations*] (Athens: Εκδόσεις Σάκκουλα, 2004)

Corten, Olivier, *The Law Against War: The Prohibition on the Use of Force in Contemporary International Law* (French Studies in International Law, Vol. 4; Oxford: Hart Publishing, 2010)

D'Amato, Anthony A., *The Concept of Custom in International Law* (Ithaca: Cornell University Press, 1971)

D'Amato, Anthony A., *Introduction to Law and Legal Thinking* (Irvington-on-Hudson: Transnational, 1996)

D'Aspremont, Jean, *Formalism and the Sources of International Law: A Theory of the Ascertainment of Legal Rules* (Oxford Monographs in International Law; Oxford: Oxford University Press, 2011)

D'Aspremont, Jean, *Epistemic Forces in International Law. Foundational Doctrines and Techniques of International Legal Argumentation* (Cheltenham: Edward Elgar, 2015)

Danilenko, Gennady M., *Law-making in the International Community* (Developments in International Law, Vol. 15; Dordrecht: Martinus Nijhoff, 1993)

De Spinoza, Baruch, *Ethik* (Berlin: Hofenberg, 2014)

De Vattel, Emer, *Le Droit des Gens. Ou Principes de la Loi naturelle, appliqués à la Conduite et aux Affaires des Nations et des Souverains. Tome 1* (London, 1758)

De Visscher, Charles, *Theory and Reality in Public International Law*, revised edition (Princeton, NJ: Princeton University Press, 1968)

De Wet, Erika, *The Chapter VII Powers of the United Nations Security Council* (Oxford: Hart Publishing, 2004)

Deng, Francis M., Sadikiel Kimaro, Terrence Lyons, Donald Rothchild, and I. William Zartman, *Sovereignty as Responsibility: Conflict Management in Africa* (Washington, D.C.: The Brookings Institution, 1996)

Dixon, Martin, *Textbook on International Law,* 6th edn (Oxford: Oxford University Press, 2007)

Etzersdorfer, Irene, and Ralph Janik, *Staat, Krieg und Schutzverantwortung. Militärische Interventionen im Namen fundamentaler Menschenrechte aus staatstheoretischer und völkerrechtlicher Perspektive* (Vienna: Facultas, 2016)

Fastenrath, Ulrich, *Lücken im Völkerrecht. Zu Rechtscharakter, Quellen, Systemzusammenhang, Methodenlehre und Funktionen des Völkerrechts* (Schriften zum Völkerrecht, Vol. 93; Berlin: Duncker & Humblot, 1991)

Franck, Thomas M., *Recourse to Force: State Actions Against Threats and Armed Attacks* (Cambridge: Cambridge University Press, 2002)

Frankel, Joseph, *National Interest* (London: Macmillan, 1970)

Fukuyama, Francis, *The End of History and the Last Man* (London: Penguin Books, 1992)

Funck-Brentano, Theodore, and Albert Sorel, *Précis du Droit des Gens*, 3rd edn (Paris: Librairie Plon, 1900)

Goethe, Johann Wolfgang von, *Faust: Eine Tragödie* (Tübingen: J.G. Cotta'sche Buchhandlung, 1808)

Goldsmith, Jack L., and Eric A. Posner, *The Limits of International Law* (Oxford: Oxford University Press, 2005)

Gray, Christine, *International Law and the Use of Force*, 3rd edn (Foundations of Public International Law; Oxford: Oxford University Press, 2008)

Gray, John C., *The Nature and Sources of the Law. The Carpenter Lectures. 1908–1909* (New York: Columbia University Press, 1927)

Grotius, Hugo, *De Iure Belli ac Pacis. Libri Tres. In Quibus Ius Naturae et Gentium: Item Iuris Publici Praecipua Explicantur* (Paris, 1625)

Halevy, Efraim, *Man in the Shadows: Inside the Middle East Crisis with a Man who led the Mossad* (London: Phoenix, 2007)

Härle, Elfried, *Die allgemeinen Entscheidungsgrundlagen des Ständigen Internationalen Gerichtshofs. Eine kritisch-würdigende Untersuchung über Artikel 38 des Gerichtshof-Statuts* (Völkerrechtliche Monographien 10; Berlin: Verlag von Franz Vahlen, 1933)

Hart, Herbert L.A., *The Concept of Law*, 3rd edn (Oxford: Oxford University Press, 2012)

Hathaway, James C., *The Rights of Refugees Under International Law* (Cambridge: Cambridge University Press, 2005)

Henkin, Louis, *How Nations Behave: Law and Foreign Policy*, 2nd edn (New York: Columbia University Press, 1979)

Hesse, Hermann, *Das Glasperlenspiel. Versuch einer Lebensbeschreibung des Magister Ludi Josef Knecht samt Knechts hinterlassenen Schriften* (Zurich: Fretz & Wasmuth, 1943)

Holland, Thomas E., *Letters to 'The Times' Upon War and Neutrality (1881–1920) With Some Commentary*, 3rd edn (London: Longmans, Green and Co., 1921)

Jaffe, Louis, *Judicial Aspects of Foreign Relations. In Particular of the Recognition of Foreign Powers* (Harvard Studies in Administrative Law, Vol. VI; Cambridge: Harvard University Press / Oxford University Press, 1933)

Jennings, Robert, and Arthur Watts (eds), *Oppenheim's International Law. Volume 1. Peace. Introduction and Part 1*, 9th edn (London: Longman, 1996)

Joseph, Sarah, *Corporations and Transnational Human Rights Litigation* (Oxford: Hart Publishing, 2004)

Kant, Immanuel, *Critic der practischen Vernunft*, 2nd edn (Riga: Johann Friedrich Hartknoch, 1792)

Kant, Immanuel, *Die Metaphysik der Sitten. Erster Theil. Metaphysische Anfangsgründe der Rechtslehre*, 2nd edn (Königsberg: Friedrich Nicolovius, 1798)

Kant, Immanuell, *Grundlegung zur Metaphysik der Sitten. Kritik der praktischen Vernunft nebst den Abhandlungen zur Philosophie der Geschichte* (Leipzig: Baumann und Modes, 1838)

Karl, Wolfram, *Vertrag und spätere Praxis im Völkerrecht. Zum Einfluß der Praxis auf Inhalt und Bestand völkerrechtlicher Verträge* (Berlin: Springer, 1983)

Kelsen, Hans, *Das Problem der Souveränität und die Theorie des Völkerrechts. Beitrag zu einer reinen Rechtslehre* (Tübingen: J.C.B. Mohr [Paul Siebeck], 1920)

Kelsen, Hans, *Legal Technique in International Law: A Textual Critique of the League Covenant* (Geneva Studies, Vol. X, No. 6; Geneva: Geneva Research Centre, 1939)

Kelsen, Hans, *The Law of the United Nations: A Critical Analysis of its Fundamental Problems* (London: Stevens & Sons, 1950)

Kelsen, Hans, *Recent Trends in the Law of the United Nations. A Supplement to 'The Law of the United Nations'* (London: Stevens & Sons, 1951)

Kelsen, Hans, *Principles of International Law*, 2nd edn (New York: Holt, Rinehart and Winston, 1966)

Kennedy, David, *A World of Struggle: How Power, Law, and Expertise Shape Global Political Economy* (Princeton: Princeton University Press, 2016)

Kettemann, Matthias C., *The Future of Individuals in International Law: Lessons from International Internet Law* (The Hague: Eleven International Publishing, 2013)

Kinley, David, Jacqueline Mowbray, and Ben Saul, *The International Covenant on Economic, Social and Cultural Rights: Commentary, Cases, and Materials* (Oxford: Oxford University Press, 2014)

Kolb, Robert, *Théorie du Ius Cogens International* (Paris: Presses Universitaires de France, 2001)

Koskenniemi, Martti, *From Apology to Utopia: The Structure of International Legal Argument*, 2nd edn (Cambridge: Cambridge University Press, 2005)

Lauterpacht, Hersch, *Private Law Sources and Analogies of International Law: With Special Reference to International Arbitration* (London: Longmans, Green and Co., 1927)

Lauterpacht, Hersch, *International Law and Human Rights* (London: Stevens & Sons, 1950)

Lauterpacht, Hersch, *The Development of International Law by the International Court* (London: Stevens & Sons, 1958)

Lijnzaad, Liesbet, *Reservations to UN Human Rights Treaties: Ratify and Ruin?* (International Studies in Human Rights; Dordrecht: Martinus Nijhoff, 1995)

Marboe, Irmgard (ed.), *Soft Law in Outer Space: The Function of Non-Binding Norms in International Space Law* (Studien zu Politik und Verwaltung, Vol. 102; Vienna: Böhlau, 2012)

McNair, Arnold Duncan, *The Law of Treaties* (Oxford: Oxford University Press, 1961)

Meron, Theodor, *Human Rights Law-Making in the United Nations: A Critique of Instruments and Process* (Oxford: Clarendon Press, 1986)

Meron, Theodor, *Human Rights and Humanitarian Norms as Customary Law* (Oxford: Clarendon Press, 1989)

Morgenthau, Hans J., *In Defense of the National Interest: A Critical Examination of American Foreign Policy. With a New Introduction by Kenneth W. Thompson* (Washington, D.C.: University Press of America, 1982)

Morgenthau, Hans J., and Kenneth W. Thompson, *Politics Among Nations: The Struggle for Power and Peace*, 6th edn (New York: Alfred A. Knopf, 1985)

Murphy, Sean D., *Humanitarian Intervention: The United Nations in an Evolving World Order* (Procedural Aspects of International Law Series, Vol. 21; Philadelphia: University of Pennsylvania Press, 1996)

Neff, Stephen C., *War and the Law of Nations: A General History* (Cambridge: Cambridge University Press, 2005)

Neuhold, Hanspeter, *Internationale Konflikte – Verbotene und erlaubte Mittel ihrer Austragung. Versuche einer transdisziplinären Betrachtung der Grundsätze des Gewalt- und Interventionsverbots sowie der friedlichen Streitbeilegung im Lichte der UN-Prinzipiendeklaration 1970 und der modernen Sozialwissenschaft* (Forschungen aus Staat und Recht 37; Vienna: Springer-Verlag, 1977)

Nowak, Manfred, *U.N. Covenant on Civil and Political Rights. CCPR Commentary*, 2nd edn (Kehl: N.P. Engel, 2005)

Ohlin, Jens David, *The Assault on International Law* (Oxford: Oxford University Press, 2015)

Onuf, Nicholas Greenwood, *World of Our Making: Rules and Rule in Social Theory and International Relations* (Studies in International Relations; Columbia, SC: University of South Carolina, 1989)

Oppenheim, Lassa, *The Future of International Law* (Pamphlet Series of the Carnegie Endowment for International Peace, Division of International Law, No. 39; Oxford: Oxford University Press, 1921)

Orakhelashvili, Alexander, *Peremptory Norms in International Law* (Oxford: Oxford University Press, 2006)

Orakhelashvili, Alexander, *The Interpretation of Acts and Rules in Public International Law* (Oxford: Oxford University Press, 2008)

Orford, Anne, *Reading Humanitarian Intervention: Human Rights and the Use of Force in International Law* (Cambridge: Cambridge University Press, 2003)

Peters, Anne, *Beyond Human Rights: The Legal Status of the Individual in International Law* (Cambridge Studies in International and Comparative Law; Cambridge: Cambridge University Press, 2016)

Petersen, Niels, *Demokratie als teleologisches Prinzip. Zur Legitimität von Staatsgewalt im Völkerrecht* (Max-Planck-Institut für ausländisches öffentliches Recht und Völkerrecht, Beiträge zum ausländischen öffentlichen Recht und Völkerrecht, Vol. 204; Berlin: Springer, 2009)

Pictet, Jean S. (ed.), *The Geneva Conventions of 12 August 1949. Commentary. Volume I. Geneva Convention for the Amelioration of the Condition of the Wounded and Sick in Armed Forces in the Field* (Geneva: International Committee of the Red Cross, 1952)

Potacs, Michael, *Rechtstheorie* (Vienna: Facultas, 2015)

Puchta, Georg Friedrich, *Das Gewohnheitsrecht. Erster Theil* (Erlangen: Palm'sche Verlagsbuchhandlung, 1828)

Puchta, Georg Friedrich, *Das Gewohnheitsrecht. Zweiter Theil* (Erlangen: Palm'sche Verlagsbuchhandlung, 1837)

Pulkowski, Dirk, *The Law and Politics of International Regime Conflict* (Oxford: Oxford University Press, 2014)

Raz, Joseph, *Practical Reason and Norms* (London: Hutchinson, 1975)

Raz, Joseph, *The Authority of Law: Essays on Law and Morality*, 2nd edn (Oxford: Oxford University Press, 2009)

Rehman, Javaid, *International Human Rights Law*, 2nd edn (Harlow: Pearson, 2010)

Roberts, Anthea, *Is International Law International?* (Oxford: Oxford University Press, 2017)

Rodley, Nigel, *The Treatment of Prisoners Under International Law*, 2nd edn (Oxford: Clarendon Press, 1999)

Rubin, Alfred P., *Ethics and Authority in International Law* (Cambridge: Cambridge University Press, 1997)

Sands, Philippe, and Jacqueline Peel, *Principles of International Environmental Law* (Cambridge: Cambridge University Press, 2012)

Sartre, Jean-Paul, *L'Existentialisme est un Humanisme* (Collection Pensées; Paris: Éditions Nagel, 1946)

Schabas, William, *Unimaginable Atrocities: Justice, Politics, and Rights at the War Crimes Tribunals* (Oxford: Oxford University Press, 2012)

Schachter, Oscar, *International Law in Theory and Practice* (Developments in International Law, Vol. 13; Dordrecht: Martinus Nijhoff, 1991)

Scharf, Michael P., and Paul R. Williams, *Shaping Foreign Policy in Times of Crisis: The Role of International Law and the State Department Legal Adviser* (Cambridge: Cambridge University Press, 2010)

Scharf, Michael P., *Customary International Law in Times of Fundamental Change: Recognizing Grotian Moments* (Cambridge: Cambridge University Press, 2013)

Schill, Stephan W., *The Multilateralization of International Investment Law* (Cambridge: Cambridge University Press, 2009)

Schmitt, Carl, *Der Begriff des Politischen* (Wissenschaftliche Abhandlungen und Reden zur Philosophie, Politik und Geistesgeschichte, X; Munich: Duncker & Humblot, 1932)

Schmitt, Carl, *Der Begriff des Politischen. Text von 1932 mit einem Vorwort und drei Corollarien* (Berlin: Duncker & Humblot, 1963)

Schwarzenberger, Georg, *Power Politics: A Study of World Society* (London: Stevens & Sons, 1964)

Schwarzenberger, Georg, *The Inductive Approach to International Law*, 3rd edn (London: Stevens & Sons, 1965)

Schwarzenberger, Georg, *Civitas Maxima?* (Recht und Staat in Geschichte und Gegenwart, Vols 413/414; Tübingen: J.C.B. Mohr [Paul Siebeck], 1973)

Shaw, Malcolm N., *International Law*, 7th edn (Cambridge: Cambridge University Press, 2014)

Simma, Bruno, *Das Reziprozitätselement in der Entstehung des Völkergewohnheitsrechts* (Munich: Wilhelm Fink, 1970)

Simma, Bruno, *Das Reziprozitätselement im Zustandekommen völkerrechtlicher Verträge* (Schriften zum Völkerrecht, Vol. 23; Berlin: Duncker & Humblot, 1972)

Simma, Bruno, and Alfred Verdross, *Universelles Völkerrecht. Theorie und Praxis*, 3rd edn (Berlin: Duncker & Humblot, 1984)

Smith, Rhona K.M., *Textbook on International Human Rights*, 5th edn (Oxford: Oxford University Press, 2012)

Soanes, Catherine, and Angus Stevenson (eds), *Concise Oxford English Dictionary*, 11th edn (Oxford: Oxford University Press, 2006)

Sørensen, Max, *Les Sources du Droit International. Etude sur la Jurisprudence de la Cour Permanente de Justice Internationale* (Copenhagen: Einar Munksgaard, 1946)

Spiropoulos, Jean, *Die allgemeinen Rechtsgrundsätze im Völkerrecht. Eine Auslegung von Art. 38 3 des Statuts des ständigen Internationalen Gerichtshofs* (Aus dem Institut für internationales Recht an der Universität Kiel. Erste Reihe. Vorträge und Einzelschriften 7; Kiel: Verlag des Instituts für internationales Recht an der Universität Kiel, 1928)

Thirlway, Hugh, *International Customary Law and Codification: An Examination of the Continuing Role of Custom in the Present Period of Codification of International Law* (Leiden: A.W. Sijthoff, 1972)

Traunmüller, Karin, *Völkerrechtliche Fragen im Zusammenhang mit der Einbürgerung von Personen mit Wohnsitz im Ausland am Beispiel der Gesetzgebung der Russischen Föderation* (Vienna: Doctoral Thesis at the University of Vienna, 2014)

Tunkin, Grigory I., *Theory of International Law* (London: Wildy, Simmonds & Hill, 2003)

van Hoof, Godefridus H.V., *Rethinking the Sources of International Law* (Deventer: Kluwer, 1983)

Verdross, Alfred, *Die Verfassung der Völkerrechtsgemeinschaft* (Vienna: Julius Springer, 1926)

Villiger, Mark E., *Customary International Law and Treaties: A Study of Their Interactions and Interrelations with Special Consideration of the 1969 Vienna Convention on the Law of Treaties* (Dordrecht: Martinus Nijhoff Publishers, 1985)

Walzer, Michael, *Just and Unjust Wars: A Moral Argument with Historical Illustrations*, 4th edn (New York: Basic Books, 2006)

Watkins, John C., and John Paul Weber (eds), *War Crimes and War Crime Trials: From Leipzig to the ICC and Beyond. Cases, Materials and Comments* (Durham, NC: Carolina Academic Press, 2006)

Watson, J. Shand, *Theory & Reality in the International Protection of Human Rights* (Ardsley: Transnational Publishers, 1999)

Weatherall, Thomas, *Jus Cogens. International Law and Social Contract* (Cambridge: Cambridge University Press, 2015)

Wellman, Carl, *The Moral Dimension of Human Rights* (Oxford: Oxford University Press, 2011)

Wendt, Alexander, *Social Theory of International Politics* (Cambridge Studies in International Relations; Cambridge: Cambridge University Press, 1999)

Wodarz, Katharina, *Gewaltverbot, Menschenrechtsschutz und Selbstbestimmungsrecht im Kosovo-Konflikt* (Schriften zum Staats und Völkerrecht, Vol. 95; Frankfurt am Main: Peter Lang, 2002)

Wolfke, Karol, *Custom in Present International Law*, 2nd edn (Developments in International Law, Vol. 14; Dordrecht: Martinus Nijhoff, 1993)

Wood, Philip R., *The Fall of the Priests and the Rise of the Lawyers* (Oxford: Hart Publishing, 2016)

Yee, Sienho, *Towards an International Law of Co-progressiveness, Part II. Membership, Leadership and Responsibility* (Leiden: Brill Nijhoff, 2014)

B Articles and Chapters Within Books

Abi-Saab, George, 'Les Sources du Droit International: Essai de Déconstruction', in Manuel Rama-Montaldo (ed.), *El Derecho Internacional en un Mundo en*

Transformacion. Liber Amicorum en Homenaje al Professor Eduardo Jiménez de Aréchaga / Le Droit International Dans un Monde en Mutation. Liber Amicorum en Hommage au Professeur Eduardo Jiménez de Aréchaga / International Law in an Evolving World. Liber Amicorum in Tribute to Eduardo Jiménez de Aréchaga (Montevideo: Fundación de cultura universitaria, 1994) 29–49

Ago, Robert, 'Science Juridique et Droit International', 90 *Recueil des Cours de l'Académie de Droit International de La Haye* (1953) 851–958

Ahmed, Tawhida, and Israel de Jesús Butler, 'The European Union and Human Rights: An International Law Perspective', 17/4 *European Journal of International Law* (2006) 771–801

Akehurst, Michael, 'Custom as a Source of International Law', 47 *British Yearbook of International Law* (1974–1975) 1–53

Akehurst, Michael, 'The Hierarchy of the Sources of International Law', 47 *British Yearbook of International Law* (1974–1975) 273–285

Akhavan, Payam, 'The Universal Repression of Crimes Against Humanity Before National Jurisdictions', in Leila Nadya Sadat (ed.), *Forging a Convention for Crimes Against Humanity* (New York: Cambridge University Press, 2011) 28–42

Albright, Madeleine K., 'The End of Intervention', *The New York Times* (11 June 2008) <www.nytimes.com/2008/06/11/opinion/11albright.html?_r=0>

Allchin, Joseph, 'Cut Down in Their Prime', *Foreign Policy* (29 May 2015) <http://foreignpolicy.com/2015/05/29/cut-down-in-their-prime-bangladesh-atheist-bloggers/>

Alogna, Ivano, 'The Circulation of Legal Models: Toward the Evolution of Environmental Law', in Maša Kovič Dine and Vasilka Sancin (eds), *International Environmental Law: Contemporary Concerns and Challenges in 2014* (Ljubljana: GV Založba, 2014) 59–69

Alston, Philip, 'Conjuring Up New Human Rights: A Proposal for Quality Control', 78/3 *American Journal of International Law* (1984) 607–621

Alston, Philip, and Bruno Simma, 'The Sources of Human Rights Law: Custom, Jus Cogens, and General Principles', 12 *Australian Yearbook of International Law* (1992) 82–108

Alston, Philip, and Euan MacDonald, 'Sovereignty, Human Rights, Security: Armed Intervention and the Foundational Problems of International Law', in Philip Alston and Euan MacDonald (eds), *Human Rights, Intervention, and the Use of Force* (The Collected Courses of the Academy of European Law, Vol. X/2; Oxford: Oxford University Press, 2008) 1–31

Alston, Philip, 'Against a World Court for Human Rights', 28/2 *Ethics and International Affairs* (2014) 197–212

Alvarez, José E., 'The Schizophrenias of R2P', in Philip Alston and Euan MacDonald (eds), *Human Rights, Intervention, and the Use of Force* (The Collected Courses of the Academy of European Law, Vol. X/2; Oxford: Oxford University Press, 2008) 275–284

Anaya, S. James, 'Customary International Law', 92 *American Society of International Law Proceedings* (1998) 41

Arangio-Ruiz, Gaetano, 'The Normative Role of the General Assembly of the United Nations and the Declaration of Principles of Friendly Relations', 225 *Recueil des Cours de l'Académie de Droit International de La Haye* (1972-III)

Barberis, Julio A., 'La Coutume est-elle une Source de Droit International?', in Mélanges Michel Virally (ed.) *Le Droit International au Service de la Paix de la Justice et du Développement* (Paris: Éditions A. Pedone, 1991) 43–52

Barme, Geremie R., and Sang Ye, 'The Great Firewall of China', 5/6 *Wired* (June 1997) <www.wired.com/wired/archive/5.06/china.html>

Bassiouni, M. Cherif, and Daniel Derby, 'An Appraisal of Torture in International Law and Practice: The Need for an International Convention for the Prevention and Suppression of Torture', 48/3–4 *Revue Internationale de Droit Pénal* (1977) 17–114

Bassiouni, M. Cherif, 'Advancing the Responsibility to Protect Through International Criminal Justice', in Richard H. Cooper and Juliette Voïnov Kohler (eds), *Responsibility to Protect: The Global Moral Compact for the 21st Century* (New York: Palgrave Macmillan, 2009) 31–42

Bassiouni, M. Cherif, 'Revisiting the Architecture of Crimes Against Humanity: Almost a Century in the Making, with Gaps and Ambiguities Remaining – the Need for a Specialized Convention', in Leila Nadya Sadat (ed.), *Forging a Convention for Crimes Against Humanity* (New York: Cambridge University Press, 2011) 43–58

Baxter, Richard R., 'Multilateral Treaties as Evidence of Customary International Law', 41 *British Yearbook of International Law* (1965–1966) 275–300

Bederman, David J., 'Acquiescence, Objection and the Death of Customary International Law', 21 *Duke Journal of Comparative and International Law* (2010) 31–45

Beham, Markus P., and Gerhard Hafner, 'Austrian Diplomatic and Parliamentary Practice in International Law / Österreichische Diplomatische und Parlamentarische Praxis zum Internationalen Recht', 17 *Austrian Review of International and European Law* (2012) 395–476

Beham, Markus P., '"Borrowed" Concepts: The Pitfalls of "Atrocity Labelling" in Contemporary Historiography', in Markus P. Beham and Marija Wakounig (eds), *Transgressing Boundaries: Humanities in Flux* (Vienna: LIT Verlag, 2013) 73–91

Beham, Markus P., 'Islamic Law and International Criminal Law', in Marie-Luisa Frick and Andreas Th. Müller (eds), *Islam and International Law* (Brill's Arab and Islamic Law Series, Vol. 7; The Hague: Martinus Nijhoff, 2013) 349–366

Beham, Markus P., 'Genocide and Crimes Against Humanity: Siamese Twins or Separated at Birth?', in Markus P. Beham and Marija Wakounig (eds), *Mind and Memory in Discourse. Critical Concepts and Constructions* (Vienna: LIT Verlag, 2014) 177–193

Beham, Markus P., and Ralph R.A. Janik, 'A "Responsibility to Democratise"? The "Responsibility to Protect" in Light of Regime Change and the "Pro-Democratic" Intervention Discourse', in Richard Barnes and Vassilis Tzevelekos (eds), *Beyond Responsibility to Protect: Generating Change in International Law* (Cambridge: Intersentia, 2016) 53–70

Bellamy, Alex J., 'The Responsibility to Protect and the Problem of Military Intervention', 84/4 *International Affairs* (2008) 615–639

Bellamy, Alex J., 'Realizing the Responsibility to Protect', 10 *International Studies Perspectives* (2009) 111–128

Bellamy, Alex J., 'The Responsibility to Protect – Five Years On', 24/2 *Ethics and International Affairs* (2010) 143–169

Bellamy, Alex J., 'Libya and the Responsibility to Protect: The Exception and the Norm', 25/3 *Ethics and International Affairs* (2011) 262–269

Bellamy, Alex J., 'The Responsibility to Protect Turns Ten', 29/2 *Ethics and International Affairs* (2015) 161–185

Bethlehem, Daniel, 'The Secret Life of International Law', 1/1 *Cambridge Journal of International and Comparative Law* (2012) 23–36

Bevilacqua, Catherine, and Scott Sheeran, 'The UN Security Council and International Human Rights Obligations: Towards a Theory of Constraints and Derogation', in Nigel Rodley and Scott Sheeran (eds), *Routledge Handbook of International Human Rights Law* (London: Routledge, 2013) 371–403

Bianchi, Andrea, 'Human Rights and the Magic of Jus Cogens', 19/3 *European Journal of International Law* (2008) 491–508

Bianchi, Andrea, 'Looking Ahead: International Law's Main Challenges', in David Armstrong (ed.), *Routledge Handbook of International Law* (London: Routledge, 2009) 392–409

Bilder, Richard B., 'The Implications of Kosovo for International Human Rights Law', in Philip Alston and Euan MacDonald (eds), *Human Rights, Intervention, and the Use of Force* (The Collected Courses of the Academy of European Law, Vol. X/2; Oxford: Oxford University Press, 2008) 139–178

Blätter, Ariela, and Paul D. Williams, 'The Responsibility not to Veto', 3/3 *Global Responsibility to Protect* (2011) 301–322

Bloxham, Donald, and Devin O. Pendas, 'Punishment as Prevention? The Politics of Punishing Génocidaires', in Donald Bloxham and A. Dirk Moses (eds), *The Oxford Handbook of Genocide Studies* (Oxford: Oxford University Press, 2010)

Bodansky, Daniel, 'Customary (and Not So Customary) International Environmental Law', 3 *Indian Global Legal Studies Journal* (1995–1996) 105–119

Bodansky, Daniel, 'Prologue to a Theory of Non-Treaty Norms', in Manush H. Arsanjani, Jacob Katz Cogan, Robert D. Sloane, and Siegfried Wiessner (eds), *Looking to the Future: Essays on International Law in Honor of W. Michael Reisman* (Leiden: Martinus Nijhoff, 2011) 119–134

Borchard, Edwin M., 'The Theory and Sources of International Law', in Charles Appleton (ed.), *Recueil d'Études sur les Sources du Droit en l'Honneur de François Gény. Tome III. Les Sources des Diverses Branches du Droit* (Paris: Sirey, 1934) 328–361

Bos, Maarten, 'The Recognized Manifestations of International Law: A New Theory of "Sources"', 20 *German Yearbook of International Law* (1977) 9–76

Bos, Maarten, 'The Hierarchy Among the Recognized Manifestations ("Sources") of International Law', 25/3 *Netherlands International Law Review* (1978) 334–344

Bos, Maarten, 'The Identification of Custom in International Law', 25/3 *German Yearbook of International Law* (1982) 9–53

Boyle, Alan, 'Soft Law in International Law-Making', in Malcolm D. Evans (ed.), *International Law*, 4th edn (Oxford: Oxford University Press, 2010) 122–140

Brierly, James Leslie, 'The Basis of Obligation in International Law', in Hersch Lauterpacht and Humphrey Waldock, *The Basis of Obligation in International Law and Other Papers by the Late James Leslie Brierly* (Oxford: Clarendon Press, 1958) 1–67

Brownlie, Ian, 'Thoughts on Kind-Hearted Gunmen', in Richard B. Lillich (ed.), *Humanitarian Intervention and the United Nations* (Charlottesville: University Press of Virginia, 1973) 139–148

Brownlie, Ian, 'Discussion', in Antonio Cassese and Joseph H.H. Weiler (eds), *Change and Stability in International Law Making* (European University Institute, Series A; Berlin: Walter de Gruyter, 1988) 108–110

Brownlie, Ian, 'The Decisions of Political Organs of the United Nations and the Rule of Law', in Ronald St. John Macdonald (ed.), *Essays in Honour of Wang Tieya* (Dordrecht: Martinus Nijhoff, 1994) 91–102

Buzzini, Gionata Piero, 'Les Comportements Passifs des Etats et Leur Incidence sur la Réglementation de l'Emploi de la Force en Droit International Général', in Enzo

Cannizzaro and Paolo Palchetti (eds), *Customary International Law on the Use of Force. A Methodological Approach* (Leiden: Martinus Nijhoff, 2005) 79–117

Byers, Michael, and Simon Chesterman, '"You, the People": Pro-democratic Intervention in International Law', in Gregory H. Fox and Brad R. Roth (eds), *Democratic Governance and International Law* (Cambridge: Cambridge University Press, 2000) 259–292

Cabranes, José A., 'Customary International Law: What it is and What it is Not', 22 *Duke Journal of Comparative and International Law* (2011–2012) 143–152

Cahin, Gérard, 'Le Rôle des Organes Politiques des Nations Unies', in Enzo Cannizzaro and Paolo Palchetti (eds), *Customary International Law on the Use of Force. A Methodological Approach* (Leiden: Martinus Nijhoff, 2005) 147–177

Camus, Albert, 'Réflexions sur la Guillotine', in Albert Camus and Arthur Koestler, *Réflexions sur la Peine Capitale* (Paris: Calmann-Lévy, 1957) 119–170

Cannizzaro, Enzo, and Paolo Palchetti, 'Customary International Law on the Use of Force … At a Time of Perplexity', in Enzo Cannizzaro and Paolo Palchetti (eds), *Customary International Law on the Use of Force. A Methodological Approach* (Leiden: Martinus Nijhoff, 2005) 1–6

Cannizzaro, Enzo, 'Customary International Law on the Use of Force: Inductive Approach vs. Value-Oriented Approach', in Enzo Cannizzaro and Paolo Palchetti (eds), *Customary International Law on the Use of Force: A Methodological Approach* (Leiden: Martinus Nijhoff, 2005) 245–268

Caroni, Martina, Lukas Heim, and Walter Kälin, 'Article 33, para. 1 (Prohibition of Expulsion to Return ("Refoulement")/Défense d'Expulsion et de Refoulement)', in Andreas Zimmermann (ed.), *The 1951 Convention Relating to the Status of Refugees and its 1967 Protocol. A Commentary* (Oxford: Oxford University Press, 2011) 1327–1395

Cassel, Douglass, 'Does International Human Rights Law Make a Difference?', 2/1 *Chicago Journal of International Law* (2001) 121–135

Cassese, Antonio, 'The Geneva Protocols of 1977 on the Humanitarian Law of Armed Conflict and Customary International Law', 3 *UCLA Pacific Basin Law Journal* (1984) 56–118

Cassese, Antonio, 'A Follow-up: Forcible Humanitarian Countermeasures and Opinio Necessitatis', 10/4 *European Journal of International Law* (1999) 791–799

Cassin, René, 'La Declaration Universelle et la Mise en Œuvre des Droits de l'Homme', 79 *Recueil des Cours de l'Académie de Droit International de La Haye* (1951-II) 237–367

Cerone, John, 'Out of Bounds? Considering the Reach of International Human Rights Law', *NYU School of Law Center for Human Rights and Global Justice Working Paper*, No. 6 (2006) <http://chrgj.org/wp-content/uploads/2012/07/WPS_NYU_CHRGJ_Cerone_Final.pdf>

Charney, Jonathan I., 'Universal International Law', 87/4 *American Journal of International Law* (1993) 529–551

Cheng, Bin, 'United Nations Resolutions on Outer Space: "Instant" International Customary Law?', 5 *Indian Journal of International Law* (1965) 23–48

Cheng, Bin, 'Custom: The Future of General State Practice in a Divided World', in Douglas M. Johnston and Ronald St. J. Macdonald, *The Structure and Process of International Law: Essays in Legal Philosophy, Doctrine and Theory* (The Hague: Martinus Nijhoff, 1983) 513–554

Chesterman, Simon, '"Leading from Behind": The Responsibility to Protect, the Obama Doctrine, and Humanitarian Intervention After Libya', 25/3 *Ethics and International Affairs* (2011) 279–285

Chilton, Adam S., and Mila Versteeg, 'The Failure of Constitutional Torture Prohibitions', 44/2 *Journal of Legal Studies* (2015) 417–452

Chinkin, Christine, 'Sources', in Daniel Moeckli, Sangeeta Shah, and Sandesh Sivakumaran (eds), *International Human Rights Law* (Oxford: Oxford University Press, 2010) 103–123

Condorelli, Luigi, 'Customary International Law: The Yesterday, Today, and Tomorrow of General International Law', in Antonio Cassese (ed.), *Realizing Utopia: The Future of International Law* (Oxford: Oxford University Press, 2012) 147–157

Cooper, Neil, 'Two Concepts of Morality', 41/155 *Philosophy* (1966) 19–33

Corten, Olivier, 'La Participation du Conseil de Sécurité à l'Èlaboration, à la Cristallisation ou à la Consolidation de Régles Coutumières', 37/2 *Revue Belge de Droit International* (2004) 552–567

Corten, Olivier, 'Breach and Evolution of Customary International Law on the Use of Force', in Enzo Cannizzaro and Paolo Palchetti (eds), *Customary International Law on the Use of Force: A Methodological Approach* (Leiden: Martinus Nijhoff, 2005) 119–144

Corten, Olivier, 'Human Rights and Collective Security: Is There an Emerging Right of Humanitarian Intervention?', in Philip Alston and Euan MacDonald (eds), *Human Rights, Intervention, and the Use of Force* (The Collected Courses of the Academy of European Law, Vol. X/2; Oxford: Oxford University Press, 2008) 87–137

Crawford, James, 'Democracy and International Law', 64 *British Yearbook of International Law* (1993) 113–133

Crawford, James, 'Democracy and the Body of International Law', in Gregory H. Fox and Brad R. Roth (eds), *Democratic Governance and International Law* (Cambridge: Cambridge University Press, 2000) 91–120

Croft, Adrian, and Aleksandar Vasovic, 'U.S. EU set Sanctions as Putin Recognises Crimea "Sovereignty"', *Reuters* (18 March 2014) <http://in.reuters.com/article/ukraine-crisis-crimea-referendum-idINDEEA2G00620140318>

Cross, Frank B., and Emerson H. Tiller, 'What is Legal Doctrine?', 100/1 *Northwestern University Law Review* (2006) 517–533

Czapliński, Wladyslaw, 'Sources of International Law in the Nicaragua Case', 38/1 *International and Comparative Law Quarterly* (1989) 151–166

D'Amato, Anthony, 'Trashing Customary International Law', 81 *American Journal of International Law* (1987) 101–105

D'Amato, Anthony, 'It's a Bird, It's a Plane, It's Jus Cogens!', 6/1 *Connecticut Journal of International Law* (1990–1991) 1–6

D'Amato, Anthony, 'Human Rights as Part of Customary International Law: A Plea for a Change of Paradigms', 25 *Georgia Journal of International Law* (1995/1996) 47–98

D'Aspremont, Jean, 'The Foundations of the International Legal Order', 18 *Finnish Yearbook of International Law* (2007) 219–255

D'Aspremont, Jean, 'Wording in International Law', 25/3 *Leiden Journal of International Law* (2012) 575–602

D'Aspremont, Jean, and Larissa van den Herik, 'The Public Good of Academic Publishing in International Law', 26/1 *Leiden Journal of International Law* (2013) 1–6

D'Aspremont, Jean, 'Send Back the Lifeboats: Confronting the Project of Saving International Law', 108 *American Journal of International Law* (2014) 680–688

D'Aspremont, Jean, and Jörg Kammerhofer, 'Introduction: The Future of International Legal Positivism', in Jean D'Aspremont and Jörg Kammerhofer, *International Legal*

Positivism in a Post-Modern World (Cambridge: Cambridge University Press, 2014) 1–19

D'Aspremont, Jean, 'If International Judges Say So, It Must Be True: Empiricism or Fetishism?', 4/9 *ESIL Reflections* (2015) <www.esil-sedi.eu/node/1134>

D'Aspremont, Jean, 'Martti Koskenniemi, the Mainstream, and Self-Reflectivity', *Amsterdam Law School Legal Studies Research Paper*, No. 2016–03 (2016) <http://ssrn.com/abstract=2718846>

Daalder, Ivo H., and James G. Stavridis, 'NATO's Victory in Libya. The Right Way to Run an Intervention', 91 *Foreign Affairs* (2012) 2–7

Danilenko, Gennady M., 'The Theory of International Customary Law', 31 *German Yearbook of International Law* (1988) 9–47

De Hoogh, André, 'Jus Cogens and the Use of Armed Force', in Marc Weller (ed.), *The Oxford Handbook of the Use of Force in International Law* (Oxford: Oxford University Press, 2015) 1161–1186

De Visscher, Charles, 'Contribution à l'Étude des Sources du Droit International', in Charles Appleton (ed.), *Recueil d'Études sur les Sources du Droit en l'Honneur de François Gény. Tome III. Les Sources des Diverses Branches du Droit* (Paris: Sirey, 1934) 389–399

De Wet, Erica, 'Holding the United Nations Security Council Accountable for Human Rights Violations Through Domestic and Regional Courts: A Case of "Be Careful What you Wish For"?', in Jeremy Farrall and Kim Rubenstein (eds), *Sanctions, Accountability and Governance in a Globalised World* (Cambridge: Cambridge University Press, 2009) 143–168

Degan, Vladimir-Djuro, 'General Principles of Law (A Source of General International Law)', 3 *Finnish Yearbook of International Law* (1992) 1–102

Dinstein, Yoram, 'The Right to Life, Physical Integrity, and Liberty', in Louis Henkin, *The International Bill of Rights: The Covenant on Civil and Political Rights* (New York: Columbia University Press, 1981) 114–137

Donnelly, Jack, 'Human Rights, Democracy, and Development', 21/3 *Human Rights Quarterly* (1999) 608–632

Dülffer, Just, 'The United Nations and the Origins of the Genocide Convention 1946–1948', in Eckart Conze and Christoph Safferling (eds), *The Genocide Convention Sixty Years After its Adoption* (The Hague: T.M.C. Asser Press, 2010) 55–68

Dupuy, Pierre-Marie, 'A Propos de l'Opposabilité de la Coutume Générale: Enquête Brève sur l'"Objecteur Persistant"', in Mélanges Michel Virally (ed.) *Le Droit International au Service de la Paix de la Justice et du Développement* (Paris: Éditions A. Pedone, 1991) 257–272

Dupuy, Pierre-Marie, 'Théorie des Sources et Coutume en Droit International Contemporain', in Manuel Rama-Montaldo (ed.), *El Derecho Internacional en un Mundo en Transformacion: Liber Amicorum en Homenaje al Professor Eduardo Jiménez de Aréchaga / Le Droit International Dans un Monde en Mutation. Liber Amicorum en Hommage au Professeur Eduardo Jiménez de Aréchaga / International Law in an Evolving World: Liber Amicorum in Tribute to Eduardo Jiménez de Aréchaga* (Montevideo: Fundación de cultura Universitaria, 1994) 51–68

Dupuy, René-Jean, 'Coutume Sage et Coutume Sauvage', in *La Communauté Internationale. Mélanges Offerts à Charles Rousseau* (Paris: Éditions A. Pedone, 1974) 75–87

The Economist (20 August 2015), 'Why the UN Doesn't Pay its Interns', <www.economist.com/blogs/economist-explains/2015/08/economist-explains-15>

Edelman, Hal, Review of Theodor Meron, *Human Rights and Humanitarian Norms as Customary Law* (Oxford: Clarendon Press, 1989), 4 *Harvard Human Rights Journal* (1991) 238–241

Elgot, Jessica, 'British Judges Not Bound by European Court of Human Rights, Says Leveson', *The Guardian* (24 May 2015) <www.theguardian.com/law/2015/may/24/british-courts-echr-leveson>

Elias, Olufemi, 'The Nature of the Subjective Element in Customary International Law', 44 *International and Comparative Law Quarterly* (1995) 501–520

Evans, Gareth, 'The Responsibility to Protect: From an Idea to an International Norm', in Richard H. Cooper and Juliette Voïnov Kohler (eds), *Responsibility to Protect: The Global Moral Compact for the 21st Century* (New York: Palgrave Macmillan, 2009) 15–29

Falk, Richard, 'Foreword', in Anthony A. D'Amato, *The Concept of Custom in International Law* (Ithaca: Cornell University Press, 1971)

Fassbender, Bardo, 'The United Nations Charter as Constitution of the International Community', 36 *Columbia Journal of Transnational Law* (1997) 529–619

Fassbender, Bardo, 'Hans Kelsen und die Vereinten Nationen', in Pierre-Marie Dupuy, Bardo Fassbender, Malcolm N. Shaw, and Karl-Peter Sommermann (eds), *Völkerrecht als Wertordnung: Common Values in International Law. Festschrift für / Essays in Honour of Christian Tomuschat* (Kehl: N.P. Engel Verlag, 2006)

Fastenrath, Ulrich, 'Relative Normativity in International Law', 4 *European Journal of International Law* (1993) 305–340

Fidler, David P., 'Challenging the Classical Concept of Custom: Perspectives on the Future of Customary International Law', 39 *German Yearbook of International Law* (1998) 198–248

Fitzmaurice, Gerald G., 'Some Problems Regarding the Formal Sources of International Law', in Frederik M. Van Asbeck (ed.), *Symbolae Verzijl. Présentées au Professeur J.H.W. Verzijl à l'Occasion de son LXX-ième Anniversaire* (La Haye: Martinus Nijhoff, 1958) 153–176, reprinted in Martti Koskenniemi (ed.), *Sources of International Law* (Aldershot: Ashgate, 2000) 57–80

Fletcher, George P., 'Law and Morality: A Kantian Perspective', 87/3 *Columbia Law Review* (1987) 533–558

Foreign Policy (Jan/Feb 2014), 'Letter from the Editors', 1

Francioni, Francesco, 'Balancing the Prohibition of Force with the Need to Protect Human Rights: A Methodological Approach', in Enzo Cannizzaro and Paolo Palchetti (eds), *Customary International Law on the Use of Force: A Methodological Approach* (Leiden: Martinus Nijhoff, 2005) 269–292

Franck, Thomas M., and Nigel S. Rodley, 'After Bangladesh: The Law of Humanitarian Intervention by Military Force', 67/2 *American Journal of International Law* (1973) 275–305

Franck, Thomas M., 'The Emerging Right to Democratic Governance', 86/1 *American Journal of International Law* (1992) 46–91

Frowein, Jochen A., 'Der Schutz des Menschen ist zentral. Der Krieg in Kosovo und die völkerrechtliche Regelung der Gewaltanwendung', *Neue Zürcher Zeitung* (17 July 1999) 62

Frowein, Jochen A., 'Ius Cogens', in *Max Planck Encyclopedia of Public International Law* <http://opil.ouplaw.com/view/10.1093/law:epil/9780199231690/law-9780199231690-e1437?rskey=uLHVY9&result=8&prd=EPIL>

Fukuyama, Francis, 'The End of History?', 16 *The National Interest* (summer 1989) 3–18

Gert, Bernard, 'The Definition of Morality', in Edward N. Zalta (ed.), *The Stanford Encyclopedia of Philosophy* (fall 2012) <http://plato.stanford.edu/archives/fall 2012/entries/morality-definition/>

Gihl, Torsten, 'The Legal Character and Sources of International Law', 1 *Scandinavian Studies in Law* (1957) 51–92

Goodman, Ryan, 'Humanitarian Intervention and Pretexts for War', 100 *American Journal of International Law* (2006) 107–141

Gouldner, Alan W., 'The Norm of Reciprocity: A Preliminary Statement', 25/2 *American Sociological Review* (1960) 161–178

Guggenheim, Paul, 'La Validité et la Nullité des Actes Juridiques Internationaux', 74 *Recueil des Cours de l'Académie de Droit International de La Haye* (1949-I) 191–268

Guggenheim, Paul, 'Contribution à l'Histoire des Sources du Droit des Gens', 94 *Recueil des Cours de l'Académie de Droit International de La Haye* (1958-II) 1–84

Gunning, Isabelle R., 'Modernizing Customary International Law: The Challenge of Human Rights', 31 *Vanderbilt Journal of International Law* (1990–1991) 211–247

Guzman, Andrew T., 'Saving Customary International Law', 27 *Michigan Journal of International Law* (2005) 115–176

Hafner, Gerhard, 'Some Thoughts on the State-Oriented and Individual-Oriented Approaches in International Law', 14 *Austrian Review of International and European Law* (2009) 27–39

Haggenmacher, Peter, 'La Doctrine des Deux Éléments du Droit Coutumier Dans la Pratique de la Cour Internationale', 90 *Revue Général du Droit International Public* (1986) 5–125

Hailbronner, Kay, and Marcel Kau, 'Der Staat und der Einzelne als Völkerrechtssubjekte', in Wolfgang Graf Vitzthum (ed.), *Völkerrecht*, 5th edn (Berlin: De Gruyter, 2010) 147–261

Hannum, Hurst, 'The Status of the Universal Declaration of Human Rights in National and International Law', 25 *Georgia Journal of International and Comparative Law* (1995–1996) 287–397

Heinrich, Walter, 'Zur Problematik des Gewohnheitsrechts', in Charles Appleton (ed.), *Recueil d'Études sur les Sources du Droit en l'Honneur de François Gény. Tome II. Les Sources Générales des Systèmes Juridiques Actuels* (Paris: Sirey, 1934) 277–301

Heintze, Hans-Joachim, 'The UN Convention and the Network of the International Human Rights Protection by the UN', in Michael Freeman and Philip Veerman (eds), *The Ideologies of Children's Rights* (International Studies in Human Rights, Vol. 23; Dordrecht: Martinus Nijhoff, 1992) 71–78

Henkin, Louis, 'Sibley Lecture, March 1994: Human Rights and State "Sovereignty"', 25/1 *Georgia Journal of International and Comparative Law* (1995–1996) 31–45

Henley, Jon, 'Why is the European Court of Human Rights Hated by the UK Right?', *The Guardian* (22 December 2013) <www.theguardian.com/law/2013/dec/22/britain-european-court-human-rights>

Higgins, Rosalyn, 'Reality and Hope in International Human Rights: A Critique', 9/5 *Hofstra Law Review* (1981) 1485–1499

Higgins, Rosalyn, 'The Identity of International Law', in Bin Cheng (ed.), *International Law: Teaching and Practice* (London: Stevens & Sons, 1982) 27–44

Hilpold, Peter, 'Humanitarian Intervention: Is There a Need for a Legal Reappraisal?', 12/3 *European Journal of International Law* (2001) 437–467

Hilpold, Peter, 'Die bedingte Menschlichkeit. Der gerechte Krieg, die Sicherung der Menschenrechte und die "vicinity" als Voraussetzung für Empathie und Aktion', in

Gerhard Hafner, Franz Matscher, and Kirsten Schmalenbach (eds), *Völkerrecht und die Dynamik der Menschenrechte* (Vienna: facultas.wuv, 2012) 313–323

Hilpold, Peter, '"And with Success Comes Pardon Hand in Hand": Some Essential Features of R2P and Humanitarian Intervention Drawn from History of International Law' (2014) <http://papers.ssrn.com/sol3/papers.cfm?abstract_id=2413184&download=yes>

Humphrey, John P., 'Foreword', in Richard B. Lillich (ed.), *Humanitarian Intervention and the United Nations* (Charlottesville: University Press of Virginia, 1973) vii–ix

Humphrey, John P., 'The Universal Declaration of Human Rights: Its History, Impact and Juridical Character', in Bertram G. Ramcharan (ed.), *Human Rights: Thirty Years After the Universal Declaration. Commemorative Volume on the Occasion of the Thirtieth Anniversary of the Universal Declaration of Human Rights* (The Hague: Martinus Nijhoff, 1979) 21–37

Hurd, Ian, 'Is Humanitarian Intervention Legal? The Rule of Law in an Incoherent World', 25/3 *Ethics and International Affairs* (2011) 293–313

Imbert, Pierre-Henri, 'L'Utilisation des Droits de l'Homme Dans les Relations Internationales', in Société Française pour le Droit International (ed.), *Colloque de Strasbourg. La Protection des Droits de l'Homme et l'Évolution du Droit International* (Paris: Éditions A. Pedone, 1998) 282–285

Ismail, Hilmy, Review of Theodor Meron, *Human Rights and Humanitarian Norms as Customary Law* (Oxford: Clarendon Press, 1989), XI/1 *Boston College Third World Law Journal* (1991) 393–401

Janik, Ralph, 'China, Russia, and the Failure of the Responsibility to Protect in Syria: Does the Fear of Regime Change Offer a Serviceable Explanation?', 58/1 *Studia Universitatis Babeş-Bolyai. Studia Europaea* (2013) 63–88

Janik, Ralph, 'Das Interventionsverbot im Zeitalter der Demokratie: Zwischen Obsoleszenz und (Wieder-)Auferstehung', in Andrea Bockley, Ursula Kriebaum, and August Reinisch (eds), *Nichtstaatliche Akteure und Interventionsverbot. Beiträge zum 39. Österreichischen Völkerrechtstag 2014 in Klosterneuburg* (Völkerrecht, Europarecht und Internationales, Vol. 20; Frankfurt am Main: Peter Lang, 2015) 107–129

Jansen, Nils, 'Rechtsdogmatik im Zivilrecht', *Enzyklopädie zur Rechtsphilosophie* <www.enzyklopaedie-rechtsphilosophie.net/inhaltsverzeichnis/19-beitraege/98-rechtsdogmatik-im-zivilrecht>

Jennings, Robert Y., 'What is International Law and How Do We Tell It When We See It?', 37 *Schweizerisches Jahrbuch für Internationales Recht* (1981) 59–88, reprinted in Martti Koskenniemi (ed.), *Sources of International Law* (Aldershot: Ashgate, 2000) 27–56

Jennings, Robert Y., 'The Identification of International Law', in Bin Cheng (ed.), *International Law: Teaching and Practice* (London: Stevens & Sons, 1982) 3–9

Jennings, Robert, 'International Law Reform and Progressive Development', in Gerhard Hafner, Gerhard Loibl, Alfred Rest, Lilly Sucharipa-Behrmann, and Karl Zemanek (eds), *Liber Amicorum Professor Ignaz Seidl-Hohenveldern. In Honour of his 80th Birthday* (The Hague: Kluwer Law International, 1998) 325–337

Jessup, Philip C., 'The Defense of Oppressed Peoples', 31/1 *American Journal of International Law* (1938) 116–119

Jiménéz de Aréchaga, Eduardo, 'International Law in the Past Third of a Century', 159 *Recueil des Cours de l'Académie de Droit International de La Haye* (1978) 1–343

Johnstone, Ian, 'The Plea of "Necessity" in International Legal Discourse: Humanitarian Intervention and Counter-terrorism', 43 *Columbia Journal of Transnational Law* (2004–2005) 337–388

Kadens, Emily, and Ernest A. Young, 'How Customary is Customary International Law?', 54 *William and Mary Law Review* (2012–2013) 885–920

Kammerhofer, Jörg, 'Uncertainty in the Formal Sources of International Law: Customary International Law and Some of Its Problems', 15/3 *European Journal of International Law* (2004) 523–553

Kammerhofer, Jörg, 'Law-Making by Scholarship? The Dark Side of 21st Century Legal "Methodology"', in James Crawford and Sarah Nouwen (eds), *Select Proceedings of the European Society of International Law: Third Volume: International Law 1989–2010: A Performance Appraisal* (Oxford: Hart Publishing, 2012) 115–126

Karadeniz, Tulay, and Ece Toksabay, 'Turkey to Ignore Court Order to pay Compensation to Cyprus', *Reuters* (13 May 2014) <www.reuters.com/article/us-turkey-cyprus-davutoglu-idUSBREA4C0AX20140513>

Kattan, Victor, 'Decolonizing the International Court of Justice: The Experience of Judge Sir Muhammad Zafrulla Khan in the South West Africa Cases', 4 *Asian Journal of International Law* (2014)

Keith, Linda Camp, 'The United Nations International Covenant on Civil and Political Rights: Does it Make a Difference in Human Rights Behavior?', 36/1 *Journal of Peace Research* (1999) 95–118

Kelsen, Hans, 'Théorie du Droit International Coutumier', I *Revue Internationale de la Théorie du Droit / Internationale Zeitschrift für Theorie des Rechts* (1939) 253–274

Kelsen, Hans, 'Recognition in International Law: Theoretical Observations', 35/4 *American Journal of International Law* (1941) 605–617

Kennedy, David, 'The Sources of International Law', 2/1 *American University International Law Review* (1987) 1–96

Kettemann, Matthias C., 'Endlich bestätigt: Menschenrechte gelten online wie offline', *jusPortal.at. Das Fachportal für Juristen* (24 July 2012) <www.jusportal.at/endlich-bestatigt-menschenrechte-gelten-online-wie-offline_matthias-c-kettemann/>

Kirgis, Frederic L., 'Custom on a Sliding Scale', 81/1 *American Journal of International Law* (1987) 146–151

Kirkpatrick, Jeane J., 'Law and Reciprocity', 78 *Proceedings of the American Society of International Law at its Annual Meeting* (1984) 59–67

Klabbers, Jan, 'International Organizations in the Formation of Customary International Law', in Enzo Cannizzaro and Paolo Palchetti (eds), *Customary International Law on the Use of Force: A Methodological Approach* (Leiden: Martinus Nijhoff, 2005) 179–195

Kolb, Robert, 'L'Article 103 de la Charte des Nations Unies', 367 *Recueil des Cours de l'Académie de Droit International de La Haye* (2013) 9–252

Kontorovich, Eugene, 'Inefficient Customs in International Law', 48 *William and Mary Law Review* (2006) 859–922

Koskenniemi, Martti, 'The Normative Force of Habit: International Custom and Social Theory', 1 *Finnish Yearbook of International Law* (1990) 77–153

Koskenniemi, Martti, 'The Politics of International Law', in Martti Koskenniemi (ed.), *The Politics of International Law* (Oxford: Hart Publishing, 2011) 35–62, originally published in 1 *European Journal of International Law* (1990) 4–32

Koskenniemi, Martti, 'The Pull of the Mainstream', Review of Theodor Meron, *Human Rights and Humanitarian Norms as Customary Law* (Oxford: Clarendon Press, 1989), 88 *Michigan Law Review* (1990) 1946–1962

Koskenniemi, Martti, 'The Place of Law in Collective Security', in Martti Koskenniemi (ed.), *The Politics of International Law* (Oxford: Hart Publishing, 2011) 79–111, originally published in 17 *Michigan Journal of International Law* (1996) 455–490

Koskenniemi, Martti, 'Between Commitment and Cynicism: Outline for a Theory of International Law as Practice', in Martti Koskenniemi (ed.), *The Politics of International Law* (Oxford: Hart Publishing, 2011) 271–293, originally published in Office of Legal Affairs (ed.), *Collection of Essays by Legal Advisers of States, Legal Advisers of International Organizations and Practitioners in the Field of International Law / Recueil d'Articles de Conseillers Juridiques d'États, d'Organisations Internationales et de Praticiens du Droit International* (New York: United Nations, 1999) 495–523

Koskenniemi, Martti, 'Introduction', in Martti Koskenniemi (ed.), *Sources of International Law* (Aldershot: Ashgate, 2000) x–ixxviii

Koskenniemi, Martti, 'General Principles: Reflexions on Constructivist Thinking in International Law', in Martti Koskenniemi (ed.), *Sources of International Law* (Aldershot: Ashgate, 2000) 359–402

Koskenniemi, Martti, '"The Lady Doth Protest Too Much". Kosovo, and the Turn to Ethics in International Law', 65/2 *Modern Law Review* (2002) 159–175

Koskenniemi, Martti, 'Miserable Comforters: International Relations as New Natural Law', 15/13 *European Journal of International Relations* (2009) 395–422

Krisch, Nico, 'General Framework', in Daniel-Erasmus Khan, Georg Nolte, Andreas Paulus, and Bruno Simma (eds), *The Charter of the United Nations. A Commentary. Volume II* (Oxford: Oxford University Press, 2012) 1237–1271

Krisch, Niko, 'Article 39', in Daniel-Erasmus Khan, Georg Nolte, Andreas Paulus, and Bruno Simma (eds), *The Charter of the United Nations. A Commentary. Volume II* (Oxford: Oxford University Press, 2012) 1272–1296

Kritsiotis, Dino, 'Reappraising Policy Objections to Humanitarian Intervention', 19 *Michigan Journal of International Law* (1997–1998) 1005–1050

Kunz, Josef L., 'The Nature of Customary International Law', 47/4 *American Journal of International Law* (1953) 662–669

Kurlantzik, Joshua, 'Opening Gambit: One Step Forward, Two Steps Back', *Foreign Policy* (March/April 2013) 20–22

Lagrange, Evelyne, 'Le Conseil de Sécurité des Nations Unies Peut-il Violer le Droit International', 37/2 *Revue Belge de Droit International* (2004) 568–592

Landman, Todd, 'Measuring Human Rights: Principle, Practice, and Policy', 26/4 *Human Rights Quarterly* (2004) 906–931

Lane, Eric, 'Demanding Human Rights: A Change in the World Legal Order', 6/2 *Hofstra Law Review* (1978) 269–295

Lane, Eric, 'Mass Killing by Governments: Lawful in the World Legal Order?', 12 *New York University Journal of International Law and Politics* (1979) 239–280

Lane, Eric, 'Human Rights Within the World Legal Order: A Reply to Sohn and McDougal', 10 *Hofstra Law Review* (1981–1982) 747–772

Lauterpacht, Hersch, 'Règles Générales du Droit de la Paix', 64 *Recueil des Cours de l'Académie de Droit International de La Haye* (1937-IV) 95–422

Le Fur, Louis, 'La Coutume et les Principes Généraux du Droit Comme Sources du Droit International Public', in Charles Appleton (ed.), *Recueil d'Études sur les Sources du Droit en l'Honneur de François Gény. Tome III. Les Sources des Diverses Branches du Droit* (Paris: Sirey, 1934) 362–374

Leiß, Johann, and Andreas Paulus, 'Article 103', in Daniel-Erasmus Khan, Georg Nolte, Andreas Paulus, and Bruno Simma (eds), *The Charter of the United Nations: A Commentary. Volume II*, 3rd edn (Oxford: Oxford University Press, 2012) 2110–2137

Lepard, Brian D., 'Towards a Normative Theory of Customary International Law as Law', 103 *American Society of International Law Proceedings* (2009) 379–382

Lepard, Brian D., 'International Law and Human Rights', in Thomas Cushman (ed.), *Handbook of Human Rights* (Oxon: Routledge, 2012) 583–597

Lillich, Richard B., 'Forcible Self-Help Under International Law', 62 *International Law Studies Series. US Naval War College* (1980) 129–138

Lillich, Richard B., 'The Growing Importance of Customary International Human Rights Law', 25/1 *Georgia Journal of International and Comparative Law* (1995–1996) 1–30

Lobo de Souza, I.M., 'The Role of State Consent in the Customary Process', 44 *International and Comparative Law Quarterly* (1995) 521–539

Luck, Edward C., 'The Responsibility to Protect: Growing Pains or Early Promise?', 24/4 *Ethics and International Affairs* (2010) 349–365

Macdonald, Ronald St., 'The Charter of the United Nations as a World Constitution', in Michael N. Schmitt (ed.), *International Law Across the Spectrum of Conflict: Essays in Honour of Professor L.C. Green on the Occasion of his Eightieth Birthday* (International Law Studies, Vol. 75; Newport, RI: Naval War College, 2000) 264–300

MacGibbon, Iain, 'Means for the Identification of International Law', in Bin Cheng (ed.), *International Law: Teaching and Practice* (London: Stevens & Sons, 1982) 10–26

McDougal, Myres S., 'Law and Minimum World Public Order: Armed Conflict in Larger Context', 3 *Pacific Basin Law Journal* (1984) 21–33

McDowall, Angus, 'Saudi Arabia Rejects Rights Criticism After Flogging of Blogger', *Reuters* (7 March 2015) <www.reuters.com/article/2015/03/07/us-saudi-rights-badawi-idUSKBN0M30SP20150307>

McDowall, Angus, 'Shi'ite Cleric Among 47 Executed in Saudi Arabia, Stirring Anger in Region', *Reuters* (2 January 2016) <www.reuters.com/article/saudi-security-idUSKBN0UG03F20160103>

McElhaney, James W., 'The Giggle Test', *ABA Journal. The Lawyer's Magazine* (1 October 1988) 90–92

McFarland, Sam, and Melissa Mathews, 'Who Cares About Human Rights?', 26/3 *Political Psychology* (2005) 365–385

McNair, Arnold Duncan, 'The General Principles of Law Recognized by Civilized Nations', 33 *British Yearbook of International Law* (1957) 1–19

Malmvig, Helle, 'The Reproduction of Sovereignties: Between Man and State During Practices of Intervention', 36 *Cooperation and Conflict* (2001) 251–272

Marboe, Irmgard, 'The Responsibility to Protect', in Karolina M. Januszewski, Tina Hofstätter, and Manfred Nowak (eds), *All Human Rights for All: Vienna Manual on Human Rights* (Vienna: Intersentia / Neuer Wissenschaftlicher Verlag, 2012) 500–505

Marks, Susan, 'The "Emerging Norm": Conceptualizing "Democratic Governance"', 91 *American Society of International Law Proceedings* (1997) 372–376

Meijers, Herman, 'How is International Law Made?', 9 *Netherlands Yearbook of International Law* (1978) 3–26

Mendelson, Maurice, 'The Subjective Element in Customary International Law', 66/1 *British Yearbook of International Law* (1995) 177–208

Mendelson, Maurice, 'The Formation of Customary International Law', 272 *Recueil des Cours de l'Académie de Droit International de La Haye* (1998) 155–410

Meron, Theodor, 'On a Hierarchy of International Human Rights', 80 *American Journal of International Law* (1986) 1–23

Moore, Gordon E., 'Cramming More Components onto Integrated Circuits', 38/8 *Electronics* (1965) 114–117

Morgenthau, Hans J., 'Positivism, Functionalism and International Law', 34/2 *American Journal of International Law* (1940) 260–284
Morgenthau, Hans J., 'The Twilight of International Morality', 58/2 *Ethics* (1948) 79–99
Murphy, Sean D., 'The Intervention in Kosovo: A Law-shaping Incident?', 94 *American Society of International Law Proceedings* (2000) 302–304
Neuhold, Hanspeter, 'Rechtsethische Aspekte des Internationalen Militäreinsatzes', in Erich Reiter (ed.), *Der Krieg um das Kosovo 1998/99* (Mainz: v. Hase & Koehler, 2000) 193–208
Neuhold, Hanspeter, 'Das Gewalt- und Interventionsverbot', in August Reinisch (ed.), *Österreichisches Handbuch des Völkerrechts. Band I – Textteil*, 5th edn (Vienna: Manz, 2013) 422–449
Neumayer, Eric, 'Do International Human Rights Treaties Improve Respect for Human Rights?', 49/6 *Journal of Conflict Resolution* (2005) 925–953
Norman, George, and Joel P. Trachtman, 'The Customary International Law Game', 99/3 *American Journal of International Law* (2005) 541–580
Nowak, Manfred, 'Responsibility to Protect: Is International Law Moving from Hobbes to Locke?', in Gerhard Hafner, Franz Matscher, and Kirsten Schmalenbach (eds), *Völkerrecht und die Dynamik der Menschenrechte: Liber Amicorum Wolfram Karl* (Vienna: Facultas.wuv, 2012) 342–369
Nowrot, Karsten, and Emily W. Schabacker, 'The Use of Force to Restore Democracy: International Legal Implications of the ECOWAS Intervention in Sierra Leone', 14 *American University International Law Review* (1998–1999) 321–412
O'Boyle, Michael, 'Torture and Emergency Powers Under the European Convention on Human Rights: Ireland v. the United Kingdom', 71 *American Journal of International Law* (1977) 674–706
O'Connell, Mary Ellen, 'Taking Opinio Juris Seriously, a Classical Approach to International Law on the Use of Force', in Enzo Cannizzaro and Paolo Palchetti (eds), *Customary International Law on the Use of Force: A Methodological Approach* (Leiden: Martinus Nijhoff, 2005) 9–30
Oba, Abdulmumini A., 'Female Circumcision as Female Genital Mutilation: Human Rights or Cultural Imperialism?', 8/3 *Global Jurist* (2008) 1–38
Öberg, Marko Divac, 'The Legal Effects of Resolutions of the UN Security Council and General Assembly in the Jurisprudence of the ICJ', 16/5 *European Journal of International Law* (2006) 879–906
Onuf, Nicholas, 'Do Rules Say What They Do? From Ordinary Language to International Law', 26/2 *Harvard International Law Journal* (1985) 385–410
Orrego-Vicuña, Francisco, 'Customary International Law in a Global Community: Tailor Made?', 38/148 *Revista de Estudios Internacionales* (2005) 21–38
Palmisano, Giuseppe, 'Determining the Law on the Use of Force: The ICJ and Customary Rules on the Use of Force', in Enzo Cannizzaro and Paolo Palchetti (eds), *Customary International Law on the Use of Force: A Methodological Approach* (Leiden: Martinus Nijhoff, 2005) 197–218
Panjabi, Ranee K.L., Review of Theodor Meron, *Human Rights and Humanitarian Norms as Customary Law* (Oxford: Clarendon Press, 1989), 20/1 *California Western International Law Journal* (1989–1990) 381–388
Pattison, James, 'The Ethics of Humanitarian Intervention in Libya', 25/3 *Ethics and International Affairs* (2011) 271–277
Paulsson, Jan, 'Scholarship as Law', in Manush H. Arsanjani, Jacob Katz Cogan, Robert D. Sloane, and Siegfried Wiessner (eds), *Looking to the Future: Essays on*

International Law in Honor of W. Michael Reisman (Leiden: Martinus Nijhoff, 2011) 183–193

Paulus, Andreas L., and Bruno Simma, 'The Responsibility of Individuals for Human Rights Abuses in Internal Conflicts: A Positivist View', 93/2 *American Journal of International Law* (1999) 302–316

Paust, Jordan J., 'The Complex Nature, Sources and Evidences of Customary Human Rights', 25 *Georgia Journal of International Law* (1995/1996) 147–164

Peczenik, Aleksander, 'Scientia Iuris – An Unsolved Philosophical Problem', 3/3 *Ethical Theory and Moral Practice* (2000) 273–302

Pellet, Alain, 'La Mise en Œuvre des Normes Relatives aux Droits de l'Homme. "Souveraineté du Droit" Contre Souveraineté de l'État?', in Hubert Thierry and Emmanuel Decaux (eds), *Droit international et Droits de l'Homme. Actes du Colloque des 12 et 13 Octobre. La Pratique Juridique Française Dans le Domaine de la Protection Internationale des Droits de l'Homme* (Cahiers du CEDIN 5; Paris: Édition Montchrestien, 1990) 101–141

Pellet, Alain, '"Human Rightism" and International Law', 20 *Italian Yearbook of International Law* (2000) 3–16

Pellet, Alain, 'Article 38', in Karin Oellers-Frahm, Christian J. Tams, Christian Tomuschat, and Andreas Zimmermann (eds), *The Statute of the International Court of Justice: A Commentary*, 2nd edn (Oxford: Oxford University Press, 2012) 731–870

Peters, Anne, 'The Responsibility to Protect: Spelling out the Hard Legal Consequences for the UN Security Council and its Members', in Ulrich Fastenrath, Rudolf Geiger, Daniel-Erasmus Khan, Andreas Paulus, Sabine von Schorlemer, and Christoph Vedder (eds), *From Bilateralism to Community Interest: Essays in Honour of Judge Bruno Simma* (Oxford: Oxford University Press, 2011) 297–325

Peters, Anne, 'Realizing Utopia as a Scholarly Endeavour', 24/2 *European Journal of International Law* (2013) 533–552

Petersen, Niels, 'Customary Law Without Custom? Rules, Principles, and the Role of State Practice in International Norm Creation', 23/2 *American University International Law Review* (2007) 275–310

Petersen, Niels, Review of Brian D. Lepard, *Customary International Law. A New Theory with Practical Applications* (Cambridge: Cambridge University Press, 2010), 21 *European Journal of International Law* (2010) 795–797

Petersmann, Ernst-Ulrich, 'Constitutionalism and International Adjudication: How to Constitutionalize the U.N. Dispute Settlement System?', 31 *New York University Journal of International Law and Politics* (1998–1999) 753–790

Picker, Colin B., 'International Law's Mixed Heritage: A Common/Civil Law Jurisdiction', 41 *Vanderbilt Journal of Transnational Law* (2008) 1083–1140

Popper, Karl R., 'Wider die großen Worte. Ein Plädoyer für intellektuelle Redlichkeit', *Zeit Online* <www.zeit.de/1971/39/wider-die-grossen-worte>, originally published in 39 *Die Zeit* (14 September 1971)

Posner, Richard, 'A Theory of Negligence', 1 *Journal of Legal Studies* (1972) 29–96

Pronto, Arnold N., '"Human-Rightism" and the Development of General International Law', 20 *Leiden Journal of International Law* (2007) 753–765

Raz, Joseph, 'Authority and Justification', 14/1 *Authority and Justification* (1985) 3–29, reprinted in Joseph Raz (ed.), *Authority* (New York: New York University Press, 1990) 115–141

Reinisch, August, 'Developing Human Rights and Humanitarian Law Accountability of the Security Council for the Imposition of Economic Sanctions', 95/4 *American Journal of International Law* (2001) 851–872

Reinisch, August, 'Value Conflicts Within the United Nations Security Council', 14 *Austrian Review of International Law* (2009) 41–60

Reisman, Michael, and Myres S. McDougal, 'Humanitarian Intervention to Protect the Ibos', in Richard B. Lillich (ed.), *Humanitarian Intervention and the United Nations* (Charlottesville: University Press of Virginia, 1973) 167–195

Reisman, Michael, 'International Law-making: A Process of Communication', 75 *American Society of International Law Proceedings* (1981) 101–120

Rich, Roland, 'Bringing Democracy into International Law', 12/3 *Journal of Democracy* (2001) 20–34

Richardson, Henry S., 'Moral Reasoning', in Edward N. Zalta (ed.), *The Stanford Encyclopedia of Philosophy* (Winter 2014 Edition) <http://plato.stanford.edu/archives/win2014/entries/reasoning-moral>

Roberts, Anthea Elizabeth, 'Traditional and Modern Approaches to Customary International Law: A Reconciliation', 95 *American Journal of International Law* (2001) 757–791

Roberts, Anthea, 'Legality Verses Legitimacy: Can Uses of Force Be Illegal but Justified?', in Philip Alston and Euan MacDonald (eds), *Human Rights, Intervention, and the Use of Force* (The Collected Courses of the Academy of European Law, Vol. X/2; Oxford: Oxford University Press, 2008) 179–213

Roberts, Anthea, and Sandesh Sivakumaran, 'Lawmaking by Nonstate Actors: Engaging Armed Groups in the Creation of International Humanitarian Law', 37 *Yale Journal of International Law* (2012) 107–152

Roberts, Anthea, 'Custom, Public Law and the Human Rights Analogy', *EJIL:Talk!* (14 August 2013) <www.ejiltalk.org/custom-public-law-and-the-human-rights-analogy/>

Rodley, Nigel, 'Humanitarian Intervention', in Marc Weller (ed.), *The Oxford Handbook of the Use of Force in International Law* (Oxford: Oxford University Press, 2015) 775–796

Roht-Arriaza, Naomi, 'State Responsibility to Investigate and Prosecute Grave Human Rights Violations in International Law', 78/2 *California Law Review* (1990) 449–513

Rougier, Antoine, 'La Théorie de l'Intervention d'Humanité', XVII *Revue Générale de Droit International Public* (1910) 468–526

Roy, Guha, 'Is the Law of Responsibility of States for Injuries to Aliens a Part of Universal International Law?', 55 *American Journal of International Law* (1961) 863–891

Rubin, Alfred P., Review of Theodor Meron, *Human Rights and Humanitarian Norms as Customary Law* (Oxford: Clarendon Press, 1989), 31/2 *Harvard Journal of International Law* (1990) 685–694

Ruiz Fabri, Hélène, 'Human Rights and State Sovereignty: Have the Boundaries Been Significantly Redrawn?' in Philip Alston and Euan MacDonald (eds), *Human Rights, Intervention, and the Use of Force* (The Collected Courses of the Academy of European Law, Vol. X/2; Oxford: Oxford University Press, 2008) 33–86

Sands, Philippe, 'The Government is Playing a Dangerous Game Trying to Scrap the Human Rights Act', *The Guardian* (21 October 2015) <www.theguardian.com/commentisfree/2015/oct/21/government-human-rights-act-legal-europe-uk>

Sassòli, Marco, Review of Theodor Meron, *Human Rights and Humanitarian Norms as Customary Law* (Oxford: Clarendon Press, 1989), 29/273 *International Review of the Red Cross* (1989) 602–603

Scelle, Georges, 'Essai sur les Sources Formelles du Droit International', in Charles Appleton (ed.), *Recueil d'Études sur les Sources du Droit en l'Honneur de François Gény. Tome III. Les Sources des Diverses Branches du Droit* (Paris: Sirey, 1934) 400–430

Schachter, Oscar, 'Towards a Theory of International Obligation', in Stephen Schwebel (ed.), *The Effectiveness of International Decisions* (Leiden: Sijthoff, 1971) 9–31, reprinted in Martti Koskenniemi (ed.), *Sources of International Law* (Aldershot: Ashgate, 2000) 3–25

Schachter, Oscar, 'The Twilight Existence of Nonbinding International Agreements', 71 *American Journal of International Law* (1977) 296–304

Schachter, Oscar, 'The Invisible College of International Lawyers', 72 *Northwestern University Law Review* (1977–1978) 217–226

Schachter, Oscar, 'International Law Implications of U.S. Human Rights Policies', 24 *New York Law School Law Review* (1978–1979) 63–87

Schachter, Oscar, 'Alf Ross Memorial Lecture: The Crisis of Legitimation in the United Nations', 50–51 *Nordisk Tidsskrift for International Ret* (1981–1982) 3–19

Schachter, Oscar, 'The Nature and Process of Legal Development in International Society', in Douglas M. Johnston and Ronald St.J. Macdonald, *The Structure and Process of International Law Essays in Legal Philosophy, Doctrine and Theory* (The Hague: Martinus Nijhoff, 1983) 745–808

Schachter, Oscar, 'The Legality of Pro-Democratic Invasion', 78/3 *American Journal of International Law* (1984) 645–650

Schachter, Oscar, 'Metaphors and Realism in International Law', 96 *Proceedings of the American Society of International Law at its Annual Meeting* (2002) 268–269

Scheffer, David J., 'Introduction: The Great Debate of the 1980s', in Allan Gerson, Louis Henkin, Stanley Hoffmarin, Jeane J. Kirkpatrick, William D. Rogers, and David J. Scheffer (eds), *Right v. Might. International Law and the Use of Force*, 2nd edn (New York: Council of Foreign Relations Press, 1991) 1–17

Schrijver, Nico J., 'The Future of the Charter of the United Nations', 10 *Max Planck Yearbook of United Nations Law* (2006) 1–34

Schrödinger, Erwin, 'Die gegenwärtige Situation in der Quantenmechanik', 23/49 *Die Naturwissenschaften* (1935) 807–812

Schulz, William F., 'Spread the Word. Organizing the Grassroots to End Atrocity Crimes', in Richard H. Cooper and Juliette Voïnov Kohler (eds), *Responsibility to Protect: The Global Moral Compact for the 21st Century* (New York: Palgrave Macmillan, 2009) 145–159

Schwebel, Stephen M., 'The Effect of Resolutions of the U.N. General Assembly on Customary International Law', 73 *Proceedings of the American Society of International Law at its Annual Meeting* (1979) 301–309

Schwebel, Stephen M., 'The Legal Effect of Resolutions and Codes of Conduct of the United Nations', 7 *Forum Internationale* (1985) 1–16 reprinted in Stephen M. Schwebel (ed.), *Justice in International Law: Selected Writings of Stephen M. Schwebel* (Cambridge: Cambridge University Press, 1994) 499–513

Schwebel, Stephen M., 'Investor-State Disputes and the Development of International Law: The Influence of Bilateral Investment Treaties on Customary International Law', 98 *American Society of International Law Procedures* (2004) 27–30

Schwelb, Egon, 'Crimes Against Humanity', 23 *British Yearbook of International Law* (1946) 178–226

Segupta, Somini, 'A Host of Possible Objections to Expanded Airstrikes in Syria', *New York Times* (17 September 2014) <www.nytimes.com/2014/09/18/world/middleeast/a-host-of-possible-objections-to-expanded-airstrikes.html?ref=world&_r=0>

Sekularac, Ivana, and Krisztina Than, 'Hungary Shuts EU Border, Taking Migrant Crisis Into its own Hands', *Reuters* (16 September 2015) <http://uk.reuters.com/article/uk-europe-migrants-hungary-idUKKCN0RE2DS20150916>

Shavell, Steven, 'Law Versus Morality as Regulators of Conduct', 4/2 *American Law and Economics Review* (2002) 227–257

Shelton, Dina, 'International Law and "Relative Normativity"', in Malcolm D. Evans (ed.), *International Law*, 4th edn (Oxford: Oxford University Press, 2014) 137–165

Simma, Bruno, 'NATO, the UN and the Use of Force', 10 *European Journal of International Law* (1999) 1–22

Simma, Bruno, 'Gestaltwandel im Völkerrecht und in der Organisation der Vereinten Nationen', in Waldemar Hummer (ed.), *Paradigmenwechsel im Völkerrecht zur Jahrtausendwende. Ansichten österreichischer Völkerrechtler zu aktuellen Problemlagen* (Vienna: Manzsche Verlags- und Universitätsbuchhandlung, 2002) 45–63

Simma, Bruno, and Stephan Wittich, 'Das Völkergewohnheitsrecht', in August Reinisch (ed.), *Österreichisches Handbuch des Völkerrechts. Band I – Textteil*, 5th edn (Vienna: Manz, 2013) 32–49

Simpson, Gerry, 'On the Magic Mountain: Teaching Public International Law', 10 *European Journal of International Law* (1999) 70–92

Skubiszewski, Krzysztof, 'Non-Binding Resolutions and the Law-Making Process', 15 *Polish Yearbook of International Law* (1986) 135–161

Skubiszewski, Krzysztof, 'Resolutions of the U.N. General Assembly and Evidence of Custom', in Alessandro Migliazza, Fausto Pocar, Pierluigi Lamberti Zanardi, and Piero Ziccardi (eds), *Le Droit International a l'Heure de sa Codification. Etudes en l'Honneur de Roberto Ago / Il Diritto Internazionale al Tempo Della sua Codificazione: Studi in Onore di Roberto Ago / International Law at the Time of its Codification: Essays in Honour of Roberto Ago* (Milan: Dott. A. Giuffré Editore, 1987) 503–519

Sloan, Blaine, 'General Assembly Resolutions Revisited (Forty Years Later)', 58 *British Yearbook of International Law* (1987) 39–150

Sohn, Louis B., 'The Human Rights Law of the Charter', 12 *Texas International Law Journal* (1977) 129–140

Sohn, Louis B., 'John A. Sibley Lecture. The Shaping of International Law', 8/1 *Georgia Journal of International and Comparative Law* (1978) 1–25

Sohn, Louis B., 'The New International Law: Protection of the Rights of Individuals Rather Than States', 32 *American University Law Review* (1982–1983) 1–64

Sohn, Louis B., '"Generally Accepted" International Rules', 61 *Washington Law Review* (1986) 1073–1080

Sohn, Louis B., 'Sources of International Law', 25/1 *Georgia Journal of International Law* (1995–1996) 399–406

Solow, Barbara L., reply by David Brion Davis, 'The British & the Slave Trade', *The New York Review of Books* (12 January 2012) <www.nybooks.com/articles/archives/2012/jan/12/british-slave-trade/>

Somek, Alexander, 'Kelsen Lives', 18/3 *European Journal of International Law* (2007) 409–451

Somek, Alexander, 'From the Rule of Law to the Constitutionalist Makeover: Changing European Conceptions of Public International Law', 18/4 *Constellations* (2011) 576–588

Somek, Alexander, 'Beyond Kelsen and Hart', in Jean D'Aspremont and Jörg Kammerhofer (eds), *International Legal Positivism in a Post-Modern World* (Cambridge: Cambridge University Press, 2014) 151–181

Sørensen, Max, 'Principes de Droit International Public. Cours Général', 101 *Recueil des Cours de l'Académie de Droit International de La Haye* (1960-III) 1–254

Stadler, Christian M., 'Rechtsethische Aspekte des Internationalen Militäreinsatzes', in Erich Reiter (ed.), *Der Krieg um das Kosovo 1998/99* (Mainz: v. Hase & Koehler, 2000) 177–192

Stadler, Christian, 'Thesen zur Rechtfertigung der Kosovo-Intervention', 1 *Juridikum. Zeitschrift im Rechtsstaat* (2000) 44–48

Stadler, Christian, 'Zur Aktualität der Theorie vom "Gerechten Krieg". Rechtsethische Überlegungen zur Weltfriedensbotschaft des Hl. Vaters vom Jänner 2000', *Ethica. Jahrbuch des Instituts für Religion und Frieden* (2000) 79–90

Stadler, Christian, 'Internationales Recht – Völkerrecht und humanitäre Intervention', in Edwin R. Micewski, Brigitte Sob, and Wolfgang Schober (eds), *Ethik und internationale Politik/Ethics and International Politics* (Schriftenreihe der Landesverteidigungsakademie; Vienna: Literas – Universitätsverlag, 2001) 19–34

Stadler, Christian, 'Military Ethics as Part of a General System of Ethics', in Edwin R. Micewski (ed.), *Civil-Military Aspects of Military Ethics* (Vol. 1; Vienna: National Defense Academy Printing Office, 2003) 3–7

Stanton, Gregory H., 'Why the World Needs an International Convention on Crimes Against Humanity', in Leila Nadya Sadat (ed.), *Forging a Convention for Crimes Against Humanity* (New York: Cambridge University Press, 2011) 345–358

Stein, Ted L., 'The Approach of the Different Drummer: The Principle of the Persistent Objector in International Law', 26/2 *Harvard International Law Journal* (1985) 457–482

Steinberg, Richard H., 'Wanted – Dead or Alive: Realism in International Law', in Jeffrey L. Dunoff and Mark A. Pollack (eds), *Interdisciplinary Perspectives on International Law and International Relations* (Cambridge: Cambridge University Press, 2013) 146–172

Strauss, Andrew, 'International Law as Democratic Law', 103 *American Society of International Law Proceedings* (2009) 388–391

Talmon, Stefan, 'Determining Customary International Law: The ICJ's Methodology Between Induction, Deduction and Assertion', 26/2 *European Journal of International Law* (2015) 417–443

Tams, Christian J., 'Meta-Custom and the Court: A Study in Judicial Law-Making', 14/1 *The Law and Practice of International Courts and Tribunals* (2015) 51–79

Teraya, Koji, 'Emerging Hierarchy in International Human Rights and Beyond: From the Perspective of Non-derogable Rights', 12/5 *European Journal of International Law* (2001) 917–941

Tesón, Fernando R., 'Kosovo: A Powerful Precedent for the Doctrine of Humanitarian Intervention', 1 *Amsterdam Law Forum* (2008–2009) 42–48

Thirlway, Hugh, 'The Sources of International Law', in Malcolm D. Evans (ed.), *International Law*, 4th edn (Oxford: Oxford University Press, 2010) 95–121

Thirlway, Hugh, 'Human Rights in Customary Law: An Attempt to Define Some of the Issues', 28/3 *Leiden Journal of International Law* (2015) 495–506

Thouvenin, Jean-Marc, 'Genèse de l'Idée de Responsabilité de Protéger', in Société Française Pour le Droit International (ed.), *Colloque de Nanterre: La Responsabilité de Protéger* (Paris: Éditions A. Pedone, 2008) 21–38

Tomuschat, Christian, 'Obligations Arising for States Without or Against Their Will', 241 *Recueil des Cours de l'Académie de Droit International de La Haye* (1993-IV) 195–374

Trachtman, Joel P., 'The Obsolescence of Customary International Law' (2014) <http://papers.ssrn.com/sol3/papers.cfm?abstract_id=2512757>

Trindade, Antônio Augusto Cançado, 'Selected Aspects of the Case-Law Under the Inter-American System of Human Rights Protection', in Paulo Borba Casella (ed.), *Dimensão Internacional do Direito* (São Paulo: Editora LTR, 2000) 493–511

Tunkin, Grigory I., 'Co-Existence and International Law', 95 *Recueil des Cours de l'Académie de Droit International de La Haye* (1958-III) 1–81

Valentino, Benjamin A., 'The True Costs of Humanitarian Intervention: The Hard Truth About a Noble Notion', 90/6 *Foreign Affairs* (November/December 2011)

Venzke, Ingo, and Jochen von Bernstorff, 'Ethos, Ethics, and Morality in International Relations', in *Max Planck Encyclopedia of Public International Law* <http://opil.ouplaw.com/view/10.1093/law:epil/9780199231690/law-9780199231690-e936?rskey=v1zt5J&result=2&prd=EPIL>

Verdross, Alfred, 'Les Principes Généraux du Droit Comme Source du Droit de Gens', in Charles Appleton (ed.), *Recueil d'Études sur les Sources du Droit en l'Honneur de François Gény. Tome III. Les Sources des Diverses Branches du Droit* (Paris: Sirey, 1934) 383–388

Villalpando, Santiago, 'The Legal Dimension of the International Community: How Community Interests Are Protected in International Law', 21/2 *European Journal of International Law* (2010) 387–419

Villalpando, Santiago, 'The "Invisible College of International Lawyers" Forty Years Later', *European Society of International Law. Conference Paper Series*, No. 5/2013, Amsterdam Research Forum (23–25 May 2013) <http://papers.ssrn.com/sol3/papers.cfm?abstract_id=2363640>

Vinogradoff, Paul, 'Historical Types of International Law', in *The Collected Papers of Paul Vinogradoff: With a Memoir by H.A.L. Fisher. Vol. II. Jurisprudence* (London: Wildy & Sons Ltd., 1964) 248–318

Virally, Michel, 'Réflexions sur le "jus cogens"', 12 *Annuaire Français de Droit International* (1966) 5–29

Vitanyi, Béla, 'Les Positions de la Doctrine Concernant le Sens de la Notion de Principes Généraux de Droit Reconnus par les Nations Civilisées', 86 *Revue Générale de Droit International Public* (1982) 48–116

Waibel, Michael, 'Interpretive Communities in International Law', *University of Cambridge. Faculty of Law. Legal Studies Research Paper Series*, No. 62/2014 (October 2014) <http://papers.ssrn.com/sol3/papers.cfm?abstract_id=2513411##>

Walden, Raphael M., 'Customary International Law: A Jurisprudential Analysis', 13 *Israel Law Review* (1978) 86–102

Walzer, Michael, 'The Moral Standing of States: A Response to Four Critics', 9/3 *Philosophy and Public Affairs* (1980) 209–229

Walzer, Michael, 'The Politics of Rescue', 61/1 *Social Research* (1995) 53–66

Watson, J. Shand, 'Autointerpretation, Competences, and the Continuing Validity of Article 2(7) of the UN Charter', 71/1 *American Journal of International Law* (1977) 60–83

Watson, J. Shand, 'Legal Theory, Efficacy and Validity in the Development of Human Rights Norms in International Law', *University of Illinois Law Forum* (1979) 609–641

Watson, J. Shand, 'Normativity and Reality in International Human Rights Law', 13 *Stetson Law Review* (1983–1984) 221–235

Wedgwood, Ruth, 'The ICJ Advisory Opinion on the Israeli Security Fence and the Limits of Self-Defense', 99 *American Journal of International Law* (2005) 52–61

Weil, Prosper, 'Toward Relative Normativity in International Law?', 77 *American Journal of International Law* (1983) 413–442

Weil, Prosper, 'Le Droit International en Quête de Son Identité', 237 *Recueil des Cours de l'Académie de Droit International de La Haye* (1992-VI) 9–370

Weiler, Joseph, 'On My Way Out – Advice to Young Scholars II: Career Strategy and the Publication Trap', *EJIL: Talk!* (18 February 2016) <www.ejiltalk.org/on-my-way-out-advice-to-young-scholars-ii-career-strategy-and-the-publication-trap/>

Weiler, Rudolf, 'Krieg und Frieden in der VR-Ethik', *Ethica. Jahrbuch des Instituts für Religion und Frieden* (2000) 177–181

Weisburd, Arthur M., 'The Effect of Treaties and Other Formal International Acts on the Customary Law of Human Rights', 25/1 *Georgia Journal of International Law* (1995–1996) 99–146

Weisburd, Arthur M., 'Consistency, Universality, and the Customary Law of Interstate Force', in Enzo Cannizzaro and Paolo Palchetti (eds), *Customary International Law on the Use of Force: A Methodological Approach* (Leiden: Martinus Nijhoff, 2005) 31–77

Weiss, Thomas G., 'RtoP Alive and Well after Libya', 25/3 *Ethics and International Affairs* (2011) 287–292

Wennholz, Philipp, and Andreas Zimmermann, 'Article 33, para. 2 (Prohibition of Expulsion to Return ("Refoulement")/Défense d'Expulsion et de Refoulement)', in Andreas Zimmermann (ed.), *The 1951 Convention Relating to the Status of Refugees and its 1967 Protocol: A Commentary* (Oxford: Oxford University Press, 2011) 1397–1423

Wight, Martin, 'Why is There no International Theory?', 2 *International Relations* (1960) 35–48

Winter, Jay, 'Introduction: Witness to Genocide', in Jay Winter (ed.), *America and the Armenian Genocide of 1915* (Cambridge: Cambridge University Press, 2013) 1–6

Wippman, David, 'Defending Democracy Through Foreign Intervention', 19 *Houston Journal of International Law* (1997) 659–681

Worster, William Thomas, 'The Inductive and Deductive Methods in Customary International Law Analysis', 45 *Georgia Journal of International Law* (2013–2014) 445–521

Zemanek, Karl, 'Hat die "humanitäre Intervention" Zukunft?', *Jahrbuch für internationale Sicherheitspolitik* (2000) <www.bundesheer.at/wissen-forschung/publikationen/beitrag.php?id=857>

Zemanek, Karl, 'Ist das Gewaltverbot noch aktuell?', in Waldemar Hummer (ed.), *Paradigmenwechsel im Völkerrecht zur Jahrtausendwende. Ansichten österreichischer Völkerrechtler zu aktuellen Problemlagen* (Vienna: Manzsche Verlags- und Universitätsbuchhandlung, 2002) 67–82

Zemanek, Karl, 'Für mehr Offenheit und Realismus in der Völkerrechtslehre', in Klaus Dicke, Stephan Hobe, Karl-Ulrich Meyn, Anne Peters, Eibe Riedel, Hans-Joachim Schütz, and Christian Tietje (eds), *Weltinnenrecht. Liber amicorum Jost Delbrück* (Veröffentlichungen des Walther-Schücking-Instituts für Internationales Recht an der Universität Kiel, Vol. 155; Berlin: Duncker & Humblot, 2005) 895–925

Zemanek, Karl, 'The Basic Principles of UN Charter Law', in Ronald St. John Mcdonald and Douglas M. Johnston (eds), *Towards World Constitutionalism. Issues in the Legal Ordering of the World Community* (Leiden: Martinus Nijhoff, 2005) 401–430

Zemanek, Karl, 'How to Identify Peremptory Norms of International Law', in Pierre-Marie Dupuy, Bardo Fassbender, Malcolm N. Shaw, and Karl-Peter Sommermann (eds), *Völkerrecht als Wertordnung: Common Values in International Law. Festschrift für / Essays in Honour of Christian Tomuschat* (Kehl: N.P. Engel Verlag, 2006) 1103–1116

Zimmermann, Andreas, 'The Obligation to Prevent Genocide: Towards a General Responsibility to Protect?' in Ulrich Fastenrath, Rudolf Geiger, Daniel-Erasmus Khan, Andreas Paulus, Sabine von Schorlemer, and Christoph Vedder (eds), *From Bilateralism to Community Interest: Essays in Honour of Judge Bruno Simma* (Oxford: Oxford University Press, 2011) 629–645

C Other

Greenwood, Christopher, 'The Sources of International Law', Original Lecture, Sources of Law, United Nations Audiovisual Library of International Law <http://legal.un.org/avl/ls/Greenwood_IL.html#>

Presley, Elvis, '50,000,000 Elvis Fans Can't Be Wrong: Elvis' Gold Records – Volume 2' (RCA Victor, 1959)

Trindade, Augusto A. Cançado, 'General Principles of Law as a Source of International Law', Original Lecture, Sources of Law, United Nations Audiovisual Library of International Law <http://untreaty.un.org/cod/avl/ls/Cancado-Trindade_IL_video_3.html>

Index

For Product Safety Concerns and Information please contact our EU representative GPSR@taylorandfrancis.com
Taylor & Francis Verlag GmbH, Kaufingerstraße 24, 80331 München, Germany

www.ingramcontent.com/pod-product-compliance
Ingram Content Group UK Ltd.
Pitfield, Milton Keynes, MK11 3LW, UK
UKHW022000180926
475701UK00003B/128
* 9 7 8 0 3 6 7 5 9 0 7 9 6 *